Allowing is a work of art. Holly's creati
throughout every page. Her words refle
piece of themselves and propel them into a direct experience with Truth. Holly mentions how the movie Leap touched her life. Interestingly, the latest version of our film has been shaped and touched by her message in Allowing. This creative expression will not disappoint. Her story provides loving support and guidance to those seeking forgiveness, truth, and acceptance.

Ashley Anderson, Co-Founder of AVAIYA Media and Co-Creator of the films Leap, A Course in Miracles The Movie, and MPower: Empowering Women in Business and Beyond

Most of us aren't motivated enough to forge through the beliefs we hold that keep us stuck and asleep. In these pages Holly peels her own skin, question by question, and gathers the personal evidence needed to heal herself from an idiopathic disease popularly labeled as incurable. Hang with Holly as she develops an original formula for healing that defies traditional medicine. This book is more than warm fuzzies. It's a journey fired with the hot coals of determination hell-bent to reconcile and elevate every relationship... be it person, ideology or object. You will identify with Holly's search in one way or another, because it's about each of us…and our never-ending becoming.

Patricia Rich, Artist, Author: *Notes of a Sane Woman*

In each of us there is a place where healing happens and Holly not only found it, she wrote the entire book from this place. The truth of this story will transform lives, reveal new vistas, and uncover inner strengths that every reader can use for healing disease and disharmony.

Kayt Campbell, MSU International Trainer in Consciousness Mechanics since 1983
Author: *The 5-Minute Interview*

This book powerfully and inspiringly communicates that you are the creative force of your own life. Holly's personal journey of forgiveness, allowing, and honor deliver you into the arms of grace.

Donald McKinnon, Author: Coach & Founder *Brain Power ON Program*

Allowing is told with intimacy and honesty… it makes the reader feel more alive and connected to what matters. Ms. Riley's wisdom, clarity and deep acceptance infuse the reader with inspiration and possibility. This is more than a book, it's an experience.

Mason Yaffee, Co-Founder, Trainer The Bonding Weekend Relationship Empowerment Workshop

ALLOWING

A Portrait of Forgiving and Letting Life Love You

By Holly Riley

Peace in Peace out®

Reno, Nevada USA

ALLOWING

A portrait of Forgiving and Letting Life Love You

Published by Peace in Peace out® Productions

To order Allowing, A Portrait of Forgiving and Letting Life Love You or the Allowing Handbook, Simple Strategies for Manifesting Dreams by best selling author Holly Riley contact: www.HollyRiley.com

Library of Congress Control Number: 2011907254

Printed in the United States of America
Ist Printing - 2010
Revised Edition - 5/11/2012

For Dad, Mom, Debbie, and Patricia

(The fodder)

Table of Contents

Foreword

My belief in miracles is renewed through the pages of this book… many times over. As if two near-death experiences aren't unique and inspiring enough, I was awestruck by the monumental value of forgiveness when compared to holding onto even one painful judgment. The healing and transformation that Holly and her father facilitated for one another, after such a violent and abusive past, is a testimony to the change that is possible for any one of us. The depth of her honesty reaches way beyond the surface of things and acknowledges the enormous part we play in shaping our own lives. Her story will inspire and strengthen you to reach for your dreams, guiltlessly! It will feed your soul in a friendly way and draw your heart into greater integrity with your own truth. Miracles abound.

Those of us whose intention is to live more deliberately will know the treasure that Holly Riley is to the planet. Her passion to awaken herself and others as though it were one song is a good way to describe her heartbeat. She has exemplified the gentlest form of ruthless pursuit I've ever felt. For those of us who have had the honor to work with her, to feel her cheek on ours, and experience her honest and open disclosures, we celebrate her existence. Together, with the roomful of beings "on the other side," we know that she is a gift to humanity's awakening. The service of her life will not be confined to anyone else's definition, no matter how well meaning. Should you be lucky enough to know her in this life and through this book, I am confident that you will be inspired to forgive and let go of judgments that separate you from your joy.

I invite you to merge with the awareness born through these incredible experiences. Feel the inspiration as it touches your soul and let it empower you to breathe your own truth. Experience the magic of Allowing.

Shakti Cain

The thing that matters most is to be awake. Believing that we have to suffer a tragedy or pay some great price for enlightenment is a belief that has been passed down for far too long. Life doesn't have to be a painful drama. I did the suffering route and I have good news, there is an easier way.

Here is my story from hard to easy, from horror to happy. My wish is for you, the reader, to recognize a short cut through your own drama and pain. My intention is, as you turn the following pages, you become increasingly equipped to hop on a more joyous ride through life. Unless of course you prefer the roller coaster route, which many people do. If that is your choice, I bet you get good at "putting your hands up" on the turns. In either case, here lies the story of the becoming where you will find a common thread (more like a rope) that you can use to pull yourself toward your preciousness.

–Holly Riley

Sweet Death

chapter 1

When you start preparing for death you soon realize that you must look into your life–now–and come to face the truth of your self. Death is like a mirror in which the true meaning of life is reflected.

–Sogyal Rinpoche

It was a tough day compared to the previous twenty-five in the hospital. Tough because the doctor came in and told my husband he'd better call the family. He wasn't sure I was going to make it too much longer. He sadly said, "If they want to see her, you better get them here." The doctor had done everything he knew to do. I had lost forty-five pounds on my already thin frame. I had been unable to eat food for over four months. My body wasn't working anymore. With the help of an IV tube connected in the vena cava near my heart, I was being fed a white concoction called TPN. Yet, I kept losing weight right along with my ambition. I had Crohn's disease and it was winning the fight. My colon was paper-thin and unable to digest water. It was the most painful, humiliating, and horrific thing that could happen to me. It was perfect.

My life up to this point included a great deal of study on the mechanics of consciousness. I wanted to know everything about reality, how it comes to be and how it goes away. I was equipped with the best toolbox known to God and man. I could meditate, chant, pray, evaluate, visualize, imagine, therapize, and process. I could use Reiki, kinesiology, color, sound therapy, and maintain a macrobiotic diet with the best of them. I had some brilliant teachers. I even went through some miracle homeopathic and chelation therapies, spending much of our savings. You name it—I did it. I knew all the most popular ways to understand, feel, and change reality. I had studied them for the last twenty-five years. I started at the age of ten.

I had many moments of total trust regarding my illness and where it was leading me. Even as I was going through the pain and suffering there were times that I felt connected to something larger than my failing body. I knew I was more than the experience I was having and this awareness comforted me greatly. I felt the part of me that mattered would always be safe even though my body might not pull through. There were many times when I became very present and aware and observed the whole thing like I was watching a movie, while another part of me was actually in the movie, resisting it. Part of me spent a lot of time observing the Holly show and had faith in the outcome even if it included the main character dying.

There were those other moments, too, when I could drop down into the deepest, densest place possible, immersed in hopeless despair. I could end up entirely stuck in a negative emotion or self-criticism that consumed me. The sorrow would take over my connection to anything other than resentment and grief. I was fascinated by my need to repeatedly explore the pain. It was seductive. When I felt strong, I often convinced myself I could safely visit this dark place for just a moment to see if the turmoil and negativity were still there. But it was a trap and I would get sucked into a mind that ended up wallowing in itself for hours if I wasn't careful. It was peculiar that I wanted to keep inspecting the negative feelings knowing they were dangerous ground, but I couldn't stop looking for them. It was like a drug my mind wanted more of and it would trick me into investigating. I had to watch out for the "failure conversation" that would sneak up on me as well. I could beat myself up real good for being sick, despite all the enlightenment work I had done! I got caught in that dialogue plenty.

I had to pay close attention to my mind and its wanderings or I could end up in the clutches of all kinds of dark thinking that would kidnap me into a whirlwind of suffering. Thankfully, I had some very sacred moments when I would instantly become self-aware and catch myself immersed in some crazy banter and be able to laugh at its meaninglessness. There were times when my mind would have me dislike anyone who could use a bathroom without needing medication and a support team. Finding my insanity humorous helped. It was fascinating to observe the mind's need to make something or someone wrong and stir up trouble.

I spent far too many precious hours looking for someone to blame for my predicament. The unlucky target was often my father. I spread it out a bit depending on my mood; alcohol and drugs were also a couple of the biggest contenders, not my use of them but everyone else's. I felt like they were my main competitors in life as they had gotten all the attention I had longed for from the people I loved. Alcohol and drugs had taken my family and many of my friends to some reality that didn't include me. I was angry about that! Too often I had a dialogue of blame going around and around in my head that reminded me of a pet gerbil running on one of those wheels that go in circles, forever, only to end up right where they started. Just like that gerbil, I was exhausted and going nowhere.

Trapped in my need to understand, I was haunted by the many faces of the question "Why me?" *Why was this happening to me? What was the point? What did I need to focus on? Was this a step to take me to my purpose? Was this a lesson that would help fulfill my dream of being a good person, an enlightened being? Could having a disease be the plan for me? And if so, whose plan was it? And why didn't they just tell me in person what the hell is going on here?* I wanted a face-to-face meeting with whoever was responsible! I was sure there had to be some mistake and we could clear it up quickly with a short visit!

I had been suffering consistently for a couple of years with colitis, horrible pain, and humiliation that eventually culminated into a nasty case of Crohn's disease. With matters continually growing worse and no answers showing up, at least none I wanted, I finally surrendered. I accepted that I was very sick and the outlook was grim. Up to that point I had been in denial and tried to overcome my misery with positive thinking. It was more like pretending to be positive. This is pretty funny when you think about it because pretending actually verifies the realness of the thing you are denying. Pretending you're going to be fine means down deep you really don't believe it's true... otherwise you wouldn't need to pretend! So, I finally began to own where I found myself and acknowledge where I was. For the very first time, I told myself the truth and surrendered. The relief was palpable. On that Friday afternoon in the hospital, I decided to stop resisting. I quit fighting. I let go of needing to know anything. I began to die and the doctor knew it.

Pat, my husband of four short years, called my mother and two sisters to inform them of my condition. He didn't think to call Dad, assuming I wouldn't want him there. Pat wasn't just my dream come true, he was my confidant and very best friend. He was the one person in the world that I completely trusted. I knew he loved me, and that is a big deal coming from my lips. He was the only man I could say that about. It was a very tough time for him as he had recently lost his father and brother. These were the two most precious people in the world to him. He'd had enough death to deal with already and there he was, heartbroken and trying to hold a smile for me while digesting the prospect of raising our two young children alone. He had our boys to think about, Travis eight years old (who he'd adopted) and Drake, almost four. I can only imagine what was going through his heart and mind trying to figure out how they'd all get along without me. I could feel his despair and it was more painful to consider his sorrow and devastation than it was anticipating my own death.

Once the family began to show up for me, things got very interesting. My family is one for the books. At the age of fourteen I took my dad to court for child abuse and won. I was the youngest of three girls and it should have happened ten years earlier than it did. None of us were close to Dad, particularly my mom, who in her mind, had the most to forgive. My sisters were not average people: one had endured quite a heavy bout with addiction and the other had mastered the challenges of HIV. They were soldiers when it came to survival, and they dropped everything to come and save me and help the Riley family handle whatever was next.

From the second she walked into the room, Mom was a tad busy blaming her self for everything that I was dealing with, so she was quite preoccupied that first day. Dad showed up unexpectedly and sparks started flying. Nobody would look into his eyes. I did; I was hungry to know who he had become. He hadn't had much to do with my personal life and zero to do with everyone else's. He was definitely the bad guy in our family movie. Patricia, the middle sister, had recently done some processing about our childhood, uncovering issues that she couldn't accept. At this particular time, she felt strong hatred for Dad and was very angry for what he had done to her, so add that to her love of confrontation as well as her uncanny wit, and there was no telling what was going to come out of her mouth next. Mom had not seen Dad at all since leaving him in Florida after seventeen years of marriage, so she was quite nervous and scattered. My oldest sister, Debbie, was the only calm one as she focused her attention on loving me. She accepted things for what they were. How weird it all was to witness! It was some gathering to be sure. But no matter what was going on in their minds, I was very grateful for their presence.

The family that had been separated, angered, and non-forgiving, was coming together for a visit. Patricia and mother tried to dodge Dad like you would a bullet. Debbie stayed pretty mellow all day. She was the peaceful hippie just quietly observing everyone. When they all showed up around the same time I loved watching them pretend that nothing uncomfortable was happening. It was like pretending there wasn't an elephant stepping on your foot. I started to perk up and wished for buttered popcorn to go with the family movies that were being performed live in my hospital room never knowing what would happen next. Honestly, it was nice to see everyone and especially nice to see them all together.

As the family settled down and directed their attention toward me, tensions began to subside. There was a letting go as everyone came into this new moment together. An *allowing* began to fill the space and the energy seemed to change. They started being more generous with one another and kinder. There was a taste of forgiveness in the air. I found myself smiling as the past began to loosen its hold on my family. They tried to let it be, at least for now. Something shifted and a softening was occurring.

When death is in your face you begin to see how being angry with someone for making a mistake is a waste of a life. Compassion was replacing the anger and conflict. The presence of care seemed to melt whatever was in its place. The space went from heavy to light, from thick to open. A healing was occurring in our family that I had longed for forever. It was almost worth dying for. Almost.

I hadn't trusted Dad for a very long time, if ever. As far back as I could remember, I was always leery of giving him any opportunity to hurt me. I kept my distance emotionally even though we had started communicating again over the last few years after not speaking for several. The guard I had always kept up was crumbling as my energy to fight was slipping away. I wanted him close to me, feeling that somehow he was the one that could keep me safe and protect me from harm. I had wanted that for a long time from Dad but was never willing to admit it until then. I was vulnerable, and more than anything, I ached for someone to hold me and tell me everything would be all right.

That night was a rough one for my body and me, but the thought of my family being together comforted me.

The next morning when Dad walked into the hospital, we were alone and I swear it felt like a mountain had moved into the room. He was a big being and I don't mean just his physical size. With death knocking on my door, my perceptual field had now grown larger. I could feel the quality of energy in things and was aware of how people and spaces contained more than just what my eyes were seeing. I looked into my father and saw him without the cloud of our past. I became aware of his essence in a way. He was so different, like I hadn't met him before. I couldn't believe it was the same guy. His shell was softer, more caring, and even scared. He was vulnerable and open in a very unusual way. He was emotionally accessible and seemed to energetically invite me into a pool of peace. I was calmed by his presence and by the idea that I could finally stop hating him.

I was getting weaker and hope was dwindling. Family stayed with me throughout the day taking shifts. Dad came back that afternoon and just sat with me, quiet, humble, and huge. His energy was sturdy and I knew he was in the hospital about ten minutes before he entered my room. I felt him; it was like a psychic awareness, a peculiar and unmistakable link. I think it had always been there but now I was acutely aware of it through some kind of transformation of my abilities. I figured it was partly due to the fact that I hadn't eaten food for four months. I had heard you could see through walls and hear people think with a long fast. I had gone so long without solid food that I wasn't inhibited or distracted by body cravings at all and clarity rose to a new level. I was so present and connected that I could feel thoughts and sometimes I even thought I could see them.

I really appreciated being with Dad when he was quiet and vulnerable. He oozed an energy that was open and honoring. It was healing much more than our relationship. It was healing my heart to feel such love. It was peculiar to me at that time, why out of everyone in the family, my connection to him felt so strong, particularly after all the abuse from my childhood. I felt quieter inside with him there. He brought calm into the room. The past began to fade like a dream. It was good to be together, a healing of sorts, maybe a completion before I finished with my physical reality.

I had become better friends with life since facing death and had become friends with my pain as well. It was beyond anything I can describe and it took me somewhere I had never been. I did my best to follow where it led so I could look it straight in the eye. I was determined to experience it all with love. I had chosen not to use any pain medications, as I couldn't manage my mind with them. I needed my faculties right then, more than ever before. I wouldn't even take the sleeping pills. No matter what, it was important to me to have clarity and be present for what was next particularly if it was death.

That afternoon, Patricia managed a "come to Jesus meeting" to coach me on the whole pain and intention situation. She was unafraid in a serene kind of way like she knew some truth I had yet to learn. She would smile her smarty-pants smile and ask me what I wanted out of this experience. "What do you want Holly?" she would sing. Always working to lasso my attention around what was possible and the fact that I was the only one in charge of directing my focus there. She was a hoot; she got very excited about operating the bedpan, and would perform a little victory dance anytime something other than blood appeared. She made me laugh in the midst of nearly bleeding to death.

Patricia brilliantly helped me go to the place where I could see that what was happening was not *me.* At least it was not all of me. I was bigger than the experience I was having. With her coaching, I had moments where I could move from being trapped inside the situation to moments of actually viewing it from outside of myself. I was able to observe a bigger snapshot of the world around me. It was a shift in my awareness, a transfer from my viewpoint of being stuck in the pain, the hospital bed, or my body to a viewpoint that included everything around me. It was a relief as it softened and expanded the point of my focus to a larger view as though I were peering through a wide angle camera lens. Everything in my perspective received equal attention. Nothing grabbed or pulled me away from anything else. It reduced the intensity of the situation. It's difficult to describe yet it helped me relax, and assisted me in navigating through my pain.

Much like me, Patricia had embraced the work of being present and responsible for her entire life. By "responsible," I mean we did our best to not blame anyone else for where we found ourselves, ever. We weren't always successful, at least not right away, and we were continually discovering more comprehensive levels of responsibility. We were eager to be free of the pain that accompanies blame. (If you blame someone for what you're experiencing, then you have to wait for them to change so your life can get better. This can be a long, long wait, a lifetime of suffering for some). We had to be source of our feelings at a very early age. We learned the hard way that good feelings weren't going to come from anybody outside of us. It was either figure out how to create being happy or get over the idea of its existence. We did our best to muster up joy in the midst of an abusive environment.

We had to figure out how to own our power because the alternative was to suffer victimhood. So, Patricia refused to offer me pity. She knew this would only pile more drama on top of drama and solidify my unwanted reality even further. Every chance she got, she'd kick my ass so I could look myself right in the eye without blaming, pretending, or whining. Regardless of what was happening, she helped me stay present. When pain would rush my body like labor minus the baby, she'd say, "Look at the pain, listen to it, and be with it. Stay present with it and it will begin to dissolve. Don't resist it. Own it, be it, feel it." She would coach me with questions to keep me in the moment, "What color is it, how big is it, how much water would it hold, and where exactly is it?" She would hold my hand and guide me. It was as though she was feeling the pain with me. She'd say, "Don't resist it. Let it be. Breathe it in and accept it like you ordered it for dinner."

Allowing the pain to be and accepting it without denial or resistance was a big step toward transforming both the pain and me.

My pain grew more frequent over the next twenty four hours and I got darn good at managing it. It wasn't so bad. I let go of hating it, or hating anything for that matter. It became obvious that resisting anything, even for a moment, only made it worse. I had become pretty good friends with all of it, and you know, it was the most compassionate and kind experience of caring for myself that I had ever known. I used the pain to become more connected to my Self. I was there for me. It was a sweet love. I was calm and trusting. Truth was present.

I decided to be there for the party, even if it included me dying. I wanted to experience it with all of me present, ready and trusting. So, I did my best to catch my mind whenever it moved toward wallowing in anything other than the moment I was in. I was getting to know who I was on a very deep level and was positive it wasn't just the person lying in bed. I was watching myself from a very loving place. I felt how inclusive of everyone and everything my world really was and it soothed me. I was much more than what was happening in my hospital room. Whenever I had a pain, I brought in that part of me that was more than my body, to be with my body. I was connected. It was like being plugged into the master energy or grid that connects all of us. This allowed me to be there for myself in a way that I had always wished others to be. I was comforted on more than just a physical level. It was complete, and there was nothing missing for me. I wanted my family to have this experience and know this feeling. I wished for them and all people on the planet to have this love because it makes everything okay. No matter what happens, it's actually okay. I knew this viscerally.

I got much worse. The doctor told my family he wanted to take another look at my colon and scope it. I didn't know it at the time because I was medicated for the procedure, but the doctor had taken Pat, my husband, into the scope room and showed him my colon tissue. It was paper-thin and the majority of my intestines resembled raw hamburger. He told Pat that if the colon ruptured during the procedure there was a slim-to-none chance I'd survive. I had little to zero of my immune system left to fight infection as a result of being on large doses of prednisone, a synthetic steroid, for more than a year.

Emotionally, my husband prepared for the worst. The doctor asked Pat to please pick a colostomy bag for me (there were several choices of design) because if I didn't improve in the next forty-eight hours they'd have to remove most of my colon. This was a horrible moment for him given that I had previously warned him I would die before allowing someone to take part of my body out or strap a feces-catching receptacle to my abdomen. I had instructed him many times that he'd better stand by me on my firm decision to never have my colon removed. Now, he was the only one who could authorize the surgery—the doctor knew I wouldn't. He had two evils to choose from. What a burden. Pat didn't tell me until years later that he'd gone into the procedure room and was horrified by what he saw and how heartbroken he was leaving the hospital that night, fairly certain he would lose the wife that he fell in love with. Even then, I could feel the weight and the pain that he carried through that time, alone.

I believe it's more difficult for someone who loves you to watch you slowly die, than it is to suffer and die yourself.

That night everyone left around 9:00 P.M. I sent them all home and told them I was fine, even though I knew I wasn't. I started meditating like I always did when it was time to sleep, totally unaware of the "Friday she loses her body parts conversation" Pat had just had with the doctor. I did my regular routine of praying, meditating, and staying present with the pain. I never quite slept due to the buzz from the prednisone, the beeps from the monitors, and the tick-tick choooooooooooweeeeeee of the feeding machine. Quieting my mind and being present with my breath was about as good as it got for me. But this night, something happened, something that changed my life, forever.

I died.

I had an "NDE" (near-death experience) or whatever you want to call it; in the end, it's all semantics, the vibration and the fabric of words. Essentially, I left. Gone. Split. As I watched the whole thing from a bird's-eye view, it was beyond belief.

I'd gotten my shot of prednisone every eight hours. If it was even ten minutes late, my body would go into freak-out mode with my mind close behind. Contractions, pain, sweat; I will spare you all the gory details. It hurt, badly. One little bubble moving through my colon felt worse than my idea of giving birth to triplets all at once. I had to breathe and feel, breathe and feel, until the bubble had traveled all the way through. I had to use every bit of me that I could muster. It was the most blessed and painful experience I have ever had.

Anyway, the nurse was already thirty minutes late for my 2:30 A.M. shot. That night, more than once, it was like Mr. Toad's Wild Ride (from *The Wind in the Willows*)—I never knew what was waiting for me around the next dark corner! So far, I had managed to white-knuckle through it. My body was so covered in pools of sweat that I could pat my hand on my stomach and the moisture would splash about two inches into the air. I had been doing every mantra, prayer, breathing and sound exercise that I knew of, in order to not bug the nurse again. She was busy and they were short-staffed that night, which meant she had more than her share of patients to handle. These attendants were all angels… seriously. So I did my best to not flip out. But on prednisone, this is no trivial task. It was common to seize any opportunity to blame, yell, or cry when the steroids grabbed a hold of my emotions. Somehow, I didn't do any of these things. I stayed as still and as present as possible, immersed in the pain. I was acutely aware, more so than previous pain episodes.

When the nurse arrived forty-five minutes behind schedule, I had already become so intensely one with the pain, that it was surreal. She said she didn't have time to check my vitals and would have to return later because a patient down the hall was in serious trouble and needed her immediate attention. She quickly injected the prednisone into my feeding tube and headed off to her next emergency. Right at the door, she stopped, turned around and looked at me inquisitively, "Are you okay?" She knew something wasn't right. Of course, I said, "I am fine, you go take care of your chores."

Within minutes my body did something very weird. It was like it had shut down and stopped fighting. I was fully alert, and became very sad. In my heart I knew that I couldn't do this anymore, and neither could my body. I was exhausted, having had little or no sleep for so very long. My heart ached for what my husband and children were going through. I could feel the weight of their pain and worry as it took its toll. It had been a two-year nightmare, in and out of the hospital. I was so tired of what I was doing to everyone else. Really, I was okay with dying now. I felt like it would be the nicest thing I could do for my family. I rationalized that Pat could find a wonderful new wife since he was a great man; that the boys could quit worrying about their sick mother, and that everyone could all get on with their lives again. I believed and trusted that Pat would be a good father to Travis and Drake, and love them with all his heart.

I closed my eyes and felt death.

I thought about God and what really happens when we die. I guess you could call it praying. I didn't really pray to a God, it was more like I prayed to "All That Is." To that thing that I knew was bigger than me or at least that I had felt so many times before, and been comforted by, throughout my entire life. Some call it the Higher Self, or awareness, or divine spirit. Some call it the Sacred with No Name. I believe you can call it anything you want to, as long as you call it. I wanted to feel that connection, so I prayed for it with all my being. I surrendered. Not just a little. It was total submission.

Then it happened. I started ascending through the hospital ceiling of my room. I went to the next floor above, eyes wide open, one more floor, and then, oh my God! The stars were in front of my face and the evening breeze filled my senses. I could actually taste the air. It was alive as it touched my face and caressed my hair. It was pure heaven compared to the air inside the hospital. Joy filled my soul and my entire body was smiling. I was floating. It was quiet, serene, and still.

Then I realized I was lying in something… I put my hands down by my side to feel what it could be. I felt short hairs like on a knuckle. Then I felt what seemed like a finger, and when I felt what was on my other side, I touched another finger. It took a minute but I finally realized I was resting in two hands—two very large hands that were holding me. I slowly craned my neck to see who was there, and it was Jesus holding me. I am not kidding… me, not religious, never been a big Jesus fan, wasn't even sure if I knew what he looked like except from old pictures on my grandmother's wall, but I was sure this was him. I am talking blue eyes of pure love. The bluest and most clear eyes I had ever looked in. The love was so vast and complete it saturated me with sensations for which I don't have the words to describe. The feelings were not of this world. My body, mind, and spirit were filled with a peace that vibrated in connection with all life, all love, and a certainty of goodness. He never spoke to me out loud, but we did speak. He held me in his loving energy and let me bathe in it for as long as I wanted. It seemed like an eternity yet in looking back it all happened so quickly. It was rich and complete with no desire left unfulfilled. After a while, he asked me if I would like to stay or go. Keep living my life on Earth or leave now with him. Because of this incredible experience of pure love, I had to seriously consider the latter. There was no pain—only joy, completion, and the overwhelming feeling of perfection in his presence.

Returning to my life on Earth had a very different energy. Not a bad one, but very different. It had a flavor of responsibility with it. I knew that going back meant more "doing" and more activity, while staying with Him had an essence of simply "being." It was like going out dancing versus going out to simply merge and float. I was given this huge space in which to contemplate my options for what seemed like a very long time. I truly did not know which one I wanted, so I waited—to know. There wasn't one second of any pressure. It was totally my call.

I expanded my awareness outward to explore. I observed and felt everything around me. It was like taking a long drink of water when you are thirsty. Every sensation brought me more peace and more connection to a sacredness that permeated everything. I noticed the softness of the light, the endless space surrounding us, the high and low tones singing in my ears, the quality of the energy flowing and embracing me, the grace of the being holding me, and I felt the harmony of all these things. It was amazing and perfect. I knew this was the truth of all beings. This knowing, this energy, this gracefulness, is the larger part of who we really are. This more inclusive sense of being was a more honest and accurate experience than the pointed encased sensations I had when totally focused in my body. This connection, this love, and the vastness is what we are all made of. I had come home.

I just wanted to stay there awhile. Then one of us (I say one of us because it felt like Jesus and I were connected with no separation) thought of my two boys and a life size impression of Travis and Drake appeared right in front of me. The moment I saw them, I knew my answer. My heart became even fuller as I gazed upon their faces. I experienced a rush of love that is wordless. I felt honor and appreciation for them in a way I had never fathomed possible as though our relationships were planned long ago and we were keeping our promise. I had a sense of the dance being human was and how it differed from the ease and flow of where I was viewing from. I felt the plight of our planet, not that it was bad, just that it was intense and swirling, and that people had very little knowing of what was real—and what wasn't. It was as though I had a peek through Christ's eyes.

My heart was overflowing. I didn't need to say anything. Christ knew the moment I knew… I had to go back. Then we shared a sensation, an awareness of sorts that my world was about to change. A comforting certainty filled the space. Then Jesus gently covered my entire body with his breath, from my head to my toes, being very gentle and thorough.

He then placed me back in my bed and left me snuggled sweetly and happily in my new world.

I knew what was coming and it was good. I slept for the first time in a very long while.

Someday, when all is gone and the body is finished carrying you within the Earth lesson, the angel inside you returns to the spiritual place called Home. When that occurs, you will find no organization or religion there—only the love of family, one for another. We have seen you there, at Home, over and over and over and over. We know your face, and not the one you think you have now. We are aware of you when you sing your name in light to us—and you wonder who came to see whom?

–From the *Kryon Channeling*
Israel, October 27, 2000

What is Real?

chapter 2

Higher self can assume any face it chooses and will dress up in the perfect form for the consciousness that is listening. Speaking to the listening present is key to being heard.

–Holly Riley

I penciled my experience of the previous evening in my journal, astonished and humbled as I wrote Jesus' name. The details were clear and crisp in my mind and the feeling deeply etched in my heart. The whole encounter left me with such reverence for this sensation called "love." All morning, I caught myself smiling. I couldn't recall ever experiencing such wholeness before. I was satisfied and complete even as I lay there hooked up to monitors and a feeding tube, surrounded by bedpans and people demonstrating the many elements of fear. The fear was so thick you could smell it: fear of dying, fear of pain, fear of not knowing, fear of finding out, and even fear of fear itself. Yet, I was fully aware of the *love* in the background, and understood without question that none of this was as serious as people were making it. What truly mattered was all in place. The events and expressions of urgency were like part of a show we were all putting on so we could discover the many possibilities of being human. Everyone was consumed in an exciting drama and I think we all just forgot we are the ones that designed it. On some level, we were actually missing the point of the show. The best way I can describe what I was experiencing is an intuitive, compassionate, and humorous honoring of everything and everyone—exactly the way it was—and I knew how the story was going to end. Everything would turn out just fine, with the world, and with us. Life had no ending, it just moved from one reality or form, to another. It was as though we were all living in a dream, like a puppet show, and who we really were was operating behind the curtain.

What was most important wasn't being acknowledged by us. We had all forgotten and made the show more real than the puppeteer.

I kept hearing Dad's words to me as a child, and it made me chuckle. He often spoke of how the invisible world was worth paying attention to, at least as much as the visible one. He lectured about this frequently. He recommended I keep track of my dreams as they would reveal patterns and teach me something about the unseen. He spoke about how the faces worn by people in my dreams were put on quite deliberately to make a point; he believed many of them were teachers. He said awareness would wear whatever face was best to get my attention so I'd heed the message. In other words, it would be someone whom my consciousness would listen to.

What happened to me the previous night was no dream, yet it definitely took place in the invisible world. It had me questioning the solidity of anything and wondering which reality was most valid. Being in the hands of Christ was as genuine as anything I have ever known, even more so. Being in this hospital bed surrounded by all this busyness and quasi-robotic motion didn't seem authentic, in fact, quite the opposite. It was as though everyone was sleepwalking. Dad used to ask, after I'd share an inspiring dream with him, "Holly, which reality is the dream and which one is real?" I had a tough time answering and so he would ask again, "How can you be sure?" Then he would laugh as though he knew something I didn't. Until now, I never figured out what the answer to that question was.

As I wrote in my journal the last details of my interlude with death, I wondered if it was really Jesus or just the ideal face for Awareness, Higher Self, God, The Tao, or whatever you call the Sacred with No Name, so I would receive the message? Jesus was definitely the perfect identity to teach me about love. All my memories from my grandmother's descriptions and the two times I went to Sunday school were of his kindness, awareness, and compassion for humanity. The guy knew how to love, no matter what, at least in my projection of him. That was exactly the feeling I came back into my body with. It was a very different sensation than the love I knew as Holly. It was much broader, more inclusive and totally allowing, without a drop of judgment. It was like one big "YES" to everything. I awoke rearranged in some manner, and I cared in a way I was unable to the day before. There was an understanding in me, a compassion for the human condition, the self-sabotage, and the suffering. I was acutely aware of the preciousness in everyone, even if they weren't. I could feel the goodness in myself, too. The truth was twinkling through.

As I thought about my family, especially my boys, I lingered in appreciation of how I had taken my job as a parent so seriously and made rules and certain ideas into such a drama. My mothering was laughable from my new perspective. I could see how hard I had struggled to control things and prevent mistakes as though errors were awful and even sometimes unforgiveable. From this new awareness, mistakes appeared as glorious creatures that helped us all know ourselves better. They were more a masterpiece and a blessing than anything else.

As I wrote, the past kept playing out in front of me as though someone else was rolling a movie. With great clarity, my lack of trust was evident now. I could see the effects of my fear and how it had rippled through the family, like the impact that every tossed stone makes in a pond. I realized how I had pushed Pat and the boys, relentlessly, to see things my way in an effort to control their decisions and choices. I manipulated with great finesse and I called it creating a happy family. I had called it love. Until that morning, who I was being had been transparent to me.

Looking through different eyes, I saw how little I had trusted everyone to live out their own unique interpretation of life. I thought I could design their existence better then they could. It was so apparent that this was a mistake, and I understood for the first time that people had their own precious code for living. I saw it, I felt it, and it was pure and perfect. To honor and empower people to discover this for themselves suddenly felt a lot more like love than what I had been doing. Just like Jesus had held me until I discovered my next step, there was no push from Him, no agenda, and no desire hanging in the air for me to do anything other than what my heart longed for. Staying in this body called "Holly" or going with Jesus was entirely my choice, and whichever one I picked, was perfect. He created a space, one I could stay in as long as I wanted, and it was made out of pure honor and compassion. The experience allowed me to intuitively know myself and my next step. It took awhile, or at least it seemed like a long time, for me to decide. But when my knowing came from within, I knew then my choice was crystal-clear, without a drop of doubt.

I loved seeing with such certainty how each human had a code or a path of becoming. It created such a feeling of trust in my heart. I wondered how humans could access this knowing for themselves and realized that being still-minded and present was key. Watching and feeling the busyness and hustling around me seemed to be a sort of distraction, almost a fever, a delirium, to avoid the truth held in each person's heart. People I watched seemed more creatures of habit then creators of dreams, mostly following someone else's path through life instead of finding their own. They were surviving humanness instead of enjoying it.

I wasn't afraid or worried in any manner. I felt honor for all of us and appreciated how determined we humans are to do something good and right. Everyone was reaching for harmony in his or her own way and it was okay if it didn't fit my picture of a balanced life. I was calmly aware and able to appreciate and trust the whole puppet show, in a way I had never known possible. Perhaps it was because I now knew the final act and understood that everyone lives on, that there was no such thing as "done," and that at some point, everyone will remember who he or she really is… the puppeteer. I felt so free, free to be me.

It was exciting imagining the family, my boys, and everyone moving toward their desires. Especially since I didn't need to control them or persuade them to adopt my truths anymore. I was experiencing such acceptance of EVERYTHING! Without an ounce of judgment or any idea that people should be different than they were. I felt so alive and happy to have another chance to enjoy the human experience! I had so much joy in me! I laughed out loud as I wondered if the feeling would last through a long visit with my family.

I didn't want to bother my nurse, but kept hoping she would pop in so I could talk to her and be intimate with another human just to see if it felt different. I was eager to touch someone and just love. I was weird, even to myself. I smiled as I imagined living my life with this feeling, celebrating who people had created themselves to be, regardless of any mistakes they had made. I felt a new kind of understanding, like I had room in my consciousness for absolutely any reality, and I thought maybe Jesus had left some of himself with me. I kept playing with my new awareness, rolling it around and looking at it from every direction just as you would a new toy—only this toy was inside.

Again, I questioned who or what had been wearing the face of Jesus! I considered the possibility that it was my Higher Self, but that didn't sit right. It wasn't mine. At least, not all mine. It was all of ours, shared and available like an electrical current that moves through the expanse of space and time. Then I thought, maybe my Higher Self isn't only mine. I chuckled as I pictured humans sharing one big Higher Self. I didn't know the answer but I was sure of one thing; the embrace of this energy was available to everyone. I felt the vastness of that connection only briefly as I merged with the consciousness that held me in its hands and it was a huge wave of energy, an "isness" that included everyone and everything.

Perhaps this is the same energy that reflects people's personal beliefs. It wisely dons a comforting face to assist them emotionally when it's time to leave their bodies and move from one reality to another. It operates like a mirror of sorts revealing what's already inside the mind. Next, I considered the many religions and spiritual belief systems around the world and imagined the variety of faces that this all-knowing energy could wear. Buddha, Mohammed, or even your momma, any icon of safety and peace could represent heaven during this transition. The symbol may be different for each person, yet hold the same wonderful vibration of complete trust for all.

Regardless of the face, one thing I was certain of was the quality of the "presence." I felt this energy completely. The preciousness is with me, now and forever, unless I choose to turn away from it. The presence would never turn away from me. This I knew.

My doctor barged in fast-paced, anxiety written all over him. He sat down, never taking his eyes off me, with quite a smirk on his face. He was a bit infected with what I affectionately termed the "God syndrome." He admittedly considered himself god of the colon, and not just mine. I got a kick out of him and playfully argued with him every chance I got. I was not an easy patient, so I had compassion for his predicament with me as we were both competing for the position of God when it came to healing my colon. I was sure that I knew what was best for my body. So did he. I was thrilled to have a visitor! I sat up in bed eager to engage him.

As I moved around to get comfortable, I remembered that the previous day, Dad suggested that I ask the doctor how many people he had cured of Crohn's disease during his long career. Dad said this question was very important and for me to be sure and ask it as soon as possible. He said it would be good for me to get some facts on my doctor's success rate with Crohn's disease. At the time, I wasn't privy to Dad's intentions and thought it a peculiar and even uncomfortable question to throw at my doctor, so I didn't really plan to pursue it. Yet, here it was, the question popped right into my head as the doctor sat in front of me. Intuitively, I was certain I was supposed to ask it.

I held my tongue for a minute because the doctor was pretty excited and I hadn't seen him like this my entire hospital stay. He looked at me like a wide-eyed little boy and said, "I don't know what you did last night but you need to keep doing it!" He constantly poked fun at me about my weird techniques for healing, and there was never any telling what new "thing" I might have tried the day before. Frequently, I would report the new processes I discovered for managing my mind, including meditating, toning, moving light through my body, and all sorts of visualizations. I was always trying to expand his horizons on healing modalities. I also did it in an effort to gain his approval. I wanted his encouragement and agreement that what I was doing was valuable. I was hungry for confirmation. On days of horrific suffering with no apparent solution I believed, more than I liked to admit, that my life was in Doc's hands. I used to wait for my daily blood-test results like an eager schoolgirl waiting to discover if she'd received a good grade on her report card. There were times I hung onto his every word, hoping he would tell me I had improved, and that I was getting better.

Doc laughed about all my idiosyncrasies and often chided me, letting me know that he didn't believe in much of anything except allopathic medicine, the Western medical prototype. Until that morning, he had never been interested in anything I had practiced. He gazed at me intently, leaned forward and asked, "*What* did you do last night?" He wanted to know because my white-cell count had dropped for the first time since my hospitalization. This meant something had started working! I think he was particularly interested because he had tried everything he had in his bag of tricks, with no improvement in my condition. My case was one of the worst he had ever seen. I wondered if he thought that whatever had helped me might be useful to him with similar cases.

I considered telling Doc about my interlude with Christ but it didn't feel right. I knew it would be disrespectful in some way, equivalent to giving something sacred to a person who wouldn't take good care of it. I stayed quiet as I observed this perfectly dressed physician before me with his file of papers neatly placed on his lap and his red tie impeccably knotted on his crisp white shirt. I chuckled at the differences in our realities. I smiled at him appreciatively, "Some magic stuff happened Doc, and maybe I'll tell you someday." And then I changed the subject and asked that question still at the forefront of my thoughts, "How many people have you cured from this disease?" He laughed and without a second of hesitation he admitted, "None. This disease is incurable. You will have it the rest of your life." I was dumbfounded. He said this with such finality that there was no room for any other option, at least in his reality. He was absolutely positive that this disease was not going away and he wanted me to know "the truth" so I wouldn't get my hopes up. He went on to say, "Sometimes, as you get older, the disease subsides, but you are a long ways off from that." I had the instant urge to cover my ears, and my jaw hung open in disbelief! Instinctively, I did not want mý body to hear those words, and I needed to protect it from the doctor's certainty.

My mind was racing, scanning for what this meant to my world. I began to restructure my thinking. I had a doctor who was not going to heal me, one who didn't even believe it was possible to cure Crohn's disease. All the while I was having a very interesting experience as though part of me was observing our conversation from the outside. Here stood my doctor in a position of authority proclaiming *impossibility* when it came to my total recovery. I knew as he spoke this was not the truth of my body. To hear him say those words, that I would never be cured, could have proved deadly had I accepted them and totally believed them. It would have been equivalent to digesting a toxic prescription within my mind that would surely spread throughout my body. I could see the ripple again: the power of words moving into reality, the reaction of a vibration on one's environment, and that the energy dance between two human bodies was stunning. From this outside perspective, I understood that the words he spoke represented his belief structure—not mine. *This saved me.* I could see his belief about the disease clearly. It was separate from me, a life form, a pill I could choose to swallow or not. It was so strange to be aware like this. I loved it.

I knew if I agreed with Doc's perspective, even a little bit, my body would have begun to comply. It was as though his reality was lingering in front of me like a choice I could make from a buffet line, his buffet. It was solid, tangible, and it was not mine.

What an epiphany! For the first time, I saw that I was susceptible to adopting a person's opinion as my own, and in doing so, this would affect my life in countless ways. If I regarded that person as an authority figure, then it was even more likely I would consider their truth as the ultimate truth. Doubly so, if I was paying them for it! This was a profound lesson for me.

Something was happening with my sphere of awareness. I was seeing how consciousness worked. I was recognizing how realities were manifested. I saw a long line of situations where I had done this in my life, beginning with my parents' beliefs, sermons at church, and even the books I had read. Then there were all the self-help courses and teachers I had paid over the years to rally stronger beliefs for myself, in hopes these would save me from myself. As I sat there in front of Doc, I wondered about everything. Where did I get all the beliefs I had raised my children with and had pushed so hard for them to adopt? I was a freak about not eating any sugar, taking vitamins, dressing in the right colors for optimal energy, not drinking liquids with meals, and not watching television (just to name a few). Whose beliefs were those? Where did I soak them up? I pondered this for a moment and appreciated the gift this interaction had given me. I saw the natural progression of the process… I would pay someone for their expertise or teachings, adopt what they profess, and then pass it on as truth, and maybe even figure out a way to market it. All without finding out what was deeply true for me! At this point, I think Jesus was smiling.

My mind questioned this thing called "truth." Did I have any of my own? Or was it only what I had picked up along the way? What a pattern to become aware of—swallowing other's truths without deliberately examining them for myself! I wondered what was really true in the world, I mean absolutely true, especially for me. I couldn't think of one thing that didn't have an opposing viewpoint. This was mind boggling and amazing, akin to a door opening into a room that I'd never visited inside my own house! I couldn't wait to explore this more. I was eager to discover some real honest-to-God truth. I was wondering what this process would look like when I heard the doctor's voice in the background of my thoughts.

I came back to the present moment and listened as Doc talked about my recovery plan, how much longer I had to wait to eat food, how much longer on the feeding tubes, and how we'd proceed from there. He didn't want to take any chances. All of a sudden, everything that came out of his mouth looked like another choice from the buffet of his beliefs. I smiled. I was touched by his care and by all that he was doing to support me. But I also knew that the mysterious way in which my health, and my life, had recovered had more to do with me than anything he was professing. My path had changed. His intention and commitment was to only manage my disease and get it under control. Curing me was not his goal and I appreciated him just as he was and understood his determination to fight the disease. I adored him for a minute and said a private thank you.

Our relationship transformed from a patient holding her doctor up as an authority figure to one human seeing another wonderful human, committed to what he called the truth. We had been down quite an adventurous road together and it was now coming to a fork.

> *The most useful piece of learning for the uses of life is to unlearn what is untrue.*
>
> –Antisthenes

From that point on, I would be careful about adopting another person's truth. I made a mental note to pay attention to this pattern of believing whatever I had heard or read. I had plenty of work to do to find out what truth really was for me. It seemed like everyone had their own version, mostly inherited rather than from introspection and discovery. I glanced around my environment for something, anything that I could call an absolute truth. The sky is blue? That's not really true from all viewpoints. I am sick? Maybe I am more whole and well than ever before. My family loves me? What is love? By whose definition, and do they actually experience love for me? It was comical to consider what was true, not just for me but also for the people on the planet. I became more aware of how I had spoon-fed my children with what I thought they should believe! Wow, my method of parenting was going to change dramatically.

It seemed like the best place to look for truth was to start noticing all the untruths I had gathered along the way. I wasn't sure who I would be without my past truths, but I was determined to find out who the real me was. This was the plan and I knew that the agreement would be kept. Everything was falling into place.

I felt the pathway to my heart widen. I was moving toward my own knowing and it was good. I was sure of the direction I was headed and confident it would lead me to where I was meant to go with my life. I was on my way to becoming more responsible for how I felt, how I thought, and how I loved. I was more aware than ever before and it was powerful to experience this kind of strength.

As the doctor left, I was in awe of how the universe gave me exactly what I had needed to take my next step. It was a turning point for me to realize how difficult it would be to change something that I didn't believe was mine to change. This applied to any predicament in life, not just my health. I could have been waiting a long time for that doctor to cure me, given it wasn't a possible outcome in his reality. That was the day I decided to own my disease and to take responsibility for my full recovery.

Intellectually, I understood that I was made up of more than my body and more than my thoughts. I had read it, studied it, and was always taught that this was true. But now I *experienced* it and had clarity of how powerful we truly are! I had a new feeling in my heart to accompany my cerebral understanding and it was now a part of me. I got to feel the peace that lives beyond beliefs, and perhaps, beyond death! Jesus' presence allowed me to experience who I was in a much bigger way. I had a choice in how my life rolled out. I was in charge of where I found myself and my recovery was more up to me than ever before. I felt inspired and ready to get to work! It was quite liberating! I had been relying heavily on the doctor to fix me and it wasn't his job. Clearly, if total healing was going to take place, I was the one to do it! I had a moment of joy and it turned into appreciating Dad for his clever question.

That was the last morning I waited for the doctor to tell me how I was doing.

When something becomes all that is with no contrast or distinction it is often accepted as truth. Simply because there is no awareness that an entirely different world exists, does not mean it isn't there.

–Holly Riley

New Eyes

chapter 3

Has anyone supposed it lucky to be born?
I hasten to inform him or her it is just as lucky to die, and I know it.
I pass death with the dying and birth with the new-washed babe,
and am not contained between my hat and boots,
And peruse manifold objects, no two alike and everyone good,
the earth good and the stars good,
and their adjuncts all good.
I am not an earth nor an adjunct of an earth,
I am the mate and companion of people,
All just as immortal and fathomless as myself,
(They do not know how immortal, but I know.)

–*Song of Myself,* Walt Whitman,

I was different. I knew that all humans were in the enigma together trying to decide what mattered most. I treasured the notion that none of us were ever alone. What could be better than a world filled with so many people offering a variety of realities to play in?

I felt a strong connection to everyone as though linked by something invisible yet tangible; much like water must feel to a school of fish. It's there, it touches them, and they respond to it; yet, if you asked a fish how the water was… they would probably say, "What water?" Water is all that they know and because it's experienced so completely, it disappears from their awareness. Many people may not be aware of this connecting current they're living in, but I know it is so. We are all held together by it. Take a fish out of water or a human out of their "human reality" and they quickly become aware that there was something there that they hadn't been seeing. (I am not sure how it's happening, but I am certain that this connection is part of what sustains all life).

I began to wonder what I was capable of becoming aware of. Clearly the obstacle to discovery wasn't ignorance as much as it was thinking that

I already knew the answer and had called it absolute truth. I was eager to move out of the hospital and into my new world to see what life looked like through these new eyes. I questioned if I would be able to see, feel, and identify the distinctions between our visible and invisible realities. I wasn't sure of the truth of physical reality anymore, what was real, what was mine, and what was most important about it all. One thing I was certain of: I wanted my connection to the sacred to last. For me, it was the most valuable use of my life, my awareness, my spirit, to do whatever was needed to keep this connection open and flowing as I went about being a body called Holly.

I let myself imagine going home and fully recovering for the first time in four weeks. Before last night there wasn't much hope to ever leave, so that dream had best been left untouched. To consider doing simple things like cooking, cleaning, and grocery shopping got my heart singing again! To experience the sensations of walking, running, or swimming sounded like pure heaven. I had been living on automatic pilot for so long, taking so much for granted that the thought of doing these simple things, I mean really being alive and present while doing them, blew my skirt way up! I imagined the joy of washing dishes and feeling the water run over my hand and giggled. To be present while scrubbing, and appreciating my surroundings without my mind on a million other things was delightful to anticipate. I hadn't been living with much feeling or awareness in my actions or thoughts for quite awhile. I'd been going through the motions without any appreciation for the miracle of all of it, and I couldn't wait to be home and experience my sweet life, the one I'd been missing.

I toyed with images of myself dressed in fashionable clothes wearing the face and body I had before I'd gotten sick. (The steroids had made me look like my head extended directly from my chest with no neck in-between, chipmunk cheeked, and very strange). Oh, how I longed to be cute again! I'm not kidding when I say that to feel and see my face, smooth and beardless, would be such a delight! (You see, steroids also stimulate hair growth with the unfeminine texture of a wire brush). I looked out the window just in time to catch a glimpse of a gorgeous woman running by in her stylish jogging suit. She seemed to be perfectly fit, strong bodied, nicely shaped, and healthy! A competitive pang coursed through me. *Down, girl, down!* I cautioned my ego. Then I imagined the feeling of a firm body and ached for a better physique. First I thought of mine, then Pat's, and then sex occurred to me, and holy moly! It had been such a long time since I'd thought about sex, that my face turned red and

I felt a stream of heat move through my body.

I was definitely feeling better. I laughed and snuck in a squeeze with my butt to check on the hardness of my muscles, but they had the texture of Jell-O, warm Jell-O. I then tried to do a few leg lifts right in my hospital bed and then laughed again at my excitability! My legs were like toothpicks but with a little flabby calf muscle that could have swung in a strong breeze. I couldn't wait to create strong legs and a happy, healthier body! Every experience that I imagined was bursting with enthusiasm and joy! I felt so alive and so grateful to have a human body to play in!

My passionate affair with my humanness came to an abrupt halt when my body interrupted me with another horrendous surge of pain. It ran through every inch of my intestines (and that's a lot of inches). It took awhile to move all the way through, and it was a jolt that seized my full attention. The pain took every bit of me with it and left no room for anything else to exist in my consciousness. My experience shifted from an expanded, inclusive, and joyful view of life to the small screaming space inside my abdomen. This happened in a flash! The rest of the world had disappeared, and the contrast was profound. I went from BIG to small, inclusive to separate, connected to alone; yet, something about it was different from all of my previous episodes. A larger part of me was now watching as I swerved from an expanded to a contracted state of being. Somehow a portion of me was outside witnessing this event, while another part of me was inside experiencing it.

I had another insight. I realized that if I could watch the experience occur, then I must be able to direct it and somehow be more in charge of it. It was my attention, my energy, and my experience, right? I reasoned that if my attention could go toward the pain then it made sense that it could also move away from it. It was a phenomenon worth exploring. When I was inside of something it seemed bigger than me, and when I was the observer, it seemed smaller than me. This shift happened very quickly as I went from observer to experiencer. Who did it but me? As I questioned all of this, I suddenly felt so present that time was standing still. That's when I knew there was something happening that I was meant to understand. The vibration of the room changed, the high pitch sound was there almost summoning me to pay attention, similar to when I was with Christ.

Determined to "get" it and be in charge of that whole process, as the pain continued, I experimented with moving my awareness back to the larger view. I used my will power to focus on life from a more inclusive perspective, rather than staying confined to the pain in my abdomen. I slowly became more aware of the bed, the room, the noises in the hall, the window, and the world outside, and I tried to include it all in each moment of pain. Immediately, my awareness grew a little more relaxed and then expanded, no longer locked up in the small space of my tummy. It was difficult to maintain this state for very long because the pain was screaming. I decided to allow it and concentrate on the intense cramping, totally and deliberately, as opposed to merely as a default response. The result was amazing; I was completely there and I was okay. I was more in charge. With each shifting of my focus, there was definitely a change in what I felt physically. Now from a more inclusive perspective, I could manage and tolerate the pain better. If I purposely felt the pain it seemed to soften. Although I was easily seduced and overcome by the intensity of the smaller viewpoint, I used my will power again to include even a tiny bit more awareness of something outside the pain, such as the sky, visible through the window, or the sounds of the feeding machine. It helped me relax. I went from an expanded to a contracted viewpoint a few more times and it was very interesting to feel the different sensations associated with each. I kept practicing. My ability to place my attention where I wanted to improved in just a few attempts. The coolest aspect was that the pain varied and shifted, depending on how much I zoomed in on either reality. I noted that my focus of attention had a lot to do with how I was feeling. I began to understand more and more of what Patricia had been trying to teach me when she had me look the pain in the eye, on purpose, as though I was the one in charge instead of the pain being in charge of me. It was making sense.

Whoever or whatever attention is placed on becomes more real.

–Techniques for Exploring Consciousness

ReSurfacing, Harry Palmer

When I was about nine years old, Dad lectured my sisters and I on how to view an emotional or physical upset as a personality (or aspect of ourselves) simply expressing its characteristics. He tried to teach us that the emotion was never who we really were; it was just something we were feeling. He said the upset would try to make us think it was us, but we were much more than the ideas or notions that the aspect was displaying. He called the upset a "not I," explaining it as a personality we were assuming and not who we really were beyond it all. Dad challenged us to catch when these "not I's" showed up and advised us to be sure and notice the part of us that was doing the catching. This whole conversation started because I had gotten into a fistfight with my best friend who, at the time, was pretty much my only friend. I was devastated over the argument and couldn't quit crying after my friend had told me she hated me and never wanted to play with me again. We were quarrelling about something stupid and she punched me in the stomach, not hard, but enough for me to strike back. I punched her hard, in the face, and she went home crying. She was very pretty and I was afraid that I'd messed up her face. I was used to being hit and hurt by someone else so hitting my friend back was my natural response. Half the time, that was how Patricia and I communicated. I think it was my friend's first time getting hit. I was devastated and really mad at myself for ruining everything. I was sure her mom wouldn't allow her to hang out with me ever again. I convinced myself I'd lost her forever. I was afraid I wouldn't have anyone to play with. I imagined the worst of the worst and believed it was all true.

Dad explained how the part of me that couldn't quit crying over the whole event was just a personality, a "not I," and when I was ready, I could take control of the situation by recognizing that my behavior and my fears weren't really me. He said calling the emotion or upset a "not I" would let that personality know I was the boss of it. Then he said that once I got that under control, I'd be able to see a new way to approach the situation one that could make a positive difference. He said responding to it from a "not I" personality only made matters worse.

Dad said using the term "not I" would help me gain some distance from the seriousness so I could understand it better and see all the parts instead of looking at one tiny moment. Then I could change things from a more balanced non-reactive place. It would also help me realize that our shake-up wasn't about who I really was; it was more like one of my personalities having an experience. He said that practicing how to make this distinction would pay off and we would eventually learn the difference between the sensations we were feeling trapped in versus who we really were—without all the drama. Even as a kid, I understood what he was saying, and it worked. I calmed down and had a sense of how all this negative emotion wasn't actually me. The very next day, my friend came by and we played together as though nothing had happened.

I continued to practice this technique for several years, but then over time, I simply forgot to apply it. Throughout my childhood, Dad was always studying different ways to manage reality. I later learned that this concept of "not I" came from two of his favorite mentors, G.I. Gurdjieff and P.D. Ouspensky. Dad considered their teachings fundamental to understanding the human condition.

As I practiced moving my awareness from one of experiencing my pain to one of being the observer of it, I began to understand, more than ever before, what Dad had meant that day. Anything that wasn't my beingness, my core self, or source, was a "not I." In other words, "it" was my personality, not my conscious presence and when I viewed it from this more inclusive perspective it lost some of its power over me.

During my visit with Jesus I had the unmistakable experience that my body did not contain all of *me*. In that phenomenal moment, I was instantly more aware of whom "I" really was and it wasn't limited to a container. From the Higher Self's point of view it was clear that pain, suffering, and turmoil were just as Dad had described, a "not I." Yet, when my primary focus was in my body, in the hospital, immersed in the pain, it was easy to believe that these upsets were truly me—all of me, and in that moment, that's all that seemed to matter. Calling these sensations "not I's" did give me a sense of freedom and clarity. Feeling the distinction between a "not I" and an "I" was a liberating practice and very comforting.

As I continued to explore all these insights with an increased field of awareness, it began to feel as though I'd mistakenly returned to the wrong body. Somehow being sick and lying in a hospital bed didn't fit with my new sense of being awake as *the* Source of my existence! Especially in those moments when the physical pain consumed me and I had to manage "not I's" prone to victimhood. It was such a contrast to those moments of grace in which I felt so expanded and loved. One reality was about accepting, understanding, and allowing; it was everything flowing in perfection. Then, there was the other reality, where I had to try and figure out how the heck I was going to make it to the bathroom in time. I knew there had to be a way to live in both worlds and allow the contrast without resisting it or making myself wrong for it being there. My mission was to gently fit them together. To feel the gifts of my NDE with Christ left me in awe—it was a high state of being and felt limitless. Yet, whenever my nothing-but-bone legs and me attempted to shuffle the short hike to the toilet, I'd be sharply reminded of my physical limitations. The simple, taken-for-granted act of using the restroom was a huge undertaking for me, and Thank God, it was also a comical event. I was witnessing the humor of the hindrance. At this point, even though I was the star of the show, I became resoundingly determined to close the curtain on this bedpan burlesque.

I was curious about how these two realities were going to merge, and I suspected that I would soon find out. Yet again I surrendered to the process, trusting that, in time, it would all emerge in clarity. I had to be okay with not knowing. I had a feeling that patience and I would become even better friends because my body wasn't embracing limitless possibilities nearly as quickly as my mind and spirit were. The virtue of patience had a similar texture to the virtue of trust, and I was optimistic about learning and appreciating the peace that comes with them both.

Many valuable lessons were coming my way on a physical level. I was sure that the gifts I had received the night before would be essential learning them. I believed that my visit with Christ, the condition of my body, the doctor, and my recovery were all part of a bigger plan than I could fully understand. There were no coincidences, and I felt prepared to meet whatever was around the bend. The mother and wife part of me was thrilled to be exactly where I was. I knew that the whole experience would bring my family and our lives to a world that was richer with what mattered. Also, there was a big part of me that wanted my physical deficiency to be totally healed and behind me. There was so much contrast it served as great inspiration to reach for love.

It felt like I had already lived a lifetime since lying in the hands of Christ, just hours before. I was anxious to get started on what was next, unaware that the time to physically heal was exactly what was needed in order to take me where I had always wanted to go—toward my fuller "becoming."

Dad burst into the room in a bit of a panic, jolting me back to the present moment. He had a woman by his side that I had never seen before and he was reeking of desperation. He was intently serious and it didn't fit well with my morning revelations. He'd brought with him an ocean of fear, disrupting my sweet little birthing process. He was definitely on a mission. So I watched, trusted, and didn't interrupt him. It was so nice to see him that my heart was filled with appreciation. I noticed I was able to adore Dad without getting drawn into his field of energy; it was a wider and more inclusive view, unattached and still loving. It was different. I felt connected to him and he seemed to calm down as he introduced me to his friend, who he proudly reported was able to see people's energy and help them heal. He announced, "This is Donna Hamilton, M.F.T.!" like I had been given a rare gift from the universe. She was a body-centered psychotherapist and taught many avenues of healing, including hypnotherapy and NLP (neuro-linguistic programming). She was also a Reiki master teacher and a graduate of the Berkley Psychic Institute. Donna empowered people to heal on emotional, physical, and spiritual levels. Dad was so proud of her and quite pleased with himself for getting her to my hospital room! I was delighted to be with them both!

Dad's intention was oozing from him; he wanted me to tackle any emotional issues that might be at the root of my disease so I could heal and not die. He was determined for me to succeed and it was heartwarming to feel his fervor. At that point, I was fine with anything and game for a new experience, especially with Dad. Having missed so many years together, I now loved learning from and about him. I had never seen him so vulnerable and open about his feelings and I treasured every second. I was anxious to let him know what had happened the night before with Christ's love so he could quit worrying about me.

I sat up to speak, but before I could say a word, Donna's determination came toward me like a fireball and filled the room. She moved in closer and was checking me out. Dad looked at her with anticipation as though she was going to perform some witch doctoring and exorcise evil spirits. I was in awe of her presence; she had full command of her energy in a way that was grounded, graceful, and wise. As she walked around my hospital bed and tuned into me, she remarked that it seemed like the wind had blown the collective consciousness out of my field of energy. It was empty—cleaned out and clear—and she had never seen anything like it. She was a bit perplexed, trying to define it. She said it was like I had received the Holy Spirit and that it had washed out my past and the illness. Turning to Dad she said, "She is going to be fine, this disease will not stay in this body." Donna faced me: "You are ungrounded," and she recommended exercises to help me correct that. I watched her with amazement. After being quiet for a moment she said, "You have issues to work on with your father." Energetically, she said she could see something blocked in my abdomen and upper legs that had to do with my dad explaining how this was an old war between us that had made a home in our hearts. I almost spoke up about what had happened with Christ, but again, something made me hesitate. I trusted it wasn't the right time. I watched, open and willing. Donna felt it was very important to address the turbulent past with my father and she wanted to do it right then. I surrendered to the moment.

I believed that whatever the universe brought me was exactly what I was supposed to have, particularly on that morning! Smiling to myself, I listened to Donna as she explained how we held emotion in our bodies and how feelings that we deny or avoid stack up, and as a result, often cause physical problems. She went on to explain that if those old negative feelings aren't released or. cleared, they will express themselves internally—until they are heard. My dad offered an analogy to help me understand: These negative feelings are like little babies you've given birth to, at one time or another in your life, and often out of fear you tucked them away and hid them. The realization that you (and only you) are the owner of these feelings is very powerful. If you own them as yours, then you can take responsibility for them, which means you can now transform them. But if you push them away, avoid them, or think they are someone else's responsibility, you can't have power over them. You end up waiting for whoever you believe is to blame for them or in charge of them to make them go away and consequently, you become a victim of what you feel. So, unless you get acquainted with these feelings, discover their hiding places, and manage them as a parent would a child, they can become unruly—taking over your mind and even your body. Dad went on to explain how these feelings would poke and prod us, non-stop, until we find ourselves trying almost anything to keep them quiet, including many addictive behaviors. All in an effort to make the bad feelings go away. He learned that acknowledging and expressing them was far less painful than spending a life avoiding them.

I realized as Dad spoke that this, on some level, was a confession. He'd dealt with many a demon and had turned to alcohol to numb the pain and battled endlessly to subjugate his feelings, only to discover that the very feelings he'd resisted had taken over his life. It's ironic when you think about how he'd resisted feeling failure all those years, and yet, he drank himself into failure. Given his explanation, it was evident that he'd come face to face with that which he'd been denying anyway. Sadly, he'd lost everything to those demons, including his home, his family, and his health.

I could see the evolution of his life more clearly now. As a young man, dad had been a professional baseball player, a darn good one, who'd lost his career to an injury. Up to that point, he'd been a happy and hopeful man with three daughters and a wife he adored. He had the world by the tail. But when he could no longer play ball, he was devastated and became angry and resistant. I believe he tried to drink away the pain in precisely the fashion he was describing. Those unacknowledged emotions had consumed his life even though he pushed them away with everything he had. They were still alive and kicking inside him, just waiting for him to let down his guard. This seemed to happen throughout my childhood whenever he took to the bottle. He was a big man, 6 feet 5 inches tall and 230 pounds with a full-blooded Chickasaw Indian for a father. You didn't want to be around Dad when he was drinking and feeling mean. I see now how it was just like he had said—the perfect time for all that pent-up emotion to explode on all of us, because he was drunk and no longer had the willpower to repress it. He ended up destroying, in a violent and verbally abusive way that which he'd loved the most. When I finally took him to court for abusing me as a child, I fled. I won the case and had always believed I could've saved my sisters from their own broken hearts if only I had acted sooner. Their precious spirits were severely damaged by the abuse; it took its toll on all of us but my sisters inherited the worst of it.

Throughout my youth, our family had been held together by a fine, delicate thread that unraveled as soon as my sisters and I were old enough to get away. We all escaped by running off and numbing ourselves to the pain, each heading in her own direction. Our concern for one another was always there but our past was a painful and difficult memory to integrate with our present. Each of us carried our anger forward in different, yet righteous ways. As a young girl Debbie ran away in search of her genetic father, whom she had never met, hitchhiking from Florida to California in pursuit of him. She had hopes for a better life and ended up sorely disappointed once she found him. For several years, our family didn't know if Debbie was dead or alive. Patricia went numb much like our father, consuming lots of drugs and alcohol. In an effort to avoid my own pain, I became a pretentious zealot of sorts, pushing some class, book, or lifestyle philosophy on everyone I knew. We were all busy avoiding our feelings and our true selves. I think our resistance to being who we were had a lot to do with how each of us developed a life-threatening illness (mine was just first to make its claim).

I contemplated the miracle my disease had been. The opportunity for all of us to forgive each other and ourselves was real. The whole family was softening as they gathered around the thought of me disappearing from the planet. We were all letting go of our need to be right and punish one another, at least a little bit. Death gifted each of us with an invitation to question what did matter and what would matter most when one of us did die. Being right or winning a lifelong fight was NOT going to comfort us or make us happy.

That morning was a pivotal moment in my healing as I listened to my father explain the path of self-destruction he called his life. Something opened up inside me even more; maybe it was the dropping of some old armor I didn't know was still there. Dad was making amends for the mistakes he'd finally become aware of by helping me avoid the same fate. I felt like it was all a prayer unfolding. As I listened to him speak, I said a silent "thank you." The morning was filled with grace.

Dad was intent on hammering one primary lesson home, as he continually repeated, "Resistance feeds the very thing we resist." I could tell it was extremely important to him that I deal with any feelings I might have pushed down or avoided. He felt these feelings were at the core of my illness, probably because after a triple bypass and a series of his own health scares, he'd become quite familiar with the pattern. He had a pile of personal evidence that pointed to the resistance phenomena, that's for sure. Feelings repressed or ignored, he believed, would eventually let you know they were there even if it meant bleeding internally to get your attention! This sounded and felt truthful to me.

Donna watched and listened intently. As she observed the interaction between Dad, and myself I sensed her confidence in knowing exactly what to do. This visit wasn't just for my benefit but also for Dad's, and I could tell she was thrilled to seize the opportunity. It was obvious he'd been caught off-guard by her request for him to sit facing me on the side of my bed. Even though he was uncomfortable with this, he couldn't avoid participating given the dialogue we were having about denial. He wasn't prepared for what came out of Donna's mouth. She was gentle and her concern for my dad was obvious as she asked us to stretch our hands toward one another touching palm to palm in paddy-cake position. Next, we were instructed to push on each other's hands, one person at a time, as we expressed our feelings out loud so they could be released. She told me to speak from my belly and explained that I had harbored most of my past in my colon.

I thought this was going to be difficult for Dad, more so than for me, because he had to listen, feel, and experience my pain right along with me. I went first. Donna was intuitive and knew this was going to open doors for both of us that had been closed far too long. With her strong guidance and clarity, we were as comfortable as possible. She asked me to feel and speak out loud whatever was true for me and to push on Dad when my feelings guided me to as this would be instrumental in excising hate from my body. Donna could psychically see how the hate had collected throughout my lower abdominal area and ran into my heart region. She said the movement of my life energy had been blocked by anger and sadness. I was encouraged to express feelings I had not been willing to express before, to let them out, to blame freely, and release any anger or hatred from my body so I could be done with these destructive emotions. I was certain that nothing too emotional or harsh would spill out of my mouth. Hate was a strong emotion and I didn't feel a drop of it near me. I was feeling connected and loved. I laughed and told her I didn't feel anything but joy. She didn't flinch and helped get things rolling by asking questions and urging me to explain to Dad what bothered me most about my childhood. She asked some very poignant questions and suggested I finish a couple of her sentences beginning with things like, *I was hurt by you because... You should never have... You should have known...*

Then I began talking... at first I spoke softly, uncomfortable and unable to look in Dad's eyes to tell him how sad I was as a child, how mean he was, how he hurt Debbie and made her run away, and how I hated being all alone. I felt anger stirring inside me and Donna put her hands on my stomach to Reiki the area and move some stuck energy. She urged me to push my feelings out through my hands and to make a growling sound to expel it from my belly. After a few moments of trying to be nice about it all, I was surprised at the venom that began to flow. My feelings started as a trickling river and suddenly turned into a nasty flood of anger. I yelled at Dad, telling him how much I hated him for leaving me and never being there for me as a kid, for beating me, and for not rescuing me from becoming a foster child. I looked him straight in the eyes and told him he was solely responsible for ruining our family, destroying my sisters, for hurting my mother, and most of all, for not loving me. I started to cry. Tears and words rolled out from deep inside me and the hatefulness and blame that spewed from my mouth was beastly. I went on and on until I couldn't push on his hands a second more. I was exhausted. I'd repeated so much of what I thought I'd already rationally worked through the previous decade of my life. I thought all of this hurt was gone. It was shocking to me that so much was tucked away, still there, stored up and quiet.

My hands dropped. I couldn't hold them up any longer. Yet, I felt energy moving through my lower body as though I had just run a few miles. Physically I felt alive and real. Expressing myself this way, so unrestrained and painfully honest, had accomplished something peculiar and wonderful. I was very present. I felt no pain or discomfort with this movement of energy and my body was tingling. It was invigorating and exhausting, all at once. I was different, more me, more open, it was real with no holding back or pretending.

Emotionally, it seemed as though I'd actually traveled back to my childhood and opened a container I had closed up tightly long ago. I let go of feelings that had been held in my body and mind for thirty-three years. Somehow they had become me, or maybe I had become them, and I didn't even know it! I thought those feelings were who I was, that they were part of what made me, and that they would always be there like an arm or a leg. I was wrong. I was feeling what it was like to be without them. I was lighter. I could see them as separate from myself now; they were "not I's." Clearly these feelings, beliefs, and opinions were not healthy to keep inside one's body and holding them there had a great deal to do with my health breaking down. I didn't realize how much of me had been tangled up with them until they were gone and, in their absence, I finally felt more like *who I was.* I wondered how I could've ever **not** known they were there! I wondered how much more of this type of energy could be inside me. I imagined what total freedom from old negativity could feel like.

I had to lie down. It was Dad's turn, but I couldn't hold myself up any longer, not yet. So we all took a moment and became still in the quietness that now held the deep emotions I had just expressed. Donna allowed the silence to do its magic and said nothing. Truth and presence hung in the air like fog. An unraveling and integration was taking place on an energetic level, in our bodies and our spirits. We all felt it and simply let it be, without resistance. Even Dad stayed still with no need to defend or protect. Humbly he was able to allow it all the space and time it needed to settle. Without speaking, Dad and I were aware of an underlying softness being birthed through the honesty. It was moving through our hearts and reminding us of the genuine love we felt for one another.

I felt Dad connect with me, without holding back. I looked at him deeply and saw him. I mean really saw him. He was aching and remorseful, perhaps owning his past fully for the first time. His spirit felt so soft to me as though a gentle breeze could easily lift him and sweep him away. His heart was open wide and the past was flowing out. *This is my father,* I thought to myself. Reveling in the idea that we would finally heal our past completely and be together for the rest of our lives as who we really were, love filled my heart.

I was ready. I took a deep breath and sat up with my hands extended toward Dad and he looked at me with a gentleness that I had waited years to experience. I whispered, "It's your turn." I watched as he dropped his head as though he was reaching inside himself for his truth. After a moment he looked up at me softly and said, "There is nothing to say." As he spoke I could feel that he had realized some deeper truth and had begun his process of self-forgiveness. Even though he had not used words, something had opened and released within him, within us. I could feel his love for me, and was certain that he had loved me all along.

We reached a perfect place to stop and witness it all. Another chunk of the past was dissolving as we viewed each other through new eyes. Donna felt it, too, and said we had experienced enough for one day. I was grateful for her intuition in guiding Dad and me to these precious moments. This was the beginning of a treasured friendship that was heaven sent. She became a big part of my awakening from that point on, using brilliant therapy techniques that allowed me to effectively tackle the store of unseen emotions that had been stuck in my body for a very long time. I have never met another like her.

I imagine that one of the reasons people cling to their hates so stubbornly is because they sense, once hate is gone, that they will be forced to deal with the pain.

–Notes of a Native Son, James Baldwin

The Great Pretender

chapter 4

Be who you are and say what you feel because those who mind don't matter and those who matter don't mind.

–Dr. Seuss

I understood the value of dishonesty early on. Frequently as a child I had to smile big and pretend my family was "normal." Otherwise, my friends' parents would never have allowed their children to come over and play with me. I had to learn how to be very clever, or else, end up alone. By the ripe old age of six, it had become clear to me that lying was a useful attribute.

Once we hit the fourth grade, my best friend Cindy wasn't permitted to visit me anymore. One afternoon as we walked home from school, like we'd done every day, we stopped by her house to see if it was okay for her to walk home with me and hang out. Her mother's answer was a quick, "NO!" She informed us that it was best to stay at their house if we wanted to play together. She was trying to be nice and smile on top of some nasty feelings that I quickly sensed as disgust and fear mixed with a little pity. Her disguise didn't work. Something was wrong and she didn't want to say so in front of me. But I knew what it was. When people were pretending or dishonest, I would frequently get a weird nauseous feeling in my stomach like something was off-kilter. I came to recognize it as a warning and even gave this sensation a well-earned name: the "gut." This familiar feeling crept through my tummy that day and I knew that Cindy's visits to my house were officially over.

Cindy's mom had to pretend. I understood. I was a fellow pretender. She believed it was more kind to "act as if" instead of telling me the truth. She didn't know how to explain to a nine-year-old that her father was too loco to continue allowing her baby girl near him. Personally, I believe it would have been far better if she had just said it out loud. At least then, I could have reported it to my mom so she couldn't deny it anymore. The truth would have been helpful and given me some hope for change (even though it may have stung for a moment).

The truth, however, never came out of any of the parents' mouths. The grownups all did the same thing: pretend and give excuses. They were never willing to look me in the eyes and say those words I longed to hear, "I am sorry honey, but your dad is a nut job and we have to keep our daughter away from him." With pretense prevailing, no door could open up to the possibility of change for my family and me. I didn't have the courage to confront any of the parents and ask for help.

I didn't hold this against Cindy's mom. She was good-hearted and gentle as was everyone in the family. Eight people lived in a tiny three-bedroom home with each bedroom equivalent to the spaciousness of an oversized closet. The house was always messy and seriously cluttered, but one obvious ingredient made their family very special and happy—love. They were all so nice to each other. I used to watch them, amazed at how they would drop everything to step up and help one another. They were a team. Often there wasn't enough food to feed all their own kids, and yet, they'd still invite me to stay for dinner. They were so kind. One of my favorite experiences at Cindy's house was when we'd have cinnamon toast with white bread, butter, and tons of sugar... with dinner! My sisters and I weren't allowed to eat white bread or sugar, so it was one of my favorite treats! Cindy's mom would always laugh, enjoying my excitement.

My sisters and I were no strangers to being rejected when it came to having friends over. Most everyone in town had heard rumors about my father and his drinking, and consequently, weren't comfortable with sending their kids to our house for playtime. Early on there were a few occasions when friends came by and Dad showed up drunk. It made for humiliating experiences at school. Classmates would spread stories about Dad, reporting how Howie Goss was running around in his underwear saying weird things about consciousness and asking kids strange questions like, "Do you know who you were before you were born?" Patricia and I would get so embarrassed. During one sleepover, Dad ripped the phone out of the wall and told everyone there would be no more calling of boyfriends. I was seven and probably couldn't even spell boyfriend. Then Dad hid in the backyard most of the night to keep watch over our windows, scaring the daylights out of my friends. Our guests weren't too eager to come back. I could only imagine what they'd told their parents. As we got older, friends rarely spent the night anymore. It was too painful.

As I aged I became very good at pretending that what people said or thought about Dad or my family didn't really bother me. I could ignore reality like no one else I knew. I became highly skilled at acting cool and uncaring. Sometimes, when I heard stories about my dad, I would join in and joke about his craziness, simply in an effort to belong to the group. I denied that I even cared about my dad. I hid my feelings in order to avoid being made fun of or left out. My friends, the people I came to care about most, despised him and there was no mistaking the anger that oozed out whenever they spoke his name. I had my share of resentment and anger, too, but another part of me secretly felt sorry for Dad and wished I could've saved him from the pain that I saw in his face and felt in his heart. I was very confused about how I should feel.

As my elementary and middle school years passed, many tall tales about my father spread throughout the halls. The most common theme included people betting big bucks on who could take down Howie Goss. Physically, he was a huge man. Some stories were downright frightening: one was about him being dragged behind a car in chains and another involved him being drugged with psychedelics. I don't know how much was true but Dad often came home with his share of unusual injuries. My guess was that when he had a few drinks in him, his mouth would get him into trouble. He was escorted home frequently. The sight of police cars parked in front of our house was a fairly regular occurrence. Living directly across the street from our high school had made us the local news event, many a morning. Mom was often bailing Dad out of jail or wondering where the heck he was. Whenever my sisters went out at night, concerned and trying to maintain some degree of normalcy, I frequently stayed home to comfort Mom. I smothered us both with the pretense that everything would soon be okay. I did my best to convince my family and myself that this lie was a truth.

Over time, I became a sophisticated pretender. I was clever at hiding the truth to get whatever I wanted, which usually included some kind of attention or approval from others. I was very good at pushing away fear and denying my emotions in order to appear lighthearted, funny, and tough. I became so efficient at denial that I'd forgotten that my suppressed emotions were still there, deep inside. Even though I could no longer feel the heartache, the truth of the pain was still directing my life. Under it all, I felt abandoned and alone and my strategy to "fake it until I make it" didn't work out so well… not in the long run.

I tried desperately to push my sisters into living in the pretense of my

"Happily Ever After" fairytale—but they wouldn't have anything to do with it. I begged and pleaded for Patricia and Debbie to stay home and make up with Dad, to accept him, to like our family, and to stop being so unhappy. It was an impossible undertaking. Patricia made great fun of me for this, sometimes cruelly laughing in my face. I didn't understand how she could be so stubborn and not want to make things work, or at least make them look like they were working by appeasing Dad. I used to explain to Patricia that if she just let him be a jerk, if she just bit her tongue, then she wouldn't get hit so many times. She wasn't willing to budge or sacrifice her truth. She was adamant about telling it like it was and was never prone to pretense. This made my endeavor all the more difficult because, in my mind, the only possibility for our family to "feel" happy was to pretend that our past didn't exist.

The more Patricia and Debbie refused to play my way, the more ambitious and determined I became to change them. I wanted more than anything to be in control and become clever enough to trick them into living my happy family fantasy. I would quickly mend every tear, fix every conflict, and struggle to convince my family that they were all right. My ability to sweep up the messes seemed to work occasionally, but then it became virtually impossible once Debbie started using drugs. My fairytale went down the tubes and the messy conflicts grew too big for me to secretly clean up. She didn't seem to care much about anything except partying and I couldn't get her to change her mind or listen to me. It was very sad. She started sneaking out the window at night, and after one or two more beatings from Dad, she stopped coming home, staying away from us for days at a time.

I was losing my big sister and hated seeing her follow Dad's path of addiction. As far as I was concerned, addiction was the thief that had stolen everyone I loved.

Meanwhile, Patricia was withdrawing. She was seething with anger and drew her line deep in the sand daring anyone to cross it. I was jealous of her ability to say "no" but hated that she could do it to me, too. I never had any boundaries and didn't understand how this was an option. I had a tendency to do whatever was asked of me without checking in with my heart to see what mattered most. Often, Mom would turn to me as the family peacemaker. She'd ask me to talk Dad into staying home and not drink. I'd do just about anything to make Mom happy. I remember my last attempt to persuade Dad to stay home; I crawled onto his unyielding lap and begged him to please not go out drinking that night. I told him I loved him and wanted us to be a happy family. He callously laughed in my face, making fun of me for being a pawn in Mom's game. Then he shook his legs to throw me off and get rid of me. It was devastating for me, because I'd made myself so vulnerable while trying to find a place to nestle safely on his legs. He and Patricia were very much alike when it came to drawing their emotional lines in the sand.

In my young mind, I was only doing whatever was necessary to avoid further conflict and pain. I was a chameleon, being and doing whatever might keep people feeling comfortable so that their anger would remain asleep. I would do whatever I needed to do to gain some control of the situation. I lied, cheated, stole, and wore any mask that maintained a calmer, safer environment. I remember stealing hundred-dollar bills from my dad's wallet once he'd finally passed out, so I could give them to my mother to buy us food. I even took the blame for things my sisters did and volunteered for spankings to save them from being hit. I was busy soothing everyone by giving them some form of emotional milk and cookies. Now I realize how much more supportive it would have been to simply allow everyone their feelings, and give them enough room to express themselves, even if it meant all of us writhing in pain for a few minutes. The irony in all this was how I promoted unconsciousness by pushing everyone around me to be happy. I was putting my family's souls to sleep by trying to soothe them and fix everything.

I was afraid of pain. I mean really afraid, like it was the monster under the bed that waited to kill me. I pushed everyone away from it believing that somehow I was saving them when actually, if I had just let the pain exist for a few minutes, without resistance on my part, it probably would have transformed all of our lives. I didn't know that you could let the pain just be present (without being killed by it). I thought if I allowed it for even one second, it would never leave me and I'd be stuck in the horror of it forever. This seemed like a fate worse than death. So I pushed against pain, discomfort, anger, conflict, and any type of unsettling emotion, in others and myself, as though our lives depended on it. I was afraid of my family being swept away by the pain boogeyman. I didn't think people were equipped to manage such hurt without falling off the deep end because that's what had happened to me over and over again. Whenever I closed my eyes at night, I'd get lost in my fear of pain and the worry and sadness consumed me. My resistance continued to swallow and haunt me.

When I was young, Debbie had been the gentlest soul in my life. She was four years older than me and calmer than anyone else. For example, when Dad would tell us to go get the belt, she did so without any emotion as though it was her daily bread. I think she'd been planning her escape since age eleven and tolerated the turmoil so well because she knew she was leaving. Debbie was very mature and street smart for her age, like a wise old woman in a young body. Even though Dad threatened her with punishments that parents can now go to jail for, she wasn't afraid of him and she wasn't controlled by his threats or anger. Debbie did what she wanted to, regardless. She lived her life her own way in spite of what others told her was best. Debbie trusted herself above anyone else. She was solid like a rock, secure in herself. It was comforting to be in her presence. I used to try and be near her whenever she was home because I felt safe. She was unwavering and less afraid of life than me; she moved through trauma like she was being guided by some ancient knowingness. Her confidence gave me hope that there was some greater truth besides my sad conclusions and that, someday, I'd find this wisdom and be stronger like her.

Debbie dropped out of high school and ran away from home the start of her junior year. Her absence left me crushed and depressed. My hope seemed to disappear right along with her. I wanted to run away, too, but had to stay and take care of my mom or else risk losing her to the pain monster, at least that is what I believed. Even though Mom called on the police to find my sister, she was never found and the search eventually ended. I feared I'd never see my big sister again and secretly began to grieve, again holding the pain inside me. I didn't blame her for escaping the hell that we lived in, but I was mad at her for leaving me behind. Debbie's strength and kindness had filled a part of my life that I didn't fully appreciate until she had left. The house turned empty, hollow, and dark, like a light had been permanently turned off. It felt like death in our home.

I slowly became hateful and bitter toward my mother for not finding Debbie. On one level I blamed Mom for everything, reasoning that if she had left Dad, put us in foster homes, or even killed him, it would have been better than the life we were living. On top of it all, I knew that Patricia was on her way out as well. She was miserable and trying to party away her pain. I was horrified at the idea of being completely alone with my mother and father. Without my sisters, there'd be no one else to be afraid with, nobody with whom to share the truth, and not a soul around to love me. I'd be the only one left for Dad to pick on and become solely responsible for saving my mother's life. I didn't think I could do it. I prayed to die.

Even as my hate grew, I couldn't bring myself to leave. I had to take care of my mother, no options. It was a strange law that came from inside me. I took responsibility for her state of being and for how well she coped with the pain. She didn't seem to have the strength to deal with life once Debbie left. She became frozen and retreated into some place that was inaccessible to anyone, including herself. I was constantly worried she'd try to escape her reality, one way or another.

Mom wasn't very confident even though she was quite beautiful. She did her best to make a home and she did darn well considering what she had to work with. She had dinner on the table every night and could make a meal out of hamburger meat and beans better than anyone I knew. She designed and made Barbie-doll clothes that we couldn't afford to buy and even made our Barbie doll furniture. In addition, she kept us busy with long lists of chores, which provided an illusion of normalcy and a false display of happiness when really we were all keeping busy to avoid addressing our pain. In my opinion, Mom suffered most because she wasn't able to tell the truth to herself—or us. She didn't think she was good enough. She never believed in herself and settled into the painful life that this kind of chronic belief attracts. Mom talked about how she should leave Dad plenty of times and often talked about how sorry she was that he hit us. She was a small-statured woman and felt terrible for not being able to stop him from beating us. Her excuse for not leaving Dad was always that she didn't have enough money to take care of us and that the little bit of money Dad gave her was enough to make ends meet so we didn't end up living on the streets. She felt trapped with no way out and often apologized, but never did anything to change her reality. Mom was depressed and afraid of what life would bring her next.

I held my mother more responsible than my father for the misery in our home. From the beginning, I rarely expected him to show up or be there for me. So when he didn't, I wasn't disappointed. However, I fully expected my mother to protect me, to save me, and to make sure I was equipped with the skills needed to survive the life I'd landed in. Because she couldn't do this for herself, my expectations were irrational. Of course, I held onto them anyway. It was as if I collected my disappointments and saved them up to hold in front of her like a proclamation proving her ill worth. Repeatedly, part of me expected her to show up and fight for me. She never did. I dismissed Dad, ignored him, and hardly noticed his cruelty over time, somehow accepting it as normal. With Mom, I was either angry with her or worrying about her. It drove me crazy that I was constantly torn between loving Mom and hating her. I was never interested in forgiving her. It didn't even occur to me. She was my mother and she abandoned me. She deserved to be punished. I felt I could get by without a dad, but not without a mom.

As a kid, I didn't understand why Mom didn't do a better job of controlling Dad. She would cry, throw things, and yell at him for having loaded guns in the house, for spending all the bill money on bar tabs, or for bringing whores home and ordering Mom to fix them all breakfast (yep, it was that bad)! But, Mom was a push over and never left him… she stayed! Dad would humiliate her and laugh in her face. I watched angrily as time and time again she'd make a fool of herself. She couldn't muster up the courage to walk out—even after Patricia almost lost her leg to a gun that had discharged in her young hands while she'd tried to hide it from Dad during one of his drunken rages.

I swore to myself as a child that I'd never be weak like my mother. I promised myself I would figure out how to make darn sure any man I was with respected and obeyed me! That was the birth of my controlling and manipulative nature regarding men and my issues with money. I was certain that if I had money, I'd be able to boss people around and have my freedom, unbeholden to anyone. I was success-bound at a very early age, taking any job I could find: cleaning, babysitting, or yard work. I saved every dime and counted it regularly. Mom said she never left Dad because she couldn't make enough money to raise three girls alone. So I decided to be rich, not for the money–for the control.

I don't remember ever turning to Mom for help or advice. She was too empty and depleted. It felt selfish to want any of her energy for myself and I struggled because I longed for it. She wasn't there for me like a mother would be for a daughter when it came to questions that a girl has about life, boys, sex, or their bodies. I had to deal with many issues alone that she might have guided me through with a simple conversation between us. I didn't know squat about the birds and the bees (or the best way to prevent being stung) and my ignorance embarrassed me. I figured it out the hard way and angrily added more blame to Mom's pile.

A huge part of my youth was spent helping Mom cope. I did it to ensure she didn't kill herself. I worried about that when the lights went out at night. I ended up being more her mother than she was mine. By the time I started high school there wasn't anything left in Mom for us or anyone else; her plate was too full of disappointments. We didn't have enough money for the bills and were often short on food. Dad spent nearly all his money on golf, booze, and strange women. Debbie was gone, Patricia was disappearing rapidly, and eventually, we lost our house to the bank. Mom barely survived. I always pretended I was fine so that Mom never needed to look in my direction or pay a drop of attention to me. I was her rock. At least, that's what I made her think. Then I turned around and blamed her for not seeing who I was underneath the mask I wore. I blamed her for not seeing through my pretense as though it was all her fault. Eventually, I gave up on her ever showing up for herself or me and began to search for other ways that I could feel loved.

My friends became my safe haven. Even though I hid my guilt and pain and kept many secrets from them, I finally felt like I belonged somewhere, and that I mattered. It seemed like we were all pretending about one thing or another in an effort to be popular and found weird comfort in our group denial. I'd silently point my finger at all of them, believing they were faking or lying. I was constantly noticing deception outside of me rather than owning that I was the one doing the pretending. I didn't know it at the time, but what I was feeling in them was actually coming from inside me; it was the filter I saw everyone through. In an effort to protect myself from people who might have been dishonest and pretending like I was, I projected pretenders everywhere around me. I didn't trust anyone (mostly because I believed they were all like me). I thought people in general were all hiding something they were ashamed of and I found solace in the fact that nobody in our little group was interested in digging up any of it. I truly thought it was they who were being fake never once looking honestly into my own eyes.

Sometimes I assumed a superior role in which I'd prod my friends to become more "real." I acted like I was the one that knew the truth and could help them find theirs. It was habit-forming because I liked feeling useful. It ended up being a clever way to keep anybody from pointing a finger back at me and asking honest questions that would have exposed my own pain and vulnerability. It made me feel powerful and in control.

In my determination to stay in control, I continually gathered more ways to conceal my negative emotions, rationalizing on some level that they were gradually fading. Over time, I became an expert at hiding my true self. It became a programmed response to pretend to be whatever would make others happy. It was part instinct because when I got spanked as a child, if I cried or showed any emotion, I'd be struck again for being weak. Not revealing how I really felt was how I learned to survive and how I got Dad to stop hitting me. Strangely enough, detaching from my feelings was a technique that had won me approval from my father. Not feeling anything negative became my twisted and confused approach to feeling loved as a child.

So, I was pretty certain it was smarter and more important to be coveted and to look good than to tell the truth about what was going on in my mind or heart. My friends and I partied, laughed, and smothered our pain in deception; at least that's what I saw outside of me because that is what was inside of me. I felt we were safe with each other as long as nobody prodded me. I had no idea how much wearing that mask added to my loneliness.

I had very little awareness of who I was underneath my outward determination to please everyone. The real me had disappeared into who I thought the world wanted me to be. The mask I wore took over and created a life of its own. I was deeply embedded in people-pleasing identities and behaviors, never allowing a moment for the privilege of listening to my heart's music, not once. I didn't even know I had a song inside me or that it was possible to honor it without being penalized or hurt.

As a child I believed the heartache that I suffered had to be a form of punishment from a mean God. A God I had made up in my mind. That was the only way I could make sense of my pain, believing somehow that I deserved whatever I got. I ended up very afraid of being a bad person for fear of getting into trouble again and being punished even further. I didn't want that mean God to take anything else away from me. As a result, most of my energy and attention went toward wanting to be perfect and saving others from misery. Somehow, I thought this would make up for whatever horrible thing I must have done. My ambition to help people served a few purposes, including creating a nice distraction from myself; but most of all, it provided the means for me to feel like I really mattered. It became a type of addiction, as though it gave my life purpose. I was consumed with having answers for anyone who needed help. Being there for others was how I got to feel important. It ended up being another painful path.

Long before graduating from high school I had concluded that my ability to know and offer solutions for people was my ticket to being accepted, and important, and that this skill would truly keep me safe in life. I was hoping that spending my time in service to others would earn me a free pass through the infamous pearly gates. Suffering was the price of admission.

To earn salvation, I was determined to sacrifice my own desires and dreams so that others could reach theirs. In my quirky way, this was how

I believed I could redeem myself. In my quest for Karma points I threw myself under many a bus in an effort to hopefully, eventually, either get run over, or be saved by God, or anyone else that fit the bill. I was determined to be "good" in the eyes of this almighty being that I imagined was in control of all life. I felt that sacrifice and suffering was THE path to heaven. I became convinced that paying attention to others' needs over my own was the way to serve my fellow humans.

As a young girl I was struck by my first meeting with a statue of Jesus. He was nailed to a cross with images of blood dripping from his hands, providing the church with huge evidence of how he'd sacrificed his life for others. In that moment, somehow, I adopted the belief that this was what caring for others looked like. In some indoctrinated fashion, it made sense for me to bleed for others, too, so I could be considered a loving person and gain the good graces of God, or whoever I imagined to be in charge of my reality at the time. Boy, was I off the mark.

Little did I know that my approach to saving people was not only disempowering, it was disingenuous. It was birthed from my own insecurities more than it ever was about anyone else.

While waiting for a Moses to lead us into the Promised Land, we have forgotten how to walk.

–People in Quandaries:
The Semantics of Personal Adjustment,
Wendell Johnson

The Seed

chapter 5

All possibilities of reality exist simultaneously; and it's your choice which one you choose to focus on.

– *Love Precious Humanity,* Harry Palmer

As layers of my past were unfolding memories were awakened in perfect order. I was beginning to realize how every word, every thought, and all the old stories were made up of energy and I was the one responsible for carrying them forward through time. I was ready to let go of the drama I had been keeping alive. Not out of resistance, not because I was afraid of it, but because it was time. It was a decision that came from my soul. It had begun and is continuing…

Having the family together in my hospital room stimulated us all to take a good look at where we came from and where we wanted to go. Each of us had our own idea of what had happened in our past and who was to blame, and each of us called it "the truth." Regardless of who was right or what was real, it was apparent we all held some horror in our bones. To consider forgiving dad was huge, for everyone. But there we were faced with a new moment, in a different time, each with years of failure at being happy under our belts. This event, my illness, brought with it a life changing opportunity, a chance for all of us to release old patterns and make room for something new. My family had a choice; they could heal the ugly past or take it home with them. Letting go required courage and trust, and I wasn't sure yet if there was room for that in the broken hearts standing around my bed.

Everyone was processing in his or her own way. Mom was struggling, unwilling to forgive herself for not leaving Dad sooner, unaware that her blame was keeping her inability to forgive in place. Patricia had a load of anger to deal with before she'd even remotely consider letting Dad off the hook, not realizing that the hook wasn't in him but in her. I could feel how underneath it all, what she really hated was the fact that she still loved

Dad. Debbie had surrendered a long time ago to what was. She wasn't holding a grudge but seemed unwilling to trust again. The four of us watched one another carefully and I had compassion for the choices each of us were about to make.

A big part of me desperately wanted to have Dad close, but another part of me still felt a little guarded around him. I had to find those pockets of fear, the "not I's," knowing they were in the way of all of us healing. The best way for me to assist my family was to release the pain locked up in my own consciousness. While lying in Christ's palms I had a strong sense that we emit a wave of energy with our thoughts and actions and they move outward from us like ripples in a pond. I was finally beginning to understand that pushing my family to change or to do what I thought was best only slowed down my healing process, and theirs. Making them be and act different was impossible. Their lives weren't mine to change. On an energetic level, taking responsibility for what I held in my body and spirit was what I had to do, for all of us. It was all I could do. I was more determined than ever to become more responsible for myself. As always, the universe complied with my wish by nudging me with a very painful memory. It was the final episode of my father trying to control our lives as children. He did it the only way he knew how, by scaring the hell out of us.

It was Patricia's junior year and my freshman when Mom and Dad decided it was time to fix our dysfunctional family. Somehow, Dad convinced Mom that Patricia and I were the part that was broken, particularly since Debbie was gone. They swept us off to a drug rehabilitation facility in Miami, Florida called The Seed. I was by no means an addict. I wasn't an angel, but I was clear that alcohol and drugs weren't my cup of tea, particularly since every person I'd ever loved was more interested in them than me. Trust me, I did the necessary investigating with drugs and alcohol to be sure about my conclusions. There were times I wished I could be totally unconscious so I could escape like others had. I could get there temporarily, but it never lasted. Things always felt worse the next day accompanied by a hangover. Patricia was experimenting a bit much for my liking and it worried me. I think she was doing whatever was necessary to appropriately punish our parents, at least in her mind. Hurting herself was all she had left. I also believe some unconscious part of her was so accustomed to abuse that it felt natural to continue it, only now she was doing it to herself with drugs.

Mom and Dad pulled up in front of the high school in a car we'd never seen. They had obviously called ahead because the Dean of girls had already pulled us out of our classes, explaining how our parents were coming to take us for the rest of the day. That was a first. We asked her why and a few other questions, but the Dean never answered, blatantly ignoring us. She was a tough woman, not someone to mess with. Both my sisters had firsthand proof of that. Patricia and I exchanged a cautious glance behind the Dean's back. I had an eerie feeling as we walked down the hall toward the school exit. The Dean deliberately walked between us so we couldn't talk. She moved quickly, escorting us down the very long sidewalk in front of the school (Dad sold cars for a living and I assumed this was a demo he was able to borrow). Mom and Dad both stared ahead, giving not a glance, a smile, a hello, or anything as the Dean opened the car's backdoor. I was confused and had a horrible feeling in my gut. I slid in the backseat. I didn't make any sense out of what was happening until it was too late. A solemn Mom and Dad didn't say a word, as the Dean (a good-sized woman) made sure we climbed in and then closed the door a little too quickly for my liking. A big "uh oh!" screamed inside my head. Dad pulled away and immediately auto-locked the car doors. Mom, without looking back, informed us we were going to the Division of Youth Services (DYS) to be put into foster homes. I had a twinge of excitement, thinking this would be a good solution for all of us. I had already secretly been gathering information on the process. But something wasn't right about her words. My mind hoped they were true and I tried to believe them, but viscerally I felt their emptiness. I got scared. Wide-eyed and close to terrified, I looked to Patricia for something, anything, an indication that we would be okay, that she had a plan, that she knew what to do. But, she was completely blank, hollow, nothing, and wouldn't even look back at me. I hated what I felt in her, it made my skin crawl off the bones. She felt dead.

When we turned right on the interstate to head south instead of downtown toward the DYS office, I knew something was terribly wrong. I saw the grin on my father's face in the rearview mirror and my stomach turned. He could be a mean, spiteful man and he was enjoying himself. Suddenly, I had an idea! If I was able to unlock the door I could jump out when the car stopped and run away. That was when I realized how stupid Patricia and I were not to notice that the door handles had been removed. I pointed this out to Patricia but she already knew. We were trapped, prisoners being transported. Mom had lied.

I didn't know where we were going but I was sure it wasn't good. We learned at a young age to not make any noise or trouble in the backseat or a swift slap would quickly meet our face. Dad locked my window so I couldn't roll it down to open the door using the outside handle, or crawl out of it at a stoplight. We were tricked, ambushed, and totally stuck. I watched as Patricia disappeared into a daze and began ripping every type of paper in her purse and schoolbooks into itsy bitsy pieces, throwing them all over the floor. My guess was it was the best she could do to express her hatred and annoy Dad since we all knew the car had to be returned in immaculate condition. I asked where we were going as often as I could without chancing an attack. They kept ignoring me until after twenty minutes or so Mom fessed up and told us they were taking us to The Seed, a rehab for heavy drug users, and infamously known for the permanent damage they inflicted on teenagers. I heard they were closed down a few years later for inhumane treatment, including brainwashing and physical abuse. I freaked out and was as angry as I can ever remember being. Unable to make a sound for fear of what would happen, I silently cried, swallowing my hate. It didn't make sense. I had good grades, was on the swim team, was there for my mother, and always did my chores. I even tried out for cheerleading! These were not characteristics of a drug addict. As far as I was concerned, my parents had lost any grasp of reality. Taking me to The Seed would kill me, and be more damaging than the hell I'd already been living in! My mother knew this, too!

Patricia never flinched; she just kept tearing up paper. She calmly oozed hate with each methodic rip and toss to the floor. She scared me. I think if she'd had a gun she would have shot my father right then and there.

We drove for an hour in hateful stench. Finally, stopping to get gas in Alligator Alley, a stretch of road with nothing in sight but swampland and alligators. Mom and Dad left us in the car and went to use the restroom. I guess they figured there wasn't any place for us to run. I saw a phone booth out near the highway when we pulled in. Emphatically I tugged at Patricia, "Come on, let's run for it!" She didn't move and barely spoke loud enough for me to hear her say there was no place to go. I searched frantically for quarters for the phone booth and as soon as Mom and Dad were inside the station I scrambled into the front seat to get out of the car. My legs were shaking from adrenalin and I ran for the phone like my life depended on it. I made it, got in, and locked my legs against the door to block it shut as I dialed my boyfriend's number. He was my first boyfriend and I was smitten. Thank God he picked up the phone. When he answered

I was talking, crying, and blubbering so much he could hardly understand me. I told him to hurry and call the DYS and explain how abusive my parents were so they could rescue us. I told my boyfriend he was our only hope and that he had to save us and get the authorities involved!

I looked up and Mom and Dad were walking toward the booth, irritated. I didn't care. It was worth being hit. I dramatically told my boyfriend that I loved him, knowing inside I was doomed and had no chance of escaping from Alligator Alley unless I ran into the woods where the gators hung out. I peered down at my flip-flops and knew this wasn't an option. One strong push from Dad on the booth door and it was open. He dragged me out by the shirt and ordered me to get in the car. "Now!" He growled, as he pushed on the back of my head. Patricia watched in amusement. Dad walked close behind me the hundred yards back to the car. The whole time I was anticipating a blow to my head from Dad's large mean hand but it never came. We all got in the car and rode in silence the rest of the way. The air was heavy with dread. I caved into a depth of pain and betrayal beyond anything I had ever felt. Anger welled up in my chest and thoughts of revenge were my only comfort.

Once admitted to The Seed, you were a prisoner until they felt you were ready to go home. Some kids were stuck there for years. I sunk deeper and deeper into my seat, knowing we were out of Lee County jurisdiction now and had a snowball's chance in hell of getting free. My hate somehow gave me strength. I started considering the idea that I could survive The Seed if I had to. I kept falling back on the fact that at least Patricia and I would be together. We'd take care of each other, for sure. It was an unspoken oath. I grabbed her hand and held it in mine. She let me hold onto it for a while, knowing I was afraid, or maybe it was because she'd run out of paper to rip.

Patricia never spoke during the three-hour drive except in the beginning when she told me to stop asking why. She never acknowledged Mom or Dad the entire ride, not once. Mom never looked at either of us. My guess was the guilt was eating her alive. Mom had repeatedly told us she wanted to leave Dad, hoping someday she could, in order to save us from him. I remember when he brought those two women home and told her to cook them breakfast, how she swore to us she was going to kill him. We even had friends she spoke with about "doing the job." It was that bad. He was an ass. So her sitting in the front seat supporting his insanity had sealed the envelope on my being done with both of them. I promised myself nobody would ever have an opportunity to betray me like that again. I joined Patricia in her numbness for the rest of the ride, turning off all feelings to the best of my ability so I could survive the ordeal.

We pulled into The Seed, walked into the administration trailer and waited. It was smoky and silent with a mix of mildew and the stench of sweat. The windows were shut and the drapes pulled tightly so our eyes took awhile to adjust. All I saw were cracks of light with rivers of smoke moving through them anywhere the curtains weren't closed well. There were three desks in the small 15 x 15 room with six chairs lining a wall to the right, and two more by each desk. Sitting at all three desks were women chain-smoking with their ashtrays overflowing. It was filthy, smelly, and hot. I felt like we'd walked into hell and these people were the demons.

You could hear every word said inside the tiny space. The counselors never acknowledged Patricia and me. They spoke about us as though we weren't actually there. Obviously, they had been expecting Mom and Dad and had them sign a contract for payment while explaining the check-in procedure. It happened fast, ten minutes max. The counselor never even looked up until she reached for her cigarette and took a long drag. While looking straight at me she told Dad he would have better luck if he split us up. I couldn't see her face clearly through the cloud of smoke, but there wasn't a drop of humanness in her voice. She recommended they keep one of us for a week or two, and then bring back the second child once the first had conformed. They claimed that sisters frequently hung onto one another, rendering the treatment less effective.

I panicked. Not out loud, but I was horrified and totally freaking out inside. Being there without Patricia would be my worst nightmare. She was so strong and bull-headed it was sure to save us from the brainwashing stories we'd heard about this place. As far as I could tell from friends who had returned from the program, the counselors' techniques had the same result as a lobotomy. The teens returned zombie-like. It seemed they'd lost themselves and had become clones. Patricia listened quietly to the debate about who to keep and who to take and then turned around to me with absolute certainty, "I will stay. You go home." She was hollow, yet firm, and I knew she would be the one they kept.

My eyes flooded with tears even though I was trying with all my might to hold them back. I didn't want to leave her. I knew in some way I would lose her. We had survived everything together, as a team. She was strong when I was weak, she taught me to toughen up when I was afraid, and she held me when nobody else was there. I always tried to make her life more comfortable, easier so she wouldn't hurt so badly. I couldn't imagine how either of us would make it alone. I believed the program was going to rearrange her world and it would no longer include me. The feeling in my heart was unspeakable. Somehow I knew the moment that was coming, leaving her there, would lead to more devastation than either of us had ever known. I wiped the wetness off my face, not wanting anyone to see me weak. Lost in my own world, I hated life, the unfairness of it, and the pain in my chest. I contemplated running out the door as fast as I could to escape right before the decision was made to keep Patricia. Mom and Dad stood up and said, "Let's go, Holly." I wanted to die instead.

Patricia and I were soul mates, often mistaken for twins. We were best friends. I grabbed her and pulled her body close to mine, sobbing. They had to tear us apart before they could take her away. She was shaken and vulnerable. It was rare to see her like that. She looked at me and promised me she'd be okay. All day, it was the only moment that she'd let her heart speak. With strong intent in each other's eyes we connected on a level not of words. I felt her love me and she felt me love her, completely and unconditionally. Then Dad grabbed my arm and pulled me out of the little building, demanding I get into the car. My anger and hatred for my parents doubled that day as my heart ripped into even smaller pieces just like the paper on the floor of the car that I stared at the whole ride home.

I didn't know it until much later but Patricia saved my life by staying. She took a bullet she has been trying to remove to this day, and she took it partly for me. The Seed was a cruel and inhumane place for addicts. I don't think I could've survived it and she knew it. The program would have killed my spirit, but on some level, Patricia would enjoy the fight. I wasn't as strong as her when it came to boundaries and in a strange way I think The Seed helped her heal an aspect of her brokenness. Maybe it was the least of many evils. She had a place to belong for a while. Even though it wasn't a good place, I think it was her first feeling of home.

Leaving Patricia there and riding back with my parents was the end of my childhood. I had to step up and handle what was coming, alone. I lost my sister for a very long time.

The ride was silent. Once we returned home I was put into a holding tank, otherwise known as my bedroom. Handles were removed from the door and window so I couldn't get out without someone opening either from the outside. They informed me that this confinement would last one week if all went well with Patricia's brainwashing. They didn't say it like that but that is what I heard. I was never left in the house alone. I didn't attend school. Instead, I had to go to work with my mother every day. I was not allowed to make one phone call, and nobody knew I was still in Fort Myers. My friends all thought I was at The Seed with my sister. I was a prisoner being held in solitary confinement. The only thing I had to talk to or work with was me, and I needed a plan!

What do prisoners do? They find a way to break out! I had one window and one door. The first night I checked the window and tried every possible way to turn the mechanism without a handle; I even tried moving it with my teeth. No luck. I took the screen off and the glass wouldn't budge an inch. I worked to get the screws loose and remove the handle case, hoping that might help the window open at least a little, but I didn't have any device that would turn the Phillips head screws. The door was my only choice, but I had to wait for the second night. I was exhausted. I put everything back in place so they wouldn't know what I was up to and fell into bed.

The next day was awful, sitting at Mom's office and being stared at like a criminal all morning. I was stashed in a back office with way too many people between the exit and me to consider making a run for it. She asked two of her co-workers to keep an eye on me and guard the door in case I tried anything smart. There was no way out, so I settled into my spot and tried to get some sleep so I'd be ready for later that night when I'd make my escape.

When we got home, I went straight to my bedroom. I never spoke. I didn't want to be anywhere near my parents. They repulsed me. I skipped dinner and despondently lay on my bed, waiting. Finally, about an hour after Dad wired my door closed, they fell asleep. I went to work figuring out how to undo the twisted wire clasp through the tiny opening. I was determined and desperate. I kept pumping myself up telling myself I'd succeed if I remained patient enough. It was my only chance for freedom. I kept looking for any method or tool to loosen the wire. I had to be very careful not to drop any evidence on the other side in case I failed and Dad might find it in the morning. That would have been a disaster.

I tried using anything that would fit to remove the wire: a mechanical pencil, a pen clip hooked on the end of a pen clasp, but nothing held it firmly enough to turn it. After an hour of tedious work, I had unwrapped only a small bit of wire and became very frustrated. I think I told myself I'd untangled some just to encourage myself, but mostly I only moved it around a little bit. I told myself to calm down and work smart. There was no giving up!

I worked on the wire some more and then took a break by searching for some other tool or object to help me grab hold of the wire and unravel it. I desperately needed a pair of tweezers. I searched every place imaginable, every drawer, all our old purses, the overnight bags, and under the beds. I decided to dig in the closet. I was so ecstatic and surprised when I found a pair of old tweezers on the floor underneath some shoes that I almost let out a yelp of excitement. It was a miracle. My hands were shaking as I held the tweezers close to my eyes, inspecting them and squeezing them to make sure they weren't broken or something. I poked them through the opening and reached the wire, no problem. It would be slow going but I could finally unravel the wire a little tiny turn at a time. I felt it in my bones, I was going to be free and I needed to plan my escape carefully. It was early morning so I decided it was best to wait one more night. I needed some sleep and had to have more time to organize my get away. I felt hopeful enough for my busy mind to actually relax. I told myself it was best to wait, not hurry and make some silly mistake. I needed to think about where I would go, how I would get there, and what I would take with me since I planned to never return to this home again. I couldn't afford to do anything stupid.

The next evening it took forever for Mom and Dad to go to bed. They were finally asleep around eleven (I could tell by Dad's snoring). I had to operate quietly and stay calm. We lived in a small condo with my bedroom door around thirty feet from theirs. They slept with their door open. I hoped Dad's noises would cover up any sound from my efforts. Mom was a really light sleeper and I imagined all kinds of crazy things: her lying there, eyes wide open waiting for me to make my move, me pushing her down as I made my way free, and worse of all, her jumping out of her pitch-black bedroom and grabbing my arm just as I was walking past. If mom turned her head just right, she could see my bedroom door from her pillow. I was hyper-alert with fear and my imagination was running wild. Any strange noise made me stop, hold my breath, listen intently, and hope my heartbeat wouldn't wake up my parents. The beating was so loud in my ears that I convinced myself mom could hear it. I was operating on pure adrenalin.

When my door popped open, I was dumbstruck and couldn't believe it had released. For a minute, I just stared afraid to move or I'd find out it was some kind of trick. I had no idea how I did it because the wire still seemed attached to the door latch. I was in utter awe but I didn't stop to figure it all out. I remembered my plan and went to work. I felt like a cat in the night, wide-eyed, ears tuned, calculating my next move, and ready to dash. I checked Dad's breathing and stayed very quiet, making sure the popping noise of the door hadn't woke anyone. With adrenalin pumping full blast and my heart pounding fiercely in my chest, I found it difficult to breathe.

I grabbed my little stash of clothes and money and bunched it all up under my arm. It was 1:30 A.M. I couldn't open the back door because it was a sliding door and they'd jammed a metal rod tightly into the groove to make sure it would make a loud clatter if I removed it. There was only one way out, I had to walk right by their bedroom door to leave the house. Mom had rabbit ears; she could hear a pin drop ten miles away and I had to walk within five feet of her head. I was prepared, wearing only underwear so she wouldn't hear any pant legs rubbing together. I wasn't taking any chances. I began slowly, taking what seemed like a full minute for just one step, eager to be soundless as a ninja. I took another step, moving very close to their door, and thank goodness the front drapes were fully open and a bright moon was shining through the living room. I couldn't believe my eyes! They had rigged a trip wire across the floor to the front door. A trip wire! I almost gasped out loud. I stood still for a few seconds oddly aware of the strangeness of my life.

Certain of my actions and feeling rather wise, I easily stepped over the wire. It was a moment for me. Symbolic, like somehow the real truth was going to be revealed. Like the tweezers on the closet floor and the door popping open, things were going to happen for me, as I needed them to. I calmed down, felt the rightness of what I was doing, and looked around to see what other trap might be waiting for me. Ten feet more and I'd be at the front door, only ten steps to freedom. Everything was happening in slow motion. I could hear the crickets outside, the clock ticking in the kitchen, and the rhythm of Dad's breathing; in that brief moment all those sounds were so pronounced. I was aware of my own breath and somehow soothed by its cadence. Three more steps. I stopped and scanned for some type of trap near the front door—a bell or a string of some kind, but the coast was clear. I slowly pushed the metal handle down and opened the door, only two feet from their bedroom window, and it made a very LOUD EEEEEKKKK noise as the hinges squeaked bloody murder! I was a deer in the headlights, frozen, reaching with my ears to see if anything had moved or if Dad's breathing had changed. Then a voice in my head yelled "RUN, RUNNNNNNN!" and I ran like a gazelle across the hundred yards of parking lot, leaving the front door wide open.

The vacant field that bordered our condo project was several acres wide with a few small bushes and no trees to hide behind, but it was my best bet. I couldn't stop running. I was too afraid. I was sure Dad was hot on my trail. I didn't want to take a second to look back because I was sure that would gain him just enough time to capture me. I kept going full blast for almost a mile. The moon was so bright I could see broken glass, cans, and lots of garbage under foot. I didn't care, barefoot, half-naked, and gasping for air, I didn't slow down. I bolted across the entire field before I had the courage to quickly peek over my shoulder, still expecting Dad to reach out and grab my arm. There was nobody there. I was free! I couldn't believe it. I was so happy and relieved. I laughed and cried altogether. I crouched behind a small bush to catch my breath and get a good look at the front door that was still open with no one in sight. I knew right then—I would never go back. I was done with that life.

I made my way to the mall parking lot. There were streetlights everywhere. It was then I realized I had better put on some clothes. I slipped on my jeans and shirt, and made my way to the phone booth across the parking lot. I'd stashed a few bucks in my pocket that I'd stolen from Mom's purse at work just in case I needed to take a cab or something. I called my boyfriend, who was ready to come to my rescue. I waited in the phone booth, squatting behind the painted part of the glass, making sure I wouldn't be seen.

My sweetheart was there in minutes. I jumped into his Volkswagen Beetle and we sped off into the moonlight. It was quite an escape. I felt strangely different from whom I had always been. It was the end of my family and my life as I had known it. I felt peculiarly and rebelliously independent, ready to take care of "me" instead of everyone else. I ended up staying at my boyfriend's house, with his parent's permission. He told them what had been happening with my family and they were reluctantly willing to harbor a runaway for one night.

The next morning I called DYS and was connected to a miracle. Vivian Foster was the miracle's name. Her presence and sincere goodness helped pull me through a very difficult time. It only took me telling her a couple of stories about my Dad hurting my sisters and me before she assured me there'd be no problem removing me from his custody to place me in a safer environment. She was very thorough, making sure I really wanted to be taken from my parents. She kept reminding me there was no going back once the judge declared them unfit. I told her I was positive about leaving them. I went down to her office and made a formal statement and she declared me a Ward of the Court until a hearing could be scheduled with my parents. I shuddered at the thought of being in a courtroom with Mom and Dad, and images of me being interrogated and beaten down by dad's glare kept flashing through my mind. Vivian was very kind and sat with me a long while, reassuring me I was doing the right thing by reporting my Dad to the authorities, explaining how it was not okay to be treated in such an abusive way. I pleaded with her to figure out a way to free Patricia as well and gave details of the abuse she had suffered. I could tell Vivian was angry at my Dad even though she'd never met him. Vivian said The Seed was out of her jurisdiction and because Patricia had already consented to the program, it would be difficult to release her. Already missing my sister and fearing the worst, I felt emptier and more alone than I'd ever felt in my life. I tried to hope, but I couldn't even do that. Patricia wasn't getting out of The Seed unless she escaped on her own. We needed more than a miracle. Vivian assured me she'd do her best, but I began settling into the idea of being without both of my sisters and going forward in life without a family.

Later that afternoon, Vivian escorted me to the children's home. She walked me in, got me registered, showed me my room, and did her best to make me feel cared for. Mom drove by the building uncountable times before and I'd always tried to catch a glimpse of the kids through the windows, wondering what it was like for them. To be looking out the window as one of them now was sad and very bizarre. The cars rolled by quickly and I wondered if they were looking in at me. I was vulnerable, unsure about where I was going to live, and I felt like an outcast.

The playroom waiting area sat sterile and empty. Everything was made out of metal and it matched the way I felt inside. I noticed Vivian's attention on me and knew it was time for her to go. I tried not to cry but the tears started falling. I prayed for numbness. I was angry, confused, and felt betrayed by everybody I considered family. I blamed drugs, alcohol, Mom, and God. Vivian gently put her arm around me and pulled me closer with a hug of understanding while saying nothing. I let her embrace me for a minute, which was astonishing. Then my embarrassment got the best of me and I wiped my face on my arm and pushed her away. I politely thanked her for all her help and turned to look around for a place I could retreat, somewhere to hide for a while. Vivian stood in front of me and promised to be there for me, every step of the way. I didn't tell her about my lack of regard for promises and simply smiled respectfully. Although I was relieved to have someone I could talk to, I knew better than to expect it. She knew my heart was broken and, in retrospect, she knew I had no idea just how broken it was.

Vivian Foster did stay by my side and taught me a way of honoring people that touched my life forever. I loved her dearly, even though I never told her.

I woke up after my first night in the children's home and made my way to the kitchen area to sit down and within seconds about twenty-five small children were clamoring for my lap. It was amazing. I never saw so many big brown eyes looking up at me longing for attention with arms outstretched, reaching and aching to be picked up. To just be held, that was all they wanted. My misery suddenly evaporated in my deep desire to comfort every one of them and make sure they knew how special they were.

Easter was in two days and I'd been invited to help make it a big surprise. I was the oldest child in the home. I fell in love with those children and wished I could take every one of them home with me. They healed me more than I healed them. They reminded me what it felt like to be wanted and special. I laughed and played with them all day long. They were happy to just hold my hands and would fight over who was next. My soul was hungry for this gift. It was the best Easter I ever had and I felt very blessed to be with so many angels. These children became the important ones and my situation seemed insignificant as I peered into their love-hungry eyes and was able to share some of the care that Vivian Foster had shown me. In hindsight, I appreciate how the Universe provided me with that healing opportunity at the perfect time.

Over the next few weeks I worked very hard to find a legal strategy to break Patricia out of The Seed. Without money for a lawyer and with the jurisdiction problems, the outlook appeared grim. Vivian said we couldn't do anything unless Patricia initiated it by a letter or some kind of communication requesting help. I called The Seed and left numerous messages, I asked friends to call and do the same, I tried to connect with my sister in every way I thought possible: dreams, telepathy, angels, prayer, you name it, I tried it. I kept hoping she would hear me and respond but she seemed to be farther and farther away from my world.

For a couple of years I moved in with girlfriends and their families until I was able to pay my own way and rent an apartment. I wouldn't have made it without their generosity and understanding. They were more kind than I deserved and I wasn't a very grateful person at that juncture of my life. I was rebellious and self-centered, eager to break rules and prove my independence. I was angry at life. I was free of having a family and I behaved like I was special because of it. I had no rules to follow except my own. I partied and did mostly whatever I wanted. I used my friends and wasn't very nice or deserving of their kindness. I did well in school and kept a job, but overall, I felt like the world owed me something for what it had done to me and I was looking to get it.

I hadn't heard from Patricia for over a year when she finally broke out of The Seed and hitchhiked across the state to find me. I was sitting on Ft. Myers beach when I looked up and saw a girl standing about two hundred yards away that resembled Patricia. I stared, unsure, waiting for her to move or do something characteristic of my sister. She was timid in her demeanor, yet frantically searching the beach blankets for someone. Her frame was thinner than Patricia's and she was crazily dressed in boots, jeans, and a coat when it was 95 degrees outside. She also had very short hair, unlike Patricia, but I couldn't take my eyes off her. I stood up to move closer and get a better look when the girl saw me and started crying. Then I realized it was Patricia and ran toward her in disbelief. We both cried and laughed as she held my face with her hands saying, "I can't believe it's you, I can't believe I found you." She was different, very thin, and had cut her long beautiful hair, as most people in the program usually did in an attempt to leave their old self behind. Patricia seemed so weak, vulnerable, and broken. She grabbed my hand and turned back toward the street pulling me to leave with her, explaining how she broke out of a house in Miami and the police would be looking for her. She didn't even want me to go and get my things until she realized I needed my keys to drive the car. She refused to meet my friends on the beach for fear of having to talk to them. She was fragile and scared, not wanting to be alone, yet not wanting to be with anyone else. This was quite a switch from the sister I'd known.

While I had become rebelliously independent and self-centered, Patricia had become withdrawn and afraid. We had reversed roles. I was eager to help and be there for her as she had always been for me. Her timing back into my life was perfect. I needed someone to help me remember who I was, beyond my personality, just as much as she needed someone to remind her how she was Source of her experience of life. We had both forgotten who we were without our stories and had become lost in the drama of our life situations. Empowering Patricia to recognize the "Not I's" was a catapult for me to reconnect with the goodness in the world. As I encouraged her to become aware of her preciousness and follow desire to her unique truth, it awakened my own knowing of what mattered. We both began to remember who we were beyond circumstance. We explored how we could choose our next experience instead of feeling like a victim.

Our reunion was profound although unwieldy in quiet moments of recognizing our strange yet familiar differences. We had to reacquaint ourselves with the personalities each of us had adopted. Patricia and I were hungry to know who each other had become. We had always been stronger together then apart and we longed to reconnect and plug back into the comfort and trust that had always aided our survival. We left the beach and talked for hours. We laughed, cried, and tenderly began opening our broken hearts to each other, cherishing the safety and strength of our love. We gently considered what might be next for her, where she would live, what she would do, and most of all what she dreamed of. A question she had rarely allowed herself to ponder. It was my turn to protect her and make sure she was safe. I mattered.

We both agreed her recovery and reintegration into life was going to be a challenge. She explained how The Seed broke her down and terrified her, persuading her to accept the "fact" that her old friends, every single one of them, were really her enemies. I could tell I had been included in that list. She didn't quite open up all the way with me. She was confused and afraid and I understood how my nonconformity could pose a threat via the unusual mode of her brainwashed thinking. Her survival in the program was based on pretending to fit in and agree. She explained how they wouldn't feed her or let her shower unless she did what they said so she acted as though she was a believer in their system. She'd pretended for so long that she wasn't sure who she was anymore. Patricia was fragmented and needed expert help I couldn't give. I didn't know what to do or who to trust with her heart. On her own, she finally decided to talk to Mom and Dad, feeling confident she could persuade them to let her return home. Unbeknownst to me, they had visited her quite a bit during her time at The Seed and she'd created a new and different relationship with our parents.

The sun was setting and after much contemplation I took Patricia to Mom and Dad's condo, she felt confident this was the best choice and that was what mattered most. I left her there without going in. It was very unsettling watching her walk through that same door I had broken out of a year earlier. My sister as I knew her was gone. Patricia's personality had been torn down; she'd been molded to become who others wanted her to be. Although he didn't use a belt, Dad beat her one last time by sending her to The Seed.

Mom and Dad agreed to let her move home that day instead of going back to The Seed. There was a positive aspect to the scenario, Patricia got off drugs and committed to school and the three of them actually had a fairly good year together. She felt they mended part of their relationship. But the few times Patricia and I hung out the connection between her and my parents never seemed authentic and actually gave me a yucky feeling in my gut every time she'd mention it. Of course, not much seemed real at that point in my life. In retrospect, my conclusions were coming more from *who* was doing the looking than from what I was seeing.

During that same period, Debbie returned on her own accord after being gone almost four years. She moved into the tiny condo with the three of them and tried to make life work. Patricia told me she had to call the police on Dad one night when he was seriously hurting Debbie accusing her of using drugs. Soon after, Deb was sent to a girl's reformatory in Ocala, Florida. Dad had her put away for being unruly. Through all this, I almost never saw her or any of them. I stayed away and tried to pretend none of it had an effect on me.

Mom and Dad split up shortly after Debbie left. He was seeing other women and Mom began drinking regularly to drown her pain. They'd had enough of each other. Patricia helped Mom leave. I don't think mom could've done it without her. They packed up and took off together, moving three thousand miles away to Nevada. Before they left, Patricia called to say goodbye, it was uncomfortable. I elected not to see them off; I had no interest in any type of contact with Mom. Patricia and I spoke occasionally but were mostly living separate lives.

Since I had no intention of having a relationship with my father, as far as I was concerned, everyone was gone. Drugs and alcohol had consumed and destroyed my family. We were all either desiring them or resisting them, which really ended up being the same thing… addiction.

I was alone and even though I never told anyone, I couldn't believe Mom and Patricia had left me. I didn't know what was real anymore. The family I'd worked so hard to save had crumbled and all my fairytale characters ended up with dripping fangs, including me. I wondered if there was any point to being alive or if anything really mattered. I was obsessed with finding out.

Open Sky

If you're not amazed by how naïve you were yesterday,
you're standing still.

If you're not terrified of the next step,
your eyes are closed.

If you're standing still and your eyes are closed,
then you're only dreaming that you're awake.

A caged bird in a boundless sky.

–*The Enlightenment Trilogy,* Jed McKenna

My Momster

chapter 6

The Thoughts I Think Determine the Relationship I Attract... *You are the thinking, Vibrating attractor of your experience; and the thoughts you think determine everything about the life that you live. As you turn your attention toward the positive aspects of the personalities and behaviors of others with whom you share your planet, you will train your point of attraction in the direction of only what you desire... Not only does the power of your thought determine which people make their way into your life, but the power of your thought determines how they behave once they get there.*

–*Abraham Hicks* by Esther and Jerry Hicks

Mom came to the hospital alone for the first time since her arrival. Even though we had spent a considerable amount of time together over the previous years, we were still strangers who never discussed the past.

It was hard for her to see me so fragile. It brought up feelings of remorse that filled my hospital room. I'm not certain if they were hers or mine. She offered to help me take a shower, the first one in a very long time, and it was kind of a celebration. The nurses had just given me the okay, after much begging on my part, to sit in a chair and let someone bathe me. It was going to be spectacular to feel water running across my face and body after a month of damp washcloths. The nurses kept poking their heads in making a big deal of the whole thing and Mom was so pleased with herself, finally being able to do something nice for my wilted body. She had a soft, sweet smile on her face and it was all peachy and wonderful until I removed my hospital gown.

Mom gasped when she saw my boney frame. I didn't blame her. I looked down at myself and screamed in an exaggerated manner right along with her, like I had no idea it was so bad. She laughed nervously at my sarcasm. My starved body was a difficult sight for anyone, particularly a mom. She did her very best to avoid staring at my protruding hips and sacrum, which were barely concealed with thin skin, and she tried to stay focused on my eyes. But you know how that goes. It's hard not to stare when something very strange is right in front of you when you've only seen it on TV. It shook her up. She turned away, fighting tears she hoped I wouldn't see.

Over the last several days, I'd been seeing angels. They hung out in my hospital room quite a lot and there they were sparkling about. The spirits or energy showed up as light and changed density and location as if they were dancing. They didn't say anything in words but I could always feel them whenever they drew near. They brought the feeling of joy with them and it warmed me from the inside. They would flash in and out of my awareness quickly and at times stay stationary as though they were preoccupied with something. There was no apparent pattern or formation and sometimes they would all disappear together like they had somewhere to go, quickly. They appeared the same way, all of a sudden and sometimes in groups. I always thanked them for coming and sent them love. There were a couple angels hovering close to me as I climbed into the shower using Mom's arm as a crutch. It seemed like they were there to help Mom more than me. She needed someone to hold her up right then and I couldn't do it the way I had through most of my childhood.

One thing I now know: a mother loves her child no matter what. She may not always do what the child thinks is best, or even what she herself believes is best, but a mother loves her child. As I sat on my little stool in the shower and mom gingerly prepared the water temperature pictures and memories began flooding my mind, as though someone began rolling a film. It felt like something important was about to happen so I inhaled deeply and trusted the unraveling I sensed coming.

When I took Dad to court for child abuse the last picture of my mom, the one etched in my mind for years, was her sitting behind Dad at the defendant's table with a vacant stare forward. She never looked at me. Not once. Probably for fear of acknowledging the pain and disbelief on my face as Dad reported with a straight face that he never did anything to us we didn't deserve. I wondered how many other parents used gardening tools as instruments for effective punishment. Mom was unable to stand up for me and tell the truth that day, just as she hadn't been able to stand up for herself throughout the marriage. Still, some part of me naively believed, even with all that had occurred, that she would run toward me and apologize the very first moment she saw me. I thought at least she would tell me she loved me and relay some message from Patricia. She knew Patricia and I were deeply connected and that her absence had been devastating for me. Mom was my only link to my sister and she offered me nothing that day in court, not one word.

Mom had an opportunity to make things right in her world that day. All she had to do was tell the truth and she couldn't do it. She would have opened a door to forgiving herself. In my opinion, that was a door she left tightly closed for many years to come.

The courtroom was filled with waiting and heavy dread. You could hear every sound and almost every thought. I sat with my counselor at the plaintiff table, placing my chair far enough back to keep one eye on Mom. She was sitting in the first row behind the defendant area where Dad was leaning back in his chair with hands behind his head in a disrespectful and impatient fashion. I turned, fully facing Mom, staring at her to get her attention and even though she was less than ten yards away, she wouldn't acknowledge my existence. I was flabbergasted and simply couldn't accept that she was ignoring me. I did everything but throw something at her, and believe me, I considered that. I couldn't comprehend what she was doing or why she was acting like I had done something wrong to her and how she could possibly justify being angry with me!

When I had been trapped in the car on the way to The Seed, I'd figured that Mom couldn't defend herself for fear Dad would hurt her. The courtroom was clearly different. Authorities were on hand to protect her. She could have spoken up and not been touched once. It made no sense to me that she didn't take this perfect opportunity to finally tell the truth. Particularly, after all the years of her apologizing and complaining about how she wanted to get rid of Dad and all the time I'd spent trying to help and console her! The whole scene was eerie. It felt like I had been transported into a Twilight Zone film and I couldn't figure out the story line! Mom was acting like Dad was a good person and that ending up in court was my fault.

I began questioning myself, wondering if I was a horrible person for taking Dad to court. I wished Patricia was there or that Debbie would magically walk through the huge wooden doors to tell me I was doing the right thing. For years I imagined what justice would look like and how Dad would be held accountable for his cruelty. This didn't fit any of my pictures. Mom's behavior really baffled me. I was second-guessing all of my conclusions and sorting through my memories for some clarity or confirmation. I reasoned, maybe Mom and Dad had made up, maybe he quit drinking, and maybe I was ruining their lives.

Within minutes I was sick to my stomach from uncertainty. I doubted everything I held as true. I even wondered if I had imagined my past. I was losing it. I wasn't sure if I could keep from throwing up before we even got started.

I had just decided I would back out, drop the charges, and run away when Vivian grabbed my hand under the table. It was as if she felt what was happening in my mind and body. In a soothing voice she said, "Everything is going to be okay, you're doing the right thing." Over the previous week I'd given her pieces of Dad's more serious rampages, though not the worst ones for fear of his being locked up forever. She felt I would be in danger living under the same roof with him and intended to make me a permanent ward of the court until I reached adulthood. She assured me I would never have to go back to him. When it came to doing the right thing that day I trusted her more than I did myself; I was too bewildered.

To be totally honest, I was confused about my feelings for dad, too. I'm not sure what I expected that day in court, but it wasn't what I got. I hated him and loved him at the same time. It was always like that. To be the only daughter who was taking dad to court felt particularly strange. Debbie and Patricia might have called me Dad's favorite and I was beaten the least of the three of us. Watching my sisters' hatred consume their lives, however, ended up feeling a lot worse than any belt physically touching my skin. All three of us were very good at withstanding torture. Our physical pain tolerance was off the charts. Due to the "don't cry or you get hit again" rule, all of us were accomplished at being tough, at least until we got back to our bedrooms. I almost never cried. Neither did my sisters. We would listen to each other's beatings hoping nobody caved in. I think we all experienced each other's trauma as deeply and painfully as we did our own. Not being allowed to express pain, our emotions hibernated until they began eating us all alive from the inside.

We'd been waiting less than five minutes for the judge to enter the courtroom but it felt like hours. Many feelings I'd worked hard to deny were rearing their heads. It all multiplied when I was forced to take the stand and testify. Dad denied all the charges as they were read, calling me a liar to the judge, which meant I had to prove my claims were true. My counselor was hoping it wouldn't come to that and reluctantly told me it was time. I got up and nervously walked into the witness stand area and did the whole place your hand on the Bible thing. I was scared, and Dad was obnoxiously laughing out loud at everything as though it was a big joke. I could see his eyes and immediately knew he was hungover. He had that mean look on his face that meant, "Get far away fast," in kid language. Mom stared at her lap the whole time. My voice was shaky and my mouth was so dry it made a cracking noise with each word. It was a horrible five minutes.

My counselor wanted me to tell the judge about the "hoe incident." So I began explaining, almost in a whisper, "Your honor, I was supposed to be home by 9:00 P.M. and I was five minutes late. My father was standing in the front yard in his underwear waiting for me with a hoe. I saw him as we went to pull in the driveway and I screamed at my friend to keep driving, to not stop. I knew Dad was drunk, which was always scary in our house. I told my friend to take me around the block and drop me off so I could sneak in the back, like we always did when Dad was on a rampage. Then my Dad chased the old Volkswagen Beetle on foot as we pulled away; it was moving really slowly about five miles an hour in first gear and my Dad caught up with us, grabbing for the bumper until we hit second gear. It was very scary for my friend." I told the judge how I was used to this behavior and continued, "We pulled around the next block, turned off the headlights, and rolled up to the house that backed up to mine. I told my friend to get away fast. I hated my friends knowing how crazy my dad was." I explained how they were never allowed to come over and hang out.

"Anyway, I got out of the car and crept through the back yard, which unfortunately was covered in leaves so every step I took was a loud crunching noise. I looked all around the tree trunks trying to see if Dad was hiding in the dark, waiting to pounce on me, but it was too black to be sure. It was frightening but not unfamiliar. I made it up to my mom's bedroom window and I tapped on it lightly. I wanted to let her know I wouldn't be home but that I was okay so she wouldn't worry." I looked over at Mom for support and she had a faraway look in her eyes, like she wasn't hearing anything I said.

"Your honor," I continued, "I would have tried calling on the phone but Dad had pulled it out of the wall earlier in the week when he was drunk, because he didn't want to hear it ring. He did this all the time. We almost never had a working phone. So I tapped a little harder on the window and the next thing I knew my feet were pulled out from under me and my face slammed to the ground, hard. It took me a minute to realize what had happened. Then I rolled over and Dad was laughing, leaning over me, asking where I had been and who did I think I was sneaking through the yard. I knew better than to talk to him when he was drunk so I quickly looked for the best way to escape. He had his foot on my leg trapping me against the ground. I don't remember what I called him or what I said but he raised the hoe up over his head as though he was going to chop my head off. I stared at him in disbelief. I thought he was joking and then I froze as the hoe started toward my head. My body wouldn't move. Then the hoe went halfway in the ground a few inches from the side of my face, some of my long hair was caught underneath it. I became animal-like and scrambled over on my stomach pulling my free leg up under my chest and kicked at him while I clawed at the ground to get a hold of some earth and grass so I could use it to pull myself forward. I pushed against his leg and moved about a foot and a clump of hair ripped from my head. I crawled away running on all fours until I could balance enough to get up. I tore off with all my might and heard Dad's laughter as I made my way through the trees in the dark."

I looked over at Mom again and still nothing. I told the feeling in my chest, "NO," so I wouldn't cry. The anger welled up and I bellowed, "Your honor, Dad did much worse than this to my sisters. He should be locked up, he could have killed me!"

The judge told me that was enough, to take my seat with my counselor. My legs were wobbly. I wasn't sure I would make it the fifteen feet to my chair. Firmly pushing back tears and doing my best to appear untouched, I moved toward my spot next to Vivian. I desperately wanted to turn toward the doors, to get away, out of the building and be alone. I didn't care what happened anymore. I decided I would run away like my sisters did if the judge made me leave with my parents. I promised myself to never go home again. I looked over at Mom one last time before sitting down to try and determine if she'd even heard a word I had said. But there was nothing, no encouragement, no softness, and no care, not even a glance.

In that moment, I hated her completely and was glad to finally realize what was happening was all her fault, not mine. I rationalized that none of the terror and pain would have occurred if she had left Dad. I wondered, if Dad had killed me that day, how she'd have lived with herself. For an instant, I almost wished he had, just so she could suffer. I was furious. In my mind, everything my family suffered from was due to her being weak. I decided again, I was done with her. I turned off my heart and committed to never opening it again. Becoming hateful was a weird relief from being a hurt, scared little girl.

It took time. But eventually I came to realize Mom couldn't

acknowledge me or be there for me back then because she was never there for herself. She had abandoned ship to safer ground the moment we walked into the courtroom, maybe long before that. She probably escaped to the same place she went when Dad was hitting us. It was her cocoon, her pretend world, where life couldn't hurt her. Mom was unable to listen to what I said that day in court. She didn't have the strength or courage. It would have been beyond painful and made it impossible to continue the safety and comfort of her denial. Hearing what I said would have opened a door to feelings that could have easily destroyed her, more than she already was. The coping mechanisms of humans amaze me.

Even as a young girl I understood fairly well that it was our choice to not feel. Mom and I were in an emotional stalemate. I intentionally told myself to stop feeling, to shut down, don't cry, save it for later, and most of all, let Mom go. It was all a young girl could do to survive the dismay. I'd shut down just like she had. It was all we knew how to do and we were both highly skilled in the closing-your-heart department. That was the only way we could endure our house of pain for so long. It was how Mom had learned to manage her world and continue to function, and it was how I'd been handling my feelings for as long as I could remember.

Dad was declared an unfit parent that day. The judge, being someone he golfed with, told Dad if he went to see a psychiatrist for only two appointments, he could have me back. Dad's response was, "Fuck her."An unexpected pain shot through my chest. I couldn't believe he said that. Worse, I couldn't deny that saying the words seemed to bring him great pleasure. I hoped Mom or Dad didn't see the flash of hurt on my face. I stared forward in pretense as I felt the strangest sensation move through my body. It was as though I had been slapped from head to toe and my insides were still stinging. While very aware of my counselor's disbelief; she was also shaken by Dad's remark, I played the perfect stoic. The judge didn't do anything but chuckle and tell Dad to watch his mouth. I closed up and withdrew even more. Promising myself to never be vulnerable again, I became empty and was grateful for the numbness that was enveloping me. I didn't think I could hate anymore, but in that moment it took on a new face. It was hollow, meaningless, like a void. I was beyond emotion. I felt my face turn to stone and it matched my insides.

I was deemed a child of the court with instructions to reside at the local children's home until a family fostered or adopted me. Mom's eyes were still a vacant pool of nothingness.

Ironically, that day was more about my mother than my father. Dad being mean and ugly was old news to us. I was already angered out on that one so I just added anything he did to the heap without much surprise about what came next. Mom, on the other hand, really surprised me and I lost any ability to trust … for a very long time. I didn't know it then, but it explained the trail of faltering relationships with the females I hung out with, on top of the already troubled relationships I had with the males I was drawn to. I attracted people who were not trustworthy… probably because I believed those were the only type of people who existed. I looked for love and ended up with partners just like ma and pa, abusive, betraying, and numb. My archetype for being cared for included being hit, abandoned, and ignored. In my world, love equaled suffering.

The pain tucked away by all of us that afternoon in court etched a path through each of our lives that was traceable to my sweet little hospital room where my mother was now scrubbing my back with remorse. There were consequences, decisions, separations, and a repeating of similar abandonment patterns in all of our subsequent relationships. Mom ended up marrying another alcoholic. Dad ended up with numerous women whom he was unable to commit to, or several he was committed to simultaneously. It all depended on how you looked at it. None of us were well versed in trusting and all of us were unaware that what we kept attracting was a match to who we were being.

After I graduated from high school I went to college via financial aid certificates. It got me started, but I never finished. After three years of part-time school I gave up, unable to pay all my expenses. Mom and I had talked a few times over the years, more to be polite than anything else. In one conversation she invited me to live with her in Las Vegas for free so I could finish school. Since I'd come closer to accepting that my pain was at least partially my responsibility, I was ready for the challenge of reconnecting. I took her up on her offer, which coincided perfectly with Patricia helping me realize that I was in a rut living in Fort Myers. She came and rescued me from my rebellion and hauled me off to the West to live with my mother. As we drove across the United States, Patricia's love comforted me through the decision to leave my friends. Truth is, I was hungry for family and the genuine connection I'd always experienced with Patricia. I also secretly hoped for a feeling of belonging when I looked into my mother's eyes.

At first, it was uncomfortable being with Mom. We never addressed our past, but we did drink a lot. People drank twenty-four hours a day in that town, at least in the bar I was frequenting! I never made it to college.

I tried to be a model, which is a short and sad story I will spare you. I ended up posing for a few ads and landed a cover for a community newspaper, but mostly I lived the fast life and freeloaded off Mom. I'd always worked hard, often two jobs, so the free-bird life was a new experience for me. Mom and I never talked much about what mattered or did much of anything that pulled us more toward truth. She wasn't into studying, unraveling, or dissecting consciousness like I was. We kept it light. I missed myself when I was with her. A year later, I barely got out of Vegas alive.

Mom had gone into a repeat of her relationship with Dad, minus the physical abuse, and married another emotionally unavailable man who treated her disrespectfully. I realized it was okay with her, normal I guess. She was satisfied with her life. I was still hungry to know what the point of existence was and I was burdened with my expectation for others to want the same. I resisted how Mom just let everything be, never reaching for more. She was an intuitive woman that had turned down the volume of her awareness and didn't want to turn it back up. Maybe it hurt too much. My unconsciousness became boring to me and simultaneously my desire to wake up began gnawing at me. I decided to move to Reno to be with Patricia. She and I always had that hunger for the truth in common.

I lived with Patricia for a while and spent time studying and deciding who I wanted to become, we grew very close. We were healing, pointing, arguing, and ultimately laughing. We both had our demons but were willing to be honest with one another. We felt safe together. It was so easy to see each other's weaknesses, not so easy to swallow our own. These weaknesses ended up being very much the same and the mutual reflection was a great blessing as it helped us take more responsibility for what we were becoming. Patricia introduced me to my first husband, Travis' genetic father. I ended up marrying a guy that was just like my Dad after all. Of course, I'd resisted and hated myself right into a perfect repeat of the past so I could learn the lesson and continue my awakening. The whole experience provided the perfect opportunity to integrate a great deal of my blame and anger, plus a little extra.

Finding out my new husband was a closet cocaine addict after I'd already said "I do" was the beginning of quite a bumpy ride. Obviously I had much to clear in the area of addiction or I would never have attracted him into my life. He ended up being unavailable just like Dad, not present, not communicative, and not home. So what did I do? I got pregnant. In retrospect, I was hungry for love and reaching for a solution. I thought a baby might wake up my husband and that he would magically quit doing drugs and want to create a happy family (my fairytale). To be very honest, there was a part of me that wanted to become pregnant so I could manipulate and mold my husband into how I wanted him to be. It was a selfish and hurtful attempt to control reality.

I was lonely and longed for a child. I didn't give enough thought to my baby or consider how my decisions could affect him and be part of what he'd end up processing throughout his life. I got pregnant for myself; my motivation was to have my way.

A part of me felt having Travis would fill my emptiness and that I'd be a good mother, no matter what happened with my marriage to his genetic father. Naively, I believed I could be enough for Travis when I wasn't yet enough for myself (doing exactly what I blamed my own mother for). I didn't think through the hardships that could show up if I ended up a single parent. I didn't think of the many times Trav could end up without a dad in school, scouts, sports, or when he had questions that a dad knows how to answer better than a mom. I didn't consider how his little heart could break because his dad wasn't yet responsible enough to be a father. I didn't think about when Travis turned fifteen and asked why his dad chose cocaine over him how I might answer or how it would feel to him. I never even considered the pain Travis' dad would likely go through giving up his son and then facing himself later. I only thought of myself. I didn't take into account that I would need to forgive myself and be responsible enough to answer all of Travis' questions about his genetic father without a stitch of blame. I never considered that someday I would need to apologize for making decisions that deeply affected the lives of others that were based only on my personal desires.

I was blinded by my ambition to have my way and didn't see what might be ahead. I was in love with Travis' dad. It was a love defined by abuse, a precise repeat of my past. He was the perfect man. He was just like my father. I recognize that I loved as much as I knew how at that time and in the only way I knew how, by suffering, being a victim, and trying to save someone. When I lost him to drugs my heart was broken. I went through the same abandonment scenario again. That was when I started to understand that this scenario would keep repeating until I realized and owned my part in it. Through unawareness and holding onto my resistance, I was the one that kept manifesting it.

That was when I started loving my mother again. Mom helped me sort through my fear and sorrow. She showed up magically right as I went into labor with Travis. Without anyone calling her, she intuitively knew to come. She had a long drive from her home and made it there as though this moment was planned all along. She comforted me as I gave birth on my living room floor with two midwives and my sister Patricia. After three hours of labor and nobody being able to find my husband, he finally showed up. Right before Travis arrived and even though I was in the heat of labor, I knew the moment he walked in the room he was high and I'd be raising my child alone. I realized as I panted and pushed what I had done. Travis' genetic dad wasn't able to give up his addiction for himself, much less for a baby or me. I knew that and never admitted it until Travis was born. Just like my dad and every guy I'd been with up to that point, addiction had won.

The blessing that snuck into my world, in spite of my mistakes, became apparent the moment I looked in Travis' sparkling, aware eyes. He mesmerized me. I became someone else, more full, more responsible and intensely determined to discover the magic of life. I had to. It was my responsibility as a mother to pass this treasure on to my child. I was not willing for this precious being to suffer like I had in a house of pain. I found tremendous strength and purpose in being awake, for Travis! His presence was astounding—pure awareness, and no busy mind in the way, our connection was heaven. I committed to do whatever it took to clean up my past and stop the cycle of abuse.

Mom stayed with me an entire week after Travis arrived and showed me how to take care of my baby. She helped me realize I could do it alone. She empowered me to trust my ability and not rely on someone else to save me, particularly an addict, knowing all too well where that could lead. It was a special time for her and me. It was the closest we had ever come to quieting our past. We stayed present and shared some very real and tender moments with our focus on the miracle of her first grandchild. He was all a person could ever wish to be in the midst of, he was pure love and he taught us both a profound lesson… to never give up because even the deepest of sadness can be followed by the greatest of joys. As I held Travis something loosened around the blame I harbored for my mom. I could feel her genuine care for me, for us. I let a little of it in that week. It was a beginning.

Sitting on the tiny stool in the hospital shower I was overflowing with gratitude for my mother. I appreciated all the memories unraveling and the ability to view my actions honestly, without any effort to be right or blame. As Mom tilted my head forward and tenderly rubbed my neck with soap, I realized how lucky I was to have her there, loving me after all I had done to her.

Mom was worried the shower was too much for me and asked softly, "You okay honey?" She was kind and nurturing, handling me like a lost treasure. It was the first time I connected with her in present time, without the past. I felt her goodness, her fragile body, and her life path. She was genuinely there for me. I imagined her motion and care were opening my heart so any remaining patterns of un-forgiveness could move out of my body. She scrubbed my back with such sweetness I imagined it was a symbol of our readiness to wash the past away. I longed for letting go, for both of us, so we could feel loved and unconditionally forgive ourselves.

Realizing the repetition of mom's "undeserving pattern" throughout her life, I saw my own archetype more clearly and how becoming ill probably saved my marriage to Pat. It would have eventually followed the same old road as my marriage to Travis' genetic dad, if I hadn't become aware and started taking responsibility for all the resistance I held inside. The pattern already had its beginnings in my fight against Pat's consumption of alcohol. He wanted to drink more every time I tried to control him. My efforts to manage his drinking backfired and inspired him to prove his independence. When I fought alcohol, alcohol always won. Focusing a bunch of attention against something merely attracted more of it.

My past was filled with people either emotionally unavailable, addicted, or both. I always thought they were the ones who were messed up! It was simply me, creating the repeat so I could learn the lesson and move on. My fear of someone liking alcohol or drugs more than me was vibrating so strongly that it acted as a magnet to the very thing I was resisting! Like Werner Erhard said long ago, "What you resist will persist."

I looked over at Mom to say thank you and couldn't help but notice all the sorrow her face carried and I had compassion for what she had attracted into her life, too. There was never anybody out there doing "it" to us. We were living, breathing tractor beams to what we had been resisting—we were abuse magnets. Every man and woman we attracted was responding to our unconscious message: I am unimportant and unworthy, and I deserve to be abandoned. A victim needs a victimizer to exist.

The greatest power that a person possesses is the power to choose.

–J. Martin Kohe

I needed to forgive my mother, unconditionally, and the path began with taking responsibility for what I'd done to her. I had to acknowledge, own, and experience my part in the cycle of punishment so the pattern could release. I knew this in the deepest part of my soul. The pain would stop when I became aware of the pain and suffering I had caused. I had to be honest about what I'd done. I believed I could finally do this wholeheartedly.

As Mom washed my hair with kind hands, I silently admitted that I'd punished her for a long time, on purpose, when I knew it was killing her. I confessed there was some part of me that felt satisfaction from her pain, like a debt was being paid and she deserved it. I admitted my cruelty, my bad intentions, and wanting her to hurt as much as I hurt. I cringed as I felt the meanness of it all and the pain I'd caused her. I felt it as my own. I felt a flood of emotion. As I exhaled I intended for the density of the sensations to let go and leave my body. I saw the line of broken hearts: we punish our parents… they punish theirs… who punish theirs… ad nauseam.

Mom carried forward what happened to her as a child, punishing her own mother just like I punished her for my pain. We cause others to suffer and then justify it with our own suffering. When does it stop? Subtly, family members hurt each other with a glance, criticism, and a diminishing comment disguised as a joke, or energetically by secretly staying separate. We cause such heartache by privately blaming our parents or some failed relationship for who we've become. Blame never solves anything and only magnifies the pattern. The affects of my cruelty to my mother were undeniable. The lines in her face told the story. She'd felt her heart break many times.

The remorse coursed through my body in waves. My chest grew heavy and my heart ached as I saw the trail of pain left in her world. I was sincerely sorry for each moment she suffered. I prayed for both of us to forgive the past, all of it, and release it to the Sacred with No Name. Then I intended and imagined all the old patterns dissolving and washing down the drain. With my hand I motioned for them to leave. I decided I was done punishing. I enclosed Mom energetically in my arms and showered her with care, knowing that the nameless filled her with love and eagerly allowed all the pain and sorrow to fall from her body and soul. I prayed for my mom to be free to love again… most of all herself.

Mom began rinsing the soap off my hair and water was running down my back to the floor of the shower. I took a deep breath and said a little prayer to the angels I'd seen earlier and asked them to help us both let our pain flow into the drain with the suds so we could start brand new. I prayed to know how to forgive her for everything, to be complete, and be able to love her without the past interfering again. I let the feeling of the Sacred fill my heart with trust.

I turned around, looked Mom in the eye, and told her I loved her and that everything was going to be okay. She started crying as though she'd been reading my mind and was also ready to let life love her. She apologized for everything and I accepted and assured her it was all perfect, explaining how in some weird way it was exactly what I needed to happen to get me where I'd planned to go in this lifetime. I whispered how everything we had been through led us to the moment we were in and that we had waited a very long time for this. I looked at her with such gratitude as I described how my love for her and others could only grow from here because I now understood what it felt like to let go of the past and forgive. She cocked her head in a funny way as if she was "feeling" to see if this was really possible. I think the angels whispered something to her because she relaxed, and accepted the idea as though she'd done something that ended up good after all.

So try to imagine KNOWING, in any circumstance,
that All OF IT, including beings in that circumstance,
IS, LITERALLY, your One Self, complete and whole.
For then, as you look upon an experience,
Which is really just your Self,
Your forgiveness will free you to experience,
With total openness and freedom,
Everything that is there.
Your forgiveness will allow you to BE,
Without thought of the past or the future,
Without concern for whatever a circumstance
might bring you.
Try, within your being,
To EXPERIENCE your One Self.

–*Journey Beyond Words,* Brent Haskell, Ph.D., D.O.

W.T.P.s

chapter 7

It is important that you here realize that you are not at the mercy of the unexplainable, that you are not at the mercy of events over which you have no control whether those events are psychological events or physical ones, in your terms.

As I have told you, there is little difference if you believe that your present life is caused by incidents in your early infancy or by past lives over which equally you feel you have no control. Your events, your lives, your experiences, are caused by your present beliefs. Change the beliefs and your life changes.

–*Seth Speaks,* Jane Roberts

Mom left with a lighter heart. It was good to be with her and relate in honor of who we were, beyond it all, instead of interacting through identities wrapped up in the past. The stillness that was born from being present was where the truth lived and we were finally able to meet there. I experienced her preciousness and cherished her openness with me. We spoke of how we cared for one another and the healing was pivotal for us both. We released a vast amount of energy trapped in old beliefs and ideas, simply from our willingness to open our hearts to one another.

As I lay down to nap I felt a tremendous surge of gratitude for what was happening with my family, my body, and my understanding of what mattered. It was a gift beyond measure. I was so different from who I had been. I sent a prayer of thanks into the room for how memories were awakened in perfect harmony with my ability to acknowledge and release them. That's all they were, memories, not truths, not cement structures, but ideas and beliefs I'd given so much attention and importance to that they'd became burdens I carried and suffered over. I was the one lugging around the beliefs so they could hurt me. It was me doing it to myself! A memory could only move forward through life with me if I brought it along. I was the carrier. I laughed at the simplicity and irony of my suffering. Who I was in the past wasn't the person lying in the hospital bed.

I could feel more unraveling in the core of my being. It was as though my body was purging old family movies along with outmoded conclusions that had grown as solid as blood and bones. My spirit was leading me somewhere new, like I was being guided through the layers of feeling in my heart by some inner knowing toward what needed tending to next.

I looked back over my life and pondered when my search for truth really kicked in, and it was definitely at age twelve when Dad handed me the book, Seth Speaks by Jane Roberts. The material fit into my style of thinking, like a key into a lock. It was food for my soul. I studied the book so often the pages swelled and fell out. As I began to explore and try on the teachings of Seth, I had a sense that most of what I thought was real or important wasn't, and the feelings I'd gotten lost in or ran from, were unquestionably beliefs and "not I's" that I'd mistaken as the real me. Even though as the pages turned I understood this intellectually, and could even sometimes apply it, I still fought myself and often forgot what I thought I already knew. I was impatient with my pace of awakening and continually struggled to be enlightened (struggling to be enlightened; an ageless oxymoron). I was constantly processing in an effort to control reality, believing I should've already been good at managing the ups and downs of childhood after only a few short years of study. I ached for intimacy with Seth's notion of being expansive, multidimensional, and a heck of a lot larger than the turmoil of survival. I was unusually hungry for the experience of who I would be devoid of the game I felt we were all hooked into yet couldn't figure out how to stop playing it.

I constantly questioned how much control we actually had over our existence and pushed on limits both self induced and otherwise to find out. I became aware of what I felt powerless over but never concluded where the limits were on what was possible, how much I could create, who exactly I was, or what my life purpose might be. There were so many miracles happening in the world that didn't have any rational explanation and I believed if they could happen in one place, they could happen anywhere. Dad always made sure we put attention on mind blowing events leaving news clips, notes, and even UFO sightings around so we would see them. One article I recall vividly told of a woman picking up a car with her bare hands when the jack collapsed and their vehicle fell on her husband. She said lifting it required no effort, it was easy and natural.

Dad maintained that miracles were the norm rather than the exception and that we need only to believe something is possible, without a shred of doubt and we could experience it. He pronounced that the woman could pick up the car because she had zero time to let her mind get in the way, she never even considered that she couldn't pick up the car. She just did it. It was a lesson.

As a child I watched many people use themselves up with their unquenchable need for things, spellbound by owning and seeming to miss the point of existence. They didn't seem happy. I didn't see the point of collecting all the "stuff" and I thought it was a distraction or a trick being playing on us humans. I wondered what it was all for? It seemed that working, collecting things, then managing them, and ultimately figuring out how to distribute it all when you died, didn't offer much of a dream. It was a weird ritual to me. Being human often reminded me of being herded, like sheep or cows, and I wondered if life was some kind of maze we had to find our way through to get to the real prize of joy.

Patricia was studying Ram Dass and we had many discussions about how little the life we were educated to succeed at was teaching what mattered most to us. She would say, "I have a bad case of the W.T.P.s," (otherwise known as What's The Point?) and we would contemplate and search for something that held great value to try and ease the pain and confusion. Our search always ended with us looking into each other's eyes, realizing it was our connection with each other that was important and most real. It was the "I AM" that could only show up when we were fully present and the feeling always brought me to my knees in reverence. It did something to my sense of self and all my troubles seemed to disappear in it. It was who we were—without our beliefs and memories. It's who the woman became when she picked up the car off of her husband. It was source energy experiencing itself. It was the substance in my world, the one constant I believed in, and it became home to Patricia and I in a very powerful way. It was the anti-venom to the W.T.P.s.

Debbie had moved to California, Patricia left with Mom for Nevada, and I searched for more satisfying answers to why things were happening the way they were. I longed for someone to connect with. I missed my sisters. I couldn't find anyone who wanted to explore consciousness with me without the use of drugs. I tried LSD, speed, and cocaine, looking for spiritual answers by accessing an alternate reality, hoping a door would open to some great truth, or maybe to my heart. I wished to find someone to share a new level of awareness with. I'd had many interesting experiences with energy and seeing molecular patterns of density, and even an occasional pink rabbit, but never found the doorway I was searching for. I didn't like the idea of hurting my body or mind, so my explorations concluded fairly quickly. Having no parents and raising myself during those experimental years, my self-discipline skills needed to be sharp and strong. It took awhile for me to figure that out. I didn't have anyone to answer to but me. My friend's dad who took a chance and let me live in his home with his daughter Kathy, while he was mostly away working, was a saint. He trusted me more than I trusted myself and it affected me so strongly that I wanted to become who he believed me to be. I went from being completely controlled by my father to having total freedom and autonomy. It took a little time to get the craziness out.

I needed money to survive and had to work for anything I wanted. Or I had to steal it. I got pretty good at shoplifting; stuffing lunchmeat, clothes, or whatever I could fit into my baggy clothing and then purchasing inexpensive items to conceal having stole the costly ones. Being a thief was a rebellious habit that I finally broke, with a little help from the police.

I decided to finish high school and go to college. I hoped this would lead me to something that made more sense than my world so far. It seemed that I needed to learn how to play the game of life, whether I agreed with it or not. I had to buckle down and figure out how I was going to take care of the essentials; food, rent, car, insurance, and enough money to have some fun. Obtaining a degree seemed like the avenue to being free.

Even though I acted tough and independent, I longed for the feeling of being cherished. The real truth is I wanted someone who cared about me to share the gigantic responsibility of managing my life. I wasn't very good at it. Nobody knew the real me. I wished for someone who was interested in what I thought, who I was, and what I dreamed of. I wanted a friend I could trust and contemplate life with. I wanted answers. I think I was too weird for most people. I was non-conforming and constantly questioning what everyone considered real. I was lonely for someone to be me with.

As I lay there looking out the window of my hospital room, watching the leaves on the trees dance to the rhythm of the wind, I felt compassion for all the suffering of humanity and for myself. Life could be very confusing. As an adult I had achieved the material life I dreamt of as a child but I wasn't emotionally fulfilled. I played the game and worked long hours, rarely allowing myself a day off to enjoy anything. I was either at work or in some kind of class every weekend up until the first day I got sick. I was rich in resources but empty-hearted and never able to let in love. I imagined all the lonely moments people experience as they move through human existence, unaware of the sweet caress of the invisible. I became sad over how much living I had missed. I never took time to be with the people I loved. My heart was aching. I must have been ready for change because another painful memory was bubbling up.

It was my high school graduation day and I had no family to celebrate with, so I decided not to attend the ceremony… even though I had my cap and gown hanging from the bedroom door in my small apartment and saw it out of the corner of my eye no matter where I sat. I hadn't been on campus for a long time due to finishing up my graduation requirements half a year early. I had given up the swim team and all school activities for work so I could pay rent, eat, and fuel my car. In my sophomore year, I'd started my first real job deep-frying chicken, which coincided with the end of my dream to someday become an Olympic swimmer.

As I checked the clock every few minutes that Saturday morning, I rationalized that nobody would care if I attended the graduation ceremony or not. I told myself it was trivial, unsure if I wanted to participate or just observe from the stands and then collect my friends and head to the parties afterward. After all, I had the weekend off! I sat, waited, stared at the green graduation gown staring back at me. At the last minute I scooped up the garb and headed to the school. I had to drive like a maniac to make it on time.

As I walked and then ran to my alphabetically placed chair, guests were filing into the football stadium like a parade. I acted like I was above it all in a very arrogant way. As far as I was concerned the graduation ceremony was more a formality than a celebration. At least, that's what I kept telling myself. I didn't expect anyone in my family to show up given they had all moved away, except Dad whom I was sure wouldn't come. I cringed as I found myself searching through the crowd every few minutes for their faces hoping someone might surprise me. I told myself, "Stop it!" Unconsciously, I continued checking out each new person. Admittedly, a big part of me hoped that my mother would make an appearance.

As I looked around the stadium at the families hugging and holding up banners, siblings hollering words of encouragement, and people excitedly motioning relatives to saved seats, the pit in my stomach became large enough for me to fall in. Everywhere I turned there was an abundance of love and acknowledgment. There was no ducking it, so I automatically went numb, always my best defense. Of course, I still put on a pretty smile.

The ceremony was quick. The most exciting part was the streaker darting through the stadium. He got quite a cheer before being caught. It brought the ceremony to a halt for a while as we all chuckled, watching the authorities try and apprehend him. Minutes later we threw up our hats and mass confusion ensued as parents shuffled to embrace their children. I stood in front of my chair and watched as everyone disappeared into the arms of someone. My crowd of friends was mostly older and had long since graduated, so there were only a few in the group that I felt a kinship with. I looked for someone, anyone to hug. Even my boyfriend was nowhere in sight. I became embarrassed, hoping nobody would notice me standing there by myself.

Then someone screamed, "My car, my car, I got a car!" A fellow classmate consumed everyone's attention as he held up and shook a set of keys. I gawked dumbfounded. What a present! My parents wouldn't be buying me breakfast, or even a graduation ring for that matter, much less a car. Right next to him a mother was holding her daughter tightly with eyes moist from crying; she was so proud and honoring of her baby girl. I kept staring at them all and realized my mouth had dropped open. The care seemed genuine but a part of me was skeptical and didn't quite believe these people were sincere. I concluded it was their job, their parental role. I watched intently, like a scientist. Yep, there was kindness everywhere; even older brothers and sisters were a tad emotional as they acknowledged their younger siblings. It was all very weird to me, surreal. I preferred to think of it all as fake. I racked my brain for some memory of an experience similar to this with my parents. My mind flashed to winning an event at one of my swim meets and neither of them had been there. I was used to not being recognized. I had even become skilled at overlooking myself in staying true to my wounded form.

Suddenly I realized I hadn't moved an inch and was standing motionless beside my chair, a lone wolf. I imagined that if someone had a bird's-eye view of the three hundred-plus graduates, they'd see everyone in clumps surrounded by people who adored them… except me. Nobody else was inside my ten-foot circle of emptiness. I was embarrassed and tried to disappear into the crowd. The groups were all complete and full. I didn't belong anywhere. At first I muttered some joke about it to myself, trying to brush it off as par for the course, but I finally had to acknowledge the lump in my throat. I quickly became very sad but then my anger saved me from crying. In mere seconds, an automatic well-constructed heap of pretense masked my emotions so no one would know. My face became calm and cool. I had a pang of jealousy running through me that turned into a stabbing sensation in my gut, yet I didn't even flinch. Many feelings were awakening that I preferred would stay asleep. I became almost dizzy as I shoved these feelings aside and began walking with my plastic smile intact. I wanted out of there fast, before I lost it. I thought I might just head to my car, the one I had saved for and bought on my own. My five-hundred-dollar olive green LTD special was waiting for me, but first I needed to find my best friend Patty because she was my party date. We were heading to the beach and that was just the remedy I needed.

The crowd seemed to open up and relax a bit, as the big wave of celebration began to dissipate. Patty's golden blond hair was easy to spot. She was the beauty of our class of '77. She was with her family, which included my boyfriend David. I slowly moved toward them, not wanting to take away from their special moment and then I saw Mommo Fiore's eye on me. I knew she was saving a space for me in her arms. I don't think anyone else that day but Mommo knew nobody was there for me from my family. Mommo had taken care of me over the last few years in her own way and even though I didn't tell her much, she always seemed to know when something was troubling me. She wasn't an openly affectionate woman, but her love was huge and unmistakable with every one of her six children as well as their friends. Mommo always had enough for everyone. A hug from her was gold and could fix anything. I walked over to her and she put her arm out while talking to Patty. Totally enclosing me in a squeeze without missing a beat, she asked, "Where have you been?" I melted into her soft, buxom form. She held me tightly making everything okay… at least for a little while.

The Fiores were my model for what was possible with a family who supported one another. The Italian in Mommo and Poppo (that's what everyone called them) created a forum for eating and talking and then eating some more. It was Italian heaven. They actually listened to their children when they spoke at the dinner table and were interested in what they had to say. It was a delightful phenomenon to me. Since becoming a foster child, although I had never lived at their house, I felt like the Fiores were my real family. Mommo took care of me more than she will ever know just by being the woman she was. She insisted I come and stay with her when I had my wisdom teeth removed and served me ice cream when I was in screaming pain. Maybe a small thing to some but it was monumental for me at that time in my life. I will never forget her kindness. The Fiores took me in whenever I needed taking care of and fed me along with all the other mouths they had to fill. They actually had dinner at the same time every night, and everyone miraculously showed up to be together. They were reliable, strict, and caring and I could drop by anytime and feel welcome. They had a place set for me at the dinner table, more often than not, and offered me a bed whenever I needed it. The food was fantastic and almost always authentic Italian. They were my saving grace and I trusted them.

As everyone began to break up and head toward their celebration parties I slid off my green gown, picked up a hat from the ground as proof I'd been there, and crunched it all into a disrespectful ball with my diploma rolled up inside. Underneath my gown I wore shredded blue-jean cut-offs with threads hanging long and straggly, a bathing suit top that showed under a loose-fitted tank top, flip-flops, and unshaved hairy legs. I was not dressed to impress. Quite the opposite, I was dressed to rebel and I liked it! Mommo's jaw dropped as she scolded me, "Holly!" I laughed lovingly and motioned for Patty to hurry up. We had a beach to get to! Patty Fe (Fe for Fiore) kissed her mom sweetly and we headed toward my old set of wheels. It had an awesome stereo that was perfect for drowning out any misery, especially when Joni Mitchell had the mike.

We headed toward the large gate and my car. I was walking fast, excited about being near the water. The ocean seemed to help heal whatever ailed me, for most of my life. I looked up from gathering the loose ends of my gown and almost fell over as I spotted my dad heading straight for me. He was just entering the stadium, about thirty yards away. I had only a moment to decide what to do. Part of me wanted to run into his arms and be told how great it was that I graduated, and the other part wanted to trip him and watch him fall flat on his face. I did neither. My heart was beating so fast and hard I decided breathing was my best choice right then. My fight or flight response was on full tilt. Then I saw him, I mean really noticed his body posture, slumped shoulders, and long face. I hadn't seen him for some time. He was red-eyed and moving slowly. Probably hungover, I quickly surmised. As we reached one another I muttered, "Hello" and stood quietly contemplating his face. He looked so old to me.

The silence between us was heavy and dense. Nervously, I rushed to fill it up by asking him to take my diploma. He was surprised I would trust him with it. I was, too. Truth is, it was the only thing handy I could use as a distraction so Dad wouldn't notice all the emotion brewing in me. He was good at feeling what was going on inside of people and could intuitively sense more than I ever wanted him to. I'd sooner die than have him realize he still had the power to hurt me. I assessed never seeing the diploma again and that was a good trade for freedom from his penetrating eyes. I'm not sure if he planned on saying anything. I didn't give him a chance to. I told him I had to leave and rushed off; afraid I might become weak and do something stupid like cry. I didn't turn back to look. I felt his eyes follow me and was glad to get away. I turned to Patty and said, "Asshole," even though I kind of felt sorry for him. He seemed like a reservoir of loneliness. More so than me and that was saying a lot. This was the second time I'd seen Howard Wayne Goss since taking him to court.

The first time had been very brief, a year earlier, when I fell into trouble and needed some spiritual advice. I was about to make the most important decision of my life. I didn't have anyone to talk to. At that time, my mom and sisters weren't anywhere geographically or emotionally close to me. Mommo and Poppo were Catholic, so turning to them was out of the question. That shortened my list of adults to confide in. I needed someone who was not subject to societal or religious belief systems and who had some connection to what I called Higher Self. Basically, I was looking for a priest-like person that hadn't been religiously indoctrinated. What an oxymoron. I hadn't attended any church since I'd been a child and I didn't trust organized religion to guide me anywhere but toward their idea of salvation. I considered myself an expert on religious indoctrination and nobody could tell me otherwise. Come to think of it, at age eighteen I considered myself an expert on pretty much everything.

In retrospect, I chose Dad intuitively because I knew he would direct me to my own answer. After all the years of him quoting scriptures and pointing to the bible, he was as close to a priest as I would get. God knows he had lectured me as though he was the Holy Spirit himself during most of my childhood, drunk or sober.

I had another agenda while seeing Dad. I wanted to connect with him and find out who he had become in the years since we'd left him. I had grown up a bit, was working at forgiving and letting go of the past, and was curious how I would respond to him. It was time to check in and see how we were both coming along. Plus I needed to know what to do, not wanting to make a mistake that would haunt me the rest of my life. I was two months pregnant.

Shortly after admitting to myself that I needed some help I was heading home from work and I thought of Dad again. I didn't do that often, if at all. Twice in a week was a lot. There were moments, in spite of all the hardships, where his awareness shined through and I would recall something valuable he had told me. He knew quite a bit about what mattered when it came to spirit and you could feel it in him, even though he was an alcoholic. Dad always said, "We're in this world but not of this world," as though he felt the meaning of this personally. He would speak of God in a way that guided me to find the truth inside instead of looking for it outside myself. He'd ask crazy questions that made me look at reality from a place never taught in schools. He was about as un-indoctrinated as one could be from my tiny view of life right then. Even as a very young girl I knew that what Dad was teaching and constantly talking about offered me freedom from the doctrines instilled by society. Sometimes, even half drunk, he could speak intelligently enough to be a guidepost in recognizing a path to what was next for me. At this juncture, I needed some of that knowingness.

My car pulled into the parking lot of the Pontiac dealership like it had a mind of its own. I walked right into Dad's office as if I had an appointment. He was sitting in his salesman cubicle and acted like he'd been expecting me. He pointed to the chair across the desk and I sat down. There were no kind words and no greeting. I had a purpose and my mind was clear about it. I didn't rehearse or plan any of it. I looked up at him and said, "When does a soul enter the fetus?" He didn't flinch. After a moment he said, "When you are ready for it to." I said, "How does someone know when they are ready?" He asked, "Are you ready?" Without hesitation or doubt I said, "No." He answered, "That's how." I stood up and said, "Thank you," and walked out of his office without a glance back.

I let what dad said sink in and questioned what to do from every perspective I could imagine. I prayed myself to sleep that night seeking wisdom and clarity.

I had a chance to marry into the family of my dreams and be taken care of forever. They would have loved me like their own. Patty Fe would have become my sister and my baby would have had the best grandparents on the planet. The problem? David was already on the path to alcoholism and exhibited all the characteristics that drove me crazy about my dad. David and I spent most of the year arguing. We had some brutal fights and many were physical. I pushed him over the edge every chance I got, almost begging him to hit me. It was my pattern. I knew in my heart marrying him would lead to nowhere good. David was my dad all over again and in my sick world the more he hurt me, the more loved I felt. I was aware of it, yet unable to stop the game or my compulsion to attract it. I obviously had more work to do and I refused to bring my painful patterns into his or a baby's life, not to mention hurting the precious Fiore family by dragging my baggage into their world.

Alone and afraid yet confident, as though something larger than myself was accompanying me, I made arrangements to get an abortion.

Apart from the pulling and hauling
Stands what I am,

Stands amused, complacent,
compassionating, idle, unitary,

Looks down, is erect, or bends an arm
On an impalpable certain rest,

Looking with side-curved head
Curious what will come next,

Both in and out of the game
watching and wondering at it.

–Walt Whitman

The Illusion of Truth

chapter 8

Illusions recognized must disappear.

–*A Course in Miracles,* Lesson 187, Marianne Williamson, Gerald Jampolsky, M.D., and Kenneth Wapnik

My hospital room had become a sanctuary of memories stirred. Each one invited me to experience a deeper level of honesty and offered a fresh appeal for forgiveness. My heart was breaking open in a very good way. As the past moved out, love and understanding flowed in. Who I was, underneath all the history and sensations, was coming forth from its cocoon. I was ready to meet myself.

Every aspect of my hospital room setting communicated something important. The gardenias spoke of love as they floated in a glass bowl wafting my favorite of all smells, roses and a variety of beautiful flowers across the room reminded me of people I adored, and my children's homemade get well cards on the wall portrayed the most meaningful stick figures ever drawn. My husband, the king of comfort, had installed a humidifier that mixed moisture with the scent of fresh flowers, which transformed my small, clinical space into a garden nursery. I gazed at the ceiling where he had duct-taped the air vent closed to prevent air from blowing on my face and I grinned. Tidbits of care were everywhere. I appreciated them all and let gratitude flow through me into my surroundings.

It was very peculiar to me that just one day ago, I had looked at everything differently, not only at my family and life circumstances, but also objects around me. Just yesterday the drawings on the wall had made me sad and stirred thoughts of guilt over my kids being without a mother. The flowers across the room made me lonely as I doubted ever seeing my friends again, and each whiff of gardenia stimulated a deep sorrow as I thought of Pat and me never having the life we dreamed of. To top it off, the only thing I could smell in the room was myself and there was nothing flowery about it. Twenty-four hours ago the room had reeked of frustrating reminders of the life I believed I could no longer live. Yet, in one day, my room had transformed into a personal church! Such opposite experiences, yet both rang of pure truth in my mind.

I realized what was profoundly different now—it was my point of view. I went from looking through eyes of preparing for death to looking through eyes of celebrating life. Each perspective felt acutely distinct from the other. It was amazing to see so clearly how the sensations I was experiencing didn't have anything to do with *what* I was looking at, but everything to do with *who* was doing the looking. Feelings never came from any object; it was my own judgment I had emotionally responded to. My perspective dictated my experience and I was starting to comprehend just how much a person's viewpoint affects their ability to be happy in life. A sick person saw something different than a healing person. How we see ourselves and our surroundings affects how we interpret reality. How we interpret reality carries a pattern of programmed emotions and reactions. From now on, I would pay closer attention to my translation of what is in front of me and choose who would do the looking. It was an essential lesson.

The intestinal bleeding had almost completely stopped since my visit with Christ and overall I was feeling spunky. Dad walked in and I was thrilled to see him! Just sitting with him was soothing to me. I had so much gratitude for his presence and our ability to connect in that place that seemed larger than personality or identity. This relationship was more real to me than the daughter-father costumes we'd been wearing. This new way of being was what mattered. It was authentic presence. When we met this way there was no room for resistance or blame—only love and honor. The session with Donna cleared the way for what was coming.

In many ways I felt like a newborn, with Dad being the one person that understood where I came from and where I was going. He was a guide on my path and it seemed like we had prepared and planned for the meeting we were about to have, a long time ago. It was going to be soul to soul and you could feel the electricity in our combined awareness. He sat down, reaching for the sesame oil so he could massage my feet. He had done this at least once a day since arriving, explaining how I needed to get my blood moving. I think it helped him relax and provided him with an opportunity to give, which he very much wanted to do. For me, it was a time of letting in his love. It was a bit uncomfortable at first, as receiving had not been my area of expertise. When it came to him I was particularly unpracticed. But I relaxed and allowed the flow. As he quietly gave to me I could feel a circle of energy moving back and forth as much as each of us could allow. It was nice to BE together.

I began to tell him of my journey into the hands of spirit and found myself feeling the strong sense of love Christ filled me with all over again. As I spoke the opening between Dad and I expanded and overflowed with a preciousness that is indescribable. I became emotional as I relived the sensation of allowing and honor that I had experienced in Jesus' presence. A couple of times I could hardly speak. Telling the story out loud to Dad added to the profundity as he experienced the truth of it with me. The nameless filled the room. To come from a place of blaming my predicament on Dad to a place of sharing the blessing I felt in my heart with him was a miracle.

This moment was sacred, dad rubbing my feet, my being given a gift from Christ, and sharing it all in a Higher Self-connection with my father. The meeting included more than what the visible world was revealing. What I was experiencing with Dad was bigger than both of us put together. The collection of feelings in the room felt like an answered prayer. Dad's eyes welled up as I described how the moment Christ picked me up all my pain vanished, and how I really wanted to go with him and be free of this life and body, until the moment I saw my children. I told Dad that the love I felt for Travis and Drake was so strong my soul was unquestioningly drawn in their direction. I shared with him how overcome with joy I was to see their beautiful faces. He looked at me and nodded his head in full understanding with tears running down his face and I realized he loved me in the same way.

Dad and I became silently aware of the bond between us. In spite of everything we had been through, it was still there. We sat quietly conscious of it, with no urge to pull away or hide our vulnerability. We were present with the mix of emotions that accompanied our willingness and honesty, allowing them to flow. I looked up at him and said, "Thank you." It was a circle of energy moving from him to me to him. He answered, "Thank you." Then I told him I loved him. He let it into his heart. We both felt it deeply and in a whisper he said, "I love you, too."

The past was not a part of this moment. We both felt its absence and the present was all that existed. It was visceral as though an old agreement had finally been kept. Some might label the feeling forgiveness, but it was more than that. There was a core understanding between us that all prior moments had led to this one and somehow there was perfection in the order. Forgiveness was irrelevant. Everything was exactly as we had created it to be and on some level we both knew that was true.

I continued sharing all the details: the Caribbean blue of Christ's eyes, the feeling of love with no expectation, and the space that was created for me to lay still in until I made my choice to stay or go. I tried to describe the feelings that didn't have words, "My favorite sensation of all was how spirit allowed me to fully be me, without a drop of judgment. The allowing felt like pure love, openness, freedom, ecstasy, and a strong trust that no matter what I chose it would be perfect. There wasn't one drop of Christ wanting me to do anything other than what I decided to do from my heart. I could feel how honoring my Self brought joy to Christ." Dad smiled, enjoying my conclusion. I could feel the knowing in him and asked, "What are you thinking Dad?" He responded, "Keep going." I explained how Jesus blew his breath from the tip of my head all the way to my toes. Then I asked Dad what he thought that meant! He didn't say a word and obviously didn't intend to. I went on to tell him about the constant hum in the background and how it was like a choir, an orchestra of tones, and asked him if he thought it was the vibration of energy in the invisible world or angels singing or what… still no answer. I watched Dad curiously as I told him about my blood work improving for the first time and he remained quiet. I mentioned how ironic it was that Donna had commented immediately that the patterning of collective consciousness had been blown out of my energy field. Dad laughed out loud.

I didn't understand what he was laughing about or why he wasn't answering any of my questions! He finally offered, "The answers you are looking for are not in me, they're in you." He said he could give me his interpretation but that I might be pulled in the direction of his answer instead of my own. Dad said the interlude was a gift meant for me and that he didn't want to cloud it up with any opinion that could distract me from fully receiving it through my own level of understanding and awareness. Suddenly I realized how different he was, all the stress had evaporated from his energy. He was lighter, happier and freed up from the fear and panic I sensed in him earlier in the day. Curiously I nudged him one more time, explaining how important it was for me to know what he interpreted my experience to mean. I questioned him anxiously as to what he believed mattered most about the event. I wanted to know if he thought I really died or almost died, or what had happened. I wanted him to give me his idea of what I was supposed to do with the information and, more importantly, who or what he thought it came from.

I pushed for some validation or insight from Dad because Higher Self and the invisible realm were his areas of study. He was the one person I trusted to lead me in the right direction. He looked at me with a wise twinkle and said, "You know the answers to your questions." I looked at him, felt his resolve, and contemplated this for a bit. He was solid and immovable and he was right. I did know. I was certain of the course everything pointed me toward, even if I didn't know what everything meant or how it would end up. I knew my next step was letting go of the past, including all grudges, criticisms, and guilt. I was sure I needed to correct *my* viewpoint to one of openness and trust and it would transform my experience. I understood how negative feelings had lodged themselves in my body and acted as the filters or beliefs through which I experienced life. I knew my job was to allow love to move through me. I was already in the beginnings of it. I believed as I followed my intuitive knowing, it would lead me perfectly to the next step. I was clear of the road ahead. I was simply looking for confirmation and acknowledgment from a dad who rarely gave it.

In retrospect, I'm grateful Dad didn't share his perspective of what was true. If he had offered any conclusions different from my own, it very possibly could have thrown me off track. I might have trusted him over myself or questioned my own knowing and lost something important in the haze of doubt. I appreciated him staying quiet and imagined how difficult that must have been. It was a valuable lesson for me to see how his not answering was much more empowering for me than his answers ever could be. He trusted me to discover my own truth and he believed in the process of self-discovery more than the human need to fix me or achieve some result! Wow! Somehow, right then, I became more "me." I took a second to etch this in my brain for my communications with my sons.

Dad looked at me with a kindness that said it all. He encouraged me to trust myself from that point on, explaining how this would be my strongest asset, not just in healing myself, but in all aspects of life. He said the most important thing I could learn was to hear the whispers of my Higher Self and that I needed to only train my listening to be quiet enough to know its voice. He explained how the more I listened to the guidance of my intuition the louder it would speak. But the less I listened to it the quieter it would become. Dad assured me I was going to be fine, better than ever. His relief was tangible. I think he and Jesus were pretty good friends.

It was getting late and I asked Dad if he had eaten yet. Food had been on my mind a lot these last few hours. After avoiding food for so long and trying to not care about it, nurturing myself now felt like an exciting subject. Dad had been fasting and not eating either. I think it bonded us in yet another way. He said he began his fast once he heard I was sick, long before he came to see me. He didn't offer how many days he had gone without food, but he and I seemed to be on the same page when it came to feeling like we were out of our bodies, ungrounded, and somewhat able to see through walls. He believed that not eating opened up channels of sensory perception that were normally clouded by the whole consumption ritual. I couldn't argue with that; I had definitely become extremely aware. All my senses were heightened. I could smell what someone had eaten for lunch when they were standing across the room. Sometimes I could hear a person's hum or vibration and sense their sound. I even had an awareness of people outside my door; I sensed what they were feeling. I could connect with their energy and frequently know who was approaching before they entered my room. I could feel and smell Dad before he walked through the door, his breath had a certain odor as a result of detoxing from the fast. That afternoon I had a sense that his body needed something and I mentioned it was probably a good time for him to break his fast and get some grub. I told him I felt it was important. With certainty he replied, "Not quite yet." He didn't have any problem with making his own decisions. I noticed how automatic and authoritative my suggestion was. It was eye opening to feel the energetic effect my comment had on the space we occupied. It created a bit of unease for a second. It wasn't natural and flowing, trying to influence him was disruptive and disempowering.

Dad was ready to go home and as he headed toward the door he slowly turned as though unsure of whether to say what he was about to say, "This is all going to make you a great teacher Holly, it's a very old plan." I laughed out loud and responded sarcastically, "Right, Dad." He smiled that peculiar smile, and winked saying, "See you tomorrow." I laughed at the idea of me teaching anybody anything. My life was totally full of who I thought I was… a mother, a wife, and a real estate agent.

I sat quietly enjoying my time alone. I nestled into myself. It was easy to just be me now. There was no resistance. It had been quite awhile since I'd had any pain, and that helped. I tried to meditate but my mind wanted to dissect all that had occurred in the last two days so I let it. I noticed how my lessons kept pointing to the same thing: finding out what truth was. Everyone had their own idea of right and wrong, good and bad, and what mattered most. It was as though the Universe was mocking how I'd spent most of my life looking for someone or something outside of me to provide the answers, the real truth, the right truth, the one that would get me a hall pass into heaven or a person's good graces. I wanted Christ to tell me whether to stay or go. I wanted my dad to interpret every little thing that was happening. I wanted the doctor to take responsibility for healing me, and I expected any one of the teachers from my vast collection of books and classes to hand me their pearl of wisdom so I could take the right actions with my life. I rationalized, I paid them for their wisdom, and it was their job to guide and on some level fix me, right?! Don't get me wrong, I loved accumulating knowledge but I had to laugh at how secretly, on some level, I had been looking for others to participate in being source of my life and at least take partial responsibility for how it was all turning out.

Another pattern began to unravel. If I implemented someone's suggestion and it failed to fix or help me, my failure could be deemed his or her fault and not mine. I could avoid personal responsibility by having someone else to blame. What an intricate and crazy system I had wired up to ensure I had legitimate excuses for my failures. I didn't do it consciously but I could see the string of wiring and it was definitely mine. I had used my tough childhood in the same manner; to blame "it" for my unhappiness instead of admitting I was in charge of how I felt.

Even though childhood sets us up to experience others (parents, teachers, government, etc.) as being responsible for what happens to us, I mistakenly carried this into adult life. I had an underlying agenda for someone, anyone—teachers, counselors, and even friends to help me make choices and be partially liable for how I experienced life and who I became. The blame option offered me an "out" from being fully accountable for how my life was going. Copying my father's dysfunctional responses to his own mistakes, I punished others for what I considered to be their mistakes, which included them not taking better care of me and not loving me the right way. Wow! Basically I believed it was my moral duty to punish any behavior that didn't go my way. The whole "search and find someone to give me an answer and then watch them fail at helping me" was a fiasco that had provided me with a scapegoat to blame and punish. It was a way for me to feel powerful and in control just as my father had seemed to be whenever he punished us. It was a repeat of the parent-child-abuse cycle of my lineage, which unfortunately included paying the pain forward.

The more people I could entice into taking responsibility for me, the more proof I had that nobody cared about me because nobody ever showed up that could save me or make a difference! Why? It was impossible. My need to be right perpetuated their failure. I wouldn't let anybody in to love me or save me. I wanted to prove my rightness about how messed up my parents were more than I wanted to fix my problem of feeling insignificant. God knows I found quite a number of great people who shared their wisdom, offered supportive advice for healing my past, and taught me brilliant techniques for taking more responsibility. I had paid many of them well for it! But of course nothing anyone offered officially worked because, on some level, I was more interested in proving life wrong than actually dealing with my issues.

It saddened me to realize that my search for help had an underlying intention to find someone to blame for my life situation. It was a sour and slippery way to orchestrate excuses. It was hard to get ahold of, but I began to see this thread through my relationships. Pat would be happy about this discovery. I was never very helpable and it was very frustrating for him. The insane part? All the energy I spent on enticing people into my drama and wanting to be right had never made me happy or made my life worth living; in fact, quite the opposite. Being right never felt good for more than a few seconds. If that! In addition I habitually focused so much attention on what wasn't working in my life and criticizing others as being inadequate that there wasn't any room for goodness to show up. I was attracting into my life exactly what I was sending out, emotionally unavailable people and a lot of emptiness.

What a waste. I was suddenly aware of how much life-force I had spent caught up in that madly insane game when I could have been directing it toward my dreams. I suddenly became aware of my list, my collection of stories to substantiate how horrible and permanently damaging abandonment or child abuse was. I read books to gather more evidence, made friends with people who'd agree with me about it, found therapists to verify its long-term damage, collected attention by repeating my sad tale to anyone who'd listen, and attended classes and processed the same old drama for days. I could examine the abuse over and over again and cleverly analyze it to death, out loud and to myself, never to fully release it, but to reinforce it. I actually kept it alive by putting so much effort and attention into it.

I thought of all the people I had hurt and let down. I didn't know I had woven such a web until now. I never saw with such clarity how wanting to appear right and all knowing had been delineating my life. I ended up very alone in my museum of wins and losses. I took a deep breath and shuddered as I continued the process of opening up and getting honest. I saw a long line of teachers, friends, and even strangers that I had, in my own way, punished. I had become the thing that I'd long despised in my father.

I saw the persistence of my story in a very comprehensive manner, including physically feeling it, intuitively knowing it, and an ability to entirely own it. The awareness transformed me as I grasped its beginning and potential end. I fully understood that as long as I believed my parents were responsible for what was happening to me or to my body I didn't have to be 100 percent in charge of what I was feeling. I could blame them forever and never take charge of how miserable I was. What an unfulfilling existence! The really crazy part was that I had been willing to do almost anything to prove how right I was about them being wrong, even if it meant a life of suffering for me.

The strongest corroboration I could offer for how bad my parents were would be by failing or getting really sick and dying. That way, I'd not only be right, I could pay back Mom and Dad with more suffering and make sure they felt horrible for what they'd done to my sisters and me. That would really show them! It would prove them incompetent once and for all, and then I'd be in the lead of this insane competition in my head, which included winning by dying. What a loony tune. What a painful and emotional trap I'd created for others and myself by wanting to be right. I couldn't believe what I was seeing. It was the ultimate self-sabotage… suffering in order to demonstrate how horribly someone had treated me.

My anger had become my parents' fault and by holding them responsible, I could justify being cruel as though I had the right because somebody owed me for what I'd been through. As I cracked the code of my dysfunction I thought of how many others on the planet are doing this right now, how many kids are angry and making someone else pay for what they feel. Story line: YOUNG, ANGRY GIRL ADOPTS BLAME TO PROVE THAT SHE WAS A VICTIM, to avoid responsibility for what she felt or how her life was turning out, and ultimately, to establish that her misery and death were someone else's fault!

Clearly as I had grown older, the blueprint of my self-destruction also grew more sophisticated and savvier, but I admitted it was the exact same intention, just in varying degrees. Others were mostly wrong and I was mostly right and whether I admitted it or not, I was thinking it. I was well practiced at noticing others' mistakes so I could elevate myself. I was adept at taking any topic—family, government, war, global warming, education systems, the media, and of course Pat, my husband—and give you several examples of what was wrong with each of them, but not much data about what was right. I went to great lengths to persuade myself I was better than most, which of course meant I never believed it of myself.

I felt the destruction of carrying resentments forward. I looked at my frail body with such compassion and sorrow for what I had done to it. I used it, almost like a weapon, and I felt a heavy sadness for all the pain I had caused everyone, along with myself. I looked down to my tummy and apologized. I made a promise to honor it as I would a dear friend who had stood by my side even though I'd mistreated them. A soulful pact was made and I became eager to be honest in all my relationships and finally tell the truth.

Perfect timing. The Universe definitely had a sense of humor. Dinner was now being served to the other guests (patients) and the food trolley was noisily parked directly outside my door to remind me: here was one way I could start being friendlier toward my body. Eat, digest, and receive some nutrition! I got it! The door was open just enough for me to get a whiff of some type of buttery, salty something. I wondered how many more days it would take before I could put something in my mouth that required chewing. Doctor's orders were to eat nothing that stimulated my intestines.

On cue, Patricia walked into my room and I hollered, "Hey grab me a cheeseburger off that cart!" She laughed and shook her finger "no way!" As I watched her walk in, I swear it was like watching myself. She was my twin in many ways and loving her was the closest I'd ever gotten to loving myself as a child. Once we even switched classes in high school but the teacher never knew. She was eighteen months older and as I observed her strolling toward me I was tremendously grateful we had each other. We had weathered many a dark storm. Looking into her eyes felt like home to me.

Patricia was calm and fearless. It was as though she knew every single thing that had been revealed to me over the last couple of days. She held no worry. She sat by the bed, took my hand in hers, and just loved me. Patricia taught me the purest concept of love I'd ever felt as a child. I believed she treasured me more than anyone else when I was little. She was the one that helped me be strong through the beatings, fear, and denial. Although protective of me, she'd always let me fall and scrape my knees if she thought it was the best method for my learning. I ended up with a lot of scraped knees. Patricia had become a strong spirit, unafraid of life or death. Still, there was no denying the pain we both carried forward in our hearts and right then, as she took my hand, I was more aware of hers than my own.

That night, she came just to hang out. We were quiet in the feeling of our love. Tears were rolling down my face and I noticed she had some of her own. She was very intuitive and quite certain I'd be fine, which meant she felt okay about heading home to Laguna Beach where she lived. She didn't say so, I just knew. It was difficult for us to say goodbye. I felt very lucky to have her in my life especially right then as everything was beginning to make sense. I told her I was going to be all right. She looked at me with a smile and said, "I know." I asked her how? She said the day she arrived she wasn't so convinced but now she was sure it would all work out. Patricia explained, in her big-sister way, that I had to experience death so I could get to where I was meant to be. I asked if she had talked to Dad and she made a funny comment about how he avoided her like someone coming at him with a sharp knife. She had not forgiven him and it saddened me. Not so much because it hurt him, but more because it was killing her. I remembered watching Dr. Christiane Northrup, *Women's Bodies, Women's Wisdom* on PBS explain how holding a grudge doesn't hurt the person you're mad at nearly as much as it hurts you for holding onto it. She said, "Not forgiving someone is like taking poison and then waiting for them to die." I now understood.

In a somewhat sassy tone, I asked Patricia what it would take for her to forgive Dad, to challenge her a bit. She gave me a superior smirk as she mentioned that I may want to work on my own issues with Mom for a while, pointing her finger right back at me. I laughed and said, "touché." I shared some of the letting go I had just experienced around Mom. I told Patricia how sweet Mom was as she helped me shower and how easy it was to release my resentment once I decided to get honest about how much I'd hurt her. I told her some of the horrible intentions I discovered in myself and how I had wanted to punish Mom and pay her back in pain. I looked her in the eye and said, "I know Mom loved me, even if she didn't do it the way I wanted her to." In an effort to soften things I added, "Dad made a lot of mistakes, but he's different now and he does love us." She rolled her eyes and dismissed the conversation as irrelevant and the door slammed shut to any conversation about Dad. She didn't want to forgive him, no matter what she read, studied, or knew about non-forgiveness. She asserted it wasn't an issue.

I explained to Patricia how I'd been working on letting go of negative feelings nonstop and how there seemed to be a zillion of them. She shared some of the tools she learned from a recent Avatar®[1] course knowing that

I'd appreciate the technology. It aligned with what we believed and made the *Seth* books by Jane Roberts and the work of G.I. Gurdjieff more digestible. She said the materials gave her easy processes that led her into some very dark places so she could release the negative feelings tethered there. She told me not to worry, professing that if people were honest, they'd all admit they had bad intentions, at one time or another. Patricia recommended that I take the class as soon as possible to further my clarity. "Don't ever give up on being happy, even if you run into something and feel overwhelmed. Back up, slow down, and take one feeling at a time, and it will unravel just right."

I explained how I became angry with myself and almost got stuck in the cage of self-pity. She answered, "Start small and keep it simple." Curious, she asked, "What experience did you feel trapped in?" I rolled my eyes as though she should have known, "high school graduation!" She chuckled and said, "You do have a mess there! You'll need to get real honest about how you didn't tell any of us when it was and never even committed to attending yourself and then blamed all of us for not showing up!" I laughed, seeing my self-sabotage again. She continued, "The more you take responsibility for creating your experience, the easier it is to feel and let go of. Be careful not to get sidetracked in self-blame either, it is an ego distraction. Just keep going and don't take the whole event at once." She explained how sensations would show up when I was ready for them and to start with whatever feeling was present first, like removing one thin layer of onionskin. She warned, "There are probably opposing and even contradicting feelings wrapped up throughout the event and you will have to admit you had both ends of the spectrum going on inside you. For example, part of you was feeling like a victim and another part of you was being the bully. There was probably some part of you wanting to be loved and another part of you not wanting to be acknowledged at all. Feel them all. Own them all." She advised me not to dive into the center until I had peeled the onion a bit, telling me to be patient and trust the process. This was great to hear because I already had so many opposing feelings inside that it could get very confusing.

We relaxed for a moment, appreciating one another and our depth of commitment to discovering joy. I was sure we were dear friends from somewhere beyond this lifetime, these circumstances, and all the pain we had endured.

1 Avatar, RsSurfacing, and Star's Edge International are registered trademarks of Star's Edge, Inc., 2004, by Harry Palmer. All rights reserved.

Patricia interrupted the silence to tell me she had worked with Travis and Drake regarding the seriousness of my illness. She asked them separately what they were experiencing and gave them room to express it. Travis was having a rough time and he asked her if I was really coming home someday. She tried to comfort him, but he pushed his feelings down and was acting tough and unafraid. She could feel his fear. Somebody probably told him to be strong, believing they were doing him a favor. He was in the second grade and I suspect many people were offering this type of advice, with good intentions. Patricia and I talked about how society taught people to avoid emotion and heartache as though it was a sign of weakness or vulnerability. We both agreed it was often a sign of strength for someone to actually allow his or her feelings to exist. Then Patricia admitted that Trav might have overheard a conversation about me dying and my heart ached. She spent time with him explaining the same principles Dad and I had worked on with Donna and I was grateful she'd seized the moment.

She told Trav, "If you don't feel the fear or pain and at least admit it is there, it can grab ahold of you when you least expect it." She invited him to express these feelings in his own time. Assuring him she was there to help him if he wanted her to. She showed him how she'd sometimes grab a pillow and squeeze it tightly to move her anger, fear, or sadness into the pillow, sometimes even yelling into the pillow. She explained that once the bad feelings leave her and go into the pillow, then the Universe could safely take them away. I loved her analogy and how she knew how to communicate to his listening. I planned to use her example with him in the future if need be. Travis seemed to understand but was shy about it. She believed he would try the exercise on his own, in private. Patricia played around with some ideas she thought Drake might also grasp but he wasn't interested. At three years old he was very sensitive and felt a lot of turmoil but I think exploring was too confusing for him. He had just started preschool and we decided this was probably a good place for him to have his attention. The Montessori teachers were incredible and very aware of what was going on should Drake be ready to express anything. He just wasn't ready to talk about my illness, not yet. I knew he missed me and felt abandoned. I sensed it in him the day they visited me. He was withdrawn and shy, afraid of the whole mom-is-in-the-hospital situation. I desperately wanted to cuddle my boys and help them understand.

Hmmm, I thought, *what a unique family.* We kept reminding one another that each of us was in charge of his or her life experience. Pity was not an element in any of our relationships with each other. As a matter of fact, we were more apt to kick a family member when he or she was down, as a means of trying to lift that person up. Or maybe kicking was just a habit we'd adopted to avoid truly caring and feeling. I guess it all depends on how you look at it as well as which aspect of us was doing the looking.

I silently absorbed Patricia, wanting to drink her in before she left me. I didn't like her leaving—ever. I tried to hang tough for a second and not release the wail building up in my chest, but I finally gave up the pretense and started to sob. We held each other close for a few minutes, saying nothing. It was a goodbye filled with love and honor for how each of us had survived. I'd be returning home soon to reinvent my life, and I was going to miss having her by my side.

Love is an expression of the willingness to create space in which something is allowed to change.

–*Techniques for Exploring Consciousness*
ReSurfacing, Harry Palmer

To Feel or Not To Feel

chapter 9

Reality is merely an illusion, albeit a very persistent one.

–Albert Einstein

From my new perch of awareness I began to quiet my mind by watching the river of thoughts roll by. I could feel the ideas, or just let them be. Each had a unique sensation and some presented a stream of the past like a vapor trail from an airplane. There were so many feelings to choose from. I had a buffet of experiences in front of me and I believed any mood could be mine simply by merging with it. As I put my attention on sadness, I felt it. If I focused on ideas of healing, I became the sentiment of them, and when merging with the idea of love, I had a more expansive sense of self. Or I could be still, neutral, and quiet. It was my choice. When I put my awareness back into what I considered my core or my heart, the sensation was solid and unwavering. It was similar to the experience I had when I was held in Christ's hands. This gift, this reservoir of conscious presence inside me was the connecting energy to that very same vibration in all things outside of me. It was the real me, aside from the thoughts and judgments my mind could get caught up in. I didn't have a name for it. The feeling was sacred.

I was deciding where to put my attention and wherever I put it, an experience was waiting for me. Cool! I played with moving my focus from feeling to feeling and realized a sensation could be appreciated rather than avoided. It was much easier and in the flow of life to breathe it in and breathe it out instead of running from it or trying to think and explain it away. There were no words here, just a communion of my soul with pockets of collected energy. I was getting to know who I was by realizing more of what I wasn't.

Clearly at some point in my life I had defined many feelings as bad, good, helpful, or even dangerous. Feelings weren't bad. They were just experiences I'd become frightened of. I practiced moving in and out of them at will, like tasting a flavor of ice cream and deciding I wanted a different one. I wasn't afraid. They were just like Dad said; they were similar to a child I'd given birth to at some point in my life. I am the one that gave them life and defined their quality and meaning. They were lurking and would be until I owned and embraced them. It became easy and natural to allow my feelings to exist. They were old friends teaching me who I was and who I wasn't. When I appreciated them, they dissolved, lightened up and could no longer consume my spirit or direct my energy. When I resisted them and considered them bad or painful I wasn't able to realize the truth of them or feel them honestly. Whenever I judged the feelings, it was as though some aspect of the sensation that was important for me to acknowledge was out of my reach. If I couldn't feel or accept them, I couldn't manage or dissolve them. I had to stop judging my feelings so I could be in charge of them. I played around with this concept and the ease of allowing them all. It was filling my body with a sparkling sense of aliveness. When I allowed them without any resistance I could recover my energy faster. If I resisted the feelings, I became exhausted and discouraged. I was amazed at the process. I was becoming more my true self with each letting go. I was becoming child like, lighter, and excited! I did discover that if I stayed in one sensation too long my mind would want to get enmeshed in the feeling and turn it into a conflict or somehow justify rather than allowing it to be what it was—an experience. My mind was such a prankster. I even found myself feeling the sensation of that!

My body and spirit were delivering my past to me in a gentler way so that I could continue to dismantle it all. My old life didn't have to be baggage that I lugged around and continued to make a part of my reality. I gratefully watched as patterns, sensations, and densities of feelings became something obviously other than who I really was.

I became partially stuck in a clump of feelings connected to the thought of abandonment. They weren't clear and they had a lot of density to them with flavors of anger and resentment. I realized a part of me wanted to ignore them and I tried to find some kind of distraction, maybe to keep them around as long as possible, like an old familiar friend I could turn to whenever I needed an excuse. It was weird to watch my own denial in action. I decided to focus on becoming more present in the moment and more aware, so I could use my will to explore these old ideas and feelings. I had to stay partially outside of myself in an expanded way, while another part of me merged with a feeling.

I knew the first sensation very well—it was sadness. I stayed aware of the thickness of it, experienced it, and watched it flow into anger. There were so many sensations and as soon as I experienced one, it led me to another feeling as though they were part of a chain formation connected by invisible links. I felt them, one by one, and they eventually landed in a big black pool of "being alone." Totally alone, empty, a void, no God, no Tao, no essence, no body. I remembered the exact moment I'd placed them there. I knew where they came from. A picture flashed before me: I was standing by myself at my high school graduation ceremony. My heartbeat sped up and my palms began to sweat as though I had physically traveled back in time to relive it all over again.

There were layers upon layers of decisions and emotions clumped together and, almost magically, I now understood that these were at the root of several of my painful life patterns and decisions. I had an overview, like looking at a blueprint of a house, only this was a blueprint of my emotional patterns through relationships and career, and how I'd stayed separate from others in order to protect myself. I was in awe of how my past was untangling in front of my eyes and astounded to witness the fluency with which thoughts had become a dense manifested reality. I imagined removing this one event and how this would change the entire blueprint of my life.

I had a visceral response. Something twitched in my belly and I knew I was headed in the right direction. As I dove in deeper I felt pangs in my lower back and then my knee. Sometimes, the feelings were as strong physically as they were emotionally. There was definitely stored energy around this event. As I explored further, the connection of my emotions to my body became astonishingly clear.

I stepped back and watched the movie. My body tightened and became uncomfortable yet I was able to remain a witness. I saw one of the extensions of the blueprint: it was constructed with all the attention I'd received over the years from sharing my dramatically lonely graduation with others. It was sticky, unhealthy, and prominent to my identity. I had mistakenly given this flow of pity toward me the definition of love. No wonder I was so determined to be right about how mistreated I was and keep the event safely tucked away for future use. My ego mind fought for control by blabbering about the dangers of allowing the painful sensations of graduation to exist, claiming they would be intolerable to experience. Then I realized my desire to hoard the past was another aspect of the cluster and the blueprint, and that it had a built-in alarm system screaming, "Warning, don't come any closer or you will self-destruct." I had wired everything from graduation to my survival. A labyrinth of decisions about relationships, love, and control, had all been wrapped up in the un-experienced pain of that day. This mass of ideas and perceptions had been controlling many of my choices.

I decided breathing would be good. I inhaled deeply and placed my attention back on my core self for a minute to stabilize and remember who I was. It was very difficult to drag myself away from this event, so I decided to relax and recharge my battery by feeling the sacredness of my hospital experience and simply lying in Christ's hands. I was thankful for everything I was now aware of. I relaxed, grew quiet and present, and sat in amazement. It was a miracle to see and experience so viscerally how the past was locked up inside my body and even more so realizing I could choose to let it all go. Emotions that had been stored up in my intestines for years were finally releasing. I believed anyone could heal anything with this knowledge along with the willingness to feel.

I was confident of my ability to be 100 percent healthy. Gratitude filled my senses and energized me. I was ready to dive back in. I invited the feelings to come forth and there they were, still waiting for me. I went into the anger because it was the first thing I became aware of and it was screaming the loudest. It was strong and encompassed most of my body. It was easiest to locate, maybe because I didn't resist the sensations and actually now found them fascinating. I played with my ability to open myself to these feelings and moved out of the anger and toward my center to make sure I wasn't stuck there, then back to the anger again. I went back and forth a couple of times until I was able to easily be with it for a while or stop. I was in control now. The rigidity or density of the emotions began to ease up and finally let go. I experimented with this, and noticed that if I didn't think of the emotion as bad it was easier to experience the sensation. I kept feeling the variety of ideas, beliefs, and feelings, until the package became insignificant and light. I released it all and was quite certain that my blueprint for being alive had significantly changed and that this event would no longer be running my life. I was dizzy and giddy with delight.

This was like taking some kind of emotional inventory and as each pocket of feeling was discovered and felt, it would soften and often totally disappear. I didn't have to wallow in pain anymore; I could acknowledge it, be aware of it, admit it, let it hurt, be uncomfortable and then let it go. It seemed too easy. I could actually free the feelings because they weren't me. They were clumps of energy I had collected. It was a choice now rather than fate. After spending a life of finagling and struggling to not feel the hurt I'd been tugging around with me, I had to laugh at how simple life could be if I just felt the horror and fear, looked it in the eye, and for a minute, simply experienced it as my baby. I realized that this is what transforms the energy and the pattern of one's life. I'd been surrounded by those pockets of resistance and avoidance my whole life. These sensations had been trapped in certain parts of my body and now I could feel the energy of them physically leave me. I knew this was key to healing Crohn's disease. Perhaps most diseases began with resistance to feeling our emotions. To finally let it all go made my body lighter and freer. My mind cooperated as things became very still, doors opened, and more patterns were revealed.

Just as everything was beginning to blend and melt, my husband, Pat, walked in. I wondered where that guy had been! I smiled and he crawled into bed with me. We barely fit, so he had to snuggle close. With all the tubes and I.V. cords it would have been easy to tangle him up and keep him for a while. We were quietly holding each other. I could feel how exhausted he was from the inside. I'd become acutely aware of the emotions and pain of other people like never before. I could feel everything! It was like his skin was my skin.

I wanted to share all my discoveries with him, but he didn't have any space left for a big conversation right then. So I held him instead. He had a lot on his plate with the kids, managing forty-five employees, a house full of in-laws, and forget about the crazy wife. Did I mention a house full of in-laws? I told him I was sorry for all of this. He said, "Stop it." I told him I was going to be the best wife anyone could have. He said, "You already are." I told him I would learn to cook. He laughed, not so sure about that one! He said, "You've turned the corner and that's all that matters." I told him I had a lot of help, and like everyone else in my family, he'd already heard the news of my travels in the invisible realm. Dad must have told him.

I explained to Pat how I thought love was what had changed my body and mind and that he was the best medicine a woman could have. He said, "God knows, you've had a lot of it with visits from here to Jesus!" We both laughed. In a serious tone I turned and asked him if he thought I was very good at receiving the care coming toward me. He didn't mince words, "No. You give it all away and don't keep much of anything for yourself." I thought about this for a minute and knew I had to learn to nurture myself and let love in.

Giving had always been easier for me than receiving. I could see how giving helped me to stay in control and how refusing to receive did the exact same thing. I could avoid being vulnerable by keeping people at a distance and not letting their kindness or care into my space. That way, I never felt like I owed anybody anything emotionally or materially. I'd spent my life petrified to let anyone else in.

A vision flashed in my mind of jewelry strewn across a purple bedspread. I had discovered shoplifting. It was Christmas, my seventh-grade year. We didn't have any money and I was determined to have gifts for my friends. I'd stolen at least thirty pieces of jewelry and was trying to decide what to give whom. I gift-wrapped every piece beautifully not keeping one thing for myself. I ogled one pair of earrings that were awesome, wrapping them last. Hanging onto them would have been a dream come true. It never even occurred to me that I could have them for myself. It was like I was still at the store eyeing something that wasn't mine and never would be. Having what I wanted was not in my repertoire of love.

I dreaded the idea of my girlfriends handing me a gift in return. I was very uncomfortable receiving presents. In my mind, it created a type of responsibility or competition. I had to give more than anyone else so I wouldn't be the weak one in the scenario. It was as though giving to another gave me a right of passage into their heart and gave me control. Receiving was the equivalent to emotional pain. I could handle physical pain but emotional pain terrified me.

Man, did I have some cleaning up to do! As I continued unraveling the patterns, more patterns emerged. Layers of realties had been concealed by unacknowledged feelings and now they were finally able to bubble up to the surface as each layer dissolved. Unfelt feelings had trapped deeper realties inside my blueprint. Memories flooding forth for release baffled me—I thought they'd been long gone.

What I didn't realize was how alone and malnourished the habit of being in control had left me. All my life I'd been so hungry for care from others. Crohn's disease reflected a body's inability to absorb nourishment. It doesn't take a rocket scientist to see that I'd been starving myself emotionally and spiritually long before the illness had manifested physically. This was a pattern I'd developed at a young age. That's why I had to get plugged into all of the feeding tubes and fluids, to refill myself, even if it was pharmaceutical love. I had to receive or die. I wanted to let everyone with Crohn's disease know that they could begin healing by learning to receive and actually fully recover without killing themselves or destroying their organs or their lives. The threads I was pulling on told the whole story. I think my receiver probably shut down during my first whipping as a child.

I kept having realizations, one after another. My body was soft and light and my awareness buzzing from all the clearing of debris! I realized I'd set up the pattern for how the world treated me by how I treated myself. In other words, people had energetically responded to my pattern of ignoring and starving myself and unknowingly joined the party. That's what happens. People are attracted to our energetic emissions and reflect our own vibrations perfectly. Then we say God is doing it to us, or our partners are doing it to us, or the world is doing it to us—when it is us doing it—to us.

My pattern of self-abandonment was a magnet to attract more of itself. My vibration attracted those who were abandoners or more interested in being numb than present. Amazed, I considered the irony of it all; we give everyone around us the instruction book on how to treat us by how we treat ourselves! Then we blame them for doing it! One of my chief complaints about life was that nobody was really there for me. I see now it wasn't them at all. It was me that wasn't there for me. I laughed at how precisely the world showed us to ourselves. To know who we're being, all we have to do is take a good look at what we're attracting.

I became more determined to let life love me. I was determined to receive and allow the love. Every self-made block to receiving had to dissolve, emotionally, physically, and spiritually. I already had a great start.

What really blew me away was how confused I'd been about the whole concept of feeling. Basically, I thought feeling was a sign of weakness and therefore should be avoided at all costs. I couldn't have been more wrong—it was the exact opposite. Permitting myself to feel again was part of the very process of letting go of the past, awakening to Higher Self, and navigating my own life. Feeling was the path to enjoying being human! When I'd decided to go numb I didn't just turn off the painful feelings, I'd turned off the joy, too.

Feeling didn't have to be an emotional drama. It was a skill of learning how to allow a sensation to simply be what it was. It wouldn't be comfortable to feel pain, be afraid, or experience deep sorrow, but it beat dying from *not* feeling it. It required staying present with the pain and realizing it would loosen and pass. *I can do this!* Like Donna Hamilton said, "The only way out is through." Experiencing was the path to being truly alive. I was sure that allowing sensations to exist as they were was part of the process of peeling away my disease, while resisting feelings contributed to the manifestation of more disease. I was clear now: my fear of experiencing the feelings of my life had almost killed me.

I took a deep breath of gratitude for this new awareness and sent a thank you to the Universe, the Tao, God, Jesus, and my precious family. I felt so humbled. My new awareness was simple, yet profound. I felt whole. An integration of mind, body, and spirit was occurring. This is where the invisible meets the visible. I had a feeling of openness, down into my bones. It was inclusive of everyone and everything. I had an expanded sense of reality and could feel the physical world in a strange and psychic way, the people walking down the hall, what the nurses were handling inside, and the other patient's emotions. The energy that surrounded each person had a density to it, some more than others. I related and cared differently now. I felt aware, loving, and understanding, yet unattached. I relaxed into it all, silently receiving the moment.

Pat was falling asleep in the quiet. I spoke softly, probably more to myself than him. I shared how open my heart felt since feeling the pureness of Christ's love. Something closed up tightly inside me had relaxed. I described to Pat how happy I was in spite of my body's condition, how my world was different, and how I could see perfection in everything. He gave me a squeeze with eyes closed. I went on and explained the treasure it was to discover family, friends, and even strangers who cared about me and how I'd never believed this was true, not really. I told him how untrusting I'd been, even suspicious of most and how I'd considered my paranoia normal human behavior (when it wasn't). I told him I hadn't realized how much I'd kept everyone at a distance until I let them come closer, I mean really close! I had a new willingness to go deep with another human, to love as much as I was able, to let them in all the way to the core of my being and no longer conceal who I am. There was nothing to lose and everything to gain. For the first time in my life, I wasn't afraid of getting hurt.

I realized his breathing had become steady and that I'd put him to sleep with my rambling… not a first. I giggled and continued my conversation internally.

To believe it was natural to be separate and suspicious of everyone just proved my water-to-a-fish theory. You can be so immersed in a reality that it disappears and you don't even know you're living in it, at least not until you're pulled out of it. Before I got sick, I'd been positive that I was a connected and caring person who let people into her heart. I never saw how untrue that was or how my behavior was engrossed in suspicion, until I experienced what was possible. Clearly, I hadn't been close to letting anyone in when I compared it to what I'd felt with Christ. I was determined now to love more fully, to love completely.

Even as I was contemplating, I was also sure my definition of love would continue to transform. Everything was changing as I became more aware. So it goes through life. There was no need to make anybody wrong anymore, including myself. Maybe all certainties should be deemed temporary. The more aware I become, the more inclusive I am. The more inclusive I am, the more understanding and allowing I feel. The more allowing I become, the more intuitive my thoughts and actions are. All of this leads to strengthening my connection to Higher Self, which results in a more intuitive life taking each step as a result of listening to the nudge of the Universe. This may result in new directions to traverse in life and in death. I draw conclusions based on my level of awareness at the time but my awareness constantly evolves. Understanding the process makes it easy to forgive mistakes, and honor where everyone is on his or her unique path.

Everything was up for examination. Truth depended on how I looked at things or where I was focusing. My conclusions had a tremendous amount to do with who was doing the looking. Maybe love was flowing toward me all along and I was too busy vibrating fear to see or allow it. I cuddled Pat and let the wonderment of it all soak in. I closed my eyes, enjoying the sound of his breathing and cuddled closer knowing I needed to wake him soon. I was sure Debbie was holding dinner for him and that the boys needed a kiss goodnight. Besides, my arm was falling asleep. I nudged him and took a moment to treasure his sleepy face. There was so much heaven I had taken for granted. Honestly, I'd be thrilled to be home and simply watch the grass grow. Pat smiled and propped himself up to look at me.

He knew he had to go. I watched as he did all the little things to make me comfy: filling the humidifier, checking that the flowers had water, and glancing around the room to make sure everything was as good as it could be. Then he sweetly kissed me goodbye. I said I'd be home in the next couple of days and he smiled, "Be patient honey. Don't rush it. You will be home in good time." He stopped before heading out the door and we exchanged a lingering glance filled with love.

I was alone and ready for sleep. What a day. From the time I'd been determined to isolate myself in preparation for death to my bedtime, a lifetime had passed. It seemed like it wasn't even me who had those self-sabotaging ideas but someone I once knew. Two days ago I believed in separating myself from others so I could die alone, making it easier for everyone. I was certain nobody wanted to take part in the pain and drama and had concluded that enduring it solo was the highest road to take. I'd instructed the hospital, "No visitors," from the first day I was admitted. Wow, I had definitely closed the door on love. What an amazing contrast to the care I'd experienced while resting in Christ's adoring hands!

My new eyes showed me that letting someone into my heart, particularly when I was hurting, created an opening for love to flow and heal us both. I realized how vulnerable and kind the act of simply feeling what was present in a relationship was, and that to share that truth with another was profound. Now, to allow any feeling to be expressed and not blamed was an act of love. It opened a heart connection that had tremendous healing powers. When truth was present transformation was possible.

No more hiding out for me, no more pretending. Pretense had kept patterns solid and stuck. Being willing to feel again was a form of giving and receiving that I'd never fully understood or experienced before. It was a generous way to move through life, allowing sensations, connection, care, and honoring the process of being human. I felt so blessed.

I could see how sharing with someone and creating a safe space for them to share as well made what mattered in life more real. The union of honest intention created a vibration of love that became available for each person to take with them into their next moment. *Allowing* was a way to pay goodness forward. Maybe when someone received, the action of letting in opened the giver's heart and allowed love to move in a complete circle. Giving and receiving required both halves to be present; it provided a window of transformation, a cycle of integrity, and wholeness. It is a way to contribute to those around us. I feel the act of receiving allows Christ's love to multiply in the very same way the act of giving does. Every time we let a gift into our hearts we have more to share. Our cup runneth over.

Life was a gift if I allowed it to be… the trees, flowers, sky, even the drama inside and around me. I appreciated how everything that was happening brought me back to myself.

I allowed the treasures of the day to fill my heart and realized how I was finally ready to let life love me. I was ready to share. My last feeling of the day was "thank you."

It is not that you must be free from fear. The moment you try to free yourself from fear, you create a resistance against fear. Resistance in any form does not end fear. What is needed, rather than running away or controlling or suppressing or any other resistance, is understanding fear; that means, watch it; learn about it, come directly into contact with it.

–J Krishnamurti

Digesting Reality

chapter 10

The important question for me is, is the body a source for creating, for realizing yourself, for realizing what life is all about? You ask this question and you go where it takes you and then you ask another question and then again you follow. So this understanding of the body, of the unity within the body and the innumerable areas which it reveals to you is what I call realization.

–Chandralekha

I am alive, more so than ever before and... I'm going home! I get to feel the wind in my face, plant tulips, and watch the roses bloom for another season. I get to cuddle my boys, read bedtime stories, and smell their sweet breath as they giggle. I get to lie in the crook of my husband's arm and be firmly held. I have another chance to wonder at the magic of a full moon and become lost in the twinkling of the stars. Death gifted me with life. I was bursting with gratitude and had a grin glued to my face. I wanted to go out into the hallway and thank every nurse, doctor, visitor, toilet scrubber, and maintenance worker in the hospital. The blue sky outside my window, the bed, the building, everyone and everything was part of who I was becoming, knowingly or not. Every drop of energy made a difference. Everyone's vibration mattered.

The doctor walked in quite chipper and asked me what I would like for breakfast. I stared at him wide-eyed and covered my mouth in disbelief. I thought it was a joke. He said my blood work had improved significantly and I was good to go home as long as I promised to take all the medications he prescribed and agreed to the very gradual reduction of steroids. He emphasized the word "very," knowing I was not one to do what I was told. I happily accepted the terms even though my fingers were crossed under the sheets. Doc said all I needed to do was eat and eliminate to be set free from the hospital. It sounded pretty simple. Sure. No problem. It had only been a year or so since I could do this like a normal person.

Instantaneously the old "fear of food" thoughts were looking for their stomping grounds front and center of my mind. If I'd really paid attention, I'll bet I could've seen my energy moving from the wide, grateful view of life just a minute ago to being lodged in a tiny space the size of my rectum. It felt like I'd been transported from a vast, open-blue sky of fresh air, to a tightly confined room of doubt. I found that whenever I was being intense about anything, my breathing became shallow or nearly stopped. It was my signal, like an alarming red flag, that I was closing down. I took a deep breath to help me relax and reminded my body to release the tension. I nudged myself to remember what I knew about thoughts. They were just thoughts. I didn't have to give them power over me. They were "not I's." I took another deep breath and slowly exhaled, with the intention that my fears leave with it. I started to unwind and become more aware. The room was full of a soft reminder that I could do anything. It was my Higher Self voice whispering and I almost missed it.

Once I figured it would take a couple days for the eating and eliminating process to run its course I started to mellow out. I'd have time to clear out my fearful debris and make it all work. Doc went on to say that if all went as he expected, I'd be going home the next morning. I squealed out loud in surprise! I asked him if he really believed I'd be able to go to the bathroom normally by then and he was certain of it! I liked his answer better than the history rumbling around in my mind. My old beliefs were lurking and it must have shown on my face. He told me not to worry because the prednisone had worked very well, the swelling had abated and my body was ready to begin digesting. He was going to keep me on TPN (total parenteral nutrition) for a while at home via the central feeding line to ensure I'd get the necessary nutrition while transitioning back to solids. I think it was mostly to make sure they had an instant feeding line on-hand in case I ended up back in the hospital anytime soon. That line was used for everything on my current menu including antibiotics, steroids, fluids, and of course, the TPN. My arms had become a myriad of wounds from the last two years of lab tests and being poked every day at 5:30 A.M. for blood samples.

As Doc kept talking, I was aware of a mixture of delight and anxiety running through my veins. I had some fear around trusting him and realized I needed to calm down and practice what I'd learned. What I needed to trust more than anything was my own ability. I reminded myself I'd been sneaking some drinks of water since the previous night without any difficulty. I'd be okay. I knew the emotional place this disease had started from and now it was healed. So I needed to allow the physical part of me to catch up. It was the calm voice of my intuition speaking. It was neutral and knowing. I settled down, drew in a big breath, and continued to listen to Doc's orders.

He mentioned the mess that my body was in when I'd arrived and made sure to explain how he'd never been optimistic about me getting out of here with my colon intact. He wanted to forewarn me that it might not be the last hospitalization. I let that belief float right on by. I watched my mind want to grab it as it moved through my body/mind. Part of me didn't want the belief around anymore, yet my pushing against it, resisting it, would've made it stick to me like superglue. I watched patiently until the negative belief flowed out of the field of my awareness. It was fascinating to watch it disappear into the ethers as though it had no place to land.

Doc was only doing what he thought was best for me. He was genuinely happy I was able to avoid drastic surgery and keep all my body parts. He knew I was adamantly crazy about them! Something seemed different about him that day; he was more human, softer. I imagined his life and how often he had to deliver bad news, not an easy reality to spend so much time in. I was glad he was able to experience giving good news for a change and feeling a positive connection with a patient.

My attention turned to going home and as I imagined walking into the door of my sweet home, joy bubbled up inside me and a chuckle burst from my mouth. It caught us both by surprise. He looked at me strangely and we both laughed. It came from my appreciation for the whole experience, for his role, my family, the staff, and my new view of life. The whole thing was so surreal, like I'd been dreaming and it was time to wake up. I invited Doc to feel how amazing the moment was from my viewpoint. Just thirty days earlier I was hopeless, empty, an emotional basket case, and dying. I explained to him how happy I was now, how free, and for the first time in my life, fully at peace.

I thanked him for putting up with me, sincerely acknowledging his care and his part in my awakening and joy. He tried to brush it off. I just watched him, quietly waiting for him to let it soak in and receive some appreciation. He couldn't allow it in, not even a drop of it. He was embarrassed and I realized *Allowing* wasn't something he'd been very skilled at. He played a huge roll in me owning my disease, maybe not the way he'd expected, but he had. I invited him again to see how much he cared and how committed he was to his patients. He started to talk again and I said, "Oh, go on and feel how awesome it feels to help someone actually leave the hospital as a new human." He turned his head as though to tune into the joy or maybe to try and figure out what I was talking about, and then quickly turned back to the moment uneasily. Obviously receiving wasn't his specialty either. I asked him if he ever just let himself feel satisfied. He didn't answer but I knew he was looking somewhere to check.

I smiled understandingly at his silence and felt compassion for him. He sensed my care and became a little fidgety. He lost his footing for a second. I looked him right in the eye with all of me present and told him it would be good for his body and heart to allow a bit of tenderness in. You could feel a level of awareness between us that wasn't based on niceties or pretense. It was real connection, being to being. I stayed still in it with no expectation or judgment, just quiet appreciation. He sat back, sighed, and relaxed a little more, like maybe it was okay.

Doc started to open up and speak of how he'd been looking for someone to share his life with but couldn't find the right woman. He verbally listed the most important characteristics of this dream woman, like he wished he could order her from a menu. He explained how difficult it was with his career and life to even make room for a partner. He had a lot bottled inside that needed to come out. *Hmmm, this need seemed to pop up a lot in my hospital room.* He was admittedly lonely and we shared his honesty for a bit like a nurturing cup of tea. I watched his body as it released density, like a balloon letting out air. He let me into his softness and it reminded me of the treasure of friendship. His guard was down and he didn't have to be anybody but himself. I knew this was what it feels like to be real with another person, free of pretense and agenda, just honoring another human in their becoming. Acknowledging feelings when another person tries to push them away or rush past them was a sweet way to be a good friend. Doc seemed to be living a life embarrassed of his humanness and, as a result, I think he was missing the joy of existence and pushing his own heart away. I listened quietly and it wasn't long before he felt relieved of an obvious unnecessary weight. His smile was different. He was beautiful in the morning light, gentle and real. He came over and hugged me before leaving. I enjoyed him and was very grateful that he helped me learn my lessons. He'd been the perfect doctor for me!

Being present, allowing and listening was my new favorite thing. It felt like love.

I was antsy. Now that I had my walking papers I wanted to eat and get the elimination project going! I started thinking about how to break my very long fast with the perfect food, gentle, nutritious, and preferably organic. So guess what was on the menu? None of that! A nurse that I adored brought in a little slip of paper and she was ecstatic. "You get to eat! Just check off the food you'd like today and I'll get it for you!" She smiled and sparkled, totally thrilled for me! It was a moment. She had tears in her eyes, "I didn't think this day was coming Holly. We weren't sure about you." She took my hand and I grabbed her and pulled her close and held her tight, long enough to make sure she felt how much she'd meant to me. I looked at the door and another of my favorite nurses was watching with moist eyes. It was a love fest. They kept me going on the days when I didn't care, told me silly jokes, encouraged me with inspirational stories, and even let me into their personal lives by sharing the narratives of their lives and photos of their children. We were family. They'd made my hospital stay bearable by filling it with genuine care. I wiped away my tears and my eyes fell to the menu she'd placed on my tray.

My jaw dropped in shock! I couldn't believe what I was reading and didn't hide my dismay. I repeated it out loud in a very sarcastic, dramatic voice, "Processed cereal, yogurt with thirty-four grams of sugar, a cheeseburger, a turkey dinner with fake mashed potatoes and gravy! Soda, tea, milk, or juice to drink!" I hadn't eaten any of those things in so long I couldn't imagine putting any of that processed stuff in my mouth, much less my body! My mood totally shifted to one of anxiety. I looked at her in a shaky, pleading voice, "I can't eat any of this! Can I get some brown rice and vegetables?" She tried to calm me down, told me not to worry; for one day, it wouldn't hurt me. "Go ahead and check a few things on the list and I'll see what I can find you." She implied that I didn't need to make a big deal out of it and that my body could handle anything on that list just fine. I reluctantly chose the yogurt for breakfast, broth for lunch, and turkey dinner and Jell-O for dessert. I was upset. The whole fiasco reminded me how easy it was for my mind to take the reins and steer me into panic mode.

I had to chill out. I was fine in my little hospital room with recordings of Deepak Chopra reciting a variety of healing methods, the Hemi-Sync® sounds and vibrations of Robert Monroe, poetry readings by Dad, and my sweet window to the world reminding me how to let my thoughts float by like clouds. But here comes life, and a perfect opportunity to see if I can hear the voice of my Higher Self through realities that had pushed against what I considered important. I needed to be able to listen to my own inner guidance, stay aware and in feel instead of going into hyper think, be intuitive, and face the challenges of eating and eliminating because much bigger challenges than using the toilet were coming my way. I needed calm, clear knowing when faced with being a mom and raising a family, running a successful real estate practice, being a wife, handling a home and all that went along with that. I told myself it didn't have to be so complicated, simply let it in, let it out and breathe! I only had to eat one meal here, not a big deal. Eliminate enough to fill my toilet hat (that's what they called the contraption used for measuring human waste). I had to produce something that the treasure inspectors would deem acceptable. I could do this. I managed to put a little distance from the anxiousness and myself and found my sense of humor again. My graduation requirements were going to utilize all my newly learned skills. The Universe had a grand sense of humor that offered a remarkable training program... it's called life!

Thank goodness Dad walked in. I was just thinking he wouldn't mind getting me some real food. When I saw him my first thought was *the Universe is so good to me!* I also had a bunch of ideas stirring and I needed someone I trusted to examine them with. Dad was perfect! I excitedly told him I was going home in the morning. I reported all my thoughts in a steady stream: the kids would have their mom again, the feeding machine would accompany me home, and the tubes would be hanging out of my chest for one more month. I said, "I need some help making something on the menu list work for my body or maybe someone could get me some healthy food, hint hint." He chuckled so I continued, "And… what about me remembering who I really am in times of turmoil?" I explained further, "I need some tools, an ABC plan, to stay connected to my knowing when everything gets loud and crazy around me. Dad, I have to maintain a calm mind no matter what's going on in my space and the effects of the steroids, well, they wire me a little bit and make the job twice as difficult!" He laughed out loud at my seriousness, "Let's take a walk." I looked into his eyes and saw his wisdom. Having him there was very soothing. I trusted him and the preciousness of that washed through me as a wave of gratitude.

Dad took my hand and helped me up. I could tell he was contemplating the best way to handle my little hissy fit. "When your mind gets crazy, get your body energy moving, take a walk, and it will open a space for clear knowing. No need to rush to some answer just to have an answer. Be patient and the knowing will come." I hardly heard a word he'd said. I was too excited about going for my first walk in a long, long time.

I went barefoot. I love the feeling of my feet touching the floor. I held

Dad's arm for support and he dragged my gurney of fluids and tubing behind us like a reluctant dog on a leash. One step on the cold tile and I could feel my weight adjust to being vertical, another step, another, and I started moving in a rhythm, my heart beating loud and hard in my chest as I pushed open the door to my room and entered the hall for the first time since being admitted. A very different world existed out here than the one in my cramped sanctuary. *So this is where I've been tucked away,* I thought to myself. Everyone was busy moving to accomplish some major or minor task, a few were running, everybody was tense and nobody was standing still. I told myself, *This is life Holly, you better get used to it.* I looked around with the intention of "allowing" and felt like I was in a zoo among animals from a different planet than mine. My energy didn't fit into the structure of noise, the clanging of trays, and the hurriedness of it all. I had to let it in, allow everything to be just as it was, and then breeeeeeeeeathe it out. No resisting. I was surprised at how it worked immediately. I began appreciating and enjoying the hustling rhythm of the people, sounds, and movements. Gradually, I'd become part of the flow. I absorbed it all and let it be as it was. Music! I was amazed at my shift in experiencing it and laughed to myself. *This human thing is so cool.*

I was spinning with excitement, it was my first walk since being admitted, I was going home, and being alive wasn't bad either. I think I was having a hallmark moment. I couldn't stay quiet or calm. I was buzzing. I turned to Dad and began telling him that I'd asked Doc how soon I could start working out and Dad laughed. I continued anyway, "If Doc had said 'whenever you feel like it,' I probably would have jumped on the floor and tried to give him ten." Dad chuckled again, "Your body will tell you what you can do. Listen to it, talk to it, and love it." Right then, I turned my attention toward my body to see what it was saying and an unexpected feeling of friendship washed over me. I was shaky, too. All my feelings were so magnified and profound. It felt phenomenal to be in my body, to have hands that could hold onto someone, and legs to walk with. To be next to Dad, traipsing down the hall in my hospital gown, knobby kneed, was a marvelous moment. The nurses stopped and watched. Going home was a miracle and they were celebrating it with us. I turned around as we passed the nurses' station and they were all standing there smiling as they watched us stroll slowly down the hallway holding hands, with me grinning ear to ear. Their faces were filled with such tenderness. They sincerely cared and I was glad they'd let themselves linger in the joy Dad and I were oozing. I loved them. Dad had a shy, embarrassed grin on his face and I could feel how proud he was of me. We were proud of each other. I looked at us through the nurses' eyes for a minute and was in awe of my relationship with Dad and how it felt now compared to a week ago.

About then my legs started quivering badly so it was back to bed for me. My body had told me what it needed and I realized it would do the same with food, noise, and the world, if I only paid attention. I got a sense of what Dad meant. My mind was swirling, partly from the prednisone and partly from all the lessons coming my way.

Prednisone was a huge challenge. It behaved as an amphetamine in my system. I became fidgety and speedy within minutes of getting the shot, which was every eight hours. Doc told me I was on the maximum allowed. I was eager to be myself again, without the drug. I believed I'd be fine cutting back but Doc wasn't as confident and he wanted to reduce the dosage very slowly. Prednisone was an emotion enhancer, at least in my reality. Whatever I felt, happy or sad and everything in-between, I felt it bigger and more extreme than normally, which was pretty hilarious since my whole life had been about avoiding feelings. It was another example of the Universe's ironic sense of humor.

While on prednisone it was very difficult for me to remain calm for any long period of time and 'one minute' frequently ended up being a long period of time. Having been on low doses most of the previous year, Pat had become very familiar with my dramatic responses. When I'd get on a rampage about something, he gave it a distinguishing name… a "steroid slam." It took me awhile to find that funny, but eventually I did, kind of. The smallest thing from my husband—a nod, giving the kids candy, or not listening to me, could ignite a Holly lecture. If Pat wasn't around to hear it, I was always ready to write a letter of epic proportions explaining all the viewpoints and, of course, persuading him to see my perspective as the correct one. He dreaded my letters, but kindly read them, and prepared for a conversation with me that would often last hours. Steroids made me bull-headed, more than I already was. I also had days of being very sad and blue. I often cried over certain commercials, sweet stories, or kind gestures, and everyone would laugh at me never having seen me so sensitive. It was very difficult to manage my emotions on the drug but Pat handled my side effects very well… he finally learned to agree with anything I said.

As Dad left the hospital, he encouraged me to trust the food they served, promising to see me at home the next day. I told him I needed him to stay with me forever, no leaving. He smiled and talked about the class he wanted me to take to help me learn to manage my mind and feel stronger. I let him know I'd love to do that, with him, as soon as I got the feeding tubes removed.

Naked, I looked a bit like an octopus. I had two 12–14-inch tubes hanging from my chest area, a stomach that looked like a beer belly from all the swelling of my intestines, a concave ass, stick legs with knees three times the circumference of my calves, and of course, chipmunk cheeks and a head of mostly fallen-out hair. But not to worry as my face tried to make up for the loss by growing a nice beard. Ahhh, the benefits of steroids! I had one friend who told me my knees looked like they belonged to a horse. It was good for a laugh but every time I peered down at them I realized how right she was. I hadn't looked in a mirror for a very long while. The last time I did, it was pretty scary. Along with resembling one of those starving children on TV with a large stomach, my breasts had disappeared. The latter triggered memories from high school and my dreaded nickname Flaticia! Now, as I looked in the mirror, all I could do was snicker and feel sorry for my poor husband and my poor body, what a ride we had all been on.

My first meal arrived and I did my very best to look at it with love. I talked to it, thanked it, and then ate the yogurt, which tasted just like I imagined plastic would. I drank some broth, which was so salty it was tough for me to swallow, and had two bites of turkey with the texture and flavor of abundantly salted cardboard. Finally, I asked for a piece of toast, lightly buttered in hopes of getting something into my body so I could begin the process of moving it out. The toast arrived and it was make-believe wheat bread from processed flour.It didn't offer much substance. I laughed at how my mouth was as aware as my spirit. I wanted my food to be real the same way that I wanted to be real. I realized how much of my eating up to that point had been unconscious, more a task then a pleasure. To truly taste, be present, and have all my attention on the flavors in my mouth was astounding, invigorating, and a new way of eating! It was exciting. Eating had a whole new vibration to it. I realized how I'd been putting food in my mouth all my life and rarely ever took time to experience it. I was always in a hurry and didn't allow time for nourishing myself. I hadn't experienced the food; it was more like I'd been eating my memory of what the substance had tasted like previously. I went through the motions of eating, chewing, and swallowing but before now, I hadn't been aware enough to receive and allow the food to nurture me. Come to think of it, I'd hardly chewed.

I experienced aspects of flavored yogurt I'd never taken the time to notice before. My entire mouth was standing at attention. I was aware of texture, an unpleasant amount of sweetness, a chemical background, and chunks of something that was supposed to be fruit. It wasn't easy to eat. My tasters were wide-awake! I whispered a promise to my body, *From now on, I will stay conscious while I feed you.* This was a very important part of my healing. I appreciated the lesson. I was sure I'd stop eating many of the things I'd been eating before I got so sick. If I just paid attention to what I was chewing I wouldn't want that food anymore. I told the yogurt to be nice to me as it passed through my body, trying to make friends with it. I had a saying, an intention Patricia taught me to use when I resisted swallowing those prednisone tablets. "God into God!" That is what I repeated as I ate the chemically processed and dye "enriched" breakfast. God into God… it was a great mantra for the moments I believed the prednisone would kill me before the Crohn's disease got the chance. It helped me make the medicine a positive part of my healing and lessened my resistance. It was a prayer of sorts.

As the day went on I'd practiced everything I knew on how to be patient as well as handle my excitement about finally going home. I had as much lunch and dinner as I could handle, did lots of praying, quieted my mind, and loved my body. I was anxious. I kept waiting for the magic moment or should I say "movement." I talked to my colon, told it to let go, comforted it with massage, and begged it to do its thing. It was comical. Finally, I quit waiting and plugged in the phone. (I'd always left it unplugged except when calling Pat and the boys). The second I reconnected the phone it rang. It was Pat asking for the poop report followed by my oldest sister, Mom, and sister-in-law, all within thirty minutes. I could've made a recorded greeting: "Partly cloudy, light breeze, and no poop yet."

I waited some more.

Then dinner arrived. I did my best to eat it all and still no luck, no rumbles, no nada. I told Pat to not bother coming by that evening since I'd see him the next day when he'd be picking me up and taking me home!

I finally gave up on going to the bathroom for the night, turned the light off, and decided to meditate myself to sleep.

Then it happened. I felt a rumbling and it woke me up. I sat up in bed. "Yes!" I declared to the darkened room. It's embarrassing but I have to tell you, I've never been so happy in my life to see a bowl of pooh. I will spare you the descriptive details but it was blood-free, as far as I could tell. I immediately called the night nurse and asked her to come and view this wonderful specimen with me. She laughed and came right down. She played with it, the way only nurses can do, and I witnessed it like it was a holy thing, almost holding my breath. She looked at me and smiled broadly. It passed inspection! I did a little victory dance right there in the bathroom with the toilet bowl and the nurse. It was a very intimate, unforgettable moment.

The next morning my eyes peeped open and all I saw was the blue sky outside my window. I had slept like a baby. Loving the moments between sleep and awake I stayed still long enough to reach for a slippery dream. It was good to be alive. There was a peaceful feeling in my heart. I summoned my memory of Christ and his love softly moved through me again. I knew he, she, it, my Higher Self, the Tao, whatever you call it, wanted me to continue flowing this love toward myself and the world. I promised to make this my practice. I put both my hands on my tummy to say thank you for its patience. I thanked it for getting well, for forgiving me, and I promised to always be a kind friend to it. No more being angry at it, like it had done something wrong.

I had come to the hospital empty and depleted in every way. I was going home with a full heart and a strong connection to my Higher Self, acutely aware of the many sacred companions assisting me on my journey. They were both visible and invisible. I felt full, hopeful, and passionate about life and the future. I believed anything was possible and that I was much more than "the container" going home. I felt I could transform reality if I was willing to admit that somehow my reality was something I'd attracted. I felt I could correct my mistakes and release the guilt and fear as I became more aware of "my contents." I felt totally responsible for where I found myself now and knew I was in charge of my future. I was free.

I smiled feeling the grace of a second chance.

I looked around the room and knew everything was complete. I intended for my little sanctuary to be as healing for the next visitor as it was for me. God lived there and I hoped they got a chance to meet her.

To me every hour of the light and dark is a miracle. Every cubic inch of space is a miracle.

–Walt Whitman

Believing is Seeing

chapter 11

Whether you believe you can or you believe you can't... you are right.

–Henry Ford

On the ride home from the hospital I hung my head out the window like a dog tasting the wind. Spring had arrived and the air was alive. I treasured feeling the breeze dance through my hair and kiss my face. I was filled with joy, smiling from head to toe. With our hands resting gently in each other's Pat and I were quietly amazed and in awe of life. Pat took one of the prettiest routes home. The flowering plum trees lining the avenue were in full bloom, singing color into the wind. They waved as though welcoming me back to the world. I waved back and wished I spoke tree.

I was acutely aware of everything—thoughts, sounds, rhythms, and sensations. The traffic, the bumps in the road, the wind, an airplane, and the hum of my own presence, it was like a symphony. Waves of emotions washed through me as I witnessed the energies of life moving, circling, and flowing, in and out and all around. We turned down our street and the happiness flooding through me extended into forever. When I saw the house, a mix of anticipation and gratitude flooded my senses. I recognized both feelings as "not I's" and understood, for the first time, that even positive feelings are clusters of energy I cling to. I smiled realizing how everything was a choice. It was okay; I acknowledged and truly appreciated the sensations and they kept on moving. There wasn't any resistance in me for anything to stick to. I realized that in many ways the house represented who I *used* to be and that person was fast disappearing. I wasn't sure how my old life would fit into my new feet but I was ready to figure out a way to dance to the rhythm that would bring both worlds together in harmony.

My body was a bit shaky so Pat carried me up the stairs to our room. I settled into bed with a colorful view of the mountains. I think I exhaled for a full five minutes as I fully allowed myself to sink into the sheets, the fresh smell, and the coziness of our bedroom. It was calm: no ticking machines, noisy intercoms, or air thick with fear and pain. The sound of stillness was heaven. I remembered hearing someone once say that silence was the voice of God and, right then, I was sure it was true.

The kids were at school and Pat had to get back to work. I assured him I'd be fine; I had my big sis Debbie to take care of me and a nurse was coming by to set up my feeding machine. Everything was right with the world.

Debbie was watching me from the doorway, checking to see how I was settling in. I felt her probing me, scanning me with her attention like a scientist. She was timid and when she shyly approached me, I pulled her in and we embraced tenderly. She promised she'd take very good care of me. That was what Debbie did best, care for people. It was a dream come true, having time to spend with her. I looked at her face and the gentle nature of her spirit cuddled me through her eyes. Debbie and her four and a half year old daughter Kym had taken the previous few days to move in with us and planned to stay as long as we needed them. She'd given up her apartment in Woodland, California, and put her life on hold for me, for our family, for love, without a second thought. There weren't many as selfless as my biggest sister. I loved the opportunity to make up for our lost time together. We had much to share.

I held onto her. "I can't believe you are here, that you moved in to help us. I am so blessed and excited we get to hang out together, get to know each other and the kids will have so much fun!" She said, "I am going to cook for you and fatten you up before anything else." She had a determined twinkle in her eyes.

A familiar voice hollered, "Knock, knock!" from downstairs and we both turned our heads toward the door. Deb yelled back, "Up here!" about the same time that Dad poked his head in the bedroom door and spouted, "Checking, this is a check." He had a big smile on his face. It was peculiar seeing him standing there in the doorway to our bedroom, in our home for the first time. I was glad he was there.

Dad walked over and sat in the comfy chair by the bed. I could tell he had something up his sleeve and was on a mission.I said, "What?" He excitedly announced, "We are going to talk about beliefs today! You need to start creating your new reality and clearing out some old debris." I laughed and asked how long that was going to take because I was tired. He said he had been working on it his whole life and we merely needed to get started so I could be aware of the next step in my healing.

The moment was so sweet with Debbie, Dad, and me in the room. All three of us were healing, not just me. We had definitely moved some life around the last few days, allowing, getting honest, expressing, and yearning for forgiveness. Sharing, exploring and discovering, with them was going to be awesome. There was so much we didn't know about each other, so much to learn and appreciate. Neither of them knew the boys or Pat very well, or me for that matter, not really. Heck, I barely knew me! It was meant to be, us coming together at this juncture in our lives. We would all move into the future with hearts more open. I imagined Sunday dinners, holidays, and long talks about what was possible. I had big plans.

As I looked at Dad's face and saw the little boy in him through the excitement in his eyes, I couldn't help but chuckle. He was happy to be with us. It was unlocking a door for him that had been closed for a very long time. At the hospital, Mom and Patricia warned me that Dad was dishonest, to watch out because he was up to something. They were skeptical of him showing up all of a sudden, committed to my well-being after years of absence. Pat was a bit cautious, too, having heard so many horror stories from all of us. I understood everybody's concern. But I wished they could see him right then, so childlike and caring.

I longed for everyone to let the past go. They didn't realize their experience of Dad was coming from their memories instead of from being present with him. The past was so solid in their eyes that it filtered any chance of seeing who he had become over the years and who he was now, here. When Mom and Patricia saw Dad at the hospital they never gave him a chance; he was viewed through their old ideas and beliefs about him. They never even spoke to him. Yet, each time they saw him, they gathered more evidence for how bad a person he was. No matter what he did or how he acted, they made it into something evil because they were only able to experience him through the filter of the past. It was fascinating to watch the energy of criticism control their ability to see what was right in front of them. Admittedly, I had done the same thing, with plenty of others. My new vow was to be in present time with people, to live in the now and stop dragging around some mistake from the past to hold against them each time I saw them.

A couple of times, Patricia and Mom were so mean to Dad it really bothered me. I tried to explain my opinions about how toxic it was for them to carry their hate forward. They didn't want to hear me and I didn't have the energy to defend any viewpoint that day. It just wasn't time for them to accept this, yet.

I wasn't worried about Dad hurting me. I trusted what was happening. Debbie did too, and it was great that she and I could share this feeling. Her belief was; what goes out comes in. She said every action we take comes back to us and it wasn't her job to punish anybody for something they'd done to her. She said the Universe automatically gave people whatever they gave to others and it had everything under control. I wish she'd taught me that when we were kids!

Shortly before I got sick, Debbie found out she was HIV positive. She'd contracted it from her fiancé Ken who swore his blood test was clear, when in actuality, he'd never had the test at all. He had full-blown AIDS. She was angry with him for a very short time and then let it go like sand falling between her fingers. He fell very sick right before they were to be married and that was when she found out he had the disease. She sat with him at the hospital several times to comfort him and he died just a few months later. She forgave him completely. She chose to. Debbie even helped him transition with peace. She said she felt like the whole incident was part of the Universe saying, "Wake up Debbie, look at what you are being!" I think Debbie may have had a self-sabotaging belief underneath it all that she needed to be punished and that she deserved to get sick. I think that particular belief ran in our family.

Forgiving Ken opened Debbie's awareness to a new level of love and honor, for others and herself. I think forgiveness was good for her health! She transformed and began paying more attention to her body, using the disease as a teacher that eventually became her friend. She said the disease was something she'd attracted by who she was being and there wasn't anybody to blame, not even herself. She was a wise gal and that day I saw it in her eyes when we spoke about Dad at the hospital. She pointed out that over the years, the stress, guilt, and grief had taken its toll on him, including a heart attack and triple bypass, the loss of his family and home, and that all of this was only the visible part. She seemed far away as she mentioned how we had no idea what he was going through, and how we couldn't know the pain or loneliness he'd experienced. Debbie had so much compassion in her it inspired me further. When she first ran into Dad, the only father she'd ever known, she hugged him with all her heart. It was sincere and kind. This was amazing to me in light of the fact that they hadn't seen each other for a number of years; he wasn't her biological father, and he'd been quite aggressive with her as child. Once he even stepped on her throat and damaged her eardrum which resulted in a history of ear issues. They'd been through a lot. Yet, she was genuinely glad to see Dad. She was a forgiving and gracious soul.

I looked over and Dad was staring at me as though I'd just said everything I was thinking out loud. I wondered if he could read my thoughts. It often seemed like it. Debbie watched silently as though she knew this, too. It was awkward for a second; Dad shuffled in his chair, cleared his throat, and tried to redirect everyone's attention by asking his big question, "Holly, what do you believe about Crohn's disease?" Obviously he didn't want to address what was lingering in the space and preferred to move on to his own agenda. I didn't answer. I watched curiously allowing the discomfort to hang in the air a bit longer. Debbie made it easy for everyone. She stood up and walked toward the door, saying she would get me something to munch.

Trusting the flow, I shifted over to Dad's reality and considered his question. "I don't know." He invited me to look and see, and waited silently. I started slowly, not sure I knew the difference between what I really believed and what I wanted to believe. "I believe my colon lining is like raw hamburger. I saw the picture. I believe I need to get hydrated and figure out how to get some excellent nutrition in me, eat foods I can absorb to heal my tissue and body. I believe I need to put kind and loving attention toward my body instead of getting mad at it. I believe there will be scary times as I wean off the prednisone. I believe I've been given the gift of a second chance and there's something I'm supposed to be doing with my life. I believe..." Dad jumped in, "You *are* supposed to be doing something with your life and if you do the Avatar Course you're going to get some tools to find out what that is!" I laughed at his cleverness. The apple didn't fall far from the tree. He reminded me of how I persuaded people to do things I thought would be good for them by enticing them with solutions. Whether it was in regard to being more conscious, selling a house, needing money, how to eat right, or advice of any kind, I had the answers. At the very least, I knew exactly where they should go to get them!

Dad went on, "Avatar will help you find and remove beliefs that are in the way of your healing." He had recently completed the course and explained how the techniques had brought his life studies together. He felt Avatar made what Edger Cayce, Seth, Gurdjieff, and Bartholomew had been teaching come to life and allowed him to speed up his awakening. I was agreeable, especially since Patricia was suggesting I take the same course. (It was amazing how much alike they were, even in their studies). I told Dad to hold on until I healed a bit more. I wasn't jumping into anything until I could at least eat and eliminate without it becoming headline news. He continued as though he didn't hear me, "It would be a powerful step for you to start recognizing how your beliefs create your experiences and recognize how everybody has their own collection of truths, particularly your doctor! Whatever you believe is going to affect what you manifest."

Then Dad asked," What does your doctor believe?" I answered, "I think the doctor believes I'll be dealing with Crohn's disease a long time and that it doesn't ever really go away. He originally told me that he'd be surprised if I still had my colon in five years. Doc also believes steroids are the quickest solution whenever bleeding occurs. He said he had a blanket treatment for Crohn's disease patients that was admittedly hit and miss. "So," Dad interrupted, "he believes you can learn to manage it, but not heal it?" I answered, "Pretty much." Dad went on, "He believes what he was taught. He paid a lot of money to understand and align with that belief system, which often makes it more difficult to see other possibilities." Then Dad reminded me of several people who had healed from cancer and diseases that were considered incurable, much worse than Crohn's. He asked me how I thought it was possible for these people to heal. I had no answer and he continued, "It's very simple, they believed they could, without doubt." He said this course would teach me to believe I could heal.

I liked where the dialogue was going. In the hospital, I saw the phenomenon of different beliefs clearly. I felt them and knew they were at the core of my habits and personality. The ideas and opinions I'd swallowed as truths were somehow held in my body and mind as energy. They had density and feeling. They affected what I attracted, how I thought, and the way I interpreted things. Beliefs were like a pair of glasses I saw life through. They needed to be examined because they consistently and automatically determined how I experienced life. Dad went on to ask, "What do you think would happen if you believed Crohn's disease was incurable and you thought about it regularly, worried about it daily, and even found information that proved that belief was true?" I answered, "Duh, I would probably be sick the rest of my life. I would be adding more of those ideas into my body and mind every time I accepted them as truth. I would make it true for myself." I finally understood this amazingly powerful connection between one's mind and body. Then he added, "You could find information to support almost any idea about disease. You can find proof for anything you want to prove."

He told me a story he'd heard about two patients of Deepak Chopra's. Both were diagnosed with cancer of the pancreas. Their types of pancreatic cancer were very similar and the health of the two subjects almost identical. According to Dad, Deepak explained to each of these patients that they had a 50 percent chance of living (rather than a 50 percent chance of dying). He said it was apparent from the very moment he delivered the news to one of them that the patient believed he could be part of the 50 percent who lived. This patient began implementing the regimes that would allow him to create a successful outcome, beginning a healing diet, exercise, therapy, and the spiritual work that suited him. The other patient, from the very moment Deepak gave him the news, believed he was in the other 50 percent group and that he'd more than likely die. He began preparing for death. He believed death was inevitable and living a slim option. He made sure his will and estate were in order and prepared for his demise. Dad explained the variable power of a belief and how our minds have a lot to do with our life experience. Dad said Deepak's story made a great point of how our bodies follow instructions from our minds and that, unconsciously, we often don't realize how much our words and intentions physically manifest. Dad finished by explaining how both patients proceeded to carry out their lives exactly as you would imagine, in accordance with their beliefs.

Dad gave many examples of how people get to believe whatever they want to believe, explaining how nobody's really wrong. "It's a free country," he chuckled. I told him it was more difficult for me to be around the nurses who believed Crohn's was incurable. They felt sorry for me and their sympathy was heavy and uncomfortable. I felt my life energy drain whenever they came in the room, even though they were simply trying to teach me ways to live with the disease. They meant no harm and were only doing what they'd been taught. But, they injected a dense feeling into my personal space that made it harder for me to maintain the high vibration of possibility. I always felt relieved once they left. I didn't realize how much beliefs carried with them an energy and how profoundly that energy could affect others. He said, "You got it, and you get to pick who you let in by tuning into what feels good and what doesn't."

We spoke about religion and how people fought over whose God was the real God and which doctrines were the "right" ones. We discussed how people make each other wrong for what they believe and often measure someone's worth by the church they attend or the deity they worship. *So much life could be wasted defending a viewpoint,* I thought. After my experience with Jesus, I was sure these rules were invented by man and were far from what mattered most. What was important was the connection we had to the Sacred with No Name. What we call it is not so important. Our ability to become aware of Higher Self energy comes from discovering who we are beyond the indoctrination and rules we are born into. It's available every moment of life; we just look for it in places that profess it unavailable to us—unless we follow their belief system. I was certain the path to the Sacred with No Name lived inside each of us and that no one had directions to it but us. A lot of people point the way, but the finding is up to us. I remember attending a sermon as a young teen, wondering what the hubbub was all about because I didn't feel any liberation or have any insights that touched my life. Quite the opposite, I left feeling like I was a bad girl and would probably be punished at some point. For me, the magic of a good minister is in his or her ability to direct us toward ourselves so we can discover our own answers.

I wondered what could be possible in our world if everyone celebrated the *concept* of worshiping different ideas of whom or what God is. I imagined how that might look in life—in schools, government, church, and even at the dinner table. Finding the God within is the path to peace, joy, and caring for one another, regardless of what we call it: Higher Self, Muhammad, Prajna, Divine Intlligence, Christ energy, Holy Spirit, or the Tao. I bet this energy answers to any label we assign it. It's like the water is to the fish—it's everywhere, inside, outside, and it connects us all. We just give it different names—it comes down to nothing more than semantics. We also argue over fabricated laws about how the Heavenly Father only provides for those who conform to a particular belief structure. I have evidence to the contrary, although this path seems to be working for a lot of other fish. I believe Spirit celebrates all life equally and is there for anyone to become aware of and direct toward goodness. It patiently waits for us to allow grace to do its thing.

Dad and I both disappeared into thought for a while before he went onto explain how our attention on an idea or possibility stimulates that very concept in our lives, to some degree, and that the degree it materializes always depends on how much we've focused on it. Attention has the power to wake up any reality we could imagine. Kind of muttering to himself, he added, "Attention is what makes things become more real and solid in our daily lives."

It made perfect sense to me that beliefs needed attention to live and thrive. It's their sustaining energy. Beliefs become more solid if more attention is put on them. "Yes," I exclaimed, "that is exactly what happened in the hospital! I found pockets of stuff I'd been literally holding inside of me with my attention!" Dad nodded in agreement as I described how I'd given the negative events from my past more power simply by thinking and talking about them, over and over again! Even resisting them with a powerful intention to control them made them stronger. My efforts actually perpetuated their survival. I told Dad how I assumed the act of ignoring things would make them go away and leave me alone. But they never disappeared. He explained, "That's because ignoring is a form of resisting." I was dumbfounded as I realized the truth of what he said. I had ignored myself right into the reality I was ignoring. I was so happy to understand this. It was going to change my world. It was becoming more and more apparent how much of my life had been spent holding back beliefs and resisting ideas and how this very act had ironically reinforced their existence. Even though I thought pushing and shoving them away from me was a smart way to stay safe, every bit of my resistance had caused them to become more consuming. Ignoring and allowing were two very different vibrations. This new understanding was pivotal for me.

As Dad continued, I had a sense of how people, religious organizations, Republicans or Democrats, or any group fighting and positioning their energy and attention against an idea or person, on some level actually fed what they were opposing. The fervent project or belief system of any group could become so fanatical that the individuals involved could lose connection to his or her life path and inner wisdom and completely miss the opportunity to really contribute to the world in the one way we all can, by following our own intuition. I wondered if any group could effectively, for any length of time, lead its participants to their own Highest Selves, to internal peace and harmony, without taking an honest and honoring inventory of each individual's viewpoint and dreams. Understandably most groups are determined to influence a person with their perspectives as this is how they become a troop, a party, an assembly, or a strong force.

I imagined what was possible for all of us if we only put as much attention toward our dreams and peaceful solutions as we did on being against something. It would have such a profound effect on humanity's health, for example, to be pro-peace instead of anti-war. When asked why she wouldn't participate in an anti-war demonstration Mother Teresa replied, "I will never do that, but as soon as you have a pro peace rally I'll be there." I realized the power in being for something that I desire instead of against whatever I think is standing in my way.

I asked Dad if he still got caught up in belief systems or found the need to defend anything very often. He said he was fairly good at letting everything be the way it was and explained how he'd pretty much stopped resisting "any reality" at this point of his life. He did say if he ever found himself in a twitter, he'd allow himself to experience whatever feeling showed up, including emotions or sensations around the idea that had triggered him in the first place. He explained how most negative feelings moved right through him and didn't stop in his body for long because feeling everything meant nothing could hijack his attention. He used his oil paintings as an example. "If I put some paint in a spot and it didn't come out the way I expected, instead of getting upset, I feel it. Usually, I let it become part of the picture and lead me to the perfect addition." He went onto say that sometimes the best part of the painting was what he initially had considered a flaw. As he spoke, it was so easy to feel that he trusted the Universe and had become a master at allowing life to flow through him.

Once again, Dad reminded me how powerful we humans are. We are the captains of our own ships and our own experiences with our beliefs and attention carving the paths we sail. Dad said, "The easiest way to climb above everything is by noticing that you are the one creating it."

He suggested I begin focusing on what was possible, not on what the doctor or anyone else thought was impossible. I agreed. He suggested I write down what I'd like to make real and practice placing my attention on those ideas by looking at them, contemplating them, and feeling what they felt like as if they'd already manifested. I liked that approach, too. Just talking about the power of my focus had lightened the energy in the bedroom. I felt possibility, and it was good. I was so grateful that I could sense the weight of beliefs and thoughts, and become aware of the vibration my body holds and exudes. I could feel the density or lightness in things and people. I was connected to everything and it was wonderful.

Debbie skipped in with a bowl of cream of wheat, grinning from ear to ear. It was like Christmas to me. I could feel how much care she'd put into the preparation just by the way she was carrying the food. My first home-cooked meal. She'd made it with tons of love and added a big spoon of ghee butter. We were experimenting with an Ayurvedic diet and this was my first experience of the yummy, buttery taste of Indian ghee, considered healing for my Pitta body type. My mouth watered as I took my first bite. It was orgasmic. My eyes rolled back as I chewed and experienced every bit of flavor to the max. I disappeared into that bowl. I knew what Heaven tasted like. I almost cried I was so happy, completely engrossed in cereal and gratitude. I'd never tasted anything like it. I took tiny bites to make it last awhile, savoring every morsel. I forgot anybody was in the room I was so consumed. Then I looked up at Dad and Debbie and their mouths were hanging open as they watched me. I think they were almost drooling. They decided they should have a bowl, too.

My love affair with food began that day. I decided to make preparing food and feeding myself a project of love. Eating was a perfect way to practice caring for and nurturing my body. Before, food had always seemed a bothersome task of stuffing something in my mouth so I could get back to more important things. This was a great way to learn how to receive and honor life. I couldn't wait to tell Pat. He'd be thrilled. He was always wishing I'd learn to cook. I stunk in the kitchen.

I heard the boys downstairs and got very excited, almost choking on my last bite of cereal. They raced up the stairs screaming with joy to see me! I was so happy, my face leaked! I just stared at their little faces, adoring their bright eyes. They hugged Grandpa and Debbie, and then hopped on the bed, both clamoring for my lap. Seeing them with my dad and sister was a treasure. I wanted them to have some of Dad in their souls and Debbie in their hearts. As I felt their presence and openness, it was just like the space Christ had offered me, pure, innocent, and sacred. I was blown away by their preciousness and couldn't help but melt into it (kind of like the ghee). I pulled them close with one on each side snuggled under my arms. I experienced the sparkle of their souls more deeply than ever. Our connection was heaven.

I looked into my sons' eyes and appreciated their pureness in a way I never had before. I sensed who they were behind it all, two Source beings in new bodies. It was the first time I'd really looked at them with such honor. They had a new mom. We cuddled, hugged, and laughed until we were all giddy with joy. The love I felt for them encompassed everything. It came from beyond time and space. It filled the room.

I looked over and Dad was soaking it all in, quietly. As I connected with his energy I could feel he was not used to being so close to this type of parenting. I had compassion for him, remembering how difficult his childhood had been with regular beatings from his own father. I was glad for him to see the boys so happy and full of un-thwarted spirit. Dad could feel that the punishment cycle he was born into had stopped with me and that it would not be paid forward in my family, with my boys. It was done.

The cycle of blame was over. Dad got up and said it was time for him to go.

I think some memories had stirred in him that needed his undivided attention in order to be set free.

> *Be present as the watcher of your mind—of your thoughts and emotions as well as your reactions in various situations. Be at least as interested in your reactions as in the situation or person that causes you to react. Notice also how often your attention is in the past or future. Don't judge or analyze what you observe. Watch the thought, feel the emotion, observe the reaction. Don't make a personal problem out of them. You will then feel something more powerful than any of those things that you observe: the still, observing presence itself behind the content of your mind, the silent watcher.*
>
> –*Practicing The Power Of Now: Essential Teachings, Meditations, and Exercises,* Eckhart Tolle

Who's Wrong? Who's Right? Who Cares?

chapter 12

You climb above everything by noticing you are creating it.

–Howard Wayne Goss

I told Dad I planned to do the Avatar Course with Patricia. It was my obvious next step: both of them had assured me great results, plus my intuition was nudging me. I wanted to experience Avatar with Dad by my side, but Patricia wasn't open to him being around while she was feeling vulnerable and processing her emotions. When I suggested he join us, she adamantly opposed the idea stating that if he attended, she would not. She was hanging onto her grudge with no intention of loosening her grip. I hoped at some point in the course she'd be open to a viewpoint other than one of blaming Dad, and we'd be able to address the underlying issue. I believed it had to do with self-abandonment. Of course, I mostly see outside of me (exterior reality) through what's going on inside of me (beliefs), so there was no telling what might show up on our adventure together or who'd be the actual owner of that perspective.

Patricia had a friend who was licensed to teach the program and he agreed to hold a class in Reno, close to home. This would make it easier on me since I'd only been out of the hospital a short time and was still fairly weak. Dad was thrilled for me to learn the techniques and understood why I'd be taking the course without him. He gave Patricia all the breathing room she needed. He was excited about the two of us doing the course together. I asked if he'd at least stop by during the week. He appreciated the invite but was reluctant to commit to anything.

I was ecstatic to have an opportunity to explore human consciousness with my sister for nine full days. Being present and honest with her had always been one of the best parts of my life and rather than doing this as a prayer or a remedy for abuse, we were going to do it deliberately, in a gentle forum, with no urgency or need to be saved. It was sure to be a blast. To be honest, I was more thrilled about being real and intimate with her than I was about doing the class. It had been several years since we'd been together for any length of time. I felt we'd empower each other by pointing out, in a kind way, what might need clearing. Patricia and I could simply look each other in the eye and fill up on love, determination, and inspiration. I believed our connection was key to healing our worlds more than any teachings could. I'd invited her to nearly every seminar I'd ever attended over the past decade and she had wanted nothing to do with *any* of them. She'd consistently made fun of me for believing I'd find some magic trick to fix all of life's turmoil. She called me: "The rabid searcher who never became a finder." I defended being a class junky by explaining my desire to connect with aware people and that I was hungry to hang out with friends who were interested in being awake for the party (i.e., life) we had all RSVP'd to.

I loved being in the presence of presence. It offered the sensation of belonging somewhere. I preferred a class experience to most vacations, which drove my husband batty. He offered Hawaii but I pushed for a weekend retreat on creating relationships with Werner Erhard, founder of the *est* program. Patricia was right though: There was part of me that did believe some great guru or teaching held the secret, the magic wand that would relieve all suffering on the planet and inside me. I just had to find the right one!

I'm not kidding when I say that I took every class I could afford and schedule time off for, since the age of 20. I started with Erhard's *est* training, including his Ropes Course and Communication Workshops and for a few years even served as an assistant, forgoing a lot of sleep, skimping on food, and learning to hold my bladder until the next break (that was a joke, sort of). For more than six years, I was a student of Arnold Siegel's Conversation, an offshoot of *est* which explored ethics, rationality, and trusting truth to be revealed in the practice of dialogue. I studied Jin Shin Jyutsu® on balancing energies in the body and learned how to move energy in Tantric classes. I followed this with A Course in Miracles curriculum and attended Deepak Chopra lectures every chance I had. I participated in study groups on a variety of subjects including the teachings of Ramtha, Transcendental Meditation, Holotropic Breathwork,™ Taoism, and repeatedly listened to Bartholomew's teachings channeled by Mary-Margaret Moore. I studied the art of using intention and energy to heal and became a certified Reiki Master Teacher. It's embarrassing to admit the amount of money and time I spent looking for a true, complete, and final answer.

Now I realize that each course I attended led me to the exactly what I was after. Each failed attempt at applying the techniques and expecting great teachers to create significant and lasting change in my life actually revealed the most important truth of all. Whether anything worked or not was entirely up to me! Disappointment after disappointment brought me to understand classes would never change anything, they were merely an invitation to become more responsible.

The connections with the companions I'd meet in these circles became food for my soul. I loved being with people who cared deeply. It was my church. I learned a lot and I was a committed student, yet, it was more as a means to belong somewhere than anything else. I took all those classes so I could be around people I could call "family." I studied so many theories and strategies for manifesting health, happiness, prosperity, and salvation that I became a walking encyclopedia of techniques. I had a multitude of processes up my sleeve for everything you can imagine. Yes, I was Mrs. Fix It! I never found the Holy Grail, but I did find a lot of companions who had their sniffer pointed toward something that mattered… at least to me.

My brain was fairly good at compartmentalizing and retrieving information and I liked the process of learning. The challenges were fun, although parts of the data I'd gathered were conflicting and, some, even competitive, claiming that their path was the best or ultimate one for saving my soul or the world. I understood the organizations were also running a business and I didn't mind...much. For me, there was tremendous value simply in being near another who was vibrating with hunger for awareness. It was home. It was the gold at the end of the rainbow. I was a junky for the energy of good intentions and being linked to others who were determined to be the best they could be. We probably could have read nothing but the phone book in our meetings and still experienced miraculous transformations as a result of our aligned desire for integrity (wholeness).

The course information rarely impacted me as much as the relationships did. In fact, some of the material became belief systems that I had to unload in order to connect to my intuitive self. The real me often got buried beneath the need to conform to the methodologies. Much of the data I'd accumulated ended up being a distraction from trusting and becoming Self aware. I got lost in needing to know. I could recite any number of teachers' beliefs quite accurately, rarely feeling what the present moment was offering for me. Knowledge and rote responses had actually created roadblocks to my intuition.

In retrospect one of the most beneficial aspects of all the courses was developing some honest ability to express myself, or at least admit to my pretense. Students were usually willing to speak their truth in a self-help class environment and it offered a refreshing contrast from my idea that everyone was faking their way through life. There were many moments that gave me an opportunity to see how my projection of pretenders was actually birthed from my own lack of authenticity. Although I wasn't keen on letting others in, over time, I became increasingly vulnerable and less pretentious. As I grew more honest there were an awful lot of idiotic actions and thought processes revealed for me to own of myself. Along with realizing no matter how much honesty I mustered... it seemed I always had further to go. I became my own entertainment for a while, never knowing what craziness I would find next.

I loved witnessing the innocence on courses. Being with students, uncovering their innermost fears and secrets while removing the mask they'd been showing the world, gave me so much hope that goodness would prevail. It was real. It created a safe space to move forward in and dig for deeper truth. I felt it was the closest I ever got to letting people know me without fear of being judged and it helped my heart open a little more so I could see inside. The whole process of distinguishing between my story and who I could be without it was ongoing. I frequently confused the two. However, when truth was present, without any story from me or my classmates, we all felt it. It was pure and precious with the same quality of love I'd felt in Christ's hands. When two or more are gathered...

Eventually, once I settled into the idea that becoming real and trusting my Self was a lifelong endeavor, I began to relax into the notion of my project literally taking forever. No matter how close I came to feeling like I had reached some pinnacle, I always found another mountain that needed climbing. I became more comfortable with the hike instead of obsessed with getting it done... at least, some of the time. I had my share of moments forgetting this.

My involvement with a few of the organizations became confusing for me. It always started out sweet and exciting but as I committed to their goals my ego would compete for approval. I'd end up operating in a spiritual environment employing the very patterns we were there to dismantle. Part of me would silently compete for the position of "most evolved" or "most integral and inspiring" and then project that onto whoever was in the authoritative position as though that person was some type of God that I needed to please and win approval from. For me, the scary and challenging part was doing whatever it took to advance and acquire a pat on the head. I misconstrued the whole game with holy work and believed that somehow, being devoted, inspiring new disciples, and sacrificing my own joy would earn me enough karma points for a free pass into salvation. And I wanted through those doors!

Usually we'd be acknowledged for the number of people we could bring to an event. In retrospect, I confused praise with love. Being the competitive type, starving for approval, and desperately wanting to be a good person in the eyes of "God," structures like these were dangerous ground for me. I too easily became a clone and a follower of someone else's ideal of what was important in the world of awakening, all in an effort to garner approval. I was looking to belong. It was seductive and I got tangled in it more than a few times, partly because I was adept at persuading people to agree with my viewpoint(s) and register for a class. Every time I dove into a new course, my long time friends made fun of me. They'd usually stop returning my calls for a while until I had cooled off from my latest and greatest passion of study.

I watched some of these organizations struggle with power and fall into the same rut society often suffered from: always wanting more, needing others obedience to survive, and justifying using people to accomplish their righteous goals without offering a true exchange of equivalent value. It felt like obtaining approval and feeling connection became conditional upon my level of cooperation and conformity. It took me awhile to realize that my love for others was founded on these very standards, if they performed as I expected I rewarded them with attention and approval. Clearly what I was experiencing with all authority was a result of my projection (a placement of old unresolved patterns and expectations onto reality and then experiencing that as ultimate truth. This concept is cleverly portrayed in the Leap movie. www.LeapMovie.com).

I am in awe of the visionaries that are able to gather large groups of people and inspire them toward their dreams. I believe it's a tricky task to manage personal power and offer exercises and concepts to people that encourage human expansion, without the intentions becoming a religion or set of strict rules that the followers must adhere to or suffer the continual pangs of inadequacy. This was especially risky for people like me who projected their unresolved childhood mother and father issues onto authority figures, and there were usually quite a few of us enrolled. Operating through these circumstances, it was impossible to feel satisfied or ever collect enough attention or approval from Ma and Pa. (gurus, organization heads, teammates, etc) We ended up looking for love in all the wrong places.

Eckhart Tolle offers a wise perspective on how our studies, classes, books, and tapes are merely pointers to be used to find our own truth. Stating how we should not stick with one methodology and turn it into a God. He speaks of students making the tools and application of the processes more important than the truth they are pointing to. I saw evidence of this when students would become devout followers of another person's beliefs, missing the purest possibility of the teaching. I discovered this in myself.

So, off to another class I went. This time it was Avatar, and I was adorned with tubes hanging out of my chest, steroids in my body, and a miniscule amount of energy. Being afraid of doing too much too fast, I moved cautiously through that first day. Pat was leery of me taking on a nine-day commitment. He didn't think I was strong enough yet after only a month out of the hospital. I think he was also fed up with my coming home from course after course with a new series of child-rearing techniques or relationship strategies, insisting we implement them. He wanted me to heal and take a look at what I'd already studied and to recognize that none of it had kept me from getting sick. I argued that I was different, more willing to be honest than ever before. I explained how I still had feelings and ideas tucked away from long ago and that my unwillingness to expose and experience them was part of why I became so ill. I wanted him to understand that Mrs. Searcher had found something in the hospital while connected to the Sacred with No Name. I was becoming a finder and I trusted myself more than ever. I promised him I'd be careful and assured him I felt safe and that I'd listen closely to my body. He threw his arms up and surrendered, knowing how stubborn I could get once I had my mind set. With great skill, Pat had learned to wave the white flag or else ignore me.

There were six of us taking the Avatar Course together. It was a very relaxed setting and students popped in and out throughout the nine days; I ended up treasuring every person. We spent most of our time outdoors in a backyard that belonged to my dad's best friend, Harry Holman. During the week, Patricia had to prod me along a few times, but I did my best to keep up on my class checklist. There were some wonderful lessons in the materials that offered easy techniques to strengthen my ability to feel, quiet my mind, and own the reality I found myself in. The materials were a perfect fit with what Dad had lectured about when I was young. The exercises helped me better understand the mechanics of attention, consciousness, and awareness and how beliefs comprised the blueprint I lived out of, usually without knowing it. I used all the processes in the course to discover and remove old ideas that had been blocking happiness and health. I released layers of patterns and Patricia and I laughed and cried as we discovered more wiring that transmitted the notion that life equaled suffering. It was good to be together and see some humor in our travels. Supporting each other in clearing out our history was profound. As we honored one another and owned the choices we'd both made along the way, there was a deep healing.

I was in awe of the way the instructor delivered the course. It allowed students to arrive at their own truth without the interference of someone else's idea of what was "right" or important. I was delighted with how it lined up with my new understanding that everyone had their own truths and the only way a person could come to know their own power and preciousness was to feel their way and then follow their own intuition to where it was leading. I no longer needed my storehouse of answers. I actually had to empty the warehouse, let go, and stop automatically supplying solutions or remedies to people like I had *their* answers! That had been a habit in my world. Telling others what I felt was important for them was disrespectful in a way and took them off their path. During the course I became honest about how it was an ego-feeding activity for me. I wasn't inspiring them to believe in themselves and discover their own truth. I could see the dynamic and had a glimpse of the damage it could do over time. After my visit with Christ I was sure we each had our own special spot in the world and if we followed someone else to their spot, ours would remain empty until we found it. Our connection to Higher Self is what offers the ideal rope to pull us toward our dreams. Using somebody else's rope will only pull us to somebody else's dream. I had thrown many a rope to others and mistakenly drawn them toward my truths and I was truly sorry for that.

This new awareness offered so much freedom. I instantly had more trust in where people were on their personal journey. I didn't need to direct them away from pain or toward some intention I had hidden up my sleeve. They needed to be where they were until they decided where to step next. I had an epiphany: in my lifelong search for the guru or great master that could give me the answer, the final truth that would make everything okay and relieve my pain, I'd become a worshiper of many human beings, believing they were the doorway to my soul. I adopted their doctrines and then took their pearls of wisdom and passed them along, with some part of me intending to be a guru for others, as though I held their secrets. My ego had wanted to be admired and coveted in the same way I had praised the teachers who gave me solutions. With this admission came a deep sense of remorse. I saw a trail of people I had led or tried to lead and how I had crossed the line, making the answers I offered more about me than them. I felt the damage I'd done and how misleading and egocentric this pattern was. In this moment of realization something changed inside me. With great certainty I knew life didn't come with a manual on how things were supposed to be and that nobody had the answers for anyone else. I didn't need to save a soul.

Everything my soul ever needed to know would always be revealed in the moment I was moving through. Any challenge I faced would come with a simultaneous solution. I just needed to be present and uncluttered enough to see it and hear my intuitive guidance. It required an ability to listen and trust. Clearing my mind, learning to be still, and connecting to the Sacred with No Name, the Holy Spirit, Higher Self, awareness, truth, etc., was the true teaching. Creating anyone or anything as an outside authority of my path was only a detour. The Avatar tools had opened my eyes in a very sweet and compassionate way.

Furthering this understanding, I experienced a poignant lesson during one of the group discussions that the truth for everyone was a little different. We were all faced with noticing how we dealt with opposing viewpoints. It was enlightening to become aware of my urges to persuade or convince others of the value of my opinion. As we discussed parenting I noticed how most of what I believed, I had considered as absolute truth, like I knew the correct way to parent! I had some very solid ideas about diet, exercise, and vaccinations and I had become protective and positional when discussing them. I spoke really fast, throwing out statistics and opinions until another person in the group calmly stated several diverse opinions, explaining that she also had facts and statistics to support those viewpoints. It was good for me to see how I got triggered by her know-it-all attitude and how my mouth started running like a freight train to prove my rightness. I watched myself unable to shut up. After a few minutes of nonstop yammering, I noticed I was dominating the whole conversation and that everyone was staring at me. Embarrassed, I closed my mouth, making a zipper motion over my lips.

As difficult as it was to acknowledge, it was a great opportunity to observe myself. It was clear that we could find facts or statistics to support almost any idea if only we looked hard enough. Even as I quieted down, a part of me was still having a bit of a tizzy, wanting to give yet another fact to prove my point. As if reading my mind, one of the gals at the table stated, "A fact is a belief that is no longer questioned." I laughed and was inspired to shush for a few minutes and contemplate.

Observing myself was very interesting. I kept realizing how full of myself I was, feeling like I knew more, had better knowledge, studied more and had read all the right books. I watched my ego wanting to argue and prove its superiority. I had a physical reaction, urges driven by adrenalin. It was crazy! I was like a mother trying to handle an unruly child. I told my mind repeatedly to relax using every bit of will I could rally to not say anything from ego. It was really hard. Finally, with a deep breath and a little bit of surrender, something happened and my struggle softened.

I saw how my judgment of the gal across the table being a "know it all" was really a reflection of myself. I was the know it all! That was how I came across. That was how I was speaking and acting and I had projected it all onto her. My opinion of her became the filter I had viewed her through. As soon as I saw myself behaving that way and managed to own my part in it, the energy shifted. The filter was dissipating simply from my being honest and becoming aware of it. I was able to connect with the person, instead of my judgment of her. I could feel the solidity of the ideas I held lighten and become thoughts instead of something I had to prove. I wasn't the thoughts or ideas that I held. The moment I remembered this, I became more aware of whom I was without them. I felt the awareness that included much more than all the bodies sitting around the table defending a viewpoint. Like the water to the fish, something much bigger than all of us was connecting us—and suddenly I felt it.

I wanted to interrupt the discussion, grab Patricia, and report my discoveries so I could show her how this was what we had done with Dad. All those bad memories of him had become the filters we experienced him through. We had no idea who Dad had become. We didn't know him in present time. Our attention toward him was all filtered via our past. Our relationship was with our filter, not him!

I also noticed how silly it was to want to be "right" about how to raise a child when every person at the table probably had different beliefs, opinions, filters, and realities about what worked. I considered how cultures across the world had extreme and varying methods for raising children and there I was in Reno, Nevada, thinking I had the best answers! What did I know? Who did I think I was? I had to laugh at my arrogance or maybe it was ignorance. All of a sudden I became light, free, and sincerely celebrated every viewpoint at the table.

I enjoyed letting go of my solid reality way more than I enjoyed defending it. It was a relief that I felt throughout my body. The tightness was gone. I was relaxed with nothing to defend. I had an idea this lesson, my letting go of being right, was something I'd get to practice a lot. I wanted to make sure I understood, so I went over it... when I realized I was stuck in the solidity of an idea, part of me was able to separate from it and it seemed to soften. First and foremost, I had to observe myself and admit what I was doing. As I continued to listen to the discussion from that newly expanded viewpoint, my position began to dissolve and I became interested in other viewpoints. I could better hear what was being said, connect, and participate when my mind wasn't protecting a position. I could actually be open and learn something new! As my attention released from my solid position, I was free to explore other opinions and move toward a more intuitive knowing. Cool! When I finally let go of being right, I could increase my awareness, include more possibilities, and access intuition.

I looked around the table at each person, the diversity, and then realized we all seemed to reach this knowing as a group. As we became more allowing, an understanding and an intuitive connection had been established. Different types of solutions began to show up that included honoring everyone. The group discussion stopped being about any one person knowing anything or being right. It was about connecting for a greater good, a higher purpose. We had a mini model of the world at our small table discussion with each person holding a unique perspective of what mattered. We could fight over it, defend it, protect it, or let it be an idea we were all committed to exploring—in order to access a greater knowing that would bring solutions to the whole. Awareness and good intentions allowed group insights that weren't available when we were immersed in protecting one idea or one identity or personality. We had come to a place where we could explore all possible viewpoints, allowing, intuiting, and enjoying one another. I imagined how this could apply to any subject in life and in the world.

The honesty and willingness in each person at the table was an open space, fun, and encouraging. To allow all our viewpoints to exist simultaneously without any need to dominate or manipulate other participants had raised the vibration of the experience. We all felt it. Each of us was appreciating the diversity without any judgment. There was a very kind, compassionate connection between us, and a feeling of respect for each person's path as a part of the whole. The gate to Higher Self was wide open. There was a lightheartedness that made me want to giggle. We all savored the feeling and found ourselves smiling at one another with no need for words.

I questioned where I collected my ideas and beliefs on love, spirituality, happiness, and even truth! I continued to realize how adopting a doctrine or set of beliefs created by someone else could never deliver me to my place in the world. Sure, I could gather information from a person that might point me in a direction, but I had to do whatever it took to listen, feel, and decide for myself or I'd be more like a herded sheep then someone engaged in discovering the joy of their own life. Choosing out of fear or a need for approval was no longer an option. I had to determine my next step from whatever degree of intuitive knowing I could summon, even if it meant making mistakes. I had to honor that process in others as well.

The ability to quiet my mind and trust my own knowing was fast becoming the number-one priority in my life. I knew it would be a challenge with all the ideals and societal hierarchies involved in raising children, and healing from disease, but I was determined. I had to stop the busyness, meditate, hang out in nature, write, pray, or do whatever would deliver me to stillness so I could hear the whispers of my own soul. My next step might not be crystal clear at first, or even all the time, but I was sure this practice of connecting to Higher Self would guide me. Even if it meant doing nothing for a while, I needed to **not** be in a hurry.

It was quite liberating to recognize the importance of empowering people to follow their hearts toward their own harmony. It was one thing to know it, a whole other sensation to experience it. As it occurred in the group discussions, it led each of us to more joy. One woman was very certain her children should be vaccinated. I was certain they shouldn't be and we both spouted off scientific data to defend our viewpoints until, finally, we both admitted that it was all just stuff we'd either read or heard and agreed with. We weren't sure that anything we were saying was absolutely true. Everyone claimed their statistics were accurate, but there was no way to verify the validity. It was all someone's conclusion based on a study that was most likely facilitated with an intention to prove a certain viewpoint. We could have argued till the cows came home to defend some idea we'd been spoon-fed. We both recognized that we could find as much evidence as needed to support either side of the argument. It was awesome to realize that phenomenon together and laugh about it!

We could have stayed in disagreement, judged one another as uneducated and even rallied fellow classmates to promote our views. We could have created separation and constructed a mini war. We could have lost all opportunity to care for one another... in our effort to prove our rightness. It felt a heck of a lot better to care than to fight.

The discussion inspired me to take a look at how I had latched onto viewpoints in my daily life. I did it often. I was positional about so many things: children learning music, managing money, growing tomatoes, not eating fruits with proteins, trimming rose bushes, and on and on and on. I defended ideas I had held as absolute truths without considering that everyone could do the exact same thing with opposing and different viewpoints. It was their right.

I realized how often I had separated from people with diverse opinions, sometimes secretly rejecting them for not agreeing with me (as though hurting or abandoning someone was a resolution). I laughed as I admitted how often I had done that over stupid issues or actions that didn't fit my own images. I punished Pat, co-workers, family, and even other drivers, for not being how I thought they should be. I even did this while shopping whenever I saw how some parents spoke to their children, or bought food that I didn't approve of, or didn't dress their kids' appropriately. Oh my God, I was a judging machine. A picture flashed in my mind of sitting in the bleachers watching Travis's baseball game. Pat and I would ridicule parents who yelled at the referees, calling them rude, crude, and loud, while some parents just sat and judged all the other parents for being so trite (uh, that would be me!). Pat and I would agree on mistakes other parents were making. We quietly criticized other parents for being so critical. Hellooooo! We didn't make any effort to understand them or where they came from. We were just like them.

People are a product of what they've been taught is true and important, and many of us are taught opposing realities. We're all a product of our beliefs and we instill them in our children just like our parents did with us. The children could feel us being critical, even if we weren't doing it out loud. Children watch and often copy their beloveds. I let out a long sigh, realizing how important the job of being a mother is, and how kind it would be to stop judging people like I knew how they should be living. Another layer of Holly was unraveling.

I thought, *Next time I judge a person for something it might be a good idea to see if I had ever considered or committed the act I was criticizing them for.* I knew I could find times or events where I'd been lost in self-absorption, being hateful, selfish, a poor mother, and for sure, acting dishonestly. By admitting this to myself, maybe I could stop pointing my finger and accept that we humans are a lot alike. I could become more compassionate. We've all messed up and we've all been ornery or positional, at some point. We've all hurt and we've been hurt. Maybe we're more similar to the people we judge than we have been willing to admit.

We've all gotten wrapped up in minds that thought they were better or more right than others. It's a disease of its own kind, a debilitating aspect of the human condition. I had demonstrated it perfectly in that morning group discussion, and we all did it in our own way. The good news was: we finally owned it and became honest about our naivety and had become aware of what we were being while we were doing it. After that, we were able to enjoy each other as students of life. We became closer and more open, without having to agree on everything. There was no need for approval and that spelled freedom to all of us.

My favorite part was when we transcended our busy minds and felt the essence we'd all shared. From awareness in the present moment, we were eager to act on behalf of everyone involved instead of acting out of self-centered indoctrinated belief systems we'd adopted. By the end of the day, we'd all decided that honoring whatever the other deemed as truth was way more valuable and enjoyable than protecting an opinion. Our worlds became flexible and open instead of positional and closed. It was an enlightening experience and we'd become caring companions on the path of awakening.

Being is not only beyond but also deep within every form as its innermost invisible and indestructible essence. This means that it is accessible to you now as your deepest self, your true nature. But don't seek to grasp it with your mind. Don't try to understand it. You can know it only when the mind is still. When you are present, when your attention is fully and intensely in the Now, Being can be felt, but it can never be understood mentally. To regain awareness of Being and to abide in that state of "feeling-realization" is enlightenment.

–*The Power of Now: A Guide To Spiritual Enlightenment,* Eckhart Tolle

Willingness

chapter 13

Focus attention on the feeling inside you.
Know that it is the pain-body.
Accept that it is there.
Don't think about it—don't let the feeling turn into thinking.
Don't judge or analyze.
Don't make an identity for yourself out of it.
Stay present, and continue to be the observer of
what is happening inside you.
Become aware not only of the emotional pain but also of
"the one who observes," the silent watcher.
This is the power of the Now,
the power of your own conscious presence.
Then see what happens.

–*The Power of Now: A Guide to Spiritual Enlightenment,* Eckhart Tolle

Dad used to say, "You can tell a whole lot about a person by their willingness to experience something." I was around five when he started pointing at folks and asking me, "Can you feel his willingness?" I noticed people who were willing seemed softer, more open, and available. While unwilling people felt more closed and tight. I didn't use those words, but the difference was obvious to me even at an early age.

I remember the first time Dad taught me a lesson on willingness. One of his really good friends was at our house one night crying on the back porch over losing his wife. It was late and there was a big pile of used tissues next to his chair. I had never seen a grown man cry so hard, for so long. It bothered me. I was told to go to bed, so I strained to hear what was happening through my open bedroom window, which was near where they were sitting. Dad kept trying to get his friend to experience and feel what he was afraid of; repeatedly asking him what was underneath his emotion.

After about an hour, Dad gave up and headed off to bed, leaving his friend sobbing and sitting alone. I quickly ran to my bedroom door to catch Dad as he headed down the hall toward his bedroom. I bravely asked why he was quitting. Without missing a step Dad responded, "He doesn't have the willingness to feel. I can't help him."

I didn't totally get it then but I do now. His friend was pushing against feeling, resisting the fact that his wife had left him. He was fighting the feeling of her being gone the entire time dad was with him and was never once willing to try on (explore, feel, taste) a different viewpoint. The experience never shifted or transformed for him because he wasn't able to feel anything except his emotional response to what had happened. He was stuck in self-pity or whatever name one gives that action of resisting; he was never willing to explore and simply feel or experience being without his wife: like taking a minute to get a sense of what it actually felt like to be alone, to live alone, eat alone, or something similar and experience/allow the sensations of what he was afraid of. I bet he would've been able to settle down and start seeing things differently if he had. It seemed he couldn't turn off his mind and became tangled up in pushing against life.

I've been stuck in that same place plenty of times, fighting the feeling of guilt or grief or whatever negative emotion was pressing in on me. I recognized my own pattern of pushing against whatever stood in front of me. I usually resisted by getting sick, angry, and even drunk. I knew how to push away feeling. The trouble was, it always waited for me and would show up first chance it had which was usually the next morning. I understood the habit of self-pity very well. I didn't blame Dad's friend for being unwilling, but I almost snuck out on that porch and told him what Dad had said. I couldn't stand seeing him in so much pain. He cried a long time that night. I wished I could make him be happy.

Humans are rarely encouraged to feel life. Maybe we learn how to be unwilling to feel as a defense mechanism of sorts. I was so glad that my ability to sense feelings in people, places, and life was awakened in the hospital. Although my father had directed me toward my feelings as a child, I'd also received plenty of prompting to resist them. There were so many instances where I was hurried or discouraged from really feeling and experiencing what was occurring. I understood how feeling could easily become squelched during childhood by people we admire, respect, and want to please. One time, I had a serious fall in gymnastics and my coach that I adored told me to ignore the pain and try again. She explained how important it was to be stronger than the pain and not let it get to me. Another time, I was hanging out with a caterpillar in the backyard, pretending I was him, feeling his life. My big sister branded me stupid. When I was about four years old I witnessed a mother slapping her child in the grocery store, it hurt me. I felt the whole thing, the emotions and the energy moving between them. I was told to stop, that I was being rude.

It was embarrassing to get caught red-handed experiencing life. It was as though it was self-indulgent or inappropriate to feel. People who took the time to feel their way through events or circumstances were often judged as day-dreamers, unproductive, or lazy, maybe because they moved a little slower through life. Even sensitive and sensuous adults were often viewed as weirdoes. Exploring or enjoying the energy of a gathering or location was unheard of. I laughed as I imagined a CEO marching into a boardroom and inviting all of the executives to feel for a moment and tap into Higher Self before they started their meeting. Feeling was something to be done behind closed doors. It's no wonder people opt to go numb.

Before I got sick, I had feeling thoroughly mixed up. It was often equated and confused with emoting—hurting, crying, being angry, happy, or sad. Experiencing reality was so much more than this. So far, I was pretty sure emotion was more a result of how I was thinking rather than how I was actually feeling. Eckhart Tolle says, "Emotion arises at the place where mind and body meet. It is the body's reaction to your mind—or you might say, a reflection of your mind in the body." Not that emotions should be ignored or unappreciated, quite the contrary. Negative emotion is a signal that there is something out of whack, it is a guiding system delivering a wake up call. It is a signal to pay attention, explore, and reconnect with our intuitive knowing so we can direct our lives toward what feels better. Sometimes a strong cry or burst of deliberate anger helps allow the underlying truth to be known, felt, and released.

In the hospital I discovered that feeling could include emotional experiences, but was not limited to them, by any means. It was much more. It was like feeling the angels in the hospital, the energy in the room, and the sense I got from people without even thinking about it—it was a knowing that came from my connection. I actually had a perceptual awareness whereby I could experience sensations, both inside and outside of me. It was akin to touching life and its contents with my attention instead of my hands. It was sensual, palpable, intuitive, and energetic. Everything visible and invisible had density and weight, and each person felt unique to me. I could feel them best if I was merely present without judgment or any filter of how something or someone was bad, good, or better than me. When I was aware, my past didn't filter my present moment.

It was amazing to be able to feel reality, life, and people around me, without resistance or desire. I think it was because there was no mind interference. Truly experiencing whatever came my way was invigorating and I believe it was healing for my body. It was joyful, playful, and accepting. Maybe that's why gurus liked to hang out on mountaintops and just "be." When I let life be, I felt expansive, happy, complete, and linked to everyone and everything.

Before getting sick, I had no idea I could learn to feel life in such a manner. I wanted to *know* everything rather than feel anything. Maybe I had thrown out my ability to honestly experience sensations along with my intuitive knowing, the first time I'd decided it was best to avoid feeling pain. I trashed the whole concept of intuition the moment I'd decided to be polite and go numb.

I loved that feeling was an integral part of the Avatar training. Harry Palmer's tools offered processes and steps that allowed us to develop these skills in profound ways. The whole approach was quite a joyous contrast next to my recent studies with Arnold Siegel, founder of the Autonomy and Life workshops. I appreciated the diversity. Arnold had taught us to use emotions as a call to think so we could deliberately use our minds to handle whatever situation we found ourselves in. It was a very logical and practical approach to succeeding in business, persuasion, and ethics. He proposed authenticity and rationality as our guide without exploring the perceptual or energetic weight of a feeling and how its existence could affect health or awareness in self or another. Arnold didn't acknowledge sensations or unverified phenomena as valid paths to attaining data or relevance. It was as though he considered feelings a type of distraction. Like most of us, I think Mr. Siegel had feelings and emotions mixed up.

From my perspective, Harry Palmer's technology applied feeling and honesty as the primary path to awareness and ownership of how your life was turning out. During the course there were many processes that offered simple steps to help me get to places where a pattern began which allowed for efficient unraveling. It was like pulling the right thread when you open up a giant bag of dog food. Pull the correct one and the whole thing opens perfectly and the contents are revealed. Pull the wrong one and well, you end up with a tangled mess. It was brilliant. Mr. Palmer's philosophy, much like Eckhart Tolle's, supported the idea that discovering beliefs you were operating out of and experiencing and appreciating those beliefs is what allowed change to occur. Very similar to The Seth Material I'd studied as a child, only now I understood more fully the profundity of ownership. Seth said, "Your events, your lives, your experiences are caused by your present beliefs. Change your beliefs and you change your life." I couldn't change any upset, belief, or feeling if I didn't first own it as mine. Ever since my hospital experience, I'd realized that the size or seriousness of the obstacle (cluster of old beliefs) shouldn't matter; if feeling worked, it could work on anything. I found the "any" part very intriguing.

It was lunchtime during the Avatar course and I'd found a tree to nestle against, away from everyone. I wanted to handle a lifelong issue and explore my pattern of addiction. I was ready to get rid of it. Being surrounded by addicts most of my life, I figured something inside me must still be attracting the repeating scenario. Fighting addiction had consumed much of my creative energy. I worried about my children being drawn into the scenario and acting it out just like everyone else I loved. There were a lot of alcoholics and addicts in my extended family, my husband's family, our group of friends, and our work environments. It was a problem that seemed to follow me everywhere. I resisted it enormously.

I pondered how society and most rehabs taught addicts to use their will to resist and fight whatever substance they were addicted to. They were often told to push against the feelings of desire and be strong. Say "no" to drugs. I understood the thinking, I used the phrase with my children and believed it worked on some level, but also wondered if resisting the whole thing didn't somehow make it bigger or store it up for later? Pushing against a desire no longer made sense to me. Fighting anything merely attracted more of the thing we were fighting. I questioned, *If I positioned my energy against drugs, which I had, wasn't I somehow keeping the reality close to me?* To keep the ideas or fears at a distance meant I had to literally push against them. To push on anything, I had to somehow touch it. This meant I had to stay right next to drugs and alcohol in order to manage and keep an eye on them. I thought about how the same principle could be explained using a door. If I wanted to keep a door closed at all cost, I would have to touch it or at least maintain some force against it. I would always have to keep some attention on the door to manage it. I would have to be near it or at least have some awareness of it to make sure it never opened again. Via my resistance to the door opening, my energy would remain connected to the door, guarding it, throughout my existence. My resistance to drugs and alcohol as I strained to keep them away, was constantly consuming a piece of me, in much the same way as the door. I laughed at the picture I had of myself using both hands and all my weight to push against drugs and alcohol. Guess what I had to be close to, forever touching, managing, thinking of, and worrying about? It was a hellish relationship! Drugs and alcohol were my boogeyman.

I began hating addiction at a very early age. Obviously, hating anything merely creates more of it. In *Seth Speaks* Jane Roberts explains repeatedly how hate merely breeds more hate. Yet I found myself doing it anyway not realizing if I had taken a few minutes and observed myself hating, and become the silent watcher as Eckhart describes and followed the hate to what was underneath, I could have become more free of it. I expended a lot of my life energy trying to keep that addiction door closed. I was constantly on alert. I patrolled and noticed drinkers and drug users everywhere. My resistance had made addiction more of a problem in my world than it was already. I wondered what I didn't want to feel, and what I was avoiding.

I was sure there was a physiological aspect to addiction that I knew nothing of. It was probably horrifying and painful. I wished addicts could be taught to "feel" in a safe environment. I imagined that if they could experience their pain and difficulty in a deliberate way, with loving assistance, maybe they could relieve some of the suffering that goes along with physical addiction. I didn't know and certainly wasn't qualified to assume anything; yet, I longed to help addicts be free. I suspected my wanting to help could be part of how I was attracting them.

I wondered how the act of simply feeling sensations could help a person manage an urge to do something they knew was self-destructive. It could be so useful to figure that out! Anything that we indulged in to avoid looking life in the eye could qualify as some kind of addiction, overeating, over-sexing, over-televisioning, over-shopping, or over-chocolating. I had escaped plenty using all the above. It made sense to me that if an addict could allow the desire for drugs to exist, even for a minute, and take some time to feel the sensation, perhaps with some help they could watch the urge, come to know it wasn't them, and then let it be, without needing to respond to it. They could finally stop the fight. Maybe with some guidance, their feelings could transform and lighten the way my feelings had in the hospital. It was all speculation but it was intriguing to me. It madé sense that somehow permitting the sensations instead of resisting them would result in a shift of energy. However, it would require enough willpower to manage one's mind, which I believed was difficult for substance addicts because their perception was usually altered from continuous abuse. I wished I had the answer. I had already witnessed so much suffering from addiction.

Clearly one thing I could do was to work on myself! I had my own issues and maybe other people's issues would start to disappear once I started to clean up my own pile of debris. If I just allowed addicts to exist, without resisting the whole scenario, it would mean freedom for a lot of people, freedom from my judgment. I tilted my head to the sky and the majestic trees surrounding me, and realized I was on one of my thinking binges and that it was time to quiet my mind and feel the stillness.

I made a list of feelings associated with addiction in my world with the intention of simply feeling them, letting them be, without resistance. They poured out onto my paper and I started out exploring how I felt when people I loved were drunk. I couldn't think of one time that I just felt the pain that I'd associated with the idea. I always fought it, hated it, and became angry with everyone, never willing to feel what was in my heart. My list began with anger, followed by alone, betrayed, abandoned, superior, unloved, and right. I think it all boiled down to blame. I felt that last idea for a moment and my focus flashed to a party I'd attended where almost everyone was drunk, ugh! I immediately tensed up and became nauseous and resistant. To regain some control and distance, I looked away for a moment, far away, at the tree line on the mountain ridge on the other side of the valley. I laughed at how crazy I was, sitting under a tree, feeling drunken people. I relaxed and dove into the sensations more playfully. I was surprised how the idea of superiority was the dominant layer. I thought I was better than everyone else at that party, smarter and more aware. I willingly experienced my narcissistic scenario. Then I let the feelings flow as I walked through the party in my mind. There was disgust, pretending, criticizing, separation, and a lot of satisfaction. I felt better than them, holier somehow. I had to laugh again. I had to admit that part of me liked having unconscious people around me so I could feel special and wiser. I applied the Avatar technology and let them all go.

I became acutely aware of my "Self" and could visually sense how my beliefs and ideas about addiction were not me. I could finally look the experiences in the eye and own them as separate from me, ideas I had given birth to. Just admitting that I was the owner of the opinions that were hurting me changed my sense of being. The tight sensation in my chest released and I felt incredibly determined and able to change my reality. I dug in and thought about childhood and my dad not coming home, night after night. A memory bubbled up and the feeling of being abandoned came next. I kept experiencing whatever showed up and as pockets of feelings dispersed, I encountered an enormous layer of anger. My face grew hot and my breath more rapid, but I kept going. I observed the feeling as I felt it and it became a sharp stabbing pain in my lower back and I stayed present with the pain until it loosened up. I'd always had lower back pain so I found this very interesting. Suddenly, a flood of emotion welled up and I started crying hard. I ended up in a big pool of sadness that diminished almost the second I merged with it and simply allowed it to be there.

It was just like the pain body that Eckart Tolle describes: "The pain body, which is the dark shadow cast by the ego, is actually afraid of the light of your consciousness. It is afraid of being found out. Its survival depends on your unconscious identification with it, as well as on your unconscious fear of facing the pain that lives in you. But if you don't face it, if you don't bring the light of your consciousness into the pain, you will be forced to relive it again and again." He continues, "Let me summarize the process. Focus attention on the feeling inside you. Know that it is the pain body. Accept that it is there. Don't think about it—don't let the feeling turn into thinking. Don't judge or analyze. Don't make an identity for yourself out of it. Stay present, and continue to be the observer of what is happening inside you. Become aware not only of the emotional pain but also of 'the one who observes,' the silent watcher."

It was as though all the feelings had been waiting for me to face and acknowledge them, so they could leave freely. In silence, I remained still-minded and became the witness, the essence of being. I was present as the observer. It was grace. I opened my eyes and saw the expanse of the blue sky and felt a wave of gratitude for the awareness that held me in that moment. I felt lighter and more in charge of my experience of life.

I continued, determined to clear out my history of resistance to addiction. I thought of losing my oldest sister next; it just showed up so I went with it, trusting my Higher Self to take me where I needed to go. My chest ached like a hundred pounds of weight was lying on top of it. I stayed present, looked right at the feeling, and felt the immense sorrow and fear collected near my heart. It was so very thick and dark. I ended up feeling isolated and alone, with a sense of wanting to get revenge. It was strange. I didn't know that was inside me. I merged and watched simultaneously as the emotion gurgled up from deep in my body. I sat still for a few minutes. Allowing. Not resisting. Almost appreciating. It dissolved so fast. Gone!

After everything quieted, I was incredibly alert. I felt bigger, alive, and giddy. I heard the birds singing and felt the wind on my face and everything was profound and beautiful. I felt free. I scanned my body one last time to see if there were any sensations in my gut that I had missed. Nope, I detected nothing. I contemplated alcohol and drugs for a while to see if they still triggered anything and it seemed different, more spacious; I wasn't stuck in it and I wasn't resisting it. I knew I was on the right track.

I wondered how far I could take the notion of experiencing and where I would end up if I just felt everything, what would be left? Or, who would be left? Would I empty out? Would I be a blubbering idiot who didn't fit in anywhere with anyone? Or, would I end up living more from Higher Self once those old patterns had dissolved? I knew one thing… going numb or avoiding feelings only made them worse. Being responsible for whatever my attention was on, is what allowed transformation to occur. To be released, pain had to first be admitted and acknowledged as my manifestation, then experienced. A part of me still questioned, *How much? How long? And would it ever stop?* I also wanted to know exactly how much of life I was in charge of, and who was in charge of the parts of reality that I wasn't. One thing was certain—I was responsible for a whole lot more of my misery than I'd ever imagined possible. I began to see how most of what I had blamed others for was a result of my unfelt pains and patterns being projected outward. It was me, re-creating my past.

I contemplated the distinction between feelings that were categorized as emotions and feelings as perceptual awareness or sensations and energy. One definition seemed more connected to the invisible realm and the other more to the material realm. Emotions were very physical for me, visceral, and if not acknowledged and experienced, could lead to great pain or a bottle of wine and a hangover. Emotions were more extreme and reactive. They seemed to have the consistency of honey or peanut butter and often stuck in my mind or my body for a while. On the other hand, my perceptual awareness, exploring and sensing the energy of things, left me in an expanded state of awareness within just a few seconds. Becoming aware of sensations on a perceptual level occurred from the viewpoint of the silent watcher, it was a lighter state, less attached, more allowing and in flow. When I was present, it seemed I could move into

Higher Self and sensations could move right through me. One thing I noticed was that no matter which type of feeling I engaged in, it required me to pay close attention to its substance and take full responsibility for whatever I became aware of.

I imagined that as life unfolded I would catch myself in many aspects of judgment. Just like in the group discussion earlier, I would recognize when I was being critical and honestly explore what was really happening. I figured I would have plenty of chances to feel ornery, critical, alone, fearful, and positional simply by being human and that each sensation would provide an opportunity to discover and take responsibility for what I was feeling or not feeling. I would do my best. My plan was to get good at observing myself, and appreciating that whatever came my way was a signpost. I didn't have to become trapped in a reactive viewpoint. *Welcome to life,* I told myself, *this is the art of creating a new habit. Relax, take a breath, and trust yourself.*

I examined the list of emotions I had written down regarding my relationship with addiction. Some feelings were showing up more than once with slightly different qualities depending on HOW they were associated. For example, failure felt different to me as a child than it did when I'd experienced it from a mother's perspective. There were many faces to the concept of failure as there were to anger, sadness, or loneliness. Each face offered me an aspect of the whole. It was all connected. I realized the name of each feeling merely opened the door to the collection of energy it encompassed.

I kept playing with my new perspectives, wanting the discoveries to sink in further. I again reviewed my years of study with Arnold Siegel, whose work was geared toward being authentic, relevant, and rational, avoiding feeling altogether. Harry Palmer's Avatar work was focused on owning everything you found inside yourself so you could actually transform it. There wasn't much rationality in Avatar from my mind's point of view; as a matter of fact, the course was designed to turn the mind off so we could access what was left once the noise stopped. Both studies included a very diligent practice of being deliberate with your time and attention. Both were structured with self-discipline being the key to any type of success. Harry's technology was about experiencing, owning your reality, and learning how to live deliberately. Arnold's work was about thinking, using the mind as a tool, practicing the seven virtues, and being in integrity. Once I stirred in the concepts I'd learned from Werner Erhard's teachings to the mix, I saw that they were all leading me to take responsibility for where I was as well as suggesting that I couldn't move forward until I became more honest about putting myself there.

The intentions of all these methodologies were to free up students from suffering and blame, and I appreciated how they each offered pieces that led me to better know my Self. It was clear I couldn't change the way I felt if I believed it was someone else's fault. If I blamed what I was experiencing on something or someone outside me, then something or someone outside of me would always end up in charge of my life experience. This meant that something or someone outside of me always had to change before I could feel better. I didn't like that. It was more empowering for me to be the one that put the bad feeling there because, at least that way, I could remove it. Clearly, whatever I was feeling was from a choice I'd made somewhere down the line anyway, knowingly or unknowingly. I had attracted what was showing up in my reality. I didn't like this concept too much at first because it made me responsible for *everything,* but I began to grasp how being responsible was actually the key to becoming totally free. I laughed considering all the ways I had skirted responsibility for my sadness, my health, my finances, or the condition of my relationships when owning the beliefs and experiences I had ingested was the very act of responsibility that could land me in my dreams. Taking responsibility for everything that showed up in my life was beginning to sound like huge fun.

When I was about ten years old, Dad sat me down and instructed me to move a pencil lying on a shelf. He wanted me to do this without touching it. I worked so hard trying to get that pencil to roll that I broke into a sweat. We would sit for five to ten minutes a stretch, focusing our attention in an effort to merge with it, become it, and create some movement. He would say, "Turn your mind off and be where the pencil is, be in that space, become the pencil and roll." I truly believed we could do it. We would sit quietly, intending together, very present, and Mom and my sisters thought we were crazy. I liked it. Dad was so determined.

That was my first effort of putting my awareness in something outside of me—without mind chatter, resistance, or words. I didn't know it then, but I was feeling something perceptually. I became the pencil over and over, hoping I would finally get it to roll or budge so I could please my father. He practiced this on his own with a variety of objects, including a spoon. He would sit for long stretches working with his attention in this manner. I believed, right along with him, that he could bend that spoon. I would frequently check his little work area when I got home from elementary school to see if there were any changes in its shape. He thought he was Neo from the *Matrix* long before the movie was known and he wanted me to be his protégé. It was meditative to work together and it was the beginning of learning how to quiet my mind and feel without language. I could sense the pencil and feel the lightness of it, but I never was able to move that darn thing.

Being able to feel was pivotal to finding out what I was holding in my body and to becoming aware of what I was resisting. I had to be able to feel my way into those energy pockets in order to discover and be done with them. I couldn't think my way into those places because, most of the time, what was bunched up there didn't make any sense to my mind. They were old ideas and beliefs mistaken for truths. Looking for resistance in a pile of stuff considered to be true didn't work too well because a mind will do its best to defend and protect what it previously confirmed as real.

I often had to move through layers of old ideas to get to the feeling I was avoiding. It was usually buried under some fairly weird conclusions. For example, I found many beliefs I had picked up unknowingly from an old 1960s television show called *Leave It to Beaver.* In my mind, the Cleavers were the model family and I was fascinated by their ideal relationships. I longed for June Cleaver to be my mother and Ward Cleaver to be my father and as a child I began comparing all family life to this ideal archetype, believing it was possible and probable in everyone's future. My sisters and parents couldn't hold a candle to these archetypes in my head; yet, I imagined when I grew up that I would be just like June. The Cleavers had a faultless and blame-free family atmosphere. They never punished, never raised their voices, treated each other with respect, and not a mean word was ever spoken! Beaver got into some serious messes, too! They were kind and loving even when he destroyed hundreds of dollars worth of property, which happened nearly every episode.

In the Avatar Course, I found a tangle of beliefs that I'd been lugging around for decades and I wanted to decipher where they came from. One very painful belief was that in order to be a good mother, I had to be identical to June Cleaver. As I let that belief go, the concept started to get funny. These related beliefs made me chuckle… my mother should've been that type of mother, all fathers should be like Ward Cleaver, good children would never tell a lie, and Pat, my husband, had to be the best Ward Cleaver of all in order for me to totally trust him. How silly of me to think that my happiness required that people I loved must behave perfectly, like fictional television characters. But I did believe it on an unconscious level.

To me, as a little girl, the Cleavers were real and depicted the perfect family. The concepts they represented had been tucked away in my mind as a certainty, an absolute truth, and used as a means by which to measure all families. The beliefs were the source of a substantial amount of disappointment and sorrow for me. Subconsciously, I'd compared all humans to these made-up characters. Nobody could ever live up to that ideal, so nobody ever fully met my expectations, including me. I didn't know *Leave It to Beaver* was my measuring stick for joy until I'd retraced my steps to where it all started. I actually experienced myself as a child, dreamily in front of the TV, concluding that when I grew up my husband and children would be just like the characters I adored. That old belief was very alive in me. It was fueling many of my interpretations, and my willingness to be quiet minded and feel was what led me to discovering it.

I understood how my childish mind had latched onto *Leave It to Beaver* as ultimate truth. I didn't know the difference between real and pretend at that young age, I was barely able to comprehend it as an adult. Once I dove into several of the old ideas and feelings I held regarding what a perfect family should look like, my relationship patterns began to make more sense. There were so many disturbing emotions attached to the conclusions I'd drawn. To see how I had been dragging them around with me and devoutly interpreting reality through them was astonishing. I could never be a wonderful mother when I compared myself to June Cleaver. The whole fabrication was wrapped in a cloud of never feeling good enough, an emotion I'd experienced frequently throughout my life. Nobody could measure up to June! She never had a hair out of place, always smiled, and never once raised her voice. She even wore tailored suits while preparing dinner in high heels, and of course, cooked magnificent meals every night. As long as that was my definition of a happy family I was DOOMED and destined to feel like a failure. I didn't even like high heels.

With the help of one of the exercises on course I began to see many things that I had adopted as truths. They were not ideas or opinions that I had deliberately examined and decided I wanted in my life. They were beliefs I had happened across, read, or was taught by someone else. Leave It to Beaver was never real, it was pretend, and I had swallowed it hook, line, and sinker. There was no rational path from my feelings of being an unhappy adult to my adopting beliefs from the most pleasant and kind family in TV land, but the beliefs I'd held were very much connected to my suffering.

Practicing how to feel and trust my intuition during the course helped me to know myself in a way I never had. I was starting to grasp what it was like to be Source of my life experience. I was so ambitious to put the puzzle pieces together and understand my old wiring that patterns showed up like magic. Grateful that my mind couldn't fool me when I was in "feel," I became more connected and aware. I was beginning to understand just how capable we are as humans.

Recognizing and feeling any resistance became a significant aspect of my ability to allow instead of control. *Allowing* had to happen in order for me to heal. My new mantra was… "I have to feel to heal!"

On the Avatar Course, I uncovered many beliefs regarding illness that I had no awareness I'd been holding. Beliefs like… people love you more if you are sick, you can control people when you are sick, sick people don't have to be accountable, sick people can get away with anything, sick people have an indisputable excuse, sick people get more attention than healthy people, getting sick is fun because you get to skip school and Mom has to stay with you, people do things for you when you are sick, people care about you more if you are sick, etc. Each idea had specific feelings associated with it along with a vibration that was attracting the reality of being sick into my life. I found the beliefs were part of me—my energy, my body, and my mind. If you had told me I believed those things, I would have argued with you. I couldn't see them on an intellectual level and would never have admitted to them before actually feeling their realness within me. They were old ideas covered over with layers of new beliefs and positive thinking. They were hiding out and doing their job, beckoning the realities they contained. After seeing how my beliefs were holding my past in place, I was excited to release them. As Harry Palmer states, "Believing defines realities, and experiencing dissolves realities—that is the cycle of creation." I was in awe of Harry's studies and how he put everything together so that students could discover how they were creating their lives with their underlying beliefs.

When I was eleven, Dad told a story at the dinner table about a monastery in the Himalayas where initiates were lined up outside hoping to be accepted as devotees. In this particular order, it was very difficult to be taken in as an initiate. The initiation process required the students to remain outside one full night while sitting in the snow, naked, in sub-zero temperatures with a bucket of water poured over their heads at sunset. If they were able to manage their minds and heat their bodies throughout the evening with various breathing techniques and meditative abilities, then they were deemed to have proven their skills of pure thought. He explained how they had to keep their attention completely under the control of their will to survive, and according to Dad, some did. They couldn't hold beliefs in their personal space regarding what temperature they might freeze at or consider beliefs that were commonly held throughout the world when it came to being cold and dying from freezing temperatures. If they slipped into those beliefs, they would never make it through the night.

Dad's point with the story was that some people believe if you go outside with wet hair in cold weather, you get sick. Others don't think the cold matters at all. He would ask, "Guess what people will experience when they go outside with wet hair in the cold?" Then he'd answer, "Whatever they believe they will experience." Dad explained how people could pretend or say they believe one thing, but you could always tell what they really believed by what experiences they were having and attracting. He said if we wanted to know what we believed on a deep level, we only had to look and see what we had drawn toward us.

My sisters and I had heard Dad tell that story at a time when we felt tortured by him. I suspected that one of the ways he justified his cruel behavior was by considering it a training program. I think on some level, Dad was trying to convince us that we attracted him into our lives and were at least partially responsible for how our childhood played out. He used to tell us that we picked him and Mom to be our parents before we ever came into our bodies and that we wanted to experience life with the opportunities our relationship with them could provide. He explained how the vibration they both emitted at conception resonated with our desires for expansion so we all beamed right in to the reality. I never bought it, not entirely. Not until now.

I experienced the movement and flow of energy Dad was talking about when I was held in Christ's hands. When I longed to be with my children and love them, the energy from that desire opened up the path to its experience. I was intending from a Source perspective, from awareness or Spirit. It was like a bubble of potential that I directed to a dream. What Dad always said seemed true. We decided to experience our incarnation in a certain way and our desire vibrated us toward it. We weren't pushed or persuaded. It seemed to me that if a reality was intended from Higher Self, we could automatically move toward that idea, effortlessly.

Dad repeatedly told us we were in charge of our own experience of life, that we attracted it by what we believed and where we put our attention. He used to tell us that people were equipped to grow a new arm or a leg, providing they trusted this was possible and believed it without a single doubt. That was a tough one for me to swallow but he'd said it often enough to make me wonder. When I was in the hospital, he and I listened to Deepak Chopra audio tapes, as he explained how we grow new organs every few days, how cells replace themselves with new cells every few hours, and how the world was filled with "pure potentiality" for creating anything if we would only allow it and access this stream of energy that was there waiting for our instructions. I wanted to believe I could grow a new colon and eliminate Crohn's disease and listening to people who believed this was possible was helping me to see and feel it as a viable option. Dad always declared, "Believing is seeing!"

On the last night of the Avatar Course, Patricia and I were feeling very expanded and playful and we had a simultaneous idea to help heal my colon. It was powerful and so very loving. It came to us while reading a bedtime story to the boys, *The Cat In The Hat Comes Back* by Dr. Seuss. We were all cuddled in my bed with the boys between us and totally engrossed in the story. In the last part of the book, there's a huge mess and not one character is able to clean it up and this is devastating to the children in the story because their parents will be home soon. The Cat In The Hat himself tried every helper he could find, from A to Z, with no luck. This was an emergency!

The Cat In The Hat had to call on the secret, all-powerful, and all-mighty help of VOOM! As we were reading the lines out loud to the kids, together in dramatic fashion, we both knew immediately this would be the perfect ingredient to heal my intestines. *VOOM!* We squealed as we looked at one another wide-eyed, and Patricia was talking really fast at the same time that I was talking really fast and we both laughed gleefully at how identical our thinking was. We agreed that VOOM was magic and that we had to have some in my colon right away!

In the story, VOOM was invisible, made up, and did whatever you intended it to do. It was the magic of intention and belief mixed together. The guy who came into the house with the VOOM was certain it would work, absolutely positively. Not a shred of doubt had he. Patricia and I knew we needed the same total belief in its power for the

VOOM to do its magic on my colon tissue. We laughed, half making fun of, but partly serious, pondering how effective our intention could actually be. We all agreed to believe anything was possible! We giggled with delight.

Being an artist, Patricia devised a creative way to use the VOOM! She suggested we all imagine riding ice cubes down my intestines like a roller coaster at the fair. She said, "We could spread happiness and light all through the tubes from top to bottom and then do it again and again. We can get the whole family riding!" The boys clapped their hands excitedly! I loved her so much in that moment, observing how serious and excited she was about how well it would work. She added, "We will shower your colon with the healing power of VOOM, all four of us, as a team, intending the tissue heals, absorbs food, and eliminates easily." I loved the idea! It was caring, ambitious, and all about me (wink-wink).

The kids got so excited, jumping around on the bed and spouting how they wanted to ride the roller coaster. Patricia had us all lie down, close our eyes and imagine my intestines. She told us all to hop onto ice cubes and ride through my belly. She guided us through bumps and turns with great sound effects. We laughed and used our arms to splash light all along the way. The kids were making awesome laser sounds like they were shooting light out of a Darth Vader lightsaber. It was wonderful. I believe it made a difference. It was pure love going into my body. We were all connected in joy and kindness. Success was a sure bet!

Thus, was the birth of our new family practice known as VOOMING! Patricia immediately shared her technique with Debbie, Mom, and Pat. I told Dad. It became a tradition that whenever someone got sick and we couldn't be close to them physically, we VOOMED them from afar! We would imagine light moving into each other's bodies, releasing hardship and loving whatever needed mending. We focused on the places in one another's body that hurt and intend for that energy to move so healing could happen. We focused on pure potentiality for each other. We visualized and imagined what it would feel like if that area were happy and healthy and connected to the stream. Our family used VOOM to connect with each other from a distance by flowing loving energy to one another with the belief that this was healing. We became official VOOMERS!

"Now here is the Z
You can't see," said the Cat.
"And I bet you can't guess
What he has in HIS hat!
He has something called VOOM
VOOM is so hard to get,
You never saw anything
Like it I bet.
Why VOOM cleans up anything
Clean as can be!"
Then he yelled,
"Take your hat off now,
Little Cat Z!
Take the VOOM off your head!
Make it clean up the snow!
Hurry! You Little Cat!
One! Two! Three! Go!"

–*The Cat In The Hat Comes Back,* Dr. Seuss

Patricia and I were a team throughout the entire Avatar course on almost every issue, except when it came to Dad. She wanted my agreement on her perspective and I wanted hers on mine. I wanted forgiveness all around and she wanted him to take responsibility for what he had done. When he dropped by the class to visit, there was no room for transformation or niceties; she was venomous. It was sad and I felt a deep sorrow in my heart, but I had to honor her process and realize how I felt was up to me. I encouraged Dad to handle his part of it and he was timid, explaining how Patricia would come to peace in her own time and that she was very much like him at her age.

My husband, Pat, was right: after completing the course I came home with yet another new set of tools to raise our children. He was a trooper and tolerated my enthusiasm. I pushed on him to align with my new understanding as much as he would allow. As a family, we worked diligently on placing our attention on what we wanted to manifest instead of on what we resisted. We worked toward feeling life, quieting our busy minds, and connecting with Source energy. Whining or blaming became darn near obsolete around Pat and me. It simply didn't work for the boys in our home anymore because we were quite sure nobody was responsible for what we were experiencing—except us.

I spent the next several months using everything I had in my toolbox to process and clear out obstacles to a healthy body and mind. I learned to be very kind to myself during that period and fell deeply in love with being a mother while learning to feel the magic of life.

Even a stone, and more easily a flower or a bird, could show you the way back to God, to the Source, to yourself. When you look at it or hold it and let it be without imposing a word of mental label on it, a sense of awe, of wonder, arises within you. Its essence silently communicates itself to you and reflects your own essence back to you.

–A New Earth: Awakening to Your Life's Purpose,
Eckhart Tolle

Trust Worth Ye

chapter 14

As soon as you trust yourself, you will know how to live.

–Johann Wolfgang von Goethe

I played with my children and loved who we were all becoming. Perhaps I was just getting to know who we were all along.

We had enough money saved up to allow me time for healing and figuring out what was next for me. Pat encouraged me to stay home and be a mom and stop working all together. Being able to do that was a life-changing treasure, for all of us. Lazy days with Travis and Drake were by far the most precious gift of Crohn's disease, and there were many. We were learning about being human together and getting to know one another as inventors of life. If I hadn't gotten sick, I would have missed the whole glorious event.

Before I'd gone into the hospital, parenting had been a "job" I took very seriously. It was part of my daily schedule, which also included ten to twelve hours of selling real estate. I was more like a machine than a human. I rarely had time to play with the boys because there was just too much to do. Parenting included a long list of chores that needed to be completed every day, rain or shine. I was not flexible about that. I did the mother thing "right" by golly. I breast-fed for one year making sure my children got their colostrum via mother's milk, used 100 percent cotton diapers, and only fresh goat's milk for at least one year once the boys were weaned (which I drove many miles through sleet and snow to buy). I had heard that cow's milk could cause allergies and believed it. I knew the story about cows having seven stomachs and humans only one, and how ludicrous it was to think our bodies could digest milk that was meant to be processed through a much more elaborate digestive system then ours. I could recite the cow-stomach story backwards and half-asleep, and often did, to any parent who would listen, peddling my superior knowledge of such matters. I knew the "right" rules for being a good mom. I read about these rules regularly and kept up on what I had to do to qualify for the decent-parent category. I had to be calm, patient, a good listener, not hit or yell (at least in public), help with homework, volunteer at school, maintain a clean and organized environment, and feed my beloveds only unprocessed foods—which meant no sugar. Also, I felt the boys should participate in scouting, restricted their television viewing to a maximum one hour per day (requiring them to sit at least four feet away to avoid any dangerous radiation) and, of course, taught all the childhood danger basics like not running out in traffic or never playing with matches. Oh, and I did flashcards with Travis from the ripe old age of one week and continued flashing him throughout his first year. I was a freak.

I had studied many techniques to multiply a child's intelligence before Travis was even born. I played baroque music for him while he was in my belly. I implemented a variety of unconventional suggestions from the books I liked best. I was set on having brilliant, five-star boys. What was important about having superior children you might ask? I wanted to be the perfect mother, more perfect than June Cleaver! But what was missing? *Me.*

After my near-death experience I was not the same mom. I was no longer obsessed with instructing, solving, and indoctrinating the kids with my personal truths. I didn't have the desire for lots of money or a bunch of "things" anymore and to Pat's dismay, cleaning dropped way down on my priority list, too. Above all else, I wanted to love and connect. I let the outer world go and just hung out with those two little beings I had birthed, feeling who they were, unpainted by my intentions. I watched, listened, and discovered in awe. I was in heaven and they were the angels I was given to play with. They were the most amazing people I had ever encountered. I couldn't get enough of them and preferred their company to anyone else's. They taught me a great deal about being real, living in the moment, and having fun being alive. They were hungry for experience, unafraid of what's coming next. The future wasn't where their attention was and they weren't stuck in the past either; they were fully engaged in the present. They were fascinated, curious, and willing to feel everything.

The boys were really good at feeling life instead of thinking it. They were incredibly intuitive and aware of the energy around them much like animals are. Frequently, they knew what I was feeling without me using any words to express it. They kept an inquisitive eye on me, not quite sure what to think for a while, exploring who I had become. I didn't look, act, or feel the same. I moved much slower than the old model and the new Holly even let them eat sugar.

I was eager to experience everything the way it was for a change, instead of missing that very important aspect of relationship where you really take time to listen, understand, and feel someone. You know, relate! I had an old habit of immediately pushing for people, situations, and circumstances to fit into my impression of how they should appear or feel. *My* relationships, the good ones, where labeled "good" because the people acted how I wanted them to act.

I longed to be more allowing and open to let everyone's dreams into my heart. One complication, however, was that I was weaning off of the prednisone, which made for some extremely emotional responses from me because reducing the dose exacerbated the already highs and lows. There were situations that were completely illogical to all three of us. I could be swept up, out of control in seconds and cry over the silliest things, such as babies, yummy plates of food, love songs, and sappy TV commercials, just to name a few. One day a Downy fabric softener commercial floated across the screen and the tiny baby was so precious I burst into tears which were abruptly followed by silly sobbing noises. The boys thought it was terribly funny. They grew accustomed to it after a while and would giggle at how my face would suddenly start leaking for no apparent reason. I felt things deeply and extremely, both from the drug and from the opening of my heart. I was a child again and we had a blast discovering life together.

I made a point to acknowledge the boys' intuitive skills and encouraged them every chance I had to listen to this type of feeling. I knew how useful intuition would become in their lives as they learned to rely on it to manifest and experience reality. I wanted them to be well versed in acknowledging their personal sense of what was happening and be connected to their inward knowing of a situation. I was committed to them learning how to trust themselves.

> **Trust** *n 1 a: assured reliance on the character, ability, strength, or truth of someone or something b: one in which confidence is placed.*

> **Trust** *vt 1 a: to commit or place in one's care or keeping; ENTRUST b: to permit to stay or go or to do something without fear or misgiving 2 a: to rely on the truthfulness or accuracy of: BELIEVE b: to place confidence in : rely on c: to hope or expect confidently.*

When Drake was just starting to speak clearly he would answer questions that I had merely thought and never said. It was as though he could read my mind. I would tell him I had never spoke the question out loud, but he continually thought I was kidding. I never made a big deal of it so he accepted it as natural and settled into the idea that he just knew what I was thinking. We had many a laugh over him answering my silent thoughts, even from another room. He would come to where I was sitting in my office or the kitchen and ask me what I wanted as though I had yelled something across the house. I started having fun with it and often tested him by asking, "What am I thinking now?" He knew the subject every single time. I consistently encouraged him to recognize and honor his skill. He could feel when something was bothering me and would come to wherever I was and stare at me as though trying to get some information out of my head. Drake was always a feeler, very connected to energy with a keen awareness of the vibrations of people. He was kinetically sensitive and would ask me what was happening whenever energy would quickly shift in our environment or someone angry would enter our space. He could feel fear a mile away. His sphere of awareness was quite expanded and I treasured becoming familiar with how he interpreted reality.

Drake was about four when we started playing a unique game in the car. I told him that whenever he felt people who seemed sad or thick, he could always send them a ball of light or energy to see if they felt it. He understood immediately and loved the idea. Just minutes later, we rolled up to a traffic light and stopped right next to a gentleman wearing a scowl and oozing seriousness. I suggested we give it a try and flow the man a love ball. Drake turned his head without another word and began flowing energy to the guy. Within seconds the man looked in our direction and obviously felt it. His expression changed, he seemed lighter and happily confused. Drake got an enormous kick out of the effects so it became our favorite pastime in traffic. He would pick people who seemed sad or worried and then we would join intention and send them a ball of light. As Drake got older he started doing this naturally, on his own, at school and with friends. I think it became a little automatic for him as a way of living. We would always get a response, a smile, a nod, or people would look in our direction with a strange expression on their faces, trying to figure out what had just happened. We laughed about this a lot.

The boys knew how to have fun and invent any character or reality they needed to set the stage for the drama they were preparing to act out next. They knew how to create. It was the same thing we were continuously doing as adults, except that the boys didn't take their roles so seriously or get caught up in another person's thought about whom or what they were pretending to be. They played. They would put on the identity of a king, a businessman like their father, a gangster, a mutant ninja turtle, or G.I. Joe, and fully become the part, playing it out full tilt, only to toss it aside for another persona when they were done. Seconds later they would be totally immersed in another personality, with great pleasure, and then discard it nonchalantly with the others once they'd tired of it. Every day was Halloween and they were forever trying on costumes to discover who they wanted to be for the next portion of life. Travis was highly skilled at becoming any character. He would have been a phenomenal actor. Trav could get into the identity so intensely it was captivating. Drake and I were riveted watching as he performed. Travis trusted his ability to be anything, even at a very young age. His charisma and authority were magnetic. Everyone loved being near him. He was a brilliant and witty little guy. He had an uncanny knack for communicating and entertaining. He believed in his ability to influence people. He would set the stage for each drama he and his brother played out, giving Drake explicit instructions and carefully describing who he needed to be, how Drake needed to act, including what words he should say, what he should wear, and how he should understand the role. Travis was very good at managing the scenes. He had a clear image of how each act should unfold and was determined to design the experience to match his visions. He reminded me of when I used to do the same thing with his father, trying to get Pat to wear the "costumes" or wardrobe I thought worked best for our performances in life. Only I wasn't playing around; I was serious.

By the age of six Travis was a master choreographer. He loved playing out a good drama. I think on some level it was a fun way of avoiding a very sensitive and profound aspect of himself. I loved that vulnerable part of him and knew it well. So did most people, but Trav just wasn't quite ready to see it in himself.

Watching the boys play act inspired me to look carefully at the characters I had been playing in my own life before being hospitalized, and how I had grabbed onto certain personalities, clinging to them as though they were the real me. All of them seemed to be adopted or designed to conform or please, rather than chosen as a true expression of my heart. I had become many identities so fully that I had forgotten these were costumes I was wearing. I thought of a few fondly… the helper, the real estate agent, the know-it-all, the nutritionist, the student, the teacher, Mrs. Conscious and Most Aware, and the romantic. Let's not forget the perfect and highly skilled mom who made sure Travis rode his bike without training wheels before any other child on the block, as though it was some reflection of my superiority as a mother. Oh, and my dear friend, the spiritual identity mask. I had worn that one so well that I was sure it was the real me for a very long time. I chuckled as I continued watching the kids "play" at being human.

> *"We spend our lives, our life-force cultivating and grooming our appearance in the eyes of others. That's how we know that we exist. That's how we know who we are. That's where we find reassurance that we are real and not just hollow dream characters. That's how the illusion is constantly maintained."*
>
> *"So, like, when they say perception creates reality...?"*
>
> *"Perception is reality. There is nothing else. Just like in a dream."*
>
> –*The Enlightenment Trilogy,* Jed McKenna

Yet, the part of each of us that was most worth knowing was the one putting on the identities and costumes. Truth lived there. We just failed to get to know the master puppeteer.

Before becoming sick I had defended and protected some of my identities as though I couldn't live without them. I was afraid of what I would lose or what might happen without the safety that I believed came from their solidity. I had no idea the freedom it would bring to set them aside. I took a moment to appreciate that I wasn't any of those costumes I had worn, but the actor putting them on. I was very grateful to know and feel the difference in my bones. I thought about how we all get wrapped up in identities and how being "someone" is a big part of the human game that we play. That's duality. No wonder we had trouble trusting ourselves; we didn't know who we really were half the time. We changed costumes from being a lover, friend, adversary, partner, novice, knower, parent, or child of a parent so many times in one day, it stands to reason we could get our personalities and their beliefs confused. You have to wonder how the many aspects of us could possibly agree with the convictions of all the others. Unless of course we learned how to keep one foot out of the game and maintain some awareness of Higher Self while we played.

As children we all enjoyed filling up the void of nothingness, the quiet, the stillness that encompasses all life. We got bored easily. We desired stimulation. We gathered data, costumes, and defended and protected our collections. We became the stuff we'd accumulated. Unfortunately, as we aged many of our beliefs bumped into other beliefs and created conflict both inside and out. This often resulted in us finding more proof for our perspectives and taking a denser stance. For what?

The ideal reality would have included parents who sat us down as we were old enough to understand and explain that we weren't the costumes we were going to be wearing. A mother or father who continually invited us to consider what we wanted to explore, helping us understand and feel our options. This way we could design our realities more from deciding what we wanted to believe and experience, rather than as a result of someone telling us what we should believe and experience. This would include a lot of fun dialogue examining what seemed important from the changing perspectives of someone growing up and learning about life. With parents guiding children to examine consequences, feelings, and speak what is true in their own hearts, and most importantly teaching them how to feel and discard what didn't seem honorable to Higher Self, our schools would be overflowing with compassion and integrity. When we act from Higher Self, we naturally act on behalf of everyone. I imagined children realizing that all humans had the right to decide what mattered most understanding the concept of consequences and appreciating the fact that all people had the power to change their minds…as many times as they liked!

Unfortunately, most of us weren't educated in the "tossing" aspect and we kept gathering more stuff, more costumes, and more controversy, thinking it would make life better to have all those solid ideas and beliefs. As Dad always said, "More isn't better. It's just more." Perhaps the peace we long for as adults comes from shedding the default costumes, loads of data, and concrete conclusions we've gathered along the way so we can get back to the empty space, awareness, and divine intelligence that is our birthright and embrace the formless that Eckhart Tolle speaks of. We can decide to create our identities deliberately as Harry Palmer teaches, and manifest our dreams from "the Vortex" that Abraham-Hicks encourages.

Why not feel the natural joy of Source energy while still inside a body instead of just surviving life and ultimately waiting for death, or something better, to rescue us.

Man has no individual I. But there are, instead, hundreds and thousands of separate small "I"s, very often entirely unknown to one another, never coming into contact, or, on the contrary, hostile to each other, mutually exclusive and incompatible. *Each minute, each moment, man is saying or thinking, "I". And each time his I is different. Just now it was a thought, now it is a desire, now a sensation, now another thought, and so on, endlessly.* ***Man is a plurality.*** **Man's name is legion.**

–*In Search Of The Miraculous,* G.I. Gurdjieff

Being human was so interesting to me after hanging out in the invisible and having seen the flow of life from a new viewpoint. Knowing there was a much more inclusive domain/reality embracing everything that occurred was helping me appreciate how my "Holly personality" was a tiny speck in the scheme of things. I had my share of challenges, still struggling with some of my strong personalities like wanting to influence Pat or any grocery clerk who would listen toward some ideal in my head. I had to work hard sometimes just to keep my mouth closed. I processed and practiced every day to maintain some connection to the Sacred because the more I dropped into my identities and got lost in the illusion of them, the harder it was to feel the joy I knew existed. One helpful practice was to appreciate the costumes and assume them as more of a choice than a default action. Sometimes I would say out loud which identity I was getting ready to become, "I am moving into my bill paying personality! I am putting on my mother cap!" This way, I was able to sustain at least some awareness that I was the one deciding who to be next. The kids thought it was normal for me to announce my next role, that's what they did all day long. I wanted to be more like them, they were having fun and playing the characters without taking it all so seriously. When I was successful at playing, it felt a bit like keeping one foot in Higher Self and the other in the costume, with the observer staying aware and on a good day, affectionate. The moment I forgot and believed that the costume was all of me, I would easily spend a bunch of energy defending and protecting the opinions of the costume I was wearing. It was very liberating to watch how easily the boys tossed aside a character, not at all confusing it with who they really were. It was a fun, naturally intoxicating game for them. I needed some work!

Hanging out with Travis and Drake when they were simply being themselves was pretty cool, too. It was pure. They were soft and open without pretense. I loved lying around with them, smelling their puppy smells, and experiencing the moments when they relaxed into the emptiness behind the game. I loved how their small eyes half-closed and how a part of them would fight sleep, not wanting to miss out on one thing. Even though sitting still was my most difficult and greatest achievement during my recovery, I cherished when I was able to relax enough to do absolutely nothing with them.

I came to appreciate that I had two realities to play in. One was transcendent and free and the other was in a slow moving weak and timid body trying to incorporate the invisible into the visible. There were times when I became consumed in one half of the equation. When visiting the transcendent half, no matter what occurred I trusted it was perfect. I coveted observing life from that unquestioning state. Reality always played out exactly as it was meant to and I didn't have any urge to manipulate or mold it. Until it was time to cook dinner, climb stairs, or use the restroom. That's when the practical human half seemed to lose that loving feeling and became consumed with being done and getting better, even if it meant controlling reality and whoever happens to be visiting mine! I kept reaching for balance and understanding of these two domains and remained optimistic about bringing them into one.

Staying home and not contributing financially was tough for me. Having been so independent, it was quite a switch letting Pat be the sole breadwinner. There were many lessons in trusting, receiving, and penny pinching. I couldn't offer much else since getting my body strong required mountains of time and patience. The medicine I most needed was a ton of rest and a heap of faith. I frequently revisited the expectation of perfection (trust) I was bathed in while laying in Christ's hands. Because, each time I felt that allowing sensation in my body, it was very nurturing and the energy became part of me. It soothed me like nothing else. My hope was to integrate that depth of knowing that everything would always be okay, no matter what, into my daily routine.

Welcoming all the generosity from Pat and learning to say "YES" to such goodness coming toward me was another interesting malady. As the universe would have it, the same day I decided to study and explore actions that let love in a friend popped by to visit, with their Labrador retriever. I watched the dog, stupefied at how she lapped up attention and love, rolling over onto her back and revealing her vulnerable tummy to all potential givers. She did this in response to every person that walked into the room i.e., her life! She **expected** love from EVERYONE and let it in all the way to her soul. If the person didn't come to her, she got up, wagged her tail (entire rear-end), and went to them offering yet another opportunity to play in her joy. She wasn't mad because they didn't come to her, she didn't punish them or hold a grudge, and she just kept on loving everybody. I wanted to learn how to **expect** people to love me and allow care into my heart like that dog did! I imagined, explored, desired, and visualized expecting love and it was phenomenal, electric, and yummy. Talk about trust… **expecting** exemplified the sensation. What a perfectly timed lesson that dog taught me, one I will never forget.

Healing required getting good at doing nothing. I believe this is one of the most difficult tasks for anyone physically recovering. Doing nothing, especially on prednisone, deserved a gold medal! I did well until a steroid slam came to visit. Then all I could see was what needed fixing, cleaning, organizing, or who needed training. I would start grinding my teeth, my mind going into hyperdrive, and all I could think of was DOING… the idea of simply being was nowhere to be found. I could feel the wave of intensity rushing toward me like a freight train and very often I was unable to stop it. My body and intuition disappeared and my busy mind took over with an urgent need to organize the garage, scrub the shower with a toothbrush, and teach. It was another lesson.

Prednisone was a crazy drug that created mood swings from joyous to dismal in seconds flat and energetic to zombie even quicker. When the family saw or felt the slam coming they magically disappeared. It's funny now but it wasn't at the time. I was a lunatic for an hour or so and the episode would usually end with me crying or falling asleep. Due to the false energy blasts from the drug, I had to pay close attention to my urge to rearrange the house, move a couch, a piano, or a bed, and top it off with a hundred or so sit-ups. My urges appeared about once every two days and I would end up taking everything out of a closet, emptying the kids' dresser drawers on the floor, or reorganizing the kitchen cabinets. Of course, if Pat was home, I would talk him into moving the larger pieces of furniture to a variety of locations to see what looked best, where. My sister Debbie, bless her soul, would just calmly head outside and enjoy a cigarette or five because she knew I wouldn't bother her there. I completely lost my connection to higher self when I was consumed with doing.

In addition, I loved getting rid of things... it was a passion. Completing something or making space gave me an adrenalin rush. Using that last drop of shampoo, the end of a bottle of spice, throwing away old files of information, releasing a mind-clogging feeling, cleaning out a drawer or closet and giving away half the contents, was all crazy fun to me. I was a completion junky and finishing became more important than being present in the moment. I would even use up extra product just so I could toss away more bottles. I drove Pat insane by mixing different lotions, shampoos, hairsprays, gels, you name it, just so I could make space and feel the satisfaction of getting rid of containers. Pat stopped using anything that poured out as a variety of colors; skeptical of what weird concoction I had blended. He was smart that way. I was frequently too creative for his liking. I loved being done with things, which is hilarious because we are NEVER done!

So there I sat with my boys, looking around the messy house. There was dirty laundry stacked around the corner, cluttered drawers and toys everywhere, and I practiced letting it all simply be that way. Every day was a challenge as my mind tried to persuade me that getting done was more important than being still. When I was successful at letting it all go, it was very cool and felt like I was making progress at relaxing, connecting, and trusting that everything would work out—without me pushing or controlling it. Before being sick I was fanatical! Every moment of my life was used for working feverishly on an item from one of my to-do lists. I had lists for the boys, Pat, my partner at work, yard work, projects, budgets, health, exercise, and even a list of how to have fun. I had files of lists. I even had a list for being a good parent including projects, spiritual lessons, goals, and books to read, classes to take, and what it would all look like when my enlightened children blossomed into enlightened adults. None of my lists were short and if anyone in my presence had time for just sitting around and being still, something was wrong because that was not on the list!

I was miraculously learning how to let the house be dirty while I played with my boys. It was a monumental achievement. There were times when it was an enormous test and required great restraint, but I was determined to succeed at *allowing!* I had to be aware of my body and its limits as I healed and not let my mind run the show. Before Crohn's disease, I'd been a well tuned machine. I could push through anything. Now, as I was practicing this new approach to being human it was magically untangling my solid stance on perfection. Something wonderful was happening. I had a new phrase that I started repeating to Pat. He would come home from a hard day's work and I'd be on the floor playing with the kids as he looked around the messy house with a "trying to figure it out" look on his face. I would spout, "I don't think we are going to die and wish we'd had time for one more load of laundry before we left!" Sometimes, when he would work really late and miss precious time with us I would say, "Honey, I don't think you are going to die and wish you'd had a little more time to work, just one more precious hour at the office before you split!" He just shook his head.

Even though I got to spend a lot of time alone during my healing, it wasn't long before I became involved in personal growth classes again. I looked for something local and started attended weekly classes and meditations with one of my favorite humans, Donna Hamilton, and a small group of her students. She was a phenomenal and very generous teacher, determined to show us how to allow magic into our lives. We knew it was possible just from witnessing her ability; she created whatever she dreamed of. Donna professed that we all had a magic wand and if we could just trust ourselves and own our power, we could manifest our dreams. One thing I began to understand more clearly from her teachings was how people sometimes preferred familiarity to change. Even if it meant continuing to suffer, familiarity was a way to avoid the unknown. For the most part, not knowing, being in limbo, not understanding, and not having an answer seemed equivalent to hell. We all wanted a clear picture of what would happen next before we were willing to commit to jumping off the cliff of unhappiness into the abyss of the unknown. But Donna said we couldn't experience what was next until we trusted enough to let go of what we were holding onto. The jump represented following our hearts, even if it meant divorce, moving, quitting a job, or giving up some indoctrinated reality that a whole life had been spent acquiring and suffering over. Much like Dad used to say, "You can't keep doing the same thing and expect your life to change." Jumping was scary business.

Donna guided us in meditations where we would get to the edge and have to trust, believe in possibility, and imagine jumping into black nothingness. She helped us recognize how silly it was to hold onto suffering and helped us trust the whole concept of not knowing. Being alone, falling into the unknown, and sitting in the dark waiting for whatever might show up, revealed a lot to each of us. It was brilliant work. She helped us experience the feeling of death so we could stop being afraid of it and begin to live. The stories were fascinating. Students were rarely able to trust hanging out in the dark, or themselves, or contemplate death. When given the opportunity in a meditation, they manifested someone to save or guide them. A guru, a wise man, or a dead relative were a few of the images that students visualized coming to their rescue after they had leapt. Every time I jumped, nobody was there but me. I wondered about that.

There was so much fear accompanying "not knowing" that many students admittedly chose repeating the past, opting for familiarity instead of change. It was intimidating to feel the vulnerability that went along with "not knowing." I decided I would try and sit in that feeling of emptiness and uncertainty until I was no longer afraid of it. Just the idea of it used to scare the crap out of me. I would fall into all kinds of weird behaviors to assuage that horrible experience of looking dumb. So it really surprised me that once I got past my idea of "not knowing" as being dangerous and painful, I actually ended up enjoying the space of nothingness that accompanied those words. It started feeling pretty wonderful.

It was funny to me how hard I had worked to avoid not knowing. I even resisted uttering the words "I don't know." I laughed at myself. Not knowing was just another feeling, a liberating one at that. I repeated the words a few times to see what sensations accompanied, *I don't know.* I had so many ideas and beliefs about the dreadfulness of not knowing that I never, ever just felt the idea. My ideas were what kept me from ever allowing it and even enjoying it. I had always thought it was unacceptable to not know and was nervous about someone thinking it true of me. When I finally melted into the idea that I didn't know much of anything, not for sure, and certainly not absolutely, it became pleasurable and soft. I experienced the openness of the concept and discovered that possibility actually surrounded the sensation. To allow emptiness without a clear idea of what should happen next was a new level of trust for me. It wasn't bad, not knowing felt exciting and actually became one of my favorite feelings to allow. It had a flavor of freedom. I felt another chunk of my "need to control" loosen inside.

Donna introduced me to Robert Kirby. He offered a unique technology called kinesiology or muscle testing, which revealed truths held in our physical body as well as our energetic body. It was an exceptional process when it came to releasing the past and moving old energy. The methodology provided undeniably terrific information for healing. I attended his first workshop in Reno, wanting to make sure what I had heard was valid. Here's how it worked; Robert would ask a student's physical body a question and it would answer via muscle testing. He would have them stand, hold their arm up in a horizontal position and when a falsehood was spoken, he would gently pull down on their arm and it would collapse. When a truth was spoken, for example me saying my name is Holly, he would try and pull down on my arm and it was solid, strong, and unmoving. It was mind-blowing, literally, and I was very excited to learn this unconventional art of unearthing truth.

Robert said whatever the body, mind, or spirit was holding onto could be discovered through his tests. It was fabulous! Without knowing anything about the students, he found beliefs at the core of lifelong patterns. Kinesiology was a method of discovering underlying beliefs much like feeling had allowed me to do; only Robert followed the feeling in and double-checked by testing where it was held dimensionally and then dismantled any physical ailments that resulted from the pattern. He assured us kinesiology was irrefutable, providing that the tester remain neutral. Initially, I wanted to be sure this wasn't some kind of trick. I volunteered to be worked on so I could try to manipulate his testing process. I needed to be sure, so I deliberately resisted Robert's attempt to get an answer from my body, holding my arm up with all my might to keep it from going down as he made the statement, "Holly is free of guilt and shame." My arm went limp as a cooked noodle and dropped immediately to my side, showing that his statement was false. No matter how hard I tried to hold up my arm, when he said those words I couldn't. I argued with him for a bit, explaining how I had handled my guilt and shame, tons of it. He laughed gently, explaining how there was obviously another pocket in me somewhere.

Neither my mind nor my body could sway the test, and that was a very good thing. That day, I was completely convinced of kinesiology's value. We unraveled an area I hadn't been able to change because it had been safely buried under a blanket of justification. Robert started the process by asking me if I would like to be free of the guilt and shame and I answered, "Sure!" Surrendering to the onion layer phenomenon yet again. He tested what the priority was, where to go first and asked a series of questions he had neatly categorized. He tested what I was strong to and what weakened me by using a list of words and phrases he had organized. He checked to see what numbers he should go to instead of having to know any answers or intuit anything. I appreciated this very much as it took subjectivity out of the equation. I questioned if opinions of the tester could energetically sway the accuracy of any test. I am not sure but I think the numbers correlated to different energetic domains and directed him where to start—physical, emotional, intellectual or spiritual—and also directed him to where the creation began, the time, age, location and beliefs surrounding it. It was a science. As Dr. David R. Hawkins, renowned lecturer and expert on mental processes and co-author of *Orthomolecular Psychiatry* with Nobelist Linus Pauling, explains in his comprehensive writings on the value and application of kinesiology, *Power vs. Force,* "This confirmability of results has been observed during the last twenty years by thousands of clinicians using kinesiology in their everyday clinical practices or for research. The results, in fact, are more consistent than conventional diagnostic methods used in traditional medicine (e.g., a weak heart never tests strong with kinesiology but may give an erroneous normal EKG tracing—a well-known fact)."

The place for us to begin healing my guilt and shame issue ended up being on an intellectual level. Silently Robert just pointed his finger at the binders of information as he held onto my arm and when my arm went weak, he knew which book to work from. Then he went down another list to understand specifically where the problem started and when he got to a number that was connected to religious belief systems, my arm fell like putty. He even found the age my feeling shameful had begun and went directly to the core issue—religious indoctrinations from the age of seven. I never would have guessed that. The couple of times I attended church, it was two very different denominations with incongruent belief structures. I figured somehow, something I had heard about being a bad sinner must have gotten in my head as a truth. Maybe it was from television, who knows.

By the time Robert had finished unraveling the stored emotions I was positive that muscle testing was accurate. His clearings opened up my past and exposed old ideas about my need to be punished in order to deserve something good. It was clear that when I was younger I had believed I needed to struggle, suffer, and work really hard in order to allow any type of reward like joy or success into my life. He said something really interesting about me being more afraid of success than I was of failure. The emotions and feelings that surrounded that stuck energy were raw yet easily released using his energy moving techniques. It was simply incredible. He checked to see if the issue was dissolved or if there was something more, and if I remember correctly, my arm went weak on an emotional level. I was fascinated as he explained how we hold the same issues in different fields of energy and in order to release any pattern, it was best to begin where the body wanted to begin and continue until all levels were 100 percent clear regarding that particular issue. More levels, more onions, and so it goes. I was enthralled.

Robert taught the students how to do the testing by having us work with one another. A critical step was to use his clearing techniques to ensure we were neutral before beginning to test or the results could be influenced by our personal beliefs. He said it was also necessary to be sufficiently hydrated so our bodies could respond accurately. It made sense. He demonstrated two very easy techniques to insure this before beginning, tapping our thymus and balancing our meridians. He explained how the test became subjective if the tester had any covert or overt intention to be right, prove a point, be superior, or sell a product of some kind. We learned how to clear ourselves of this so we could ask fellow students a question without any hidden agenda or attachment to a particular result. It produced a very kind way to be with one another. Once we reached neutrality it seemed like we were more connected to Higher Self, and everything flowed. I had a new appreciation for the profound perch being objective was to view and explore life from. The more I did it the more I trusted that what showed up would lead me to what I needed to address next instead of trying to force or control how I wanted things to turn out. It felt like I trusted the Sacred with No Name to guide me and work through me when I operated from this neutral perspective.

Robert's system handled potential obstacles by using numbers correlated to issues, illnesses, emotional blocks, relationships, or financial stability, instead of using his opinions or past experiences as his reference point. The number system eliminated an ego's need to be superior, right, or in control. For example, rather than asking someone a subjective question like, "Are you a control freak?" which I happened to personally know could cause someone to energetically resist, hide, or become defensive, he would go to one of his manuals and move his finger over the broad list of possibilities by testing the numbers in the margin to locate an area where clearing was needed. His findings had nothing to do with supposition and were spot on every time. The person's body became instantly weak on the exact subject they needed to resolve. Using numbers to locate issues allowed him to remain neutral.

I had an idea stirring. I wondered if Robert could check my body for how many milligrams of steroids I needed for proper healing. I became so excited at the possibility I think I was hyperventilating. This had been a constant battle for me! Not trusting the doctor. Not being unable to feel an intuitive answer to how much prednisone my body truly required to recover. Not wanting to relapse. Not trusting myself. That's a lot of knots! I didn't know how to get off of the prednisone without fear of hurting myself. I worried each time I reduced the dosage. Worry is akin to expecting a problem, which to me meant it could attract one. I repeatedly used my spiritual tools to try and let go of the haunting feeling but there it was, recreated every morning when I went to swallow my self-prescribed lower dose. The doctor's words warning me not to take the weaning process into my own hands and his admonitions would flash through my mind almost every time I reached for the prescription bottle. Doc was adamant about me reducing no more than five milligrams at a time and gave me several case examples where fast reduction had caused a relapse even worse than the patient's initial episode. He wanted me to wait two to four full weeks before cutting back each time. I was going batty and couldn't imagine it. That would mean a whole year to get off that mind altering drug!

I understood Doc did not want to take a chance on a relapse. Still, I didn't agree with him and in spite of my turmoil had been silently reducing my dose by more than he had recommended all along. I couldn't tell Pat because he was siding with the doctor. The whole process became an even bigger issue because I was doing things my way, secretly. Secrets always made issues bigger because you had to constantly keep attention on them to manage them, thus feeding them. And besides, it hurt to have them. It was standing in between me and my man.

I was blessed to have Robert help me by testing every aspect of the prednisone situation. I was hopeful that my body would know the truth way better than my mind. He started out by asking me if I had any of the pills with me, which I did. He had me literally hold the steroids next to my lower abdomen near my colon with one hand and then had me put my other arm up and hold it in that position. He asked my body if it needed the steroids to heal and pushed down on my extended arm and it didn't budge, it stayed stiff. The answer was a big "yes!" Then he asked how many milligrams were needed for optimal health as my colon heals and explained that my arm would drop at the point where it was weakened and that would reveal the amount. He started at five milligrams and from there went up incrementally. At twenty-five milligrams my arm fell. I had been on forty milligrams per day so this was an astounding reduction. I jumped up and down with enthusiasm, flabbergasted as I contemplated what this could mean. Robert wasn't done though; with extreme thoroughness he checked other organs to see if the reduction would be safe. He got a "yes" from every viewpoint including my liver, heart, kidneys, and adrenal glands. I asked if he could give me a schedule for cutting down in the future and he very confidently responded, "Yes!" I squealed ecstatically! Prednisone had affected my emotional balance with everything—relationships, health, sleeping, sex, eating, and most of all, my awakening. Trusting Robert implicitly I reached for a pen and paper. He tested my mind and my body from every viewpoint regarding each step of the weaning and I jotted down the schedule that my body agreed with. I was excited to share my notes with Pat, admit my secret, and hoped he would support me and appreciate the technology.

As I went back to my seat that day in class I was overwhelmed with gratitude for kinesiology. All of the students in the circle were transformed, happier and more hopeful. Their issues of loneliness, depression, abundance, or not being able to lose weight had been as debilitating to them as Crohn's disease was to me. Being unable to trust our personal power and allow life to love us was in some way the culprit in each person's suffering. We were all learning to face our self sabotage and take ownership of our peculiar collection of beliefs. Each person's revelations became everyone's inspiration.

I couldn't believe it! I was going to be free of prednisone in less than six weeks. I was astounded at how optimistic and secure I felt with the plan. I believed in its success and realized how powerful that moment of trust was. I felt surprisingly confident, without any reservation. I made a point to wallow in the feeling as long as possible so I could summon it later. I said a smiley thank you to All That Is.

After class, Robert took a few minutes and showed me how to do the testing on myself so I could check every product I was putting in my mouth and find out if it was actually good for my health or inhibiting in some way. He took less than five minutes and tested, using the lists of products in his binder, to discover which supplements I should take to speed up my healing. Then he had me test myself. I was getting it! My body responded powerfully to amino acids. When he double checked my results my arm became solid like a rock and he couldn't push it down. He laughed, saying he could probably hang on my arm with all his weight and it wouldn't budge. It was good news for me because amino acids would help me with so many things, including hair growth, tissue regeneration, and balance, as well as give my body the basic building blocks it needed to create energy. I was protein deficient and had been for a very long time.

I went on an entirely new regime immediately upon leaving class. I ingested only what my body stayed strong with using the diagnostics of kinesiology. I walked around the house using my thumb and first finger as a loop and my first finger from the other hand as a lever against the edge of the circle (the self test method). If the circle separated it was a sign of weakness. If the circle stayed strong against my press, it was a sign of strength. Going weak was equivalent to a "no" and staying strong was a "yes." Applying this method, I could test EVERYTHING! I went grocery shopping and looked quite strange, I kept holding items against my body (under my arm) testing each fruit and vegetable to discover what was excellent for my colon and organs to heal. When I got home, I checked the water I was drinking, the vinegar I was taking baths in, and even started checking books I should read to see which was most healing for my heart. Pat again, just watched his nutty wife in action.

I felt stronger physically after only three days on the new diet and supplement program. I was even more trusting this was the right path. The trust itself was healing. My energy stabilized and the steroid slams began to mellow. In retrospect I really appreciated how Robert wasn't trying to sell me anything through his kinesiology testing. I probably would have bought anything he recommended. He was clear energetically that truth needed to be found in each individual and that he was merely an instrument for that discovery.

I know this is a shock, but after just two weeks I wanted more, quicker, stronger, and enormous! I was lucky enough to obtain a private session with Robert due to a cancellation. Even though my family was by me every step of the way I fell into a funk now and then and wondered why I kept being so hard on myself. Recovering my full strength was taking a long time and I was impatient. *I wanted my thick hair back! I wanted breasts! I wanted muscles to water ski with and my Jell-O butt was beyond annoying. I wanted to look human again and make mad passionate love to my husband!* Unfortunately, I still ran out of breath climbing the darn stairs. I was tired of being wimpy, it had been almost two months since I left the hospital. This was the conversation I wanted to stop!

I lugged in bags of vitamins, medicines, protein powders, aloe juices, and even foods and fresh vegetable juices for Robert to check. I set them down irritably and confessed that I was in a slump. I told him I had become discouraged and needed some reinforcement. That I had some tough days when I had to drag myself out of bed and use every ounce of my will to seek Higher Self. I admitted there were times I just wanted to wallow in misery for a while, and did. I further explained how I didn't trust my tests as much as I did his… he sensed all the emotion brewing. He was quiet as though waiting to know which avenue was best to address my concerns. Then, he just talked to me in a very intuitive and selfless way. Robert reminded me of something I very much needed to hear that day. He said the process and speed of my full healing was actually the gift and that on some level of awareness I knew this. He explained how this slow path to physical recovery offered a spiritual and emotional healing of insurmountable love, if I let it. A healing he said, that included being completely free from my past and an ability to contribute to others. He assured me the result would be self-trust like I had never known. He suggested that I enjoy this time of study, introspection, and family and continue processing and working toward more faith. Faith in my own knowing, faith in God, and trust my inner guidance. He said I would come to realize this trek toward wholeness was the most sacred of all journeys and that it would provide me with the quality of living I longed for. This conversation was spirit to spirit and invited me toward the holiness of my illness. Gratitude replaced my negativity and Robert began the session.

While testing products, Robert double checked for any self sabotage by having me say, "I want to be healthy," as I held a particular product over my colon. If my arm went weak we needed to clear something or not use the product. Whenever we found a product or food that was beneficial for my colon, he would verify it by asking my body, "Digestion, assimilation, and elimination?" He made sure that the entire process, from chewing to eliminating, was health restoring for me. If my arm became weak on any of those aspects (digestion, assimilation, or elimination), it meant I wasn't yet ready for the product. I was dumbfounded to discover that much of what I'd been taking was not helpful and, in fact, had been inhibiting my healing. Robert helped me create a very specific healing protocol. He even tested quantities to see what amounts of protein powder I should consume each day and how many times per week. He checked to see when it was time for me to retest a product or a diet, helping me to realize that our bodies are always changing and what was important on one day, could become less significant the next. I wished everyone healing from some disease or issue could have this technology.

I had been a vegetarian during the previous few years and when Robert checked my body to see how that diet was serving my healing, unexpectedly we discovered it was actually slowing it down. My food was not providing me with what I really needed! Holy Moly! I recounted all the "How to have a proper diet" lectures I had preached to my kids or anybody who would listen as though there was some blanket solution for good health, and I had it. Of course, you can see by now, this was not a new pattern, just a new subject. I laughed, realizing yet again, that each person's body is different. Similar to everyone having his or her own path spiritually, perhaps they had a unique physical path, too. As Robert continued to test, he discovered that my body was starving for meat… and was ready to assimilate it. In fact, he said I needed fat. When he got to butter, I couldn't believe it when my arm held strong and firm through every question on digestion, assimilation, and elimination! Yeah! My body *wanted and needed* butter! In my world, that was nectar of the gods.

I went home that night and devoured a steak cooked in butter. Maybe that was a little overboard but it was yummy! The best part was that I allowed myself to enjoy it. I was unafraid. Pat couldn't believe I was consuming cow. He watched in disbelief and finally he asked, "What is kinesiology?" I did my best to explain it to him hoping I was making sense. I explained to him how Robert could check to see if a body liked something simply by asking the body directly and bypassing the mind. I further explained that my intention was to use this information to wean myself off steroids, to confirm the best products and food for me, and ultimately, to heal my colon. I told Pat how perfect this muscle-testing technique was because our minds typically defended some idea just because we were taught to believe or perceive something a certain way. I admitted that my vegetarian diet hadn't been optimal for me. But I had adopted the idea so completely, put so much attention on it being the best lifestyle, studied the positive effects and gathered up the proof, even to the point of persuading others to eat that way, too. Now I could see that this had been more of a decision of my mind versus a result of knowing and feeling what my body actually needed. His face scrunched up in confusion.

I decided to show him how kinesiology worked, using him as the student. The kids watched, seeming entertained. In the middle of dinner, I asked him to stand up and told him to put his arm out and say, "My name is Pat." He did and his arm was strong as a board; I couldn't get it to move even an inch. Then I had him say, "My name is Jose." His arm went soft and everyone was surprised. I told him truth makes your body strong and falsehoods make it weak. We played around with a few more questions and I told Pat that I could uncover anything out about him! The kids laughed and wanted to take their turns to see if it worked. By the end of the night, Pat couldn't argue with it and started to appreciate its simplicity and accuracy. I confessed to having kept my reduction of steroids a secret from him and promised not to do that again. He scowled for a second and then mumbled something about me never following anyone's orders. I stared up at him with my best puppy dog eyes and he grinned sweetly, forgiving me. I showed him my written schedule to steroid freedom explaining that I had to test myself again before reducing each time to see if anything had changed. Hesitantly, he aligned with my ambitious plan, providing I committed to move forward slowly and thoughtfully and keep him informed.

Prior to working with Robert and kinesiology, I had often been fearful of eating, so afraid that I would hurt my tender intestines. I didn't automatically trust the whole process of nurturing myself the way I had hoped I'd be able to. Eating with trepidation in my gut was harmful, and like many other feelings, I didn't know how dominant that fear was until it had disappeared. I was timid and scared when it came to food, not wanting to eat very often. It was a quandary. It was difficult for my body to heal while suffering from undernourishment. Yet, I was concerned about eating new foods so, up till then, I'd had a very limited diet. It was a never-ending loop and kinesiology had corrected it! I had been following an Ayurvedic diet and, through the years, eaten a truckload of basmati rice. I had consumed it almost every day since leaving the hospital, along with tons of cream of wheat. Believe me, this regimen was getting old. Being able to muscle-test food and trust the results became a life-altering blessing.

I took one more class with Robert before he headed off to Australia. We'd become friends and I was so grateful to have met him. It was a joy to be around his kindness. Class was always fun because the truth was revealed no matter how deeply buried it was. The class setting was a circle and, repeatedly, one student would stand in the middle of the group convinced of an idea, such as wanting to heal and be healthy, and then Robert would test their arm to see if it was true. Whenever a student's arm would easily fall, it revealed some falseness in the person's statement. Then he would test and discover and further unravel some hidden self-sabotage. It was humbling to admit how unaware we could be. Each of us was joined by our desire to know ourselves better. I loved being part of that circle and watching everyone let go of old ideas, each moment was a healing for us all.

When it was my turn to stand in the circle's center Robert checked my desire to succeed, my commitment, my inclination to self-sabotage, and tested for obstacles and fears, asking several questions that would reveal anything blocking the way to perfect health. I was blown away by the guilt that was still cleverly tucked away along with my unconscious belief/feeling that I deserved to be punished. Robert tested to find where to go to resolve the issue and found I'd had guilt around Travis and didn't believe I was a very good mother to him.

I felt the truth of the test but I couldn't refrain from defending myself. So I rushed to tell "my story" about being a single mom during Travis's first years, describing the struggle to make ends meet and how I wasn't there for him the way I'd wanted to be. What a story it was… I explained how Trav was in childcare way too much the first three years of his life so I could get my real estate career going. I needed everyone to know how sorry I was and how I'd had a tough time forgiving myself. As I was speaking, I was blaming myself, falling deeper into "the story" and resisting the shame. I spoke in quick succession, perhaps talking more to myself than others, as I offered all the reasons for my actions. I couldn't stop! I described how Trav's genetic dad and I divorced shortly after he was born and how he never took much of a part in his life. I hurried on, a bit more dramatically, to explain how Trav didn't have much of a dad for those first few years and I had nobody to help. I told the group how I suggested Trav's dad give up his parental rights because he wasn't paying child support or showing any real signs of wanting to be a father, and I wanted to make sure that if I died, Travis wouldn't end up in an unhealthy home.

Everyone politely watched as I attempted to justify my behavior like a criminal pleading her case. I realized they appeared neutral toward my story, and it bothered me. I wanted some type of reaction, empathy or sympathy would have been good. I wasn't getting a drop of anything! I noticed how still and present everyone was and how my drama kept losing steam in the face of their objectivity. It was a powerful space. I calmed down, took a deep breath, checked in with myself and acknowledged the denial I was standing in. Then, slowly, I began to tell the truth. I explained how Trav didn't have much of a mother either. All I did was work. Even when we were home alone I didn't play with Travis enough. I was on the phone prospecting all the time in order to pay bills. I mumbled, "He was hungry for love and I failed to give it to him."

After all those years of personal development and spiritual work and practicing everything I knew about experiencing my feelings as a method of release, there I was, caught up in my head like that darn gerbil again on the spinning wheel in his cage, defending "my story" like it would get me somewhere. It was another lesson. Whenever I try to persuade people to see my viewpoint, or insist on justifying some action on my part, there's a good chance that I'm avoiding feeling and denying responsibility for something. I realized how I was making "my story" more powerful than the present moment. I was letting the past be the ruler of my life. I finally stopped talking and felt the room and the presence was vividly pulsing. There was a space being held, like a sphere of alert awareness surrounded me, waiting for me to see myself, without a drop of judgment. Nobody spoke, nobody moved, everyone observed. Internally, I acknowledged that I was afraid. Not knowing where it would lead, I surrendered and became more willing. I had to feel and allow what was churning inside of me so it could come out and dissolve.

As I stood in the center of that circle, in front of everyone, I dropped into a mountain of old despair. I felt a huge weight on my chest as though someone was standing on it. I began to weep. Robert was patiently allowing, and trusting I would become present again and see the story, without pushing the matter. He began testing quietly, not interrupting the silence, and used his books to uncover the root cause. Within a moment of allowing the pain it began to dissolve. Robert found a tangle of shame regarding being a mother. He tested for the origin of the guilt, and without knowing it, he landed on the very month I'd become pregnant with Trav. He skillfully kept testing and guiding the session. He addressed many aspects of fear, guilt, self-criticism, and self-sabotage connected to my relationship with Trav's dad from that time in my life. I watched speechless as he uncovered and released belief after belief. I became aware of how unconsciously I'd held myself back from experiencing joy and success as a way of redeeming myself for the pain that I felt I had caused Travis. *What a strange way to try and make life better, I thought, hurting one's self to pay for the pain I believed I caused another.* It was clear to me that I had adopted that self-punishment pattern from childhood, and it seemed to keep popping up in so many parts of my life.

In our family, punishment had been the only means for redemption. I was merely trying to pay for mistakes made as a wife and a mother the only way I knew how, by suffering and feeling pain for what I had done. Once Robert had finished I felt innocent and free like a young girl. It was so fast and accurate, less than ten minutes to let go of so many years of trauma. We were all amazed. There were many mothers in the room and a wave of understanding swept across the entire group.

Robert let us all have a moment to ourselves before asking, "How is Travis?" I immediately felt some discouragement. It was a dreaded failure kind of sensation wrapped in avoidance, like admitting that I was worried about him was admitting my own failure. It must have been the next layer inside me because it reared its head once the guilt had been cleared. I told Robert that I felt Travis was one of the wisest souls I'd ever met, yet, he couldn't seem to let himself experience the depth of his heart. I further explained how hungry Travis was for attention and care, but he didn't allow in love. I told the group how sometimes I would wake in the middle of the night and Travis would be standing there, staring at me. I would sweep him up in my arms and cuddle him back to sleep but he seemed vacant, like he wasn't even there as though he was sleepwalking. I explained how I had processed my feelings repeatedly, but they would be triggered and recreated whenever Travis acted emotionally distant. I told Robert that I also had tried to work with Travis on this, having him feel his feelings, or at least identify and admit they were there, but the next morning he never remembered what had happened the night before. Strangely, he was happy the next day, genuinely, almost as if he were living two lives.

I continued sharing with the group how just a couple of weeks earlier, Travis had been walking around in the middle of the night again. I asked my son if he knew where he was, who he was, or what he was doing. Travis answered everything correctly so I asked him what he was feeling and he answered, "Sad." I tried to get him to go to the sensation and describe it to me but it was like talking to a ghost. Travis responded to each question but there was no feeling there; he was empty. The next morning I asked Travis if he remembered what we'd talked about in the middle of the night and he had no idea that he'd been walking around our two-story house or even had a conversation. He thought I was kidding. During the day, he was smiling and playful again as though none of it had occurred. It scared me.

Then Robert did something very interesting. He said he was going to have me energetically be Travis for a minute and instructed me to relax and think of my son, to connect with him and feel him. Robert helped me to stay neutral. He wanted to check something regarding Travis, but did so silently and didn't tell the group or myself what it was. Robert asked questions of my body, explaining that because I was deeply connected to Travis, he could easily get answers about what was happening with my son's energy. As Robert worked on me, my body responded without my mind having any clue what was going on. It was peculiar and invited an awareness of how everything is an element of the divine intelligence holding us all. It was energy interacting. After a couple of minutes of testing, Robert said he could help Travis let go of what was pressing on him if I wanted to arrange a private session with just the two of them. I was very curious what he had asked and what my body had answered, but it wasn't the time to address it. The class was ending and Robert began closing the day. I sat back down in my seat, wondering what the heck had just happened. My mind went a little crazy trying to understand it all… until I remembered to trust.

As soon as everyone in class had left, I reached the person handling Robert's appointments, thinking it would be a miracle if there were any openings, given that he had been fully booked several weeks before arriving in Reno. As the Universe would have it, there was one spot open in the schedule due to a cancellation earlier that day. I took it! Synchronicity!

When I arrived home, Travis met me at the door. I seized the opportunity to be alone with him, and explained a little about my day, how Robert worked, and asked my son if he was interested in trying his own session. Within seconds, before I even finished my blurb of the experience, he agreed to go. It was as though he'd been hoping I would ask.

> *When I first encountered kinesiology, I was instantly amazed at the potential I saw. It was the "wormhole" between two universes—the physical world, and the world of the mind and spirit—an interface between dimensions. In a world full of sleepers lost from their source, here was a tool to recover, and demonstrate for all to see, that lost connection with the higher reality.*
>
> –*Power vs. Force: The Hidden Determinants of Human Behavior,* David R. Hawkins, M.D., Ph.D.

God...ness

chapter 15

When you plant lettuce, if it does not grow well, you don't blame the lettuce. You look into the reasons it is not doing well. It may need fertilizer, or more water, or less sun. You never blame the lettuce. Yet if we have problems with our friends or our family, we blame the other person. But if we know how to take care of them, they will grow well, like lettuce. Blaming has no positive effect at all, nor does trying to persuade using reason and arguments. That is my experience. No blame, no reasoning, no argument, just understanding. If you understand, and you show that you understand, you can love, and the situation will change.

–Thich Nhat Hanh

When children find trouble, society provides mothers with plenty of ammunition for self-blame. We are quick to point our fingers at the *parents* of criminals, abusers, and unhappy and unsuccessful people, so hungry for someone to blame. We are experts at condemning. The perspective that blames the child is just as rampant. Looking for fault from any viewpoint is often a distraction from resolution and a wasteful detour that consumes lives. Learning to take responsibility for what *we* manifest in our personal reality allows transformation—for all.

The moment Travis and I walked into Robert Kirby's office it was as though Travis had found an old friend, one he'd been searching for. The same was true for Robert. I felt something between them that was not definable. Being very intuitive, Trav allowed the connection and was instantly comfortable. He was quick to recognize different energies in people and had a good radar when it came to feeling intentions. He trusted Robert immediately. It confirmed that their meeting was meant to be.

First, Robert asked Travis if he wanted me present or would prefer if they work alone. He answered that he didn't care. Robert tested his body to see if that was true and it was genuinely okay with him, so I stayed. I was nervous though, like I was going to find out that Trav had already been damaged by my beliefs. The ones I had lugged around about being an unfit mother since the day he was born almost eight years earlier. I wondered if holding them in my blueprint had somehow harmed him. Thoughts of what I could have done better flashed through my mind... I should've spent more time with Trav, attended fewer classes, not worked weekends, played more, been more patient, encouraged him to feel his pain more than I did, etc. Then I remembered, stop yammering! We were in the right spot at the right time. There was no arguing with Robert's findings. Travis' body was about to reveal what was inside. The moment of truth had arrived.

I reached for the Sacred to join us. I relaxed and actually looked at myself from another viewpoint and saw me, sitting in the corner of the large space, worried about my son, and loving him completely. As I watched Robert work on Trav's small body I was humbled. The appointment was a miracle. I melted into the good intentions and love that surrounded the three of us. I filled up with the hum and watchfulness of the invisible.

Suddenly, all my attention went to a question I overheard Robert ask Travis. "Do you miss your father?" Robert didn't know all the details of Pat adopting Travis at age three and that, to him, Pat was his dad. I listened intently to see how Travis would answer. Without hesitation Travis responded, "I see my dad all the time." Robert looked at me confused and said, "His body is saying he needs to see his father." Unsure of what to say or do, I did nothing. I kept quiet and let the silence be, not forcing any of my answers or opinions into the space. I let go and hoped it would move forward as it needed to with Travis directing the session. My heart was beating fast.

Travis piped in, "I have another father but I don't know him." I was nervously anticipating where the question could lead, wondering if I had missed something by not talking to Trav more about his genetic father having only discussed it a couple of times. It never seemed like it had bothered him. Then Robert asked Travis if he would like to see his other father and Travis innocently questioned, "I wonder what he looks like." Robert asked him how he felt about this other father and Travis answered shyly, "Fine."

As Robert spoke about different feelings, he continued to test and move energy on Travis. He was working silently with hands moving as though he were conducting a symphony. Finding patterns, turning pages, messaging meridians, and never stopping the comforting way he spoke with Trav. He was definitely guided by the divine, it was amazing to observe. Robert then turned to me and described, "Travis's heart and solar plexus are closed from holding in feelings he's not expressing while awake. He's processing and letting them out at night, in a dreamlike state." He went on to say, "Sleepwalking, crying, emoting, and wanting you to hold him are a few of the ways he is trying to deal with his unconscious pain." As Robert spoke I felt the truth of it in my gut.

Robert muscle tested to discover what Travis needed to help him clear this stuck energy. He turned to one of his manuals and came across several emotions and ideas that needed releasing. He paused for a moment and then pointed to a paragraph that had tested very strong, indicating that Travis should read it out loud to assist in his healing. The writing encompassed the unspoken emotions I had been feeling in him. The words invited the acknowledgment of sadness, the separation, the longing, and also the fear of love. As Travis spoke the words, I sensed the energy in the room shifting. The space became crisp, more intense, yet lighter at the same time. Robert asked Travis if he wanted to let the painful feelings go, explaining that the choice was his. Travis nodded, "Yes." His eyes were moist as the emotions released. He looked up at Robert embarrassed and said, "I don't know why I'm crying." I watched in awe, feeling the preciousness of the moment and the power of truth. Robert hugged Trav and assured him it was okay explaining that sometimes when old pains release they come out in tears.

The reading from the book was so simple it gave Travis a new way of seeing things. It explained healing such that a child could use the understanding for a long time. Robert described the content further to Travis so he could make the words his own and apply them to life through a child's eyes. He strengthened Travis energetically to receive the goodness coming toward him during the reading and cleared obstacles to accepting the love that was all around him. Robert looked in my direction explaining how Travis was shut down when it came to accepting and letting people and love in. That's part of what the reading was about, letting people love him, trusting they would always be there, and accepting that the Universe longed to give joy to him. Robert took great care to give Trav examples of how the Universe could only mirror Travis's wish. He had a very sweet conversation with Trav to help him grasp the concept of being source of how the world treated him. He asked Trav if he wanted to be loved. Trav was quiet for a few seconds as though he was considering what that might feel like. Then he smiled up at Robert sweetly and answered, "Yup."

Robert then walked him over to a roller resting on the floor about twenty feet away. As they walked I couldn't help but notice how they seemed like brothers. Robert was so tender and kind, it was very touching. He had Travis lean backward over the roller (a cushioned cylindrical apparatus about two feet long by two feet wide) in a backbend posture explaining how it would help open up his closed areas and allow a release where he was physically holding emotion. Robert knelt down close and had Trav stay in that position while he cleared trapped energy. Robert cleared his chakra points, supporting the integration of the session to occur on all levels including past, present, and future. Travis was so willing and open, eager to do everything Robert suggested, as though he knew he needed it. I was blown away by the ease of it all. I was witnessing precious perfection.

Upon completion, Robert had Trav stand up so he could test for anything else that might be contributing to his sleepwalking. Travis's body answered every question so authentically. Robert surprised me by checking Travis's body to see if he needed to see his genetic dad. His body answered a very strong "Yes." I was thinking I would have to dig up some of the photo albums I had saved for Trav so he could see a few pictures. As though Robert read my mind, he tested to see if Trav had to see him in person, and it was another strong "Yes." Then Robert asked, "Does it need to be up close, eye-to-eye?" Travis arm was firm, another "Yes." That's when I started freaking out, not having any idea where his genetic dad lived. Robert turned to me and asked if I knew where to find him and I said, "No." Then he tested Travis for the time frame, asking his body how soon he needed to see his genetic father. His body answered within seven days. Travis had to see him within seven days and I hadn't seen him in seven years. Robert said Travis would stop sleepwalking completely if they met within that time frame. I had never heard of any sleepwalking cure like it. Skeptical or not, the meeting had to happen and I was going to do everything I could to ensure it did!

We left the session. Travis was happy. It was good for both of us, in more ways than we understood right then.

As we drove home, he and I discussed what had occurred and reviewed it to see if he had any questions. We were very present and connected. The air was crystal clear between us and it seemed anciently familiar. I asked him if he knew how much I loved him and that I had forever and always would. He said. "Uh huh." I asked him if he felt the experience with Robert was good and he nodded his head yes. I told him how glad I was for him to be able to open his heart and how sometimes doing that could be scary. I shared with him how I'd had trouble trusting people when I was a young girl. Then he asked me several questions about my childhood that I answered gently, guiding him to see that as we grow up we all learn how to love and be loved.

I assured him it was safe to care deeply and that it was the most fun thing about being alive. I gave him reminders of this yummy feeling by asking him how it felt to be adored by his little brother and he laughed. I chided, "How about when your father cuddles you, reads to you, and tickles you till you scream with joy?" He smiled. Then I asked, "When I look you in the eye and open my heart as wide as I can so you can crawl in, how does that feel?" He became shy and said, "Good." I reached over to find his little hand and didn't let it go until we got home. He was glad. My heart was full.

After a few minutes, Trav told me how his friends had made fun of him for talking in his sleep and walking around inside the tent during the last scouting campout. He said they were mad at him because he had stepped on everyone and woke them up. Trav said he didn't remember doing any of it. I think things were coming together for him and beginning to make sense. I asked him if he had any problems when he'd spent the night at his best friend John's house and he said he didn't think so. I suspected he did, but was unaware of it. I told him we were going to do what Robert said and use all the magic stuff we had to help him feel what was inside; that way, we could let it out so he wouldn't have to suffer in the middle of the night anymore. I could tell he wasn't so certain that it would work. I promised him things would change and get better and invited him to trust what Robert had told him and, more importantly, to trust himself that he was very intuitive and would know exactly how to release anything he decided to release. I expressed how confident I was in his ability to do anything he dreamed of doing. I reminded him: *he* was the boss of his experience. He relaxed.

All the way home I assured Travis, everything that happened would flow perfectly to what was next and that somewhere in his new awareness there would be a present waiting for him. His eyes lit up like he was about to get a new toy. I laughed, explaining that it was a different kind of gift, one that was sometimes hard to see because it was more of a feeling or a knowing, than an object. I told him he would recognize it when it showed up. He wasn't very excited about this type of present and looked at me like

I was a weirdo. (Not an unfamiliar experience for me.)

I loved having a captive audience and went on to explain that when an obstacle to our happiness shows up it can be a really positive thing because that's when we begin reaching for what we want. We move closer to our dreams simply by longing for what we prefer. When we imagine and feel what it would be like to have situations the way we would like them, the Universe gets all excited, eager to give us whatever we want! "The Universe is waiting for you to decide what you want honey." I looked at him and said, "Maybe this all happened because you wanted to feel something different than what you've been feeling! Maybe this was a clever way to figure out how to be happier! How about this perspective; you attracted Robert, the session, and your Higher Self had you sleepwalking so you could change things! You are pretty powerful buddy!" He giggled and lit up, seeming to like the concept. Travis had a very sharp mind. I was continually mesmerized as I watched his thinking process. He was quick and when it came to connecting the dots, wayyyyyyyyy ahead of me.

I continued, "Now that you got a peek at what you have been carrying around in your body and heart and felt how it was hurting you, maybe you're ready to pick a feeling that would be more fun to have?" His expression totally shifted to seriousness, as he asked, "Which one should I pick?" I answered, "That is one of your presents, you can choose any feeling you want! You decide."

Travis grew quiet, looked out the window, and after a couple of minutes said, "Mom, who do you think God is?" I enjoyed the stillness of the moment as we drove down the street, smiling as I felt the Sacred with No Name in the trees, the clouds, the blue of the sky, and became aware of the presence of our two beings connected. I looked into Trav's eyes and asked, "Who do you think God is?" Travis was silent for a long couple of minutes. I could hear the hum of awareness in our space, a high pitch tone that I often became cognizant of when connected to Higher Self. It felt like the touch of love. It held the pureness of Source energy and had a sweet gentleness to it.

Travis finally turned and with great determination said, "I want to know what YOU think Mom, what do YOU believe about God, not what I believe!" I stayed quiet a bit longer wanting to open a space for him to say something else, but he didn't. I nudged him one more time by asking, "Honey, why do you want to know my belief? Do you think I know the real truth about it?" Travis knew I was leading into telling him that he needed to decide for himself and explaining, yet again, how everyone thought they knew the truth but only he could discover the answer for himself, a lecture he'd heard repeatedly. (Anytime he was looking for an answer, no matter what the question was, I would say look inside first then we'll talk). He interrupted quickly trying to cut me off before I even started and spouted, "Mom, you can just tell me for once. I want to know your opinion. I may not agree with you. I just want to hear it!" He was clever in conversation and I adored his inquisitive nature.

Since leaving the hospital, I'd taken Travis to nearly every church in town, looking for one I could align with—Methodist, Buddhist, Science of Mind, Christian Science, and a few non-denominational groups. We never made it to a Catholic sermon. The churches I missed, Dad had probably taken him to. They often went on Sunday mornings when I wasn't physically up to it. So when it came to God, Trav had quite a few perspectives under his belt to ponder already.

One Sunday was very different than all the rest. I took Travis to a small, humble house on the outskirts of town where I heard there was a very special woman, Connie, the minister who performed psychic surgery and could give sermons that moved mountains. I told him about it and asked if he wanted to go and he said, "Yes!"

We arrived a bit late, having followed a dirt road through the middle of pastureland to a beautiful spot with a farm like house with an outbuilding that appeared to hold about forty people. We walked in the square barn like building and the place was full, standing room only. It was quite a gathering with all types of people from doctors to hippies. Everyone was very welcoming and seemed very appreciative to be there. Prior to the service, Connie announced that after each sermon, she did healing work for Christ. She explained that in order to participate you had to sign up, pay a $20 offering, and head to a small back room, put on a sacred gown, and wait your turn. He wasn't sure what to think about all that. I watched him curiously as he took it all in, never leaving his side.

Travis had a phenomenal memory. For a while I thought it was photographic. He could look at something for just a moment, the details, driving directions, study sheets for school, and recall any of it verbatim. The odd church in the middle of nowhere was very peculiar for an eight-year-old to experience. He was very observant, looking around and absorbing everything like a brand-new sponge.

Connie was simple, clear, and poured love into the space with every word she spoke. She'd spent her life traveling the world and helping people. She explained how she only had an eighth grade education because that was when she got her calling and discovered her path to serve Christ. Travis found her interesting. He was wary but also willing.

As Connie spoke I sensed the energy that moved through her and I recognized it as home. It barely mattered what words she used. The room filled up with the Sacred with No Name. For a while, it became my favorite place to spend Sunday mornings and Travis went with me several times. He decided to have a hands-on healing with Connie, once, but after he saw her hand disappear into his body and come back out with blood on it, he didn't want to do it again. He said it was too weird. Trav had been around the church circuit, and not an ordinary one either.

So, when Travis asked me to tell him who I thought God was, his question came from a very unorthodox and eclectic perch. In all our church wanderings, I had made it a point to never, not once, tell him what to believe—only that he should decide for himself.

Only Breath

Not Christian or Jew or Muslim, not Hindu
Buddhist, Sufi, or Zen.
Not any religion or cultural system.
I am not from the East or the West,
not out of the ocean or up from the ground,
not natural or ethereal,
not composed of elements at all. I do not exist,
am not an entity in this world or in the next,
did not descend from Adam or Eve or any
origin story.
My place is placeless, a trace of the traceless.
Neither body or soul.
I belong to the beloved,
have seen the two worlds as one
and that one
call to and know,
first, last, outer, inner,
only that breath breathing human being.

–Rumi

I gave in and answered Travis's question about God with an invitation, "Okay Trav, if you want my opinion then you're going to need to feel it in order to understand it. The words aren't going to describe it very well because it is a sensation both inside and outside of me and words always fall short. I am not all of it, but it is all of me." He said, "Huh?" I explained, "It's everywhere, present all the time, and I am only a small part of it, but it is all of me." Then I said, "Feel my words instead of trying to understand them. Let them guide you to your own knowing so they can help you discover what is true for you." I let that sink in for a minute before I went on. Speaking softly I pointed, "See that huge tree? Imagine having its life for a minute. What would it feel like to have deep roots digging into the ground and branches blowing in the wind while reaching for the sun?" Pointing to the sky, I spoke softly, "Now, let yourself imagine the life of that wispy cloud." I watched as he fell right into the spirit of things. Then I continued speaking slowly to give him time to feel the sensations, "See those birds flying? Imagine that is you flying." He was into it and a little smile crossed his face. I suggested, "Now feel the energy of these things, the life in them, the vibration, with no words. Can you do that?" He said, "Yep."

I let him linger in this feeling before I shared, "When my mind stops yakking and I just be with life, I can feel what I call 'God' in everything. I feel it in my body and it includes my awareness. It is everywhere. When I connect with people I can sense it in them, too, especially when we are present in the moment together. I paused for a bit before I said, "I feel it in you now." He smiled. I asked him if he had a sense of it and he nodded his head yes. I explained further, "I always feel content when I connect with that energy. It comforts me. I can feel the goodness of life when I take time to do that. I trust what happens and can usually see the perfection, even if things aren't going my way." Trav didn't say anything and I remained quiet, giving him a chance to connect with the majestic row of flowering plum trees as we drove past them.

"I don't think there is any man in robes up in the heavens deciding if we are good or bad people. I believe the kingdom of heaven that people are looking to reach is available right now, here in the present moment. It's both inside and outside of us. We get glimpses and sensations of it when we feel love, and also when we are totally okay with the moment we are in. We feel it when we accept what is happening and trust it to lead us to the perfect next spot. You can feel it when you merge with what is in front of you, a tree, a bird, a sensation, and just let it all be. It's a very peaceful and alive experience of acceptance. Have you ever felt like that?" Trav muttered, "A little." I suggested, "Be still now, and take a few deep breaths." I spoke slowly and invited him, "Quiet your mind's need to know. Feel sitting here with me, driving down the road, the breeze on your face, and let everything be just the way it is for a minute with no need for it to be any different. Let it be okay to not have an answer to your question and just feel the space in the car that is all around us, sort of holding us." I paused a few minutes. "Now listen to the hum of life." I felt him get it and he looked up at me surprised. We sat quietly in the silence. It was a treasure.

I invited him one step closer to himself. "One of my favorite feelings is to imagine being like the tree is being, feeling its stillness, its presence, and how it's living its tree life. It isn't thinking it is unloved or not good enough or worrying about what is next. It isn't wishing it was a frog or something else." He laughed. I went on, "The tree is a great teacher to me Trav, and when I get frustrated or sad I look at one of my big leafy friends and remember to practice being like them. I love how trees teach me to allow life. Trees experience whatever comes their way, sunshine on their leaves, wind tickling them or blowing them over, snow coating them, rain washing them, and heat warming them. They allow and feel all of it with no worrying, no hurrying, and no resistance, always reaching toward the sun, the light. That's what God feels like to me Trav, a kind of still presence that caresses everything." I felt Travis expand and connect. He had a sweet grin on his face, enjoying his experience. We rode in silent awareness while holding hands.

When we turned up our street I added, "When I pray, that's what I pray to Trav, that feeling that everything lives in, that awareness that moves through us. It is all around us and holds us dear. It has all kinds of names. The Tao, Holy Spirit, Krishna, Jesus Christ, Mother/Father God, Divine Intelligence, Awareness, Heavenly Father, Allah, and Higher Self, are just a few. Feeling your connection to this Sacredness with No Name is way more important than what you call it or how you define it. Those times when you trust your intuition and just know you are making the right decision are often God or your Higher Self acting through you. You are learning how to do this, we all are, and it's a lifelong practice. I learn more about this every day. We can get better and better at it forever." As we pulled into the driveway I finished up by saying, "Your grandpa Howie says a prayer is actually your intention summoning the Universe and that the Universe always answers. I reached over and tickled him saying, "It's okay to ask for what you want in life Travis. The Universe loves giving it to you! You just have to truly believe and feel you deserve it for the magic to happen!" He was ready to go play and had enough of my philosophizing. He opened his door as soon as the car stopped and yelled, "Thanks mom," indicating he was full, for now.

I walked in the house and went straight to the phone book to see if I could locate a number for Trav's genetic dad. No luck. I phoned his last known place of employment hoping they would have some information on his whereabouts. I hadn't stayed in touch with any of his friends and that was all I could think to do. It was another miracle. The gal that answered the phone said he had just started working there again. After moving away for quite a while he had recently come back. I heard from one of my friends who saw him out one night, years earlier that he'd remarried and had another child. He had repeated the exact same scenario, losing his family to his battle with cocaine. The drug had won again. He was a good-hearted man, he just got lost in a painful addiction.

I left a message and he called me back that very afternoon. It was wonderful to speak with him and he was happy to come by and meet Travis. I didn't give him much information but did tell him Trav was sleepwalking and I thought seeing him would help settle some things that were disturbing Trav. He was very kind. I leaked some happy tears when I hung up the phone. Something was so right about it, so perfect, and I was thankful for an opening that could allow love to flow between all of us.

I was anxious to see if Travis slept through the night.

I let Pat know what had occurred with Travis's session and he was a little nervous about the meeting, but bless him, he trusted me. I was sure it was a good thing and he sensed that. We were all set to meet at the park down the street from our house. I gave him the details, letting him know our neighbor was going to keep Drake, and that Trav and I would walk to the park around noon. Drake, being almost four years younger than Trav, was jealous and not only wanted to have a session with Robert and find out secrets that his body was holding, he also wanted to go to the park and meet the mystery man. Drake was so cute about it at dinner, pouting because he didn't sleepwalk, saying it wasn't fair that he didn't have a problem. I thought of how beliefs like, "I wish I were a sleep walker," gave birth to some interesting creations. It reminded me of wishing I could be sick as a child like my sister because she got to stay home from school all the time. I talked to Drake about sleepwalking so he could understand it better and not hope for it. Pat said he wondered what ordinary people were discussing, reminding me once again of his wish to have a normal wife. It never happened. With a big smile on my face I teasingly reminded him that he loved me anyway! Pat settled into the kinesiology, the sleepwalking remedy, and his spaghetti dinner. He kindly asked what he could do to help with the meeting the next day, wanting to make sure I called him if there was any problem at all. I told him, "No worries."

Trav slept without interruption. I had my ears bent in his direction all night. We slept with the bedroom doors open so I could hear my sons breathe if I wanted to. Like my mother, I had good ears.

The next day, as we were getting ready to go to the park I got a little nervous. I wished Dad were there. He had been traveling for quite a while, driving across the country to attend an Avatar Master course in Florida and I missed him. I said a prayer to calm myself. I was kind of shaky and worse than that, I wasn't sure what to wear. I looked thin and fragile, still puffy cheeked, but not nearly as bad as a few weeks prior. I just didn't look anything like myself and I felt unrecognizable. I used to be cute and I missed it. I wasn't accustomed to looking in the mirror and seeing myself so strange, so I avoided mirrors. I liked how I felt inside, but wasn't crazy about my appearance. I looked weird. There went my mind... *blah, blah, blah.*

I put down my brush after running it through my very thin hair and said out loud. "Stop it! This isn't about you." I had to shift my attention out of the doldrums. I remembered Dad telling me about a new Avatar exercise that was being introduced suggesting that flowing kind attention toward the body could help restore well-being. I didn't have anything to lose! I stood up and walked over to the full length mirror. I examined my body slowly, very purposefully, from head to toe and couldn't believe how automatically I noticed everything wrong with my appearance... too skinny, too flat, no butt, baggy eyes, bad dress, goofy swollen face. "STOP IT!" I roared, "See something good!"

I inhaled fully and looked again. I modestly smiled at my reflection and was able to feel grateful for having my body to live in. That helped. Then I decided to focus on how far I had come and what a good friend my body had been. I scanned my body from top to bottom searching for something more to say nice things about and be thankful for. I congratulated my body for recovering, and apologized for not being more appreciative of how much it had endured. I stood there... searching for goodness, it took a couple of uncomfortable minutes but then I admitted my unquenchable desire to be a good person and it was a physical rush.

I smiled authentically at my reflection. I let it in! Then I felt my ambition to heal and then my determination to be a good wife and mother, and I acknowledged them all. It felt very different than putting my attention on what was wrong with me. It changed my energy so completely to a higher vibration that I was amazed. It was very kind and self empowering to be nice to my body. I stood there blank for a few seconds more as I gazed upon my still fragile frame and I thought of how much I was learning and how I was getting stronger every day. I smiled caringly at my body. I felt genuine compassion for *me!* I whispered to my reflection, "See, you're not so bad. How would I do all this without you?" I felt more grounded, more real, and way more appreciative of life. I looked in the mirror and winked, then laughed at myself.

I turned my head to the door and Travis was standing there staring at me with his head tilted strangely and a confused look on his face. I thought, *Oh Lord, my kids are going to end up in therapy,* and I chuckled again. He was a little embarrassed for me, "Mom! What are you doing?" I went into full lecture mode and explained how I needed to put some attention on good things about myself instead of always focusing on the negative. I told him that whenever my attention was jammed in negativity I just made that aspect of life bigger and I suffered from my own actions. But, if I looked for something to appreciate I felt way better. He rolled his eyes and said, "Okay, whatever, let's go." I think he learned that eye rolling maneuver from his father!

Travis was calm and cool. We had a five-minute walk, so I used the time to encourage him to feel what he was feeling and have fun with this whole thing. He was fine. I mean really, he was unbothered by the whole thing. It was me that needed the lecture. It was a beautiful day and he went right over to the jungle gym and played. His friend John showed up and they were doing the boy thing while I sat and waited. I thought, *Uh oh, he isn't going to show up*, and then a car pulled up and out stepped my tall, very handsome, ex-husband. I felt his presence and absorbed him as he swaggered over and sat very close to me. We hugged and were fairly comfortable. It was polite more than intimate. It was nice to be with him. I found myself excited to share with him all the joys of his son. I wanted him to feel that he had given me something wonderful. I wanted him to feel the amazing being Travis had always been, how intuitive and bright he was, rattling on about how he's in the 97th percentile of his class, extremely coordinated, and had a little brother… I realized that I was rambling and we both chuckled thoughtfully.

I called Trav over. He was a bit reserved as he joined us, keeping a little distance. I introduced them and Travis said, "Hi," as he sat down on the grass across from us and just stared, not saying much else. They talked about horses for a couple of minutes. Trav got invited to go ride someday and seemed to like the idea. Then he jumped up and said he wanted to go back and play with John on the swings. They barely talked, less than five minutes total. I shrugged my shoulders and said, "That's Trav." We sat quietly and watched him play for a while, visiting politely before we went our separate ways.

Trav and I headed home and the first thing out of his mouth was, "Mom, what happened to his teeth?" I said, "Honey, he didn't take very good care of himself or his body." He asked, "Did he forget to brush his teeth?" I said, "I would bet yes, but I don't know for sure." (His teeth had dark spots on them and were discolored). We walked silently and right before heading up our driveway I asked Trav if he wanted to talk about anything at all and he said, "Everything is good Mom." I prodded one more time and asked if he was curious, had any questions, or felt anything weird. He said, "Nope." Trav was more interested in playing with John than talking. He felt calm and centered to me, and it wasn't like he was avoiding feeling anything. I expected it to be more complicated. But it was so easy.

I wondered if that was all it would take. I hoped this meeting settled some of Trav's curiosity. I was surprised by the lack of interest he showed in the whole thing. He ran off to John's house and I went home. That was the end of the story and, amazingly, the end of his sleepwalking. Trav would say things out loud now and then while dreaming but to my knowledge he never again wandered around in his sleep.

Much happened over the following year. My healing continued slow but sure. I weaned off of the steroids, the schedule Robert gave me worked perfectly. I found the best homeopathic M.D. on the planet to empower me. At least, that's my opinion. We were very much in alignment about the healing process. Dr. John Diamond knew you had to heal emotionally and spiritually as well as physically and he had a keen awareness of how energy moved or became stuck. I worked with him to create a life of balance. He helped me identify areas I needed to address on all levels of existence. He used applied kinesiology, his intuition, and a Dermatron machine, a miraculous device that could measure if and how much a product was healthy for a particular organ or one's overall health, and also determine what virus or bacteria was present in an organ so it could be balanced with the necessary remedy. The machine also had the capacity to test and make sure a specific product was the optimal ingredient for healing. It was 1993 and Dr. Diamond was way ahead of his time.

Dr. Diamond said the priority for me to stabilize emotionally was to tame my need for control. To demonstrate just how accurate he was, I persuasively and insistently defended myself, professing I had completely handled that… until we both started laughing at my obvious attempt to influence his conclusions. I became very fond of John. His method of looking at health multidimensionally was enthralling. We shared many stories of our becoming and swapped viewpoints on the invisible realm; he was open and willing, a very gracious human. John became a dear friend and our family physician. He was the only doctor the boys knew growing up. He spoke of balance often and suggested I consider not working for a while to focus on things I loved to do explaining how that was the most healing activity a person could ever engage. He said my biggest challenge was to allow nurturing from others and to also receive it from myself. I think we had that challenge in common.

I decided to take Dr. Diamond's advice and not go back to work for a while. It was difficult to give up my real estate life and my delightfully eccentric business partner, he and I were a zany and powerful team. And hey, the money wasn't bad either! There was a lot of cash to be made and I had a five-year plan for success that was bulletproof. The way I saw it, Pat and I could have retired comfortably. But I stepped away from the whole thing, including being a co-host on the local TV Real Estate show, which had brought many a snack to my ego! Pat didn't care about the money at all. He wanted me to be happy and healthy and was very supportive of me staying home and being a full-time mother and wife. It wasn't easy giving up everything I had worked so hard to become and establish. My ego screamed for survival but my heart longed for stillness and clarity. My heart won.

I intended to use my time to learn and teach everything I could to the boys so they could experience life the joyful way I knew possible. My intention was to live in "feel" and integrate any resistance, while sharing the whole process with them in a language they could grasp—kid's language. Debbie was able to return to her life after loving my family back to health. She and I grew very close and I couldn't have managed my healing without her. It was another gift of Crohn's disease. I got my big sister back.

Even though I practiced feeling connected to the Sacred with No

Name each day I still found myself lost in thoughts or identities more often than I liked. I had to let that back and forth process be okay or change it. Learning to balance the awareness from the invisible realm with the mechanics of the visible world was ongoing for me. I had one very important regime all day every day… to pay close attention to where I was placing my focus. This was crucial for allowing, for peace of mind, and for taking responsibility for what I was attracting. My waking moments were full of self-diagnosis and processing. I studied, wrote, and questioned everything. I drove the family and myself a little crazy with my determination to be an aware and fully responsible human. I had a busy mind and was adamant about meditating twice a day to get some peace. It was a relief for me and probably everyone else when I disappeared for a while. I took time each day to feel the world around me and quiet my mind by merging with the clouds, the sky, the love of my family, and the sensations in my body. Feeling was key to my peace of mind. It was my sanctuary. I found merging with noises, trees, or whatever might be in my sphere of awareness offered a precious connection with the Tao. It was how I coalesced with the part of me that was a part of all things. It was where I felt God.

Dad returned from his trip and came over nearly every day. We chanted, practiced sound therapy from Deepak, processed with the Avatar tools, laughed, painted, cooked, read poetry, and if I whined just right, he'd rub my feet. Every moment with him was a lesson. We discussed and explored possibility every time we were together, always dreaming big and empowering each other toward our goals. He was a master at allowing life to be easy. He became my best friend. Our relationship was more comprehensive than just daughter and father identities, we were companions on the path of awakening. We were two Source beings exploring our humanness. The wisdom he shared touched all our lives deeply. He became an integral part of the family. The boys adored him, trusted him, played baseball with him, laughed at his stories, and missed him when he wasn't around. Pat and he became good friends, developing a great deal of respect for one another.

I witnessed total transformation in my father. As he forgave himself and allowed all of his feelings to exist he blossomed into who I'd always dreamed he could be. He got a second chance at fatherhood and embraced it fully. He made up for his mistakes and ended up with a very big bonus prize—two great boys to play grandpa with.

I earned my license to deliver Avatar so I could better understand the magic of the materials and teach alongside my Dad. It was his dream for us to be partners in providing a space for others to know themselves more fully. The many classes we attended brought us endlessly closer. We processed and applied the Avatar tools in pursuit of healing, forgiving, and developing our intuitive skills (connecting to Highest Self). Continually discovering that the more we took responsibility for in our lives, the more we understood and experienced joy. We cherished assisting others in knowing the same. Harry Palmer's enlightening technology charted a sacred journey and the love Dad and I evolved into is wordless. I healed, became stronger, learned the techniques, studied, and wrote, but more than anything, I had a ball hanging out with my Dad in the realm of becoming. We practiced being in charge of how we experienced reality and chose the path of very dear friends and a supportive team. We explored, grew, practiced, held many Avatar Courses in the Reno community. We laughed a lot and became increasingly aware of our many selves, remembering not to take any of them too seriously. We became the puppeteer of our lives instead of the puppet.

Within less than a year of my near death experience I had regained all my strength and enjoyed total health with no remnants of Crohn's disease lurking in my mind or body. I was no longer afraid of its return. I volunteered at the boys' school, taught art every opportunity I had, and to Pat's delight, became a fairly decent cook. Life was heaven, a completion and the beginning of something new was being revealed.

It just so happened to be golf.

There do exist enquiring minds, which long for the truth of the heart, seek it, strive to solve the problems set by life, try to penetrate to the essence of things and phenomena and to penetrate into themselves. If a man reasons and thinks soundly, no matter which path he follows in solving these problems, he must inevitably arrive back at himself, and begin with the solution of the problem of what he is himself and what his place is in the world around him.

–*Views from the Real World: Early Talks of G. I. Gurdjieff,*
G.I. Gurdjieff

Fore What?

chapter 16

Golf is a game to teach you about the messages from within, about the subtle voices of the body-mind. And once you understand them you can more clearly see your hamartia, the ways in which your approach to the game reflects your entire life. Nowhere does a man go so naked.

–*Golf in the Kingdom,* Michael Murphy

Dad loved to golf. As far back as I can remember he spent more time at the course than at work or home. It was his personal joy, along with painting and teaching. Teaching was in the background of everything he said or did. He was always telling somebody how to do something and frequently handed out flyers inviting people to attend a meeting at the local diner but only if they were interested in learning how to create magic in their lives. His charisma attracted a variety of characters and it never mattered to him who came as long as they brought their willingness. He loved them all. He'd begin each forum with some question about Source, beliefs, awareness, or being on Earth and manifesting dreams. It was his goal to help people understand the mechanics of consciousness and share a cup of bean soup (his term for coffee). He invited each visitor to explore their ability to design life as they desired it to be. Everyone loved hanging out with Dad because he truly lived as an example of someone who did exactly what they felt like doing… he exuded possibility from every pore. I enjoyed watching him in action. From the very beginning, he was determined to show people the way.

Dad was set on getting a golf club into my hands once he found out I couldn't hold a paintbrush very well. One afternoon he started nudging me toward golf by swearing it was a game of attention and feeling, and he promised my swing would be natural if I just let the club fall and didn't try to control it (me not controlling something was a feat in itself). Golf just wasn't something I was interested in. I wasn't crazy about the water and land waste and had boycotted playing the game for that very reason.

Dad didn't give up. He explained how the game was all about being able to manage the mind and how illuminating it was because it revealed aspects of our thought processes we might otherwise miss. Now that got my attention! He went on to explain, "You get to know yourself very well on a golf course because habits and personalities that are on unconscious automatic are sure to show up." I was intrigued and trying to feel if he really meant it or was just trying to sell me and get me to golf with him. Then he teased me by saying that if I wanted to measure how well I could put my attention where I decided to, then I should pick up a golf club. Well, that was it! I took the bait. Being a tad competitive and eager to impress my father, my mouth started watering! Thus, my first problem… my ambition was smothered in wanting my father's approval. I can tell you right now, you can't swing a club when your attention is focused on what someone else is thinking of you.

As Dad described what was needed to be a good golfer, I reasoned that if I could feel, manage my mind, and put my attention where I wanted to, I would do all right! Maybe even beat Dad at his own game! I laughed at the thought and decided it might be fun to give it a shot. I loved the challenge of being in charge of where every drop of my attention went!

The function of will is to decide, place, shift, or remove attention.

–ReSurfacing: Techniques for Exploring Consciousness,
Harry Palmer

I started hitting golf balls with Dad pretty regularly, at least once a week. At first, the whole idea was just weird to me. Trying to make a tiny ball find its way into a small hole wasn't attractive or exciting to me. I didn't get the point. But, watching and experiencing Dad hit a golf ball was definitely a spectacle. The joy he got from swinging a club was captivating. He would go into a zone and disappear into some feeling that I'd become quite curious to visit and understand. He'd say things out loud, not to anybody in particular, such as, "See that yellow clump of grass?" Then he would land his ball within a foot of it. He did this darn near every time, muttering where he thought his shot would land and then hit it over there. Every ball in his large bucket ended up very close to where he told it to go. Sometimes he would whisper, "Hit ball, get check." I would laugh and he would suddenly realize he was speaking out loud. The phrase was a remnant from his baseball days.

Now and then, Dad used to go with me to elementary school whenever I volunteered to teach art, which was really a disguise to coach the kids in attention management. We came up with some very creative ways to empower the students in all grades and enjoyed learning how to speak to the young ears. Dad would say the only way we can make a difference is to **talk to the listening present.** It was fun because we had to be in "feel" to do this. We had to really hear what the children were saying, understand how they thought, and do our best to feel what was in their hearts. Our connection to them was our guide with no planned result. We let our dialogue and experience in the moment reveal the perfect next step. Each class was different and what we said or did came more from the group's feel and openness than anything by rote. The kids were amazing, totally willing and eager to explore possibility. Most of them hadn't yet been taught the concept "can't." So unlike many of us adults, they were limitless.

I would introduce Dad as a baseball player who once played for the Pittsburgh Pirates. The kids would go wild! Dad could easily attract every drop of their attention and then tell his story. I'm not sure if it was real or made up, but the tale was perfect when it came to teaching a lesson. Dad was a very skilled storyteller.

On one occasion, in a very animated way, Dad told the story of his chance to break a Runs Batted in Record (RBI) held by a well-known baseball player. I don't recall the numbers or the names he used but I knew the message well. We were in Drake's first-grade class and the kids were ecstatic that dad was there, Drake had been bragging about him for a while. Dad started out by asking the children if they liked baseball and how many played, and the boys were in total awe from the moment the six-foot-five Pirate entered the room. Dad set the stage by describing the excitement and intensity of all the players in the game that day: the full stadium, the press, and the anticipation of Howie Goss breaking a longtime RBI record.

Dad explained the pressure and the roaring noise from the cheering crowd, painting the picture with lots of emotion to get the kids pumped up. The story was about his relationship with his favorite bat. He called it his magic bat. Dad told the kids how much he loved the bat, how it never let him down, and gave some examples of how he could rely on it to hit a ball out of the park when he really needed it to. He told them of its golden color, the wording on it and how he would rub his hand over the lettering for good luck. He explained how much he loved that bat and how he had used it for a very long time. He talked about how this one game was the BIG game, the one that would finally make him famous and known all across the land, and this was his last chance to prove he could do it. The kids were wide-eyed and the room got so quiet when Dad stopped talking, all you heard was breathing. He continued to describe sitting in the dugout waiting, nervous, sweating, and scared! The boys in the class are nodding their heads. He tells how he's up next, knowing this is the big moment, the chance he had been waiting for all his life. How he had to hit just one more runner home to beat the record. One more and he would be top dog!

He described to the kids how he felt in great detail, how he thought, and how important it was to be in control of his mind and his attention during those few moments. He revealed his feelings, his nerves, and how his mind wanted to say things that were scary or recall mistakes of the past. He emphasized how he wouldn't listen to the negative thoughts. He told them that he kept repeating, "I can do this." He illustrated how much better it felt to think "I can," than "I can't." Dad tells them how it's his last game, his last opportunity before the season ends and he has to do it now or start all over the following year. He painted the picture of the stadium and of all the eyes watching him. He has the kids imagine fifty thousand people staring, screaming, and every one of his teammate's eyes locked on him. He described the pressure he felt and how he had to put it all aside and focus his attention or he would've felt weak and maybe given up. He explained how his palms were sweaty but his mind was focused and clear, and most importantly that he felt confident because he had his magic bat! This was the bat he had used all season and it had never let him down. That bat was his baby.

The kids were mesmerized, so was the teacher, and so was I.

Once Dad had us all riveted, he explained how he was on deck swinging and placing every drop of his attention on feeling his bat hit the ball, and how he imagined it flying out of the park, and believed he could do it over and over again with the help of his trusty bat. Finally, it was his turn to hit, he walked to the base, and the crowd is shouting wildly with many of them coming that day solely to see if Howie Goss could do it! Dad tells them how he didn't hear anything except his own breathing because he was so focused totally on the ball, on his bat, on being ready and totally present. He described how he blocked out everything except the ball flying toward him. "CRAAAAAAACK!" He exclaimed loudly and startled the kids! He continued… "I hit the ball hard and it headed left, just outside the base." "'Foul ball, strike one!'" yells the umpire! "I gathered myself and the next pitch is coming in fast and I swing hard and hit the ball *SMAAAAAAACK!,* only this time the bat splintered into several little pieces and was strewn all over the field in front of home base. The ball headed into the stands as a foul." "'Strike two!'" screams the umpire as the batboy runs to pick up the pieces of Dad's magic bat.

Dad looked up with a sad face at the children and explained how a murmur went through the crowd as he looked at the small piece of his magic bat, still in his hand. Dad dramatized the scene and told them how his magic bat was gone now, shredded, broken, and how he had to collect himself and swing again. That meant he had to select another bat. He sulked as he walked over to the collection of bats and couldn't find a single one that felt as good as his precious magic bat. He felt afraid and less powerful with the loss of his special bat. He almost gave up. At this point, the children were devastated. A couple of them yelled out encouragingly, "You can do it!"

Then, Dad explained how something amazing happened. All of a sudden he realized *he* had a choice. Dad told the kids he had to decide to believe in himself. He described how he'd made a mistake thinking the bat was magic—instead of him! He really helped them understand that *he* was the one who had decided the bat held the magic and that he was also the one who could decide that *he* held the magic! He told them he had to make up his mind, real fast, whether the magic was in him or if it died with the bat. Then he asked them, "Where was the magic, where was my magic?" They screamed, "In you, in you!" He confirmed, "That's right," and pointed to them, letting them know how brilliant they were to recognize this.

Dad continued, "The magic was in me and I had to realize that in order to succeed at my goal. I had to own the magic, claim it as mine, or I would never be able to hit that ball!" He had to believe in himself the way he believed in that bat, even more so. He shared his thought process and how he had to own his magic in seconds because he had to get up there and hit that last pitch out of the park and break that record! So he took a deep breath, decided he could do it, and picked a bat (it didn't even matter which one). He talked about how he felt big and strong and realized he was the one that made the bat work so well, it was his strength, and the power was inside him. He felt it! Dad explained how he got up to base, the pitch zooming toward him, and hit that ball long and hard into left field, just over the third baseman's reach. It was barely inside the line. Fair ball! Dad made a running motion imitating the guy scrambling for home as Dad ran with all his might for first base. He moved his hands in the motion and yelled, "SAFE!" to show the kids how he did it, and the room broke out in wild applause.

Once they calmed down he spoke softly, almost as a whisper, to bring their attention back to the importance of the magic being inside Dad. He told them how he didn't believe the magic was in him at first, but that he finally realized it had been all along. We explained how the bat breaking into pieces was the best thing that had ever happened to Dad and how sometimes a mistake or an accident could open a door to something wonderful. Dad ended the story by creatively showing the kids how the same magic was inside them regarding having good grades, getting along with their parents and becoming a spectacular athelete. The visits ended with the kids feeling like they could do anything as long as they put their attention where they wanted to, kept their eye on the ball, and remembered the magic would always be inside them.

So whenever we were hitting golf balls and Dad muttered, "Hit ball, get check," I always got a kick out of it. It was how Dad focused and blocked out the fifty thousand thoughts that could run through his head while swinging at that tiny white ball (similar to the fifty thousand people yelling and screaming whenever he was up to bat). He was good at putting his attention on the ball and only the ball. He was a master of the zone. As we practiced on the range, we would talk about how you couldn't hit the ball where you wanted to unless you were present and could imagine and feel the ball land where you envisioned it going. He'd say, "You have to believe! There's no pretending in golf. Wherever the ball ends up tells a story about your attention." Dad said "feeling" was what made the ball go where he intended it to. He'd feel the ball landing on his target before he'd ever swung his club. It was different than *thinking* the ball there. It took a lot of practice for me to understand what he meant. It was very much the same as manifesting something in life, health, abundance, relationships, or love… I had to *feel* it happening, believe in myself, let go of fear, and trust my good intentions to land me in my dream.

Dad was right about one thing, golf revealed parts of me to myself that I had no idea were so ingrained. At times, I wanted desperately to impress him. I would swing really hard to try and hit the ball as far as he did, and completely whiff it, missing the little white bastard all together. By the way, calling it names never helped—it was like it heard me! It was hilarious. Golf gave me great insight into my humongous approval pattern. I began seeing how much of my actions in life, at home, with the kids, teaching, etc., were wired into wanting to be recognized or admired.

Swinging a club and trying to hit a puny ball had revealed entirely new levels of my competitive, judgmental, and egotistical nature. I embarrassed myself frequently, and it was good. The game of golf was the best ego crusher I'd ever met, quite humbling. It was enlightening.

We played our first nine holes together at a small course in Reno called Brookside Golf Course. It was a perfect beginner's spot with just the right amount of challenge. With two holes running parallel to the Reno Airport, it offered some interesting distractions, not that I didn't have enough trouble already stored up between my ears.

When we walked to the first tee box I noticed quite a number of people were waiting to play. Brookside was structured on a first-come basis, no tee times or schedules, so everyone just waited his or her turn. People were lined up right next to where we had to hit from, sitting on benches, or just standing around. They were way too close to the tee box if you asked me. If they looked hard enough when it was my turn to hit, they probably could see me perspiring as I hovered over the ball. Did I say there were a lot of people there? Watching intently as everyone else hit his or her very first drive of the day? I noticed every single one of them. My ego was a hungry maniac and I wasn't doing very well at quieting it down. In the long twenty minute wait to tee off I was able to find some humor in my desire to reach fame on the first tee.

Finally, it was our turn and I think about a thousand more people had arrived. At least, it felt that way to me. Dad hit first and it was a perfect shot, a gentle swing, long and straight, right down the middle of the par five. *He'd be on the green in just two shots,* I thought. I wanted to smack my ball hard and get close to where he was (bad idea). I felt I had to keep up with him (another bad idea). I walked up to the ladies' tee box, shaky and nervous, hoping my knees didn't buckle. I was watching my attention and feeling my body freak out all at once. It was hilarious to see how cognizant I was of the people around me. I was so full of myself, imagining everyone watching me and waiting to see how good I was. Then I said to myself, *Holly, like they even care!* I had a mini argument with myself as I put the tee in the ground. Nobody won that fight. I couldn't even get the ball to sit on the tee. I was totally embarrassed. After several attempts with a shaky hand, I did it. I almost expected applause from a laughing crowd, imagining that they all knew what I was going through. I was afraid to look. I got ready to swing and I swear, when everyone got quiet, I fantasized they were anticipating something wonderful. My mind was nutty. I pushed the idea away and ordered my body to focus on the ball and stop the nonsense. It seemed like I had stood over my ball for about a week trying to shut off my mind. Then I started talking to myself about how long I was taking and that everyone was thinking how slow I was and checking their watches. I was a complete nut case and the banter would not stop!

The more unfortunate news was that when I addressed the ball, I could just see a blur behind my right shoulder and knew it was Dad standing there, staring. Just what I needed. My mind was spinning and thank God some part of me was able to watch it all in disbelief with a tiny bit of humor, very tiny. Finally, I gave up on getting quiet minded, took a deep breath, and told myself to just hit the damn ball (cussing was a satisfying golf condiment, at least for a few seconds). I decided to swing my arms, and trust it. No need to impress anybody (I think I said that out loud). *Breathe and swing, breathe and swing,* I repeated in my head. I'm not sure if I closed my eyes or kept them open as I took my arms back so far, I almost hit myself in the leg. I swung hard and fast and had no idea where the ball went, but I knew it wasn't good.

I looked at Dad immediately with a surge of desperate hope that maybe it landed somewhere half-decent, in spite of all my attention being stuck on how I looked and what others were thinking of me. He smiled knowingly. I didn't like that he smiled.

I quickly reviewed what just happened, hoping to correct something, anything, before my next shot. That was another mistake. I fell even deeper into the caverns of my mind. I went into a new kind of mental frenzy trying to figure out what I had done wrong. After much internal bantering, I decided I was too stiff and had tried to control my swing instead of allowing it. I concluded I wasn't present at all but had mentally wandered off to some faraway land. I documented several reasons for my poor display of athletic ability, including complaints about all the people watching. I immediately began griping about how golfers should all have to wait up at the clubhouse, far away. The monologue rambling in my head about pure nonsense was steady and amazing to witness. The whole episode occurred in just a couple of minutes, yet, it seemed like an entire day had passed since we pulled into the parking lot for my first round of golf. That was about the time I realized that I was still standing on the tee box. Hurriedly I decided I better get moving so others could have their own turn on this delightful ten-by-ten square of grass.

As I walked toward my golf bag my mind didn't miss a beat. The difference was I had become critical of myself for the rambling. I was trying to figure out where all that nonsense in my head was coming from, and felt like I should've known better. I laughed, thinking that was another hook, a trick, and if I tried to decipher that one, I would be lost in thought for my next shot as well.

I looked back at Dad in dismay and he laughed out loud like he'd been a spectator in my head. It was about then that I realized this game was going to kick me in the rear like nobody ever could. I calmed down and considered what a perfect way this was to gain awareness of my habits and get to know myself better. Dad knew exactly what was going on with me. Finally, I chuckled, shaking my head and lightening up a bit. It was interesting to see how overly serious I was when it came to the challenge of managing my mind.

Dad pointed in front of us like I better get moving. He showed me where my ball landed a whopping thirty yards in front of the tee box in deep grass. *Perfect,* I thought, *I get another chance with an audience.* I grabbed a five iron and did my best to relax and be present. I actually hit the ball fairly well. My mind had as much to say when I hit the ball well as when I didn't. Yikes! I had a whole committee in my head, and some cheered, some criticized, and some blushed! We were off to the next shot and the next opportunity.

The lessons from that day were astounding and quite applicable to what I needed to own and clear out of my personal blueprint to really enjoy life, and not just on the golf course.

Brookside was a nine-hole course and that was plenty for my first outing. I'd had maybe two golf shots that afternoon that felt pure. The rest, well, there were many times we couldn't even find my ball. My sense of humor ended up being the most valuable club in my bag. I discovered so much about my mental and emotional habits over those two and a half hours I wished I'd taken a notebook to write them all down. My tendency was for my attention and thinking to get stuck on a past shot when it was bad a one, but I realized I'd had very little memory of a decent shot and often trouble even recalling one. *Hmmm... that sounded much like my day-to-day life.* I could always tell you what was wrong, while putting attention on what went right each day wasn't something I had practiced. Wow! Given that the more attention I put on something, the bigger it grew, this was extremely valuable information. Dad and I continually talked about what I was seeing and feeling and he offered me a great piece of advice, "Put your attention on what you want not on what you want to avoid."

When we stood on the tee box of the second hole, which was a par three. Dad pointed to the bunker and said, "If you stand over your ball and say to yourself 'I don't want my ball to go in the sand trap,' your attention is already on resisting and avoiding a trap. Resistance is like a magnet. So guess where your ball is likely to end up?" It made sense, just like life. He pointed to the pin and said, "Decide where you want it to go and everything else will disappear except your goal. Your goal will become the magnet!" He reminded me how this was true with my health, too, how I had to keep my eye on what I wanted to experience and not on what I was afraid of. I started to relax and really understand his words. I hit a pretty good shot off the tee and made it to the green. It was sweet!

I had one shot that helped me recognize the difference between feeling my golf swing and thinking it. My mind instructed me to hurry up and swing and I did, automatically fast, like obeying an order instead of relaxing and allowing the feeling to guide me. I totally sensed the difference between being jammed up in my head and rushing my swing versus feeling relaxed and inclusive. They were two totally different experiences, one much more effective and way more fun than the other. Frequently, I hurried through life, often missing the joy of what was right in front of me. Golf was a great opportunity for me to recognize and let go of this pattern of rushing everything and not appreciating it. If I hurried my golf swing, the rhythm was missing, I was missing, and my ball could easily end up missing. Golfing on autopilot didn't work. I had to be there. Similar to my hospital experience when I was dealing with the pain, I had to include, and allow, with no resisting.

The process was very similar with golf only quicker and more obvious. When I was expansive and inclusive during my swing, I felt relaxed and could focus easily. I was in the zone of the moment accepting whatever was happening around me without resistance. Noise didn't bother me, nor did people. When my attention was lost in thought, I was easily distracted, worrying about EVERYTHING and blaming. Swinging the club from this viewpoint felt contracted and small. It had an edgy, tense feeling and it wasn't fun. In contrast, I loved the expansive feeling. As I became more familiar with the contracted feeling it became useful, like a red flag signaling that I was trapped in my head, and not just on the golf course.

The most evident pattern revealed to me that afternoon was how much of my attention was occupied with what my Dad and others were thinking of me. I got distracted from my focus and my goal, repeatedly wondering if someone was noticing me, criticizing me, or admiring me. I'd had no idea that my appetite for another's energy was so huge. My scan for potential attention, before even hitting a ball, was fast as lightening, very automatic. I caught myself wanting to perform for anyone who might be watching. There were times my mind tried to seduce me by sneaking in a, "They're looking at you," and my focus would quickly search for human bodies. Hello egomania! I had to share that one with Dad and we laughed for the next two holes as I continued to report the dialogue from the committee in my head and the "not I" inside me that had an obvious ambition to be famous. I described how I was unconsciously monitoring golfers on the surrounding holes to see if they were stopping to watch me hit the ball. Dad and I were laughing so hard a few times he had tears rolling down his cheeks. We had great fun making fun of me.

It was hilarious and also true. I had been overly concerned with what other people felt or believed about me my whole life and desperately wanted to be special. This was simply another belief structure I looked forward to getting more honest about and unraveling.

I discovered one other archetype that afternoon, a slippery one. When I hit the ball poorly, particularly in front of people, I tried to turn my "care button" to the off position, pretending as though it didn't matter to me at all. That way I could act as though I was in control and had messed up (sort of) on purpose. I would announce loudly that it really didn't matter to me where the ball went and that was why I failed. But that was a lie. It did matter. The bottom line of my discovery was yet another level of, "If I didn't let something matter, nobody could touch me." The problem with that strategy was it meant holding those feelings inside. Ouch.

With golf I was the only one responsible for where I found myself... all day long. Whether in a ditch, under water, lost in my head, worrying about what someone thought of me, not feeling good enough or stuck in a pout, I had put myself there and had to admit it so I could begin to undo it. I had to be responsible for every single thing I put my attention on and experienced, moment after moment, or suffer the results. It was challenging, frustrating, enlightening, and funny. It was discouraging at times realizing how immature I still was. Becoming aware of my costumes was humbling. It inspired me to go further, become more real in my daily life, and learn to love myself instead of always wanting others to do it.

I caught myself trying to blame anything outside of me, more than a few times that day. It was instantaneous and laughable. I didn't know that was so ingrained in me. Anything handy was the perfect culprit for my bad shot, the poor maintenance of the golf course, a noise from a fellow golfer, a buzz from a bug, an airplane, a divot, Dad staring at me, or some innocent soul blowing their nose. I cracked up watching how my mind would search for a reason to justify a bad swing so I could avoid full responsibility. It was awesome to catch this because if you had asked me, I would have confidently stated that I was not a blamer, ever! My blaming was happening so fast that afternoon I had almost missed it. I appreciated seeing myself more clearly.

The quality of my golf game, very much like the equanimity of my life, had very little to do with what other people thought of me, unless I let it. I was the one deciding where my attention went, which left me solely responsible for how I experienced life. Period! It was a fun lesson!

> *Golf is a game that is played on a five-inch course—the distance between your ears.*
>
> –Bobby Jones

What I loved most about golf that first day was learning to let the game and the time I spent playing it be all about me. It was a self-ish experience. It was a very big deal to allow two hours completely for me, regarding me, and filled with me. Not because I was sick or broken, or because I had worked really hard or suffered to earn it, but because I decided to. I think Dad knew this would be helpful for me when it came to creating the rest of my life from a more self-honoring place. He was right.

As I golfed over the next year it became a welcome mirror and offered great insights. The game revealed many an urge to pretend, avoid, or deny. It was all there inside me and I got to know myself in a way I hadn't. Realizing how every shot and every experience was a result of my thoughts, habits, and motivations was very honest and empowering. The more I golfed and became self-aware, the clearer the distinction between living from my Higher Self and operating out of ego became. When the feeling of connection and presence mixed with golf, nature, and friendship, it was pure grace on the greens and I was frequently overcome with appreciation. When my ego was running the moment, I was self-absorbed, judgmental, and disconnected from nature. Golf helped me create the peaceful mind that comes with understanding that there would always be further to go, more to learn about kindness, honor, and taking full responsibility. No matter how well I managed my mind on one hole, the next one could be a total spinout. Just like life! Golf helped me to learn patience and appreciate the process, recognizing that life was never "perfect" for very long. Allowing the peaks and valleys of golf was an enormously valuable skill for creating a harmonious life.

I loved the challenge to become totally present, forever exploring what that meant. Sometimes my ego would puff up with a good golf shot as much as it would get perturbed with a bad one. My ego loved to make a big deal out of anything it could get a hold of. Sometimes I would get angry that I'd made a mistake and watch my reaction multiply the original mess. It was a grand discovery to realize how ridiculous it was to think I shouldn't screw up. Many of my faces showed up on game day!

One day I caught myself wanting to make sure everyone I played with was okay, as though peace on the golf course was my new job. There was some conflict in the air with the gals I'd been playing with and I let it get to me. It took over my game and I got tangled up in wanting my fellow players to realize how precious they were and simply get along. That day, I couldn't golf worth beans. It irritated me that others couldn't just be happy and play the game without judgment. So I judged them for judging. I got all caught up in that drama and forgot about my own joy for the entire four and a half hours. Hello! Another great mirror of my life! I couldn't play golf or handle my own reality while obsessed with fixing someone else's. I felt the depth of the pattern that day and how it filtered my perception of humanity in so many areas of my existence. I got a glimpse of the intense pain I personally had associated with saving people, saving the planet, and making everything peaceful and good as though I knew what was best for others. My focus was always on what was wrong when this "not I" was at the helm. I had worked on the issue so much over the years that I was surprised by its power over me that particular day. It was painful how lost I'd gotten in wanting everyone to be happy. It triggered a familiar pattern, like an old movie from my past, and I felt afraid that I would lose what mattered most to me if my friends weren't happy.

I had an insight once I got home. I realized that the best thing I could have done for the whole group would be to feel my own joy, be present in my own game, and stay connected to my Highest Self. I realized that keeping my own vibration higher would have been more powerful than anything I could have said. Taking care of my own attention felt like an honest way of respecting another person's experience, even if what they were going through appeared to be difficult. Particularly, since I had some very strong belief filters regarding it being my job to save any suffering human that crossed my path, as though world peace depended solely on me. Saving someone was an ego endeavor for me. Becoming honest about this helped me recognize deeper beliefs around pushing, shoving, and manipulating people to see my viewpoint (kindly, of course), as though mine was the best. At times, letting people experience their own struggles might be the kindest thing to do. Unless someone reaches for help, they may not want any. That day was a gift.

To Pat's chagrin, I found myself wanting to golf all the time. As far as I was concerned, it was the best self-help course on the planet because I was the teacher and the student, the blamer and the blame-ee, and it was all about me. It was the perfect setup for a control freak, with nobody telling me what to do except me, and nobody to point at but myself. I was hooked. Eighteen holes of getting honest was a good day's work toward becoming real. There was no denying a pattern or a feeling and I had to relax into the flow of learning and not knowing. I had to own and let go or things quickly worsened. The day always ended with more insight and some much-needed humor. Pat would have preferred me to have a real job, but I was set on my path of waking up… even if it meant golfing everyday!

Golf opened the door to guilt-free pleasure for me, something I had never experienced in my entire life. I always felt I had to work hard to be happy, struggle to deserve it, or at least suffer a little before I could have any time to myself. It never occurred to me that I could just experience pleasure or joy as a decision. On some level, I knew being happy was one of the most powerful ways to contribute to the world and my family, but I had never quite made it all the way there. I had to deal with mounds of guilt and feelings about it being selfish to want freedom. I had to pay for joy or sneak it in. God knows, being happy wasn't on my daily list of chores. Being joyful simply because I *could* had never occurred to me. I believed I had to get everything else done first and that was insane because everything is never done. Giving myself permission to enjoy being me and appreciate who I was no matter what I had, how I screwed up, or if I was totally healthy or not, changed my world. It affected every aspect of my life. Allowing happiness into my daily schedule, without some monumental achievement to warrant it, resulted in me encouraging others to do the same. Pat and the kids didn't know what to think of me. My new motto was, let the laundry go for a day, enjoy the delicacy of food, play hard, and love like there's no tomorrow.

I had a passion for asking others what they loved, what they treasured doing, and what brought them the most joy. I began asking myself this question daily and repeatedly discovered more about my dreams, the ones I had set aside to be successful. When asked this question people rarely had an answer. It required some consideration. Another's willingness to honestly contemplate his or her answer always felt incredible, and would lead to my next question, "What do you need to do next to get there?" It's a delightful experience to share company with those who are willing to give their attention to what they love and dream of.

It was quite a shift in my perspective to realize that I didn't have to suffer a certain amount before I was due some joy. Somehow I got wired up thinking that as long as one person suffered, we should all suffer, as though that was honorable and respectful of another human, when quite the opposite was true. I realized that bringing one drop of happiness to any relationship added to the overall joy available in the invisible realm that connected us all. Being happy was a great way to contribute to the world. It felt like love, honor, and truth. It became my responsibility to enjoy being human.

Dad had been clever about drawing me into a love affair with golf. He had used the game to teach me how to trust myself and learn that it was okay to care about my happiness as much as I did everyone else's. He knew golf would be food for my soul and provide me with a mirror that nobody had been able to hold in front of me before. I frequently caught him smiling in my direction when we played. We had so much fun together, laughing and pointing to what we discovered, playfully poking at each other every chance we had. He would always inspire me to stop and feel the beauty of the course we were on. He would whisper, "God lives here," and he would remind me that we needed to be present to meet Her.

A lot more happened out on the golf course than hitting a small ball into a hole.

The greatest gift that you could ever give to another is your own happiness, for when you are in a state of joy, happiness, or appreciation, you are fully connected to the stream of pure, positive Source Energy that is truly who you are. And when you are in that state of connection, anything or anyone that you are holding as your object of attention benefits from your attention.

–*Ask and It Is Given,* Esther and Jerry Hicks

Perspective IS Everything

chapter 17

If the doors of perception were cleansed, everything would appear to man as it is, infinite.

–William Blake

Travis and Drake were arguing one afternoon over how to do a trampoline flip, and my father stepped in to give us all a lesson on viewpoints. The disagreement got a little heated because the boys were certain they were right about the absolute best way to approach an airborne somersault. They had very different opinions on how to achieve the highest bounce possible. Dad pulled out a piece of paper from the notebook he was carrying and told the boys to follow him to the table. The boys continued their bickering all the way from the backyard into the kitchen where they found themselves huddled around Dad.

Dad drew a big star and had the boys help him color it in so they'd calm down enough to hear what he was about to say. All three of them chose different colors and sometimes scribbled together in the same leg of the star. It was a unique and colorful design for sure. Then Dad folded the star perfectly in half so both sides had the exact same geometric shape, albeit with different colors. He then had the boys stand and face each other, holding the folded paper between them so they both had a clear view of the same shape at the same time. He asked Travis, "What do you see?" Travis responded, "It looks like a ghost," and laughed. Dad asked Drake the same question and being four years younger with a great imagination he said, "A person singing with two arms and a head on top." Dad said, "I see, and which one of you is right?" They both said nothing for a moment. They were stumped. Dad continued by asking, "Which of you is certain that what you just named is what's here in my hand?" "Is this a person singing?" he asked as he pointed to Drake's view. "Is this really a ghost?" Who has the right answer?" The boys grew very quiet.

Dad invited them to switch places and look at the object from where the other had been standing. As soon as Drake went to the other side he giggled and said, "It isn't a ghost." Travis went to see Drake's singing person and scrunched up his nose trying to get it. He said, "I can see it a little, but not really." We all laughed and Dad asked again, "So who is right? Is there a singing person or not?" Trav said, "There is to Drake!" Then Dad asked, "And do you really see a ghost?" Travis slowly nodded his head yes, unsure. Dad continued, "Would you like to get in an argument and have a fight with Drake, make sure he knows he is wrong, that he isn't seeing somebody singing? Or Trav is it okay for Drake to see what Drake sees?" Trav was watching Dad curiously. He went on, "Would you like to spend your afternoon fighting and arguing to get him to see your ghost? You can do that if you want. It's your choice. But realize he may never see it exactly the way you see it." Smoke almost came out of Trav's ears he was thinking so hard.

Then Trav said, "I get it Grandpa. People see things differently." Dad patted him on the back, "Exactly! You two are looking at the same thing; it's a folded star, but you both see it differently. You see it through different eyes, nobody is wrong. So Trav, the question is, do you need him to see things the way you see them in order to get along? Are you the guy that knows the best way to get a high bounce, or are there others?" Travis laughed, totally getting it. Dad asked one more question, "What is the best way to do a flip on the trampoline? Trav answered, "However you want to, Grandpa." Dad hopped up and started dancing around the kitchen making a big deal of Travis's perfect answer and finished up by saying, "Drake may really see a way that is better to him and you may have an idea that is better to you. People get to have different ideas and see things differently and we can just let them. We can always share our viewpoint, but if a person doesn't like our opinion we don't need to fight with them over not agreeing." Then Drake said, "See Travis," like he knew this all along. We chuckled. Travis got it and Drake was glad to just go jump some more and didn't really care if anyone liked how he did it or not... and they lived happily ever after, at least for a while.

It all depends on how we look at things, and not how they are in themselves.

–Carl Jung

Dad and I started a conversation about attention and how easily it became stuck on certain viewpoints and tough to budge. Our opinions seemed like THE truth to each of us. It's all we can see. We defend it and protect it as though our life depends on it, but it's just an idea that our focus and energy got tangled up with along the way. Dad said, "Everybody's doing the same thing we are, with different and opposing ideas. Then the game ensues and we search for agreement for our belief, proof for our ideas, and disproof for those that oppose us. We read books about how right we are and find books about how wrong others are, and if it becomes something we think about all day long and half the night, we can do some disturbing things and end up really hurting each other or even taking someone's life, all over an idea of someone being right and someone being wrong." He was on a roll.

Dad continued, almost talking to himself, with that faraway look in his eyes, "Getting caught up in a viewpoint and not being able to feel, understand, or allow other viewpoints, is the cause of most arguments in relationships between siblings, families, and even countries. An inability to look for something we agree on is the cause of most divorces." He muttered, "That's what happened with your mom and me." He became real quiet for a minute before describing how they were stuck in different worlds, positional about what was true and who was right, and how they had neglected looking for what they both wanted, and what they both felt was important when it came to life, kids, and love. Softly he said, "People can have different opinions about how life should be lived and still get along. People don't have to agree with you in order for you to love them." I knew he was talking about Mom and Patricia.

Dad felt badly about hurting them. Through the years, they had both continued to keep him at arm's length. He could talk a blue streak about life and what mattered, but he wasn't very good at telling people he loved them or that he was sorry. Affection was not his specialty. This was a pattern passed down from his father, and we worked on these areas now and then over the years. Yes, he was better, but I could feel how there was more to let go of. I continually understood that we could always take more responsibility for our life situations, depending on our sphere of awareness. I planned on mentioning this to him next time we sat down to do some processing. Dad finished by saying, "We aren't our thoughts, we aren't our opinions, and we aren't what happens to us. We are much more than all of that."

As Dad spoke, I had an idea brewing about how to take his

"perspective application" into the boys' school. I imagined the inestimable value for all children if the lesson was presented in a fun, playful way. Maybe this new perspective on perspectives could help curb bullying, fighting, and relieve some of the suffering for victims of tragic situations, such as the Columbine High School shootings. Perhaps even prevent them from happening in the first place. Taking responsibility for a viewpoint could help people to understand and forgive, and hopefully, see a path to freedom from pain. I got very excited envisioning how, if used early enough in a child's education, this more tolerant approach could have a great and lasting impact on one's life.

An exercise was forming in my mind that would allow the kids to experience how everyone looked at things differently and that everyone was able to choose his or her own opinion. It borrowed a smidgen of everything I had learned over the past few years with Dad, plus some concepts from Harry Palmer's ReSurfacing® workbook, which Dad and I both treasured. I sketched out my plan and Dad was delighted. The following weeks we practiced and perfected the process with everyone who gave us the opportunity, including family, friends, potential Avatar students, and anyone who was struggling emotionally or needed a new perspective on life. When an opportunity came to use it in Travis's fifth-grade class, I was ready.

The previous day, there had been a devastating fire in our elementary school's neighborhood. Several homes were threatened, including ours and some had partially burned, with pets and farm animals in desperate need of rescuing. Sadly some livestock didn't make it. It was frightening and traumatic for many in the area. The children had witnessed or were involved in a great deal of the evacuation process. I got a call from a friend who told me the children were really struggling in school, emotionally, and had been unable to shake the fear or devastating images from their minds. I offered to work with the students in Travis's class in hopes of offering them some healing and relief.

Dad had a big golf game scheduled that day, so I went alone. I was a bit nervous but very excited. I loved working with children. It was my favorite consciousness to explore because they were so willing and open. Most were friends of Travis's and had worked with me before in art classes. I was very comfortable trusting that my connection in the moment would lead me toward what needed to happen. I didn't have to know everything, which was good, because I wasn't exactly sure how it would all come together. I believed that once I felt the kids' energy and focused their attention, my Higher Self would do the talking. I trusted that.

As I entered the school, I could feel a bundle of emotions swirling in the air. There was an unsettled, fretful energy that hung in the hallways and painted the faces of those I passed as I made my way to the classroom. The fire had been unnerving for the whole community. I invited Trav's teacher to include any students or instructors from other classrooms that she felt could use a little encouragement—the room was full.

I calmly walked to the front of the class and dove in, asking everyone to put his or her attention on me, on my words, and to focus the very best they could on what I was about to say. I paced back and forth playfully and even ducked and pointed out any student's whose eyes I had lost, as I explained how important it was not to miss a single word. They laughed. I told them we were going to do something very special, something they had never done before. I explained how it would allow them to feel however they chose to feel. I repeated, "Today you will learn how to feel the way you decide to feel, if you pay attention." I asked them *if* that sounded like something they would enjoy and they bellowed a cheer in unison.

I assured them, there was just one very important thing they needed to do to make this work for them: for the next few minutes, stay with me, and keep their attention on what I said, and not get distracted. I encouraged them to do their very best, and not waver from listening. Immediately, I noticed a couple of kids who were daydreaming and less present. It was a perfect opportunity to gently acknowledge their absence, inviting them to feel what it felt like to not be present with me as I spoke, but to be somewhere else. They understood and instantly became more aware of what I was saying. I asked them to notice what had taken their attention, what it had strayed to that seemed more important, so they could catch themselves if it happened again. I noticed that the entire room was taking note. I then asked the two children if they wanted to set their distraction aside for the next few minutes and be with me instead, explaining how deciding to do that would really help them accomplish their goal. They committed to it and both took more control of their minds.

As I continued, I explained how they would know if their minds had wandered off again: they might find themselves thinking about lunch or someone they thought was cute, or what they were going to do after school. They all chuckled. "If you catch yourself doing this, come back and focus on what is happening in the room so you can learn this magic trick of becoming the one in charge of the feelings you have." I told them they were going to like what they were about to experience, but they had to rely on their willpower to stay present with me in order to open the gift they were about to receive. I asked everyone if they could commit to doing that. Of course, since they were excited to escape math class and do something strange and fun, there was a loud and spunky, "Yeah!" I teased them again by asking if they'd like to decide how they were going to feel at home, with friends, and in life. In concert, they all said, "Yes!"

I then made another point and asked the kids to describe what paying attention felt like. I went around the room and had each student describe their personal experience out loud so everyone could witness a variety of viewpoints and come to understand that people truly paid attention in different ways. The answers included phrases such as, "It's when I sit up straight and listen," "It's when I don't play with my pencils," "When I totally focus," "and When I decide to look and listen." One child said, "It works best when others are quiet so I can hear everything," and one of my favorites, "It's when I give all of myself to something."

I expressed how they had all answered perfectly because there are a variety of ways to pay attention and it was very useful for each person to recognize what worked best for them. "Everybody's answer is right and nobody's is wrong." They liked that!

I continued, "I have an object in this room that you have never seen, touched, smelled, felt, heard, or have had one ounce of attention on. Not in your WHOLE life. Could you describe it to me, tell me about it, and while you're at it, tell me how you feel about it?" They looked at me in disbelief, very confused. One gal asked me what in the world I was talking about.

I asked again, "You mean just because you haven't seen it and you've never put one bit of attention on it, it doesn't exist for you?" Another gal blurted out, "How can it be real, we don't even know what you are talking about? We have never looked at it." "So," I asked, "if you can't see this thing and haven't ever seen it, is it real for you?"

They answered a very adamant, "NO!"

I then asked if they would like to see how to make something real, if they would like to make something exist that had never existed for them before! I repeated it another way so they would get it, "Do you want to know how to make something real in your life that isn't real yet?" They nodded slowly, totally engrossed and curious to see how that could be possible.

I said, "Alright, you have to follow my directions." They agreed. I told them I was going to give five minutes for them to describe an object. (I'd brought a very unique art piece and had it tucked away). I repeated, "Only five minutes, so be on your toes!" I explained how I would walk around the room and show them the object and invite them to try and find some detail that nobody else in the room had found. I inspired them by suggesting there were several hard-to-find characteristics. I asked them to say the details out loud so everyone could hear each discovery and to keep looking because rarely did anyone find them all. (I used a precious object that Drake had made for me. It had many unusual aspects, and resembled a vase, a face, an airplane, and some even said they saw a palm tree. It was made of papier-mâché, with wing-type structures on top with reds, yellows, greens, mixed and matched, sequins and pearls glued randomly, and nearly indecipherable lettering painted into all the colors; "mom" was scribbled on the side and people rarely discovered it). The group was very alert and determined, and the energy in the room was electric. I asked, "Are you ready?" I pulled the object out of the bag and started the timer.

They identified almost every detail and as each child spoke, I repeated what they had said to make sure everyone's attention would be included in the findings. Every person in that room was intently focused on the object. Thirty-five sets of eyes followed it as I held it up, moving between the rows of desks of the large room. Even the teachers got involved and focused their attention on the strange object, looking for something that the kids might have missed, forgetting for a minute they were teachers. It was fun for all of us and everyone was determined to find every single detail!

Our five minutes were up and I hid the art piece back in the bag. I turned to the group and asked them to close their eyes and see if they could find any impression of the object in their minds. They all nodded or yelled, "Yes!" Then I invited them to keep their eyes closed and focus on the visual impression and say, out loud, what specific detail stood out the most for them. They had a variety of answers including, the eyes, the volcano (that was a new one), the leaves, the yellow, the word mom, the pearl, and the glass bottle that could be used as a vase. The teachers were totally involved as well, and I treasured the experience, knowing it would offer each instructor a new viewpoint for teaching as well.

Next, I had everyone open their eyes. I scanned the room asking students how long they thought they could keep recalling the object. I asked if they believed they'd remember it in six months, a year, or five years. They all said they thought they'd remember it for quite a while. One girl promised she would remember it for the rest of her life. I jumped at the opportunity and asked her how she could do that. How she was able to make something that had not existed for her at all, not one bit, into something so real that she would remember it for the rest of her life? Then I turned the question to the room, asking all of them how they were able to make an object real when it hadn't existed for them just five minutes before!

They said things like, "I looked at," "I talked about it," "I examined it," "I described it," and then finally Eric, one of the boys in the back of the room whom I adored said, "We put our attention on it!" I danced a little jig, "You got it!" They all laughed.

I then raised a very important question derived from Harry Palmer's *Techniques for Exploring Consciousness Workbook, ReSurfacing.* "Where does your attention come from guys?" They looked at each other confused and then one girl reported that it came from her mind, and another said, "My eyes, my head." Someone else yelled out, "My heart."

"So it comes from you?" I asked. They all agreed without any doubt. I invited them to explore, "Who decides where your attention goes?" A little uncertain they glanced around at each other and, finally, in many different ways replied, "We do?" I pushed a bit, "What if the teacher tells you to put your attention on the chalkboard and you do what she says, who decided to put your attention there?" Some answered, "The teacher," and some felt it was them that had chosen. I asked, "Have any of you ever pretended like you were putting your attention on the chalkboard but really you were thinking about something else? Who decided where to put your attention?" They giggled knowingly. I continued, "You could be thinking about where you are going after school, or what you brought for lunch, and all the while looking right at the teacher acting like you are doing what you were told." They laughed again. "So really, honestly, who is always in charge of where you put your attention?" They all answered, "Me!" I reaffirmed how they decided all day, every day, what they were going to focus on. You know what? They got it! They liked the idea that they were in charge!

I repeated, "So you guys put your attention on something for five minutes and made it real for a very long time. Some of you made it real for the rest of your life." I added slowly, really wanting them to get a sense of the control they have over their experience of life. "If your attention comes from you, like you say it does, and if you are the one that decides what your attention focuses on," I looked deeply into their eyes and paused to make sure each student was with me, "do you see how in charge you are of what you make real? You are powerful! You put your attention on something for five minutes and it goes into your world for the next year… or maybe forever?

"Your attention is important stuff! You make things real with it. Wow! That is pure power!" I encouraged. You could have heard a pin drop.

"I wonder what you all are making real in your life with your attention." I stayed quiet for a minute and let them ponder the question before I continued, "You may be putting a lot of attention on certain ideas that make you feel unhappy or bad. Imagine putting a bunch of your focus on not being smart enough, cute enough, tall enough, or good enough." I smiled at a short boy in the front row. "I wonder what happens when you put five minutes of attention on sad or scary things in your life, how real you make them, and how it affects what you are feeling." Then I asked the kids if they would like to find out. The teachers were very quiet. I could tell they were realizing how their attention was creating their own worlds. They were beginning to comprehend the power of their focused (or unfocused) energy. Once the five-minute phenomenon had been experienced, people could quickly spot the areas where they had fixed their attention and how it affected their experiences of life. The teachers were a step ahead of the children.

Now we were ready to address the fire. I asked the children if they had anything that had been getting the bulk of their attention lately, something they couldn't stop thinking about. There were a couple of answers, such as homework, my dog, and lunch, before one student exclaimed, "The fire!" They whole room agreed. I said, "Perfect! Let's explore the fire."

I wrote "FIRE" in the center of a large circle on the chalkboard and made lines around it like rays of the sun. I asked the kids to start giving me beliefs, opinions, or feelings (on one level, all the same thing) that they had about the fire, so I could write them around the circle. They offered, "I was upset…" "My family totally freaked out…" "I cried and felt angry…" "It was bad…" "I couldn't sleep…" "I got sick and threw up…" "I thought it was exciting…" This last positive statement came from the back of the room, and everyone's head turned. The student defended himself by explaining that he got to be in charge of a hose and help water down his friend's house with his dad. He'd had fun doing it and he was very close to the danger. It was interesting how this notion changed the energy in the room as the other kids considered the prospect of a fire being fun.

As I finished writing down the last thought on the circle, I asked the students to consider which viewpoint was most true. We had about ten opinions on the board. As I went around the room and each student expressed what felt true, they began to see that what was true to them was the same idea on which they'd placed most of their attention. They started to understand how every person had made their own idea more real by focusing their attention on it. One girl interjected, "For a lot longer than five minutes!" It became increasingly apparent that everyone had a particular viewpoint of what was true about the fire, which also revealed that there was no absolute truth about any of it. It was more a choice than a fact. A few of the boys had heroic and positive experiences with the fire, so it offered a great contrast for us to experience the event. One child even spoke up about the benefits of fire and how it created new growth in the soil. It was amazing to feel everyone expand and include more than just his or her viewpoint.

I explained that sad things happen, and that pain is real and needs to be felt. But, when they are tired of feeling the pain and ready to feel something different, they can select a viewpoint that they'd enjoy making more real. I repeated, "You guys decide where your attention goes!" I asked if they would like to change where they were putting their attention regarding the fire. I told them they could decide which viewpoint they preferred and that being sad was definitely one of those choices. I gave them a few moments to choose whatever they wanted to focus on and manifest and suggested they write it on a piece of paper.

People see only what they are prepared to see.

–Ralph Waldo Emerson

One child, being funny and sassy, announced that he would be keeping his attention on the idea that we are all doomed and there was no hope. He was the prankster of the class and I loved that he said that. I used the opportunity to invite the kids to explore the possibility that people will choose a viewpoint like that in life, and really prefer it. I further explained how some people choose to suffer for a while. I asked if they knew someone like this. Many raised their hands. It was awesome how almost all of them recognized that suffering could be a choice. Then I asked if someone they knew was choosing that viewpoint to experience life through, would it be okay with them? Being somewhat of an expert on resisting people's pain, I think I was trying to save them from many years of hurting unnecessarily. They thought about it for a moment before one student answered wisely, "Everyone gets to decide how they are going to experience the fire and their life!" I wished someone had taught me that as a young girl. I was deeply touched by her wisdom.

We then encouraged the boy who wanted to experience the doom, to go home and announce to his parents that he had deliberately decided to suffer a tad more over the fire and to please just let him do it! This was his choice and he liked it that way! The kids all laughed! The little guy loved the idea of being able to feel doomed if he chose to! I think he genuinely enjoyed knowing he had the power to decide and be in control. Using a contrasting and seemingly absurd viewpoint had provided him with the means to feel in charge while also attracting a lot of attention. I couldn't blame him for that! We all love attention and learning how to attract it in a healthy way can be a process.

I invited everyone to share his or her new viewpoints out loud. It was amazing. As the students expressed them, one by one, I could feel a wave of comfort move through the room. I threw out the question, "If you put more than five minutes of attention on your new perspectives what do you think will happen?" By then, this was old news. They responded in several different ways that what they focused on would become what they *felt*. Everyone's attention in the room started moving toward *possibility* and realizing they had a choice in the matter. It was a profound experience. Then I wrote a viewpoint on the board that I'm rather fond of, **"everything works out fine!"** I drew a line from the word "fire" to the new viewpoint and asked them if they had any idea how I could make that perspective more real. They answered with certainty, "I have to put more attention on it." To drive the point home I asked, "How?" They answered brilliantly with suggestions such as, talk about the good parts, nobody's house burnt down, nobody died, we are all alive, our families are alive, and one child said to quit thinking bad things and to think good things, and then make a list of solutions.

Each time someone spoke I circled the phrase "everything works out fine" to make it more pronounced than the other viewpoints around the circle. The phrase ended up with a thick line around it from all the circling and I pointed to it, "This is your attention. Every time you put more of it on an idea, it becomes more real, more obvious, and bigger." I then drew a star around the phrase and invited everyone to feel what it was like when that perspective was the one they chose in life. The energy in the room had dramatically transformed into a wave of calm and trust and it moved through each of us. We felt the difference immediately, like a truth had just settled in and it was coming from our hearts. Maybe it was everyone's decision to simply be happy that had filled the space.

I nudged them a tad more by erasing the word "fire" from the circle and writing the word "school." Then I said, "Look and see what you keep putting your attention on regarding school." They laughed out loud and made sarcastic comments about not liking it, not being good at it, not wanting to do homework, and that school takes up their whole life. Then I walked toward one shy child in the back who hadn't participated much and seemed a little separate and alone. I asked him, "What is your opinion about school?" He answered timidly, "I don't know, I don't like it." He exuded discomfort. It was hard for him to answer or connect with me. He was nervous and embarrassed.

I gently asked him how much attention he had put on "not liking school" over the last couple of years and he said, "A lot." I asked him what he thought it might feel like to move some attention over to an idea such as, "I am smart," or "I am a good person." He looked up at me puppy-eyed and said, "Good!" I offered, "You know, you could do that whenever you want to feel something a little differently, it's up to you."

He looked at me so sweetly. I knew he had some pain locked up in his body. I felt it. Then I said, "I have a cool idea. Would you like to hear it?" He nodded yes. I knelt down by his side, "Write a feeling you would like to make more real about school on a piece of paper. Keep it by your bed. Before you go to sleep at night focus on what you want. Imagine what it would feel like to totally believe it, in your mind see a picture of you experiencing school that way. Imagine living like that, while talking, having lunch, and hanging out with friends. Use your imagination! You know what I mean?" He laughed. "Put more attention on the idea every time you see the paper by your bed.

You could write it on a notebook or something so you also see the word a lot during the day. Every time you see the word, let it remind you that you get to decide what you put your attention on and make more real! *You* are the boss of your focus of attention!

At the end of seven days, I bet it's pretty neat." He smiled up at me and I felt all the attention in the room on us. I invited him to close his eyes and see if the object was still there that he had described earlier and he nodded "yes." I urged him, "See if you can make it go away." He cocked his head to the side as though surprised and opened his eyes and said, "No." I encouraged, "See how powerful you are at making something real. You did that!" I touched his shoulder and gave it a squeeze making sure he felt my care. Then I finished up, "I know putting your attention on what you want to feel will work for you. It worked for me. You can make the feeling you want real just like you did the object. It just takes practice. Don't give up. Do it forever!" I winked at him, assuring him that he got it.

Everyone felt the moment between us; he and I were intensely connected, they couldn't avoid experiencing it. My hope was that these children would realize how cruel making fun of someone or excluding someone could be and how attention of this nature affected whomever it was focused on. I turned to all the students and added, "You might want to make a note of what you would like to make more real about school, or about certain people, or about your life. The more attention you put on what you don't like, guess what? The more you're going to make it real and experience it." I reminded them yet again, "*You* get to have the feeling you want; it's up to you where you focus!"

Then I erased the word "school" and wrote the word "YOU" boldly in the middle of the circle, which was still surrounded by many negative beliefs so it had a strong visual impact and their eyes opened wide in recognition. "What do you think about when you look at yourself in the mirror? Do you put attention on the good things, do you see something wonderful about yourself, what a nice person you are, how you work really hard to make your moms, dads, and teachers happy? What do you see every day when you look in the mirror? Whatever it is, you are adding more attention to the idea. It will get bigger and more real each time you give it your energy. What would it be like if you did this for ten years? You only looked at the object for five minutes and you made it real for a very long time. What is going to happen if you put your attention on things you don't like about yourself every single day? What are you adding your energy to and making more real about your body?"

They were all silent and wide-eyed, including the group of teachers, which seemed to have grown in number. Nobody could answer. "You guys are the ones in charge of the experience you are having when you look in the mirror!" I glanced at the teachers and they were very present and soaking it up. I was so grateful that they could pass the information on to their students from that day forward, they could touch many young lives.

I assured everyone, "If you have been putting your attention on what you don't like about yourself, don't worry, you get to change your mind and correct the past. You can move your attention over to what you *do* like. Your attention will obey your instructions." Palpable relief rippled through the room and everyone relaxed. I wished I'd had forty-some mirrors to hand out so I could introduce each one of them to their new best friend.

One last time, I reminded the group, "You put your attention on that object for five minutes and made it real for five years or more. Only five minutes of your attention was needed to do that. What you make more real in your life is totally up to you. You get to decide!"

Then I summed it all up with one last question, "Who decides where your attention goes guys?" They all yelled, "We do!" I smiled, deeply adoring them, especially Travis, who looked at me with his knowing eyes. I gathered my things and began walking toward the door. As I waved goodbye, I turned and added, "You are some powerful dudes!"

I meant it, too. They had become wise little beings in a very short time.

> *When you do The Work, you see who you are by seeing who you think other people are. Eventually you come to see that everything outside you is a reflection of your own thinking. You are the storyteller, the projector of all stories, and the world is the projected image of your thoughts.*
>
> *Since the beginning of time, people have been trying to change the world so they can be happy. This hasn't ever worked, because it approaches the problem backward. What The Work gives us is a way to change the projector—mind—rather than the projected. It's like when there's a piece of lint on a projector's lens. We think there's a flaw on the screen, and we try to change this person and that person, whomever the flaw appears to be on next. But it's futile to try to change the projected images. Once we realize where the lint is, we can clear the lens itself. This is the end of suffering, and the beginning of a little joy in paradise.*
>
> –*Loving What Is,* Byron Katie

SELF-ish

chapter 18

The most valuable skill or talent that you could ever develop is that of directing your thoughts toward what you want—to be adept at quickly evaluating all situations and then quickly coming to the conclusion of what you most want—and then giving your undivided attention to that. There is a tremendous skill in deliberately directing your own thoughts that will yield results that cannot be compared with results that mere action can provide.

–*Abraham* by Esther and Jerry Hicks

Dad and I were nearing the end of delivering a weeklong Avatar Course when a pretty strange and wonderful interlude occurred. It was guided by the invisible.

I was startled from a deep sleep. It was early, pitch-black outside and I felt a 5:00 A.M. nudge to head over to our course site. We'd been holding the class in the backyard of Dr. Battiglino, one of the students and a dear friend of Dad's. The students arrived each morning by 9:00 A.M., and Dad and I had an agreement to meet by 8:15 to get organized and create our intention for the day.

I conducted my morning routine quietly, so I wouldn't wake the family. I ate, stretched, took vitamins, made lunches, and left Pat a good morning note with a request to please take care of my parenting duties. By 6:30 A.M. I was making my way to the course, surrounded by a sunrise that was one of the most spectacular I had ever seen in my life. Multiple shades of orange and red painted the clouds scattered across a vast blue sky that hung over the Sierras. It was breathtaking. I was very glad to be alive and in the presence of such magnificence. I was feeling so grateful and connected, delighting in my life and being able to spend the day with my father as we delivered the Avatar tools to the people we treasured. It was heaven. The setting was sweet and the students adored having Dad as a teacher—something we all had in common!

It was a short drive, and minutes later, I was carefully making my way to the backyard so as not to wake anyone. Our chairs and class supplies sat on the porch, and I gently grabbed a seat and made my way to a spot that allowed me to view the mountains and sky clearly. I was eager to just sit and feel, quiet my mind, and breathe in the stillness of the majestic morning. I was exactly where I was supposed to be. It was grace. God was everywhere. It was my time. It was a SELF–ish time.

Less than ten minutes passed before I heard Dad's car pull into the driveway, and I smiled inwardly, somehow knowing that he would be here early, too. On some level, it was a planned meeting and I realized that was why I was there. I had learned to listen to my intuition. When I receive a nudge like that I know something important is coming. I was very grateful I got the "memo." Dad walked around the corner, saw me sitting there, and grabbed a chair without missing a beat. He moved swiftly through the large field that served as a common area and set his chair squarely facing mine, not speaking. I watched as he pulled his seat so close our knees were almost touching.

The background was a beautiful open field surrounded by gallant pine trees and grandfather oaks. We sat facing one another, both framed by a changing sky. Although we looked into each other's eyes, we didn't speak. We didn't need to. I felt an urgency in Dad, along with a soft humility. The being in front of me was not like I had seen before.

I waited and watched. His heart was open and it was pouring down his face. He timidly pulled a little piece of paper, all crumpled, from his pocket. He was emotional and unable to speak. I held the space for him and I wasn't alone; we were embraced by the Nameless. The hum, the feeling, the openness, and the presence permeated that entire field. The trees were gods and the sky was the music. I was still. I appreciated and honored him to a degree that words cannot convey. I trusted everything that was happening. Somehow, in some part of me, I understood what was coming. He calmed down and we both took a long, deep breath and then exhaled slowly; he let a small laugh escape and I smiled. He gathered himself and whispered, "I was given these last night." He opened his tiny note and pointed to seven scribbled phrases. They looked as though he'd written them in the dark or half asleep and I couldn't tell what it said, but I could feel how precious these jottings were to him. I stayed very present and connected and he was barely able to utter his plea, "I need you to be totally present with me while I manifest a new way of being. It has to be this morning. It has to be now."

To act in an independent manner, you must begin to initiate action that you want to occur physically by creating it in your own being. This is done by combining belief, emotion and imagination, and forming them into a mental picture of the desired physical result.

–*Seth Speaks,* Jane Roberts

Those scribblings held Dad's new world and he handled that tiny square of paper as though it was a holy scroll. It held the next life he was moving into and a farewell to the one he'd been living. He wanted me to experience with him what the words were pointing to. He felt it was crucial for me to be part of the process and was confident this was meant to be. He asked me to intend his new realities alongside him, to join him in experiencing them fully without reservation. Dad was counting on me to intuitively stay linked to him and help him focus, explaining how he needed every drop of his intention and attention to cooperate in order to claim his new life. While intently looking into my eyes my father said he trusted me to remind him who he really was beyond his body. It was a profound moment. I felt so blessed to be there for my father and I whispered, "This is my pleasure Dad." There was a crisp clarity in the air, the kind you feel when you sense an important agreement being solidified or satisfied. The sound of awareness hummed unmistakably in my ears and as my eyes met Dad's there was a merging of our beings that was not of this world. The ocean of energy that connects all things expanded, bonded, and embraced us. Something was opening in our consciousness.

As Dad stated the first phrase out loud, "I have all my attention particles," he became pure experience, with no mind, and his ability to merge with his Highest Self and actually *be* his intention was profound. We both were amazed at how the feeling of his words reverberated through our beings and beyond—without the interference of a mind busily analyzing, interpreting, or judging. He looked at me, startled by the solidity of the reality on only his first attempt to experience the scribbled words. He said them out loud again, "I have all my attention particles" and rolled it around in his consciousness like the first taste of spectacular gourmet food. There wasn't one ounce of resistance present in him. As he began to feel the reality of possessing all of his attention particles, he smiled, deeply enjoying this new level of ownership. He seemed to puff up as though the attention particles that had been dispersed and left behind over the course of his lifetime had now returned to him, to their rightful birthplace. We were both enchanted by the sensations.

Feeling very satisfied he spoke the next phrase, "I am a free being at Source." Immediately, it felt as though he'd expanded and become huger than life. Those words had so much intention and power in them that they almost knocked me out of my chair. It was astounding how the energy was buzzing. Then in seconds, he was back, focused and in his body again, smaller somehow. It was wild. He played with the sensations that the words pointed to repeating them several times until he'd felt them completely. I listened without judgment as he continued discovering, acknowledging, and releasing attention that had been stuck in areas of his body for a very long time. Some of the obstacles he dealt with were about being trapped in a body, a broken one. He accepted them, felt them with ease, and then sent them on their way. He smiled. I remained silent.

His next phrase flowed out softly, barely audible, "My sense of being the total creator of my reality is complete," and tears began to trickle down his face. His awareness remained strong and steady. I felt his new reality with all my heart. He owned it as his, and I was mesmerized by his presence and state of being. I didn't pay as much attention to the words he was speaking as the feelings they birthed. There was such a sweetness moving through me from his intentions, they enveloped both of us. He was so real and aware the best words to describe him are total, complete, knowing, accepting, allowing, and humble.

Dad continued to the next scribbled phrase, "I have integrated all creation." It was smooth and natural, like he was speaking about what he'd just eaten for breakfast. It was unmistakably his new truth, there was no doubt in him. For a second he seemed to merge with the space around us and his face blurred, as though he'd lost his definition. Maybe it was me who was blurring. The space we were in seemed unearthly. I stared at him trying to focus as he said the sentence again, "I have integrated all creation." He felt it so deeply that we both broke out laughing, giddy and drunk with awareness.

He became one with each phrase, in ease and willingness, opening, connecting, and trusting as an awakened human consciousness. He effortlessly merged his intention with the full potential of each word he spoke. Magic was happening, the kind that you only read about or see in movies. His words were wings taking him to places I hadn't imagined possible while still in a body. We both felt the realities come into being, and the truth of what each one pointed to, filled the space between us. The invisible and the visible were merging right in front of my eyes.

When he spoke the next statement, "I manage all my identities lovingly," there was a feeling of trust, forgiveness, wisdom, and honor for Self and all humans as though he had understood the charade and adored the perfection of all its players. Each statement flowed in divine order, adding to the richness of the energy surrounding us. The cumulative result was growing larger than either of us could comprehend during the interaction since we were focused on the individual intentions. Something amazing was happening. As he spoke the next phrase, "I am able to change my interpretation of reality instantly," the wind blew through as though the Sacred with No Name had answered him. He chuckled and repeated, "I am able to change my interpretation of reality instantly! I can make it mean anything I want to." I felt how sure he was. I loved experiencing him so happy, so free, and inclusive. The totality of the being in front of me was so much larger than the physical body sitting before me. So much more than the person I had called my father and come to know as my companion.

I still couldn't see what was written on the crunched-up paper in his hands. Each statement was a surprise and when he expressed the final one, "I have a great life full of satisfaction and accomplishment," I became uncomfortable and a weird feeling zigzagged through my entire body. The humming sound changed in my ears to an alarming pitch and the silence surrounding Dad and I became intensely alert and penetrating. He was watching me curiously, more so than paying attention to his own words. I tried to shake it off and stay present for him but I got a little lost in some kind of weirdness, almost a restructuring of reality. It was as though someone had removed a concrete block from the bottom row of a wall and now all the other blocks had loosened and were falling to a new place. Something wasn't fitting right and I was pretty certain it was in me, not him.

Dad watched what was happening to me, and in retrospect, he knew I couldn't quite let that statement into my soul. He left that for me to deal with and understand on my own, not allowing much interruption in his intention. It took me a few minutes to shift my focus back to him and off of myself. He repeated the statement. "I have a great life full of satisfaction and accomplishment." A strange look came to his face, almost a grin of understanding as though he got the message the words were meant to give him. He allowed himself a moment to absorb the experience, owning the words and what they pointed to. He seemed to fill with what I will call affection… for himself, his life, and the body sitting in front of me. It was the strongest sensation of self-love, forgiveness, and appreciation I had ever witnessed. I felt him bathing in gratitude for his life, his entire life. He was fully satisfied… with everything.

As you read the words upon this page, you realize that the information that you are receiving is not an attribute of the letters of the words themselves. The printed line does not contain information. It transmits information. Where is the information that is being transmitted then, if it is not upon the page?

–*Seth Speaks,* Jane Roberts

Dad's list was complete and so was he. With moist cheeks and a vast awareness, he stood up and turned away from me as though I was no longer there. He seemed shaken on an earthly level but deeply settled in an angelic way. We both felt the energy of his new world. It was a completion, a letting go of identity, and an opening of his heart that satisfied his soul.

Dad turned and looked into my eyes, yet spoke more to himself than to me, sharing how when he received the message to create the realities, the words he whispered into the darkness were, "Divine God Of My Being Come Forth." He explained how the words had came *through* him rather than from him. When Dad repeated them softly, "Divine God Of My Being Come Forth," a chill danced up my spine. His intention and energy felt clear, tapped into the invisible, and enormous. He turned to me and with a faraway voice said, "I am going to go for a little walk." He needed to integrate what had occurred and regain his footing. We had a class to teach.

The students began to arrive in perfect harmony, and I got the morning program started while Dad merged with the unspoken. From that day on, he was different.

The word enlightenment conjures up the idea of some superhuman accomplishment, and the ego likes to keep it that way, but it is simply your natural state of felt oneness with Being. It is a state of connectedness with something immeasurable and indestructible, something that, almost paradoxically, is essentially you and yet is much greater than you. It is finding your true nature beyond name and form.

–*The Power of Now: A Guide to Spiritual Enlightenment*
Eckhart Tolle

Going Home

chapter 19

Death is a friend of ours; and he that is not ready to entertain him is not at home.

–Sir Francis Bacon

It had all the markings of a great day. Dad was playing catch with Travis in the front yard, Grandma was keeping the boys for the weekend, and Pat and I were packing our bags for an all-expenses-paid weekend at Lake Tahoe. As we loaded up the car, Dad asked me if I had a minute to follow him back to my office. He was a bit shaky and his voice cracked as he spoke. I immediately turned to follow him into the house even though Pat was in a hurry to start our trip, and waiting for me. Something was up and I probed Dad with my invisible feelers as he walked in front of me. He dashed into the small room tucked away from the noise and clamors of a busy household and pointed to a briefcase sitting on my desk. He said without turning, "If anything happens to me, be sure to find this." He opened it slowly and pulled out a file. He went on to say, "There is a signed check in here you can use to empty out my bank account. Split the money with your sisters. There are some papers in here you will need." He avoided looking at me as he spoke so I leaned forward to look up at him, wrestling to get his eyes to meet mine. He wouldn't let me in. While continuing to look down at the case, still avoiding my eyes, he reached into his pocket and handed me a cassette tape. "I recorded some of my favorite poems for you, Holly," he said softly.

Time stopped. I tried to feel him and get a sense of his intention. The moment was very important and real to Dad. His energy was deliberate and certain, like he had witnessed what was coming and, in some span of time, it was already done and these were just the details. He wouldn't connect with me, not completely. When he finally did, I understood.

The second he dropped his guard and let me in, I knew he was leaving me. It was like someone removed my spine and my body couldn't stay upright. I leaned on the desk and our eyes locked. I was upset, almost angry, and he knew I knew. That was what he needed to happen. We both stood in the reality of death, not sure what to do with it. Five seconds, no more, and my world was reconfiguring around what dad had done and said in those two minutes. I desperately wanted to erase them and forget everything that had just happened. The interaction was undeniable, the way all communications are when truth is present. Dad was leaving. Resistance was futile, arguing that his death was a ridiculous notion, and even asking why was pointless. I did it all anyway. I hated that I had just experienced that clarity and I stubbornly dropped into a mind fully armed to convince, persuade, and pretend it wasn't true, that he wasn't going to die. For those next few moments, denial was my dearest friend, or so I thought.

I said, "I don't need this cassette, I have you." He looked at me with pure love and said nothing. My mind hurried with another attempt to brush the whole thing under a rug and get it away from me as fast as possible, like it was poison. I got bossy and shook my finger at him saying, "We have another course coming up and you can't leave until we are done, you have students coming!" I knew this was nearly the most important thing in his world, teaching and helping people to wake up, so naturally, I used it. He attempted a smile and compassionately watched me push against his certainty with every aspect of argument I could muster. "Please don't leave me now, not yet." I pleaded. He looked down, tucked his chin and exhaled long and slow as though he wished he didn't have to hurt me but he was going to do it anyway. I looked him deeply in the eyes and told him I loved him dearly. He looked right into my soul and said, "I know."

We both felt the depth of our connection and the honor that came with it. It was sacred and old as though we had been together for more than just this one lifetime. We were companions empowering each other through this space and time, posing as father and daughter. Who we really were included a knowing that came from the invisible world and an identity-less-ness that encased all we had ever been. From the viewpoint of an abused child and an alcoholic father, our relationship was a miracle. It had always been exactly as it was meant to be from the perspective of a Higher Self exploring and learning about existence as a human. One thing was clear to both of us… a promise had been kept between us, regardless of when he decided to make his exit.

On some level I was certain I would see Dad when Pat and I returned from our short excursion. I wanted to believe we could remove this crazy idea from his head with a little alignment and processing. I believed I had time. I refused to comprehend that he could leave when he decided to. It didn't make sense that he could die in the next three days. Dad was the happiest I had ever known him and his life was filled with faith and an uncanny ability to create whatever he wanted. I reasoned... *why would he leave now when life is so good, when we're so close?* He was enjoying his grandkids, he was in love with life, did only what he wanted to do, and was playing the best golf he'd ever played. He had a dream life! *There,* I convinced myself, *there was no way Dad would give up so much joy.*

I talked myself into believing my mind's story over my heart's knowing at about the same time that Pat had honked the horn and yelled for me to hurry up. I hugged my dad extra long, and held him tight. Authoritatively, I told him I would see him in three days and to just hang on so we could fix things. In the moment I turned to leave, I saw sadness in my father's eyes. As though I could fix it, I encouragingly added, "I know exactly what process we can use to get that crazy idea out of your head."

In that moment, enough of me believed Dad would be there when I returned to get myself into the car. I turned to walk out the front door and then something made me spin around and look back at Dad before losing the line of sight that connected us. He was standing still, staring at me. Our eyes locked. It was love looking at love. He felt soft and vulnerable like a child, yet wise, full, and rich with awareness. It was the last time I would ever see my father in a body. Forever I will treasure the kindness I saw on his face. In retrospect, whenever I relive that moment, I could see in his eyes that he wasn't going to be there when I got back. I didn't want to acknowledge it then. I couldn't. I didn't know how.

I wasn't meant to be there when he left, or I would have been.

The next day on the sixth hole of a beautiful golf course by Lake Tahoe, around 1:45 P.M., I heard my dad's voice. Maybe a better description would be, I *felt* his voice. I was aware of him being close and the coolest thing happened—he was telling me which golf club to use! Not by outright numbers. It was more like I was being intuitively directed. I would reach for a club and for no reason at all grab a different one on all three shots to the sixth green. Pat wore a confused look as I putted in for a par on a very difficult hole. "It's him," I told Pat. "My dad is here telling me what to do." He laughed, "I believe you. You can't play this well!"

I knew Dad had a high skill level when it came to putting his attention where he wanted it, allowing no distractions. I believed he was so powerful that he was able to communicate with me somehow and assist me with my game. I was playing lights out. I can assure you I was not a good golfer and really didn't know how to play smart. My practice on the driving range and the few rounds I played was mostly to hang out with my father and learn from him. Scoring well was never my goal. I played more as a tool for improving my ability to manage my attention rather than fulfilling any notion of winning. But that day, I played better than anyone in our foursome and there were a couple of decent golfers, far better than me. It was strange. Dad hung around for the completion of the round, popping in and out of my awareness. I didn't think it was too unusual; over the years, he had visited me that way from time to time. Now and then, he would flash into my attention and I would feel a nudge. One big difference that afternoon is that he hung around longer and was more vividly present than any previous visit. I could feel him move in and out of my attention. Sometimes it was almost an interruption. It was potent.

Pat had been given a suite on the twelfth floor of Harvey's Hotel and Casino with a spectacular view of Lake Tahoe. Our room was like an apartment. Upon entering after golf, Pat quickly dashed to the back bedroom to retrieve the phone messages and handle some work that was pressing on him. I stood by the window mesmerized by the blue sky topping the dust of snow sprinkled on the peaks of the Sierras. I was enthralled with the cobalt blue of the lake. Pat came back hurriedly and told me, "Call Harry, some kind of emergency!" He spun around and stared at me weirdly. I hadn't budged from gazing out the window. Harry was my father's very best friend and I loved him like a second dad. They had studied, meditated, and walked the path from student to teacher, side by side for many years, a pair to be sure. They had attended a variety of courses together and examined any possible path to enlightenment. They really were community saints, forever helping people, holding meditations and meetings for Q&As with intentions to assist everyone in awaking and becoming the Source of their lives. I turned to Pat and said, "My Dad died today." My experience on the golf course fell into place and made complete sense. Pat stopped in his tracks, and then walked toward me, "Don't be crazy, call Harry." He had a fire to extinguish and needed to make some calls and disappeared into the other room.

Afraid of my own certainty, I sat on the edge of the bed and closed my eyes to see if I could feel Dad. The second I did, he was right there. He came into the room with such a gust of energy that I found it hard to breathe for a minute. There was swirling electricity moving all around me, refusing to be still. I tried to follow it and couldn't, it was too quick. I immediately got angry with him and said out loud, "Why did you do this?

I can't believe you did this! What am I going to do?" I tried to take a big breath and it was not easy. It was as though there wasn't enough oxygen in the room, like the air was thin and something was pressing on my chest. I had to keep turning my head to follow the dancing energy. There were visible small lights twinkling together in comet fashion, flowing and turning quickly much like the angels I had seen in the hospital. I didn't have one shred of doubt that it was Dad. I wished it wasn't, but I knew it was. He came close to my body and the nearer he got, the harder it was for me to breathe. He seemed to know this and had to keep a little distance from me, so we could talk or connect or whatever you want to call it. He told me, not in words, but in some kind of intuitive way, that death was amazing, incredible, and phenomenal, and that he was ecstatic.

Dad had so much joy in him he couldn't contain it. I don't know if he told me or if I just sensed him feeling it, but it was permeating the entire room and probably beyond. It was hard to know the difference between what he was saying and what he was feeling; it was all one expression. He moved the joy as near to me as he could, or maybe he was the joy. It was a very high vibration, one that a human body can't easily hold. It seemed as though he wanted to get the joy as close to me as my physical form could tolerate. My body didn't know what to do with it. It affected me physically and threw me off balance. It was foreign, highly electric, and buzzing. Joy is the best word I can use to describe the energy, but it was also too much joy, if that makes sense. He was in total delight and was determined for me to experience it with him. I did the best I could to allow and embrace it. He was relentless about me understanding and feeling it. It was Dad in his heaven and as soon as I got the message and accepted the truth of it, he seemed to calm down.

Dad transmitted the idea that he was finally home and had been hungry for that experience for a long, long time. I became very sad, caved into myself and crawled up onto the bed in a fetal position to hold myself. I was confused, sad, and feeling selfish. My heart was panging hard in my chest. I wanted to be happy for Dad but all I could think of was myself. Out loud I said, "Dad, who's going to love me as much as you?" I started imagining my life without him. He was the one person I could count on to be committed to awakening as much as me. I relied on him to remind me who I really was whenever I forgot and to nudge me whenever I became lost in costume. I melted into a pool of self-pity, my awareness shrinking into my own density, identity, and body. I bounced from one bad thought to another in a downward spiral.

Suddenly, I realized that I was alone and could no longer feel Dad in the room. I became aware of how selfish and self-absorbed I was being and startled myself with the thought that this could be the last time I'd ever get to be with Dad. I struggled to stop my whining and the negative self-talk so I could move my attention and awareness back into the room, and away from my mind. I needed to relax. I sucked in a deep breath and focused outward with my awareness expanding and searching for some feeling again of Dad, and then there he was, smaller and less electric, less obvious, but he was there. I asked him to come back. I asked him to stay… forever, or at least for a while. He immediately moved closer as though waiting for my invitation. He didn't promise anything. I became aware of how he was moving some wave of goodness and love toward me. I tried to open and receive it with my breath but didn't know how. I wanted to be with him, connect with him, and tell him how much I loved him. There was so much happiness in Dad's space that, for me, it was devastating.

I desperately wanted Dad to assure me he would always be there and that I could find him anytime I wanted. I wanted him to promise me he would never be far away. I intuitively sensed that he knew how badly I wanted that, but he couldn't promise anything. Somehow I knew that too. He would be there for a while. He was here now, and that was what I had.

I scooted back to lean against the headboard and peered up, trying to stay present and not miss any part of connecting with him. I had a few seconds where I felt genuinely happy for him because it was impossible not to, as he flitted around the room. Still, when his energy came close to my physical body, it actually hurt and felt uncomfortable. That was peculiar and I noticed that it happened every single time. I thought perhaps a human body was too dense to house such a high frequency. He was so free and alive, and I could only imagine where he was able to travel that I wasn't. Dad finally kept his distance and we were together quietly for a few moments. I flowed in and out of waves of sadness and he comforted me more by sending his love than his words. I think he was doing something to help me because I could feel him busy and it seemed to have something to do with me. I began integrating and letting the idea of his death sink in deeper and deeper. I stopped resisting and began to allow it all to wash through me. I freely wept.

I believed that Dad and I would stay connected even after one of us had dropped our body. I believed this about my sister Patricia, too. It had been our agreement, our pact since forever. The three of us had said it out loud a few times to one another to ensure we were all in alignment. Here it was and it was true. I was dealing with my feelings, going in and out of the emotions of abandonment, but Dad had kept his part of the agreement.

For a minute, I got a glimpse of myself as though looking through Dad's eyes. I was sitting their pouting about not dying first and the whole scene woke me up. It was surreal like I was watching a play or a movie. For a second I remembered and felt how my body wasn't all of me and that this was all going to work out okay. A cry-sob-laugh sound flew out of my mouth and I felt Dad move close, encouraging me in the direction of becoming more aware and widening my view of what was happening. It was challenging. I had so many feelings moving through me and I kept getting snagged in them. I wondered if he knew everything I was thinking and feeling. I wondered how transparent I was to him. Most of all, I wondered how much longer I had him. I wondered if my inability to connect with him was inhibiting his process in some way. I concluded that he obviously knew whatever I was thinking because he kept instantly responding to it.

Pat walked in and Dad quickly retreated to the left corner of the ceiling and I whispered, "Dad is here, can you feel him?" Pat stopped, looked up as though tuning into his receiver, and even remained still for a minute before turning back and saying, "No" to me. It was strange; the moment I told Pat about my father, it seemed as though Dad had left the room as though he knew it was time for him to go. I couldn't sense Dad anywhere. Pat looked at me in a way that said, *you are a little nutty Holly,* and then asked, "Did you call?" I was shaking and a bit fragile and Pat felt it; he sat down on the bed, put his arm around me and asked if I was okay. When Pat had walked in, oozing of work mode, it reminded me of the world of form... sisters, briefcases, the boys, and what arrangements needed to be made. I thought about taking care of Dad's body, helping the boys deal with their pain, and contacting my father's many dear friends. I felt a mountain of sorrow overpower me as I realized that we'd all have to move forward without my Dad.

These were two very different worlds, the invisible and visible. I was in a hotel, sitting on a bed with my husband holding me while my father danced around the invisible in ecstasy. I was still in a body and needed to deal with my reality. As much as I didn't want to, I moved toward the phone and dialed Harry Holman's number. Pat sat with me and waited.

As soon as Harry's wife, Mary, picked up the phone she gasped, "Oh my God, Holly, I am so sorry." Between tears she blurted out that Dad had died about 1:30 P.M. on the twelfth hole of Rosewood Lakes while golfing with her husband, his dearest friend, Harry, and two other buddies.

He hit the straightest, greatest drive ever hit by a human, the way it was told. It had to be all of 360 yards, according to his friends. I think the drive gained footage with each telling. Heartbroken, Harry shared what ended up being a life changing experience for him... "Your Dad started walking down the fairway after he'd hit his spectacular drive. I drove toward my own ball in the cart we were sharing. For some reason I turned to look back at Howie just in time to see him slowly sit down on the grass as though to take a rest. I turned the cart immediately to go to him. I knew something was wrong. Then I watched him about 50 yards in front of me gently lay all the way back onto the ground placing his head on the earth as though falling onto a soft pillow. It was in slow motion. Then, he tilted his chin upward like he wanted to take in the blue sky one last time… then he was gone." Harry said he jumped out of the moving cart and ran to Dad's body. Then climbed onto his big frame to try and revive him by pushing and banging on his chest. He said he was hoping he could somehow make Dad come back to his body. He relived it as he told the story, softly repeating, "Don't leave me, don't leave me. But your Dad had already taken flight. I knew when I got there he was gone. His face was peaceful and he seemed so… so… complete. I yelled at him several times for leaving me. I was supposed to go first." His voice trailed off. I listened and quietly wept, appreciating his friendship with my father as I felt the treasure they were to each other.

Later something peculiar came to light… Dad had been on that exact same course a week earlier with the same group of guys he'd played with every Wednesday for years. Harry never showed up, which was very unusual. Dad quit playing that day and didn't finish his round, which was something he never did! He announced to the guys before leaving, "Something doesn't feel right." Dad left on the tee of the twelfth hole. The exact same place he died on the following Wednesday.

I believe part of the reason Dad held off his departure was so Harry could be present. I also have a feeling that when Dad approached the tee he had an intuitive understanding or glimpse of what was coming and realized he had some details to settle and organize.

As Harry witnessed Dad leaving his body, something happened between the two of them that can't be explained. They were connected so deeply and energetically that Dad's transition assisted Harry with his own personal transformation in inexplicable ways. From my viewpoint, Harry became more himself and more connected to the Divine as he courageously dove into the energy Dad invited him toward as he transitioned. The unconditional love Harry had always shared seemed to take on a new vibration from this point forward. Holding my father in his arms while his spirit merged with the miraculous was not a small thing for Harry.

Dad couldn't have picked a better person to be with as he departed. Harry held more compassion in his heart for humanity than anyone I knew, and he especially treasured my dad. He adored him as though they'd spent several precious lifetimes together. Harry always had a strong connection to the invisible and I imagine he summoned all of his angel friends to meet Dad that afternoon on the golf course. I'm very thankful they were together and that Harry was the one holding my father as he met the larger part of himself. Harry always seemed to feel and appreciate the magic of death in ways most of us don't know how to. Although upset with Dad for dying first, Harry was the one person in the world Dad had always counted on to be there for him, no matter what. I believe it was perfection and my dad was held in the arms of grace.

As a healed adult, I'd had an amazing three years and eleven months with my dad, Howard Wayne Goss, before he left Earth. We were able to release our anger and blame, and heal a father-daughter past that many abusers and victims would die with. Our time together was a blessing guided by our commitment to know our Selves beyond the game of life. It led to a deep understanding, which some might call the power of forgiveness. For a long time, that's what I called it. When you know you are not your body, your identities, your mistakes, or your treasures, and that you're actually connected to all things, forgiveness isn't the goal of existence—it's the result. Understanding replaces blame. There's a unity and flow that inspires the becoming of all things and when it is seen, felt, and/or embraced, inner peace ensues and there isn't anything left to forgive. We were eventually able to trust the process of our relationship and life. Dad and I became allies in our search for what mattered and explored many questions together. If we were blocked or stuck, we did our best to empower one another toward trusting our Highest Selves, above all else. My dad and I became dear friends and he helped me to realize that I mattered. He inspired me to create my dreams.

My father studied his whole life to find the truth of existence. It was more important to him than family or money, and even life itself. All his studies had brought him to know one thing: the answers were inside him, not in a book, a class, or from someone else's lips. The treasure came from knowing him SELF and being him SELF. My father was one of the happiest people I knew. He did what he loved every day. He didn't do anything that wasn't in alignment with his heart. Dad experienced life, he felt it, enjoyed it, didn't judge it (much), and celebrated all its parts. He knew that *he* wasn't the things he owned or his successes and failures, and that managing his mind and learning to trust Higher Self held the only key to his soul's truth. Dad knew that being a great teacher, having good health, creating honest relationships, and being a provocative artist, an excellent golfer, or anything else he dreamed of, always depended on his ability to place his attention where he chose to. He had fun experimenting with this ability in every waking hour. He wasn't an expert at anything and didn't claim to be. He had a ball testing reality and discovering just how capable he was of manifesting his dreams. Dad looked for limitations just so he could remove them.

Dad understood how easy it was to get trapped in the distraction of something shiny, and avoid any feeling by using alcohol or medication. Being able to will himself through obstacles and go further was what lit up his path to freedom. He was playful with problems and appreciated the contrast dilemma offered. He knew any upset was merely a signal he was distracted off his mark and a reminder that he needed to reach more determinedly for his dreams. His difficulties were his directors, a present of sorts because they gave him an opportunity to become more responsible and seek a different direction. Turbulence was the catalyst to dad's joy. Each mountain he moved brought him more toward himself. He never gave up on having the life experience he intuitively knew was possible by living in integrity with SELF and following his own heart. He fully believed the Nameless always led him to the perfect place for awakening, so he listened to the whispers. Dad never lived his life by what someone else believed was important.

Dad loved painting outside the lines and showing others that the lines they were trying to stay inside of were self-created. I believe Dad would consider his life a success, mostly because he learned to love, be forgiven, and helped me to live instead of die. He might not say so but I will: *I think his most remarkable achievement was forgiving himself and trusting the process of life... and ultimately death.*

Dad was profoundly grateful for the Avatar tools and for being able to call Harry Palmer his friend. Harry had provided a methodology that brought all of my father's life studies home. Harry's exercises on managing attention were a treasure to Dad, one that he worked very hard to share with anyone within talking distance. During my short time with

Dad, he taught with a healed heart, committed to people recognizing how powerful and precious they truly were. He was the best teacher I ever had. But the most difficult lesson he taught me, by far, came with his death.

Look not in the direction of woe
for it will surely come
So let thy days be full with joy of the heart
for all is but a little while
and then we depart—

To come again
another where

–Howard Goss

Alone

chapter 20

> *Aloneness simply means completeness. You are whole; there is no need of anybody else to complete you. So try to find out your innermost center, where you are always alone, have always been alone. In life, in death—wherever you are you will be alone. But it is so full—it is not empty; it is so full and so complete and so overflowing with all the juices of life, with all the beauties and benedictions of existence that once you have tasted your aloneness the pain in the heart will disappear. Instead, a new rhythm of tremendous sweetness, peace, joy, bliss, will be there.*
>
> –Osho

I made the arrangements for Dad's cremation and requested they complete it as soon as possible, wanting to get this part of death—done. The crematorium said they could schedule it right away and take care of everything as soon as his body arrived, which was scheduled for that afternoon. A short time later, I received a call explaining that Dad had arrived but the oven malfunctioned and wouldn't be fixed for three full days. It turns out that with Dad being involved in the order of the Masonic Temple, he wasn't supposed to be cremated before seventy-two hours had passed. The belief had to do with a spirit needing time to complete its connection (or rather, dis-connection) with the body before it could be burned and the consensus was it took three full days. So Harry Holman and I figured that Dad had something to do with the oven breaking. There were rumors of Dad hanging around and tampering with things, such as moving a book, closing a door, and a photo of Dad falling off Harry's shelf with nobody near it while Harry was sitting across the room thinking about him. There were also quite a few reports of Dad visiting friends in their dreams. He had some very close companions that loved him dearly who had similar belief systems regarding the invisible so the reports didn't surprise me. The first few weeks after his death, Dad sure got around! He had visited so many people that they started calling them "Howie sightings." I received messages on my phone almost daily with reports as far away as Hawaii that

Dad had appeared to someone and seemed quite happy.

The first couple of weeks following his death, Dad visited me often. I would be cooking, writing, or whatever, and get this sudden sense of him, unsolicited, and I knew that he was close. He also showed up in my dreams, frequently. Usually offering me some kind of instruction on how to become more responsible for my own experiences, he was relentless in his effort to assist me in enjoying life.

In one dream, which spoke volumes to me, Dad took my hand and guided me to a line of people standing shoulder to shoulder and facing us as we approached them. There were about fifty people lined up, beginning with the elderly on our left and gradually the younger ones to the right until it ended with small children around four or five years old. Starting with the elderly, Dad had me stand very close to each body, face-to-face, eye-to-eye, instructing me to feel them, experience them, and genuinely love them. As I practiced doing that, he revealed to me the colors and quality of my energy as it moved toward the people before me. I could see that whenever the energy looked sparse and thin, it contained some kind of judgment on my part and it was almost a burden for the receiver to be around and painful to accept. But when I could truly love whoever was in front of me, they'd light up and we'd both match vibrations. Dad wanted me to flow love and appreciation to each soul from my entire being, and not just from my head. At first, I stunk at it. He patiently stood by my side as we moved from person to person, coaching me on how to be more pure and present with each new human. He helped me to get familiar with what love felt like without judgment, saying, "Connect with the being inside, feel their essence and how it is the same as yours." Many had strange and wonderful physical characteristics that challenged me. Some were disfigured, crippled, and hurting badly and pushed all my saving-and-helping buttons. The crazy thing was that whenever I responded with pity or a need to save them, my energy would stop flowing outward and instead move inward. My sympathetic response drained them. It was amazing and so obvious how judgment prevented any flow of love and only added density and heaviness to the space for all of us.

In the dream, I realized that when my focus was on a person's exterior or their circumstances, I was unable to appreciate the being before me. I had practiced on the entire lineup without measurable success until nearing the end, when I approached a young blond girl, maybe five years old. She was scared and lonely, and as I faced her, either I shrunk or she grew because we ended up face-to-face. As I looked into her eyes I felt tremendous care and affection. I easily merged with her spirit. I became her, feeling her preciousness and awareness from both inside and outside. The light from the energy of our connection was blinding, awesome, fulfilling, and pure. It was unconditional love and my heart flooded with an overwhelming feeling of appreciation that enveloped us both. The feeling was much like what I had experienced while lying in Christ's hands. In the dream, after I connected with the little girl, Dad turned to me with the most amazing smile on his face, "Now you got it, that's it, that's how to love."

I am fairly certain the girl in the dream was me but I didn't know it until I woke up. I interpreted it to mean many things, including that I had to appreciate myself in order to truly love anyone else and it worked best if I could love with the trusting heart of a child.

In my dream, the practice of flowing love to others had filled my soul at the same time it filled theirs. Being critical toward someone also filled both our souls, except with the dense energy of judgment. It was another lesson. Dad used to say, "You won't get sick again if you master self-respect and honor." I practiced feeling kindly toward myself, wanting to comprehend what honoring one's own being felt like in daily human activity. Before the dream, I felt I comprehended how to sincerely care about others and myself, but upon awakening, I realized there was a level of appreciation and honor that I'd had no knowledge of. No words can explain the feeling of responsibility in my heart once I became aware of the affect that my thoughts had on energy. I was more determined than ever to offer something kind to others and myself. I believe the feeling that Dad wanted me to experience was how everyone was equally precious in our world—and the same on the inside. Everyone was a source being, connected to all that is, larger than their body, exploring and experiencing different ways of being human. The dream revealed how distorted my connections to people were because of my opinions of the containers they wore and how frequently my attention got stuck on mistakes or stories and had missed the essence of the content.

I wished Dad was here to talk to. I was happy for him to be free and for all his friends being able to connect with him and feel comforted by him, for a little while at least. I started getting a bit jealous after hearing of all the visits and conversations others were having with Dad, especially when he'd visit them more often than me.

The celebration of dad's life was beautiful, friend filled, and oh so precious. People spoke their hearts, told stories, and several even read poetry they had written for him. The love that was flowing between everyone was all encompassing. Mom, Patricia, and Debbie decided not to attend and felt satisfied with where they were in relationship to him. The boys sat with Pat and me during the gathering, watchful, feeling, and seeking understanding. They were hurting but allowing the pain and adjusting to the reality of dad being gone, as we all were. Travis and Drake kept me going over the next couple of weeks. Their resilience and presence was healing to both Pat and I. I would often catch myself lingering in the preciousness of their sweet faces while longing for them to never feel pain like I was feeling. They were taking off for a week of church camp and I was going to miss them enormously. It ended up, however, being good timing because they wouldn't witness what was coming next.

The day the boys had left, I crawled into bed and dropped into an endless pit of sorrow and self-pity. I sat home all day, alone, wallowing in a myriad of negative emotions, and not feeling them but resisting them. I was angry that Dad left. I grew more and more agitated with all the reports flying in from people seeing Dad. I wanted him here, across the table from me. I sulked, didn't eat, and focused on the void in my heart, making it worse.

Since my stay in the hospital, with the exception of the month dad was traveling, we had been together a few times a week, if not every day. Doing everything I loved, exploring consciousness, teaching, golfing, and figuring out how to be who we were meant to be. Now, I had nobody to do that with, and I felt so alone. Dad had been my closest confidant besides my husband, and Pat wasn't much into dissecting consciousness. He was into living and tasting all the delights of life, and a master of enjoying being human. Dad and I loved learning how energy worked and how attention created experiences. Pat put up with me yammering about consciousness all the time because he loved me and knew how important it was to me. I drove him crazy with all my studying, processing, and deciphering things, and forever pushing him to get involved. He'd ask, "Why can't you be a normal wife, and just live a happy life without questioning and processing everything?" We would laugh yet again at the idea of a normal anything and, of course, I would ask him what his definition of normal was and he would roll his eyes knowing he was in for another lecture if he answered that one because there was no such thing. So I didn't bother Pat too much with my discoveries. I saved that for Dad. I convinced myself there was nobody to play "life" with anymore since

Dad was gone. I was lonely and quickly became depressed with no plans to get out of bed.

I could have gotten myself out of the hole I had dug. I knew all the right things to process, the right actions to take to help integrate the loss and sadness I was buried in but I didn't want to do any of them. I was hurting and didn't feel like budging from the pain. I settled deeper into it. I started sinking into feelings of abandonment and resentment mostly because I wanted to. A small part of me watched as old patterns began to take over my mind. I became angry, blaming, and mean, and I professed I didn't care. A very ornery part of me was enjoying being a brat. So it was no surprise that within two days of this, my colon began acting up.

Even though on some level of awareness, I knew I was hurting myself, getting sick provided me with the ammunition for blaming some source outside myself (like an external punishing God) for the mess of feelings I was having. I wanted to hold someone responsible for Dad's death, my illness, and the horrific pain I was avoiding. A part of me watched how intently and stubbornly I wanted someone else to be responsible for my world right then. I did *not* want to be in charge of my life anymore. I wallowed in victimhood. Within a few short days of my withdrawal into density, unexpressed feelings, and denial, I started bleeding intestinally. The power of unreleased emotions stored in my body astounded me. My colon was my measuring stick, my denial meter, and I couldn't get away with avoiding ANYTHING for too long without it bloody screaming!

I knew that I better be careful and not push myself to the edge or I'd end up in the hospital again. I could feel how close I was to making that happen, and it wouldn't have taken much more effort. Truthfully, I almost wanted to see how far I could go and what would occur next. Part of me was directing my own movie and wasn't quite sure how I wanted the last scene to play out. I was pissed off and pushing against reality, getting angrier the more time I let pass without expressing and owning the feelings that weighed heavily on my heart. Right then, dying didn't sound so bad.

The piece of me that was watching myself enact the drama was the part that was awake and would never go back to sleep. I tried to shut it off and couldn't. Seriously, I tried to pretend that I wasn't creating my own situation, but I couldn't fully do it. It was almost humorous watching myself pout because I no longer could trick myself into being a total victim. There was no way I could deny the fact that my body was responding to how I was handling my own attention and energy. I couldn't

UN-know what I knew. I realized it was very much like learning how to ride a bike and not being able to unlearn that either. Knowing how to ride a bike is part of me now, and it's the same with knowing I am Source of my life. Once I get it, feel it, and live it, it's in me forever. I couldn't drink it away, medicate it away, or pretend it wasn't there. This Truth was in the background of every thought, deed, and experience I was having lying in that bed. I knew that getting sick was an obstinate way for me to sulk, a stupid one, but I was set on doing it. Part of me wanted to be free like Dad. Another part of me knew that deliberately holding onto negative emotion lacked integrity with my heart. So, it was a standoff.

I wasn't sure what to do about myself, so I waited for an answer to be revealed, hoping my intuition had a very loud and inspiring voice so I would hear and follow it through the white noise of my clamoring mind. I crawled back into bed, headstrong, barely eating, with horrific pain in my gut, and trying my best to reek of victimhood. I waited for my Higher Self to show up (sort of).

The symptoms of Crohn's disease came on fast and hard and I knew I better make a decision to be healthy or I was in for a long road of suffering. That sounds easy, but it wasn't. I was angry. I reverted to an old pattern and thought by getting sick I could somehow change things by punishing Dad, God, and everyone I loved. I did this by simply giving up. But there was only one person I was punishing.

Pat was the most clear and steadfast I had ever seen him. He knew intuitively what I was doing. After a few days, he walked into the bedroom with an energy that got my attention! That afternoon, when I told him I was on the edge of needing to go to the hospital, he didn't offer me one drop of sympathy. He told me I had better take a look at everything—my husband and sons, the rest of my family and friends, and the wonderful life we had together. He said I had better make up my mind about what I was going to do, live or die. He reminded me that I was Source of my experience and that I knew *exactly* what I was doing, pointing out that I could take responsibility for what I was creating and get back in the driver's seat of my life. He said I had better stop being angry about Dad dying, that everyone's going to die, and I had no right to make it all about me. Pat had handled enough death to know exactly what was happening.

My husband warned me not to blame someone else for whatever I was experiencing because we both knew: I was the one manifesting it. My eyes widened and I was blown away by his clarity. He felt betrayed and was angry with me for being so selfish and I appreciated him telling me the truth. He was right on. Pat knew that my getting sick was more of a decision than a health problem and that the best way to support me was to say it like it was. If he were sympathetic at all, it would have validated my actions and added more attention to my self-made drama making it much worse, bigger, and more real. Sympathy merely added more mass and negative energy to victimhood and Pat knew it. He startled me with the truth and the second he walked out of the room I got more honest with myself. That's real friendship.

I wallowed less intensely for one more day, testing to see if Jesus, Buddha, or maybe Dad would come save me. Obviously, Pat wasn't going to do it, so I had to try and entice someone else. I wondered if that was my motivation all along, to be rescued. By that afternoon, when nobody showed up, I finally figured out once again that it was me I had been waiting for. Sitting up in bed I said, "Okay!" out loud, to nobody in particular. I knew I needed to get to work before I really screwed up my body with my orneriness.

So I began quieting my mind and opening my awareness, along with the drapes, to let some light into my dark cave and wash away the gloom. I had to in order to draw my attention away from the pinpoints of pain throughout my body as well as the sadness in my heart. I had to expand, feel, and become aware of my whole Self, my energy, my body, and my spirit, so I could capture an intuitive sense of where to begin to heal. I had to get honest and real about what I was doing. In stillness, I sat on the edge of the bed, intending for a feeling to show itself so I could work with it. I scanned my sphere of awareness, increasing my focus to include anything, everything—allowing, appreciating, and beginning to feel. I admitted and felt my stubbornness. The tension in my body began to dissipate almost immediately. I relaxed, deciding to surrender to my feelings, no matter what.

A wave of sensation emanated from my chest, beginning with sadness and then closely followed by anger, which, after just a moment of letting it be there, melted into a feeling of being completely alone. Without blame, I accepted that all of these feelings were my doing, my manifestations, and as soon as I admitted full ownership of them, the energy easily transformed and my space seemed to open and breathe. I became transparent to myself and the presence of honesty allowed a natural release of feeling after feeling. I opened my heart a bit more by trusting and appreciating my sense of who I was, separate from all the feelings and emotions flowing through me. I pondered briefly what I might prefer to create at this juncture of my life noticing the enormous contrast between manifesting dreams and waiting in unhappiness. The next wave of sensation rolled in gently and I became aware of a few viewpoints of anger and blame, along with some old feelings of being a victim. They hurt. I let misery exist. I stayed with it and rolled with it until it evaporated, then waved goodbye as the pain dispersed. It was easier than I expected because I surrendered and stopped blaming. I knew it was all *mine.*

I kept at it and worked through a few more sensations and found that nothing was too heavy or difficult. Then a feeling of wanting my own way regardless surged forth and as I explored and stayed present with it, a flavor of manipulation and using people was revealed to me. It was connected to a part of my past that I hadn't been willing to admit before. I flashed to a time when I had taken advantage of an old friend, in a very righteous way. I had lied and feeling threatened by her, had purposely shut her out of my life. I relived it all over again; only this time I was experiencing what had happened from her viewpoint as well. I selfishly wanted to hurt her and tried to get others to join me. Our friendship never recovered. I was unable to admit what I had done to her. I felt how devastated she must have been and how, until then, she had trusted me completely. I wished I could call her but when she was very young, she had been killed in a car crash. I wept. I emptied what seemed like a reservoir of pain from regret, loss, and loneliness.

Operating out of my need to control, I had hurt many people much like what I was doing to my family now by wanting to get sick. It all had a feeling of being <u>owed</u> something for all I had been through, as though I was entitled to special treatment because of all my suffering. This pattern held quite a few pockets of energy. I took a deep breath and was very determined to feel whatever was there. I wanted to be totally honest with myself about being manipulative in order to get my way. Immediately upon acknowledging what I had done to others the release began. The process was quick and seemed to flow relative to my honesty. I was so thankful to remember these ideas and sensations were all "not I's" and that I could correct myself, improve, and atone for all of it.

I lay quiet for a while, listening to the song of the birds outside my window. I felt remorseful but there was a peace that came with the awareness. It was time to grow up and take full responsibility for what I was adding to the world. I apologized to my friend, and the Sacred with No Name, and called Pat to apologize and thank him for loving me enough to tell the truth. I assured him I would be fine, admitting my selfishness. I promised my husband that I would make it up to him. He was grateful and relieved.

I reminded myself that I could do the work and keep waking up without Dad. I wrapped my arms around myself in a very loving way and felt what it was like to hold and care for me. It was a new experience. I sat like that for a long time moving through waves of appreciation and emotion. A shower of kindness washed through me. It filled me up and warmed my spirit and it wasn't from outside of me, it came from inside. Along with it came more trust in my ability to recognize whatever might be next for me. "Me," I said out loud, "I am the one that needs to know and decide from here on out."

I had a sense of how Dad leaving the planet was one final way he could empower me. Not that he died because of that, but it made it easier for him to leave knowing on an intuitive level that his loss would be good for me and for all of us who loved him, eventually. Leaving was his last nudge, moving me toward trusting myself and becoming more Source of my own reality. I had relied on his knowing. We discussed everything—thoughts, dreams, raising the kids, health, books, what and how to write, and what he thought I was meant to be when I grew up. I was attached to him being in my life and expected him to be there for a very long time. I held his viewpoint in high esteem, over my own. I never saw it as inhibiting; quite the contrary, but I could see a new world emerging. I felt different, more in charge, more responsible like it was time to step up and be more of me. Dad knew.

I had to love myself just like the little girl in the dream had shown me, not a small thing. I don't think there's any better medicine for dis-ease than that. Figuring out how to feel that way about myself through the process of living was my goal! Love's definition was constantly changing, too. For so long and in so many ways I had the feelings of love so mixed up with feelings of approval and being guided, believing that if someone told me what to do and helped me, then they must really care about me. No wonder I told everyone else what to do! It was also how I felt I could love them more and show them I truly care. What an eye opener!

I imagined life without that notion, and how freeing it would be to let go of the idea that someone outside me had an answer that would lead me to myself. I think I confused my Higher Self with outside guidance, like Dad or a great teacher had a better idea of what I needed than I did, and that they all had a more elevated Higher Self then mine. I laughed, seeing what I had done with my dad, cleverly making him responsible for much of what I was deciding in life. It was vividly clear again, yet another layer of the onion was making my eyes water.

Taking responsibility for everything, every feeling, every word, every thought, and every action was an amazing concept (one that continually included more of my reality). Feeling what that felt like tickled me. It was a moment. I had never experienced anything quite like it. I smiled and felt my connection to the holiness of becoming and whispered a happy "Thank you," to the Nameless. It lives in me as it lives in all of us, and I was reminded to trust that it comes as inner guidance and inner knowing, providing I was quiet long enough to listen.

I was beginning to trust that I would be fine without Dad and that, somehow, his leaving would settle in and open a new door. He was complete and had business elsewhere. That was my belief! He was ready to go and prepared well for it. Everything was in order, his mind, body, and spirit along with his money, car, and the few worldly belongings. Even his easel that he loved and had used since I was a young girl, along with all his paints, had been stolen a couple of weeks before he died. He never replaced them and Dad had painted every week of his life. It was a very sad day for him when his paint supplies all disappeared he felt he had lost his oldest friend. I think that was when he knew the Universe was calling him home and so he began readying himself.

Dad lived a meager life and achieved a state of happiness and acceptance that inspired many. He knew who he was and who he wasn't. He even died the way he always said would be best. I think he had it planned somehow. Dad was intimately connected to the Sacred with No Name.

The coroner asked if I wanted them to conduct an autopsy because they weren't sure how Dad had died. According to all the signs, the coroner said it wasn't a heart attack. I laughed to myself fairly sure that Dad's exit was more deliberate than accidental. He was able to expand out of his body and let go. He always said it was possible. Dad was a young man, only sixty-three. The previous few months before he died, we'd had several conversations about death. He said he would stay in touch and that we would meet again, reminding me more than once of his belief that we are not our bodies and that who we are never dies.

From early on I prayed for a God to save me, never comprehending that God was the flow of energy that was there all along to support me in saving *myself*. It was time to trust myself and stop looking for answers in others. I got it. I saw the long line of organizations, teachers, books, tapes, and people that I had counted on my entire life to tell me what was most important about my own existence. This started with my sisters at a very young age and extended to spiritual gurus. Dad never counted on anything outside of him for his truth and you could feel it whenever in his presence.

The week before Dad died, he and I were sitting at the kitchen table and I was pushing him to hang out for a bit and help me dismantle an issue *I thought he was having.* Key being an issue I thought he was having. I told him he wasn't committed to our upcoming class because he didn't have any students signing up. He just smiled at me. Dad never committed to very much of anything. Even when it came to attending holiday dinners he said he would know when he knew. People that hung out with dad understood this. To have him around at all was a delight, so whenever he showed up it was a welcome surprise. This was tough for me because I was one of those people (drill sergeants) that typically had a year planned in advance. Dad and planning didn't go together in the same sentence. It was comical how often I had pushed him to be like me, and how he would appreciate my problem, but never consider it his own.

Dad rarely agreed to do anything or go to any event that someone else structured unless he felt it came from his own intention. He wasn't a member of groups and never got swept up in anyone else's cause. His actions had to come from his own feeling, not someone else's idea of what needed to be done. When we were young and certain television commercials caught our attention, he would use them to demonstrate how often people wanted you to believe what they believed and would do anything to sell you their idea. A beautiful girl would recline on a car and Dad would say, "Do you think if you buy that car you'll look like her?" "Or if you smoke cigarettes, do you think you'll look sexy like the girl in the commercial and a man will want you because smoke is coming out of your mouth?" We would laugh, but he was serious. If anyone tried to convince him of an idea or belief, he would steer in the opposite direction explaining that if someone has to persuade you, they don't believe in it themselves. Dad investigated reality for him SELF. So there we were sitting at the table with me ready to guide him to freedom from his inability to commit with a process I had selected. I was terribly excited for him to handle this annoying issue because it would make my life so much easier. Unfortunately, he never even remotely considered it a problem. When I invited him to get started he laughed and announced, "I'm not resisting anything and there's nothing to fix," raising an eyebrow at me like maybe I was the one that had the issue. Then he added, "The students will be there, Holly." I argued with him, telling him he had to work harder at it, put his actions behind his words, and clear out any limiting beliefs. That was when Dad explained something to me that changed my world.

First of all, let me tell you, I was a processor. I was always investigating better ways, shortcuts, and techniques to dismantle issues and problems and get to the bottom of things in order to clean out the past. Dad would usually play along but his role amounted to him handing me the shovel. That afternoon, Dad reported he was all done processing. He explained that all he needed to do was experience fully whatever feeling came his way and that allowed any obstacle to dissolve. He said he didn't need to spend hours looking for *why* he was the way he was and that he didn't need to find out where anything came from. He said softly that he now understood all he needed to do was be present in the moment and the kingdom of heaven would meet him there. He said that whenever upsets or emotions showed up or came to his field of awareness, he would just experience them so fully that they had nowhere to go, but to transform. He firmly announced, "I am done processing." I remember the conversation clearly because it was uncomfortable for me to feel how certain and final Dad's conclusions were and how opposing they were to my own conclusions. (Not to mention the threat to my years of expertise in unraveling life's riddles!)

Since manifesting his new realities during the last course we'd taught together, Dad had been different and was speaking from a more inclusive view. He was wiser and more complete. Dad finished our conversation that day by saying, "Avatar is great, Holly, but something else will come along, it always does, and that's life." I didn't like what he'd said and argued with him. He laughed at my reaction, pointing it out to me. In retrospect, I think Dad knew he wasn't going to be around much longer and worried about me becoming a zealot again. He knew I had a habit of that. I suspect he felt that he should bring it up before he died since he might not be able to help me notice it later. Dad loved the Avatar materials; he just wanted me to understand that even the greatest of tools are merely pointers. He knew I had a tendency to worship whatever or whoever was doing the pointing.

As I recalled that conversation with Dad, I had a new impression of his meaning. I was different and healing was different. Letting go was easier for me than before. I allowed things to move through me more freely instead of trapping notions, feelings, ideas, or beliefs, in a mind desperate to understand. I wasn't excavating the way I had been my entire life. That afternoon in bed, I had healed my wounds by breathing in the feelings and then breathing them out. It was more *intention* than processing and required less understanding, and less effort and struggle. It was more kind. I was simply being with the feelings as they arose, in the moment, experiencing them more like Dad suggested, as wind traveling through my awareness. I was ready to stop putting so much of my attention and life energy into what I didn't want. I was ready to practice deciding what *I* did want. I had always been in such a frantic hurry to get rid of problems or bad feelings that I actually added more energy to them in the process. I dissected, rummaged through them, and worked really hard to interpret some hidden message or meaning. All this instead of simply allowing them. Allowing was a kinder, softer, and easier approach.

I appreciated Dad, and felt the tremendous blessing of all that had occurred with him: the lessons, the forgiving, the way he worked with the children and Pat, and how the few years that we had together completely changed my view of life. Dad inspired me to become who I was meant to be. Even through his death, he was moving old mountains.

I trusted the events of my reality and the Universe more than ever and believed it was all showing me to myself. It was the great mirror reflecting my innermost beliefs.

What you are comes to you.

–Ralph Waldo Emerson

I contemplated how often I changed my view of what was true and how people saw God, truth, light, and goodness only as their eyes had been trained to see. We all did it perfectly in harmony with where we were on our unique path.

I was beginning to understand that change was constant and that it really was the law of the Universe. Everything transforms and nothing remains the same. Just like my understanding would continue to evolve as I became more aware and that some truth I'd held as a certainty could easily end up crumbled or discarded. So it goes, everything changes. There was no point in trying to make some relationship or reality be permanent anymore. My fairytale truly was a fairytale, but, "happily ever after" was more apt to come from letting go than holding on. Wanting to force life around me to fit into some image I had of "perfect" was an insane behavior. Understanding that situations and relationships would change, that there would be easy days, hard times, up and down emotional experiences, and moments of great sadness that came along with being human made a lot more sense. Feeling my way through life and taking as much responsibility as possible for what I was experiencing was the key. I also realized that certain situations or events might take longer to move through than others. *Ahhhh,* letting go of control, so difficult sometimes but always so liberating… eventually.

Thoroughly unprepared we take the step into the afternoon of life; worse still, we take this step with the false assumption that our truths and ideals will serve us as hitherto. But we cannot live the afternoon of life according to the programme of life's morning; for what was great in the morning will be little at evening, and what in the morning was true will at evening become a lie.

–Carl Jung, "Stages of Life"

I was somewhat proud of myself for how I had explored on my own, without Dad or anyone else, and felt satisfied with my discoveries. I decided (again) that the God I had been looking for was the Universe and it responded to whatever I was vibrating and emitting. As Gregg Braden so kindly illustrates in his *Speaking the Lost Language of God* series, whatever I am feeling **is** my prayer. I believe the Universe, God, or Spirit, will always respond in kind by bringing me exactly what I'm singing of, be it pleasure or pain. The Universe isn't discriminatory; it merely wants me to have more of whatever I vibrate at.

To hear the song of the Tao was to feel the wind on my face, swim in the rhythm of the waves, and dance in the light of the stars, trusting the flow of the Universe. I felt the privilege and honor of being Source of my own experience and I was beginning to get a larger glimpse of what that meant. I was happy.

Oh Great Spirit hear our prayer
as one of the dear ones passes through the portals of eternity;

Dear Father, Dear Friend, Dear Teacher,
We bid you love and farewell in your new land.

In the no place every place of before during and after
where the totality and greatness of your spirit is at hand.

You are gone, yet not
Felt, but unseen
The you that appeared outside is now inside
I hear your words
Now my words
I decide!

Your life here touched many beings and lit up the path. Your mission on this planet carved an opening. In the illusion of time you changed the past.

Who we are you are also. Where you are I am too.
Gifts of your isness are now integrating, in this now and all through.

Howard Wayne, a wizard in the web of time and space.
You accelerated the evolution of mankind and touched us all with your grace.

We drink in your joy and celebrate your delight
as you create the bridge with your dance through the valley of night.

You are here, I feel you.
Thank you for your love and for giving me my wings.
When I listen closely I can hear you; I hear the music as your heart sings.

May your journey be forever sweet with ancient companions close.
I will meet you in the light dear friend.

I remember how it goes.

–Holly Riley

Big Guy in the Sky

chapter 21

"Scoop a jar of water out of the ocean and put a lid on it," I tell them. "Study it in its segregated state. Where is the ocean in that jar? Where are the tides and the currents? Pour it back into the ocean and it returns to its integrated state. The temporary entity no longer exists."

"Entity?" Ronald asks.

"By scooping it into a jar, you've created a new entity, a sub-ocean. It's not possible to subdivide infinity, of course, but try telling that to your new entity. It has all the properties of the ocean from which you scooped it, in no way greater or lesser than any other sampling you might take, yet it bears little resemblance to its authentic oceanhood. It has an independent existence, yet as soon as you pour it back, it merges seamlessly back into the integrated whole. Where is that particular sub-ocean entity after you pour it back in? The same place it was before; everywhere and nowhere. It didn't exist before you scooped it up, but you didn't create it. It doesn't exist after you pour it back, but you didn't destroy it. So what was born when you segregated that jarful? What died when you reintegrated it?"

–*Spiritual Warfare,* Jed McKenna

After Dad died, I decided to quit teaching for a while and spend some time discovering what translated into joy for me. I had some breathing room since Trav had obtained his driver's license and the boys were busy exploring their independence. I had a heap of alone time over the next year. Each day I gave myself a little space to sit quietly, have a cup of tea, maybe feel the sunrise, and roll some word like "love" around on my tongue. I came to believe, if I was clear headed and clear hearted, that I could design a new life experience that was fun and adventurous. I was certain this was what "Godness" wanted for all of us, to be happy. I felt the truth of that in my bones. I just had to figure out what I wanted and then put attention and effort in that direction—and never give up.

One morning I was missing Dad more than usual. I wished he was there and tried to imagine his body sitting across from me. *Just one cup of bean soup with him,* I envisioned. His visits were dwindling along with dreams of him. I so yearned for one of our inspirational powwows. Dad and I on a quest for clarity was a festivity. I loved how he'd cleverly untangle anything that I considered serious and transform it into a light, humorous nudge of becoming more responsible. He had a great skill. I loved reaching for truth, taking it further, deeper, wider… and did I say further?

I would have given darn near anything to understand why Dad had died when everything was so perfect, when he wasn't sick or complaining about any physical pain or health issues. I wondered what he was up to! His leaving didn't compute for me, other than rationalizing it must have been his time. I wondered about God and how to fit what I believed about the Sacred into Dad's departure and all his visits since then. The visitations had become less tangible, as though he was further away now, less dense, and harder to feel. I continually explored and experimented in an effort to comprehend how to connect the spiritual and physical realms, and how they intertwined and related, so that death would make sense to me. I questioned whether all humans were able to move around in the invisible after dropping their bodies or if this was only possible for people who'd cleared away limiting ideas about not being able to, prior to death. I knew Dad's visits were authentic. It stood to reason, since other beings I considered fluent in energy and feeling had seen or heard from him, too, that he was indeed out there somewhere, somehow, cruising around.

Perhaps Dad and I were able to still communicate partly because our connection was clean. We had become aware of each other's essence and related through that more often than through the personalities we wore. Plus, we both carried a strong desire and belief that we'd be able to sense one another after death. Perhaps every little thing had made it possible; our past, our relationship, shared beliefs, a strong connection, unconditional love, our promise, or maybe it was always possible for everyone. I didn't have the answer. I wondered if forgiveness played a role; Dad had forgiven everyone and everything as far as I could tell and he didn't hold a single grudge. He was complete, very satisfied, and content before he left. That probably freed up his attention so he could travel the cosmos as a free being, as Source. That was one of the realities (intentions) he'd given life to, right before he died.

I realized I wanted to know the unknowable. What happened as he left, where did he go, who did he see, and did his life roll out in front of him like a movie? I wondered how he was able to flash into my awareness at unexpected moments and if there was some specific intention or message I might be missing. If there was, I'd better hurry up and get it because as I kept connecting with Dad and focused my attention on him, I was sensing his presence fading. I was pretty sure it was only a matter of time before he merged with the invisible and no longer existed as a separate entity.

I contemplated who God was yet again. The attraction to rely on Dad was passing, as I focused more honestly on my own truths. I was determined to feel my own heart and what it was saying. I sorted through several of my old beliefs regarding God. I differentiated between those I felt had been indoctrinated by an outside authority, such as "I would go to hell for committing adultery" versus those beliefs that I agreed with and that had served me in becoming more real and honest, such as "All beings are made up of Godness" or "Do unto others as you would have them do unto you." I explored quite a few old ideas and simply acknowledging them all as beliefs was healthy. I hadn't done this in a while and it was liberating.

My questions about death were not being answered on a mental level but a calm feeling was coming from within. I was opening up and experiencing what was underneath my beliefs and the serenity was always there, waiting for me to remember. As I reached for knowing in the quiet the Nameless met me. It was as though the answers to my questions, the presence of the Nameless, and my own being, were inseparable. I didn't understand how the physical world met the invisible world, but it felt like that was what was happening inside me. I stayed very still and felt the pulse of energy moving through my body, my awareness, and even through my mind. All noise had stopped. I didn't know physics or any laws governing this type of interaction or even if there were any, but I knew that the feeling washing through me was the same intimate flow of love I had felt in the hands of Christ. It was familiar, precious, and unmistakable. I was so blessed to recognize it. It was a moment of pure grace. I sat in the feeling wondering where it began, where it lived, and if there was any end to its vastness. I wondered if it lived inside of me, outside of me, or was just everywhere all the time easily accessible when people become aware enough to serve as a window between the visible and invisible worlds. It lasted for several minutes and I was very grateful that I was able to experience it. I wondered if Dad was there.

All the names I could have used to describe the feeling were insufficient and could only point to the all-ness, everything-ness of it. The energy was constant. Seemingly, it was in the background of my opinions and busy mind, and if I got caught up in the lather of life, it didn't disappear, but I did. Was whatever I was feeling in those moments something most people called being connected to God or Holy Spirit? It was very similar to the feeling I'd noticed in Dad when he was manifesting his new realities on the last Avatar course we'd delivered together. The invisible realm met the physical realm and the union transpired through Dad's words. It was the same feeling I'd had many times in my hospital bed. It was comforting, loving, inclusive, and filled with a calm appreciation for EVERYTHING! Dad used to say, "The kingdom of heaven is right here, right now."

I explored further, contemplating the rules and weird beliefs around whom God really was and what he or she was actually doing up in the heavens while supposedly watching over us. To project a God who sat in judgment over us was ludicrous to me, particularly since I was no saint and clearly unworthy of being "saved" by traditional born-again standards. Yet, when Jesus scooped me from my hospital bed, I felt nothing but pure love. I had ended up in the vast and unsolicited care of Christ's amazing energy and it was definitely not hell.

Dad never made it into the believer category either, at least, not by many Christian fundamentalist standards. When he visited me at Tahoe, after dropping his body, he was in a state of pure ecstasy with no hellish or fearful energy in his midst. In my mind, Dad was in heaven and he hadn't followed the rules that many people of faith believed one had to comply with in order to get there. Sure, people could claim I had made up the whole thing and it's okay with me if they do. I understand how we have to make reality fit into what we hold as true. Dad's visits after he passed were as real to me as the chair I was sitting in and they happened enough times that I stopped being surprised by them.

Dad and I didn't seem to qualify for access to heaven when it came to adhering or believing in the Ten Commandments or any religious doctrines, for that matter. By traditional standards, Dad and I fell more into the category of sinners. To boot, we were sinners who never believed that Jesus Christ was our lord and savior. So if you had to be saved or tap your heels together three times, whispering, "There is no place like home," or know some other secret code to get through the pearly gates, then how did I end up in the palms of Christ's hands being soothed with enormous love and the offer of eternal peace? How did Dad, an abusive alcoholic, end up so darn happy in the afterlife? I considered this from several viewpoints: 1) Jesus wanted me to feel the joys of his unconditional love before he threw me into the depths of hell so I would always remember what could've been had I worshipped correctly. 2) Even though during my lifetime I wasn't up to snuff… in previous lives I was good and had accrued ample Karma points. 3) It was the devil dressed in a costume trying to trick and seduce me. 4) I made up the whole notion of good and bad and on some level manifested the only impression that could absolve me. 5) There is no "judging God" except in the minds of men. 6) God is energy and will always reflect our innermost beliefs.

I remember an image that was somehow planted in my head when I was young. It was of God (a tall man) sitting on a throne up in the clouds, adorned in white robes with a crown and he was holding a big stick (I always questioned what the heck he did with that stick). I may have gathered this vision from my translation of a Sunday sermon. Or, the picture may have come from a book, a movie, a story, or some indoctrinated soul knocking on my door that was handing out pamphlets in an attempt to save me by convincing me of a lonely death if I failed to conform to whatever truth they were very sincerely peddling. That image of God had been in my mind a long, long time.

I concluded my inquiry by deciding it's basically insane to believe that the most powerful, omniscient being of all time condemns and punishes non-believers, keeping some organized list of all the "good" or "conformed" souls so they'd pass muster and gain entry into heaven. The kicker was, if people were indoctrinated to believe that scenario, then the act of judgment itself could easily be considered a sign of power, holiness, or shrewdness. So guess what ambitious humans would naturally strive for? Being shrewd, powerful, and if we're honest, a desire to be holier than thou, too. In our passion to be upstanding, we assume the posture of the God that we've invented. We become the judger and condemner. We want to be the best we can be and if we imagine the most amazing being of all time to behave like that, then it's natural, whether deliberate or not, to imitate the behavior of our idol. We want to be good people. It's innate. We hold God to be the best of all. God is good! So, if we believe God judges….

It's just weird to witness a judgmental and critical archetype moving from parent-to-child, era-to-era. It's so barbaric and thwarting when it comes to waking up and being Source of where we find ourselves. I imagined how relationships could be transformed if we learned to replace our habit of judging one another with the habit of being present and responsible for what we felt (as our own creation). If we allowed *that* to move through us and out into the world our relationships would be more authentic. We would become quite honest with others and ourselves. It's not rocket science. We don't have to love and adore every single thing or person, but getting trapped in judgment is an obstacle to a peaceful soul. It's a habit worth breaking because it's a distraction from knowing and believing in the goodness of life, each other, and ourselves.

I had no doubt that the love I felt while held by the Sacred was there for all of us, both sinner and saint, all of the time. Allowing us to know ourselves more fully so we could clearly see from an intuitive place whatever was next. There was no push or pressure for me to go in any specific direction. My next step was *my* choice, based on *my* feeling and *my* knowing. I was celebrated and loved… no matter what I did.

Honesty, awareness, and connection allowed for Higher Self decisions. As I lay in Christ's hands, there was pure acceptance and it didn't matter what mistakes I had made or who I had been. My past, my heart, my world was stretched out in full view and there was nothing in the space but compassion and care. The notion of pretending never fits in the presence of sacred energy. While resting in Christ's hands, I couldn't be anything but truthful; the Nameless was in me, my head, my soul, and it knew *everything*. We were one—in awareness. I have come to understand that being completely honest and showing my insides to the outside world leads to the perfect next step. Not always easy as a human but definitely awakening when implemented. I am eternally thankful that once I recognized my choices, I decided to finish this life as Holly. I liked being me.

The idea of imagining, creating, or believing in a punishing God seemed totally crazy to me even though many authority figures had mastered "control" and "devotion" using that same belief structure. I needed only to consider the punishment in my childhood to understand how deliberately hurting someone could crush their ability to believe in themselves or trust their own feelings. I reasoned that the threat of punishment was considered useful to people who needed control. But it often created humans in its wake who were afraid to be honest or reveal their true selves, for fear of further pain. Dishonesty became a means to avoid being hurt. Many of us had mastered pretending and lying in an effort to avoid punishment. I did and my kids did, too. At a very early age they learned to pretend that they "didn't do it" to avoid getting into trouble. They wanted everything their way. I understood. Unfortunately, lying gave birth to accumulated guilt, and that guilt vibrated outwardly and beckoned the Universe for more of the same.

What an epiphany! I saw how the projection of a punishing God was a major obstacle to manifesting our dreams. Anyone indoctrinated to believe in a judging God would rarely feel like a good enough person. How could anyone measure up?! They'd have to be damn near saintly. I imagined that most people didn't truly believe they deserved what they prayed for. And… if people didn't deeply and honestly expect their requests of God (or the Universe) to become reality, then they wouldn't. Prayers we were hoping or wishing to be answered couldn't be as long as there was a big pile of guilt screaming and vibrating to the Universe (or God) that we are un-deserving.

Prayer, as Gregg Braden describes, is what we really *feel* behind any words we speak or think. Prayer is our innermost beliefs vibrating. The Universe's job is to respond to the energy we emit. So, whenever a prayer doesn't get answered and we think the reason was some projected God punishing us, more than likely we are the ones actually doing the punishing via our beliefs of not being good enough. Perhaps we haven't learned how to pray or haven't realized (yet) that we've been praying every moment of everyday according to what we believe and feel, which is often guilt or unworthiness. I bet divine intelligence (the Universe) wishes we'd figure this one out.

> *A prayer is a request made from a small part of God to a large part of God.*
>
> –*How to Know God,* Deepak Chopra

As I was exploring, I realized how much punishment filtered into so much of our lives. Often when people get angry and resist the idea of someone controlling them via threats of punishment, they do awful things to prove they can't be caught or controlled. While punishment is practiced as a measure for civilizing children, adults, and criminals, sometimes it seems to have the opposite affect and angers people to the point of making them even more unruly. I could trace this phenomenon throughout history, especially my own. Punishment didn't civilize me. As a child, I assumed an angry view and did things just to prove nobody was in charge of me *but me.* I punished them back and learned clever ways to break the rules. I made plenty of bad choices and hurt many people simply to prove my independence and the inadequacy of others. Punishing others was one of the ways I got to feel God-like and in control.

As I searched for a solution, I pondered and felt the ramifications. I admitted how I had punished Trav and Drake in an effort to totally control them. On many occasions I wanted them to make decisions and express themselves in ways that made me happy and I often guided them with a firm hand. I wished I could take it all away. I decided to speak to them about it and help them understand the mistake I had made and how important it was not to pay punishment forward the way I had. Even though I had rarely spanked them, I realized I had punished them in other hurtful ways, including withholding affection and connection. Admitting this to them will help bring light to any of the pattern they may unknowingly carry into future relationships. We model people we love.

Over time, things changed (in me) and I realized it was more empowering to give the boys a few choices within the realm of the household rules and let them participate in forging our agreements. They liked being in charge and this helped them manage their own choices. They pushed on all the limits, as children do, but the more aware I became, the more I was okay with the learning process and trusted it would lead the boys into taking more responsibility for their decisions. They made their share of blunders and I was able to direct their attention to what they had chosen and agreed to. Unless they presented a perspective that could change my mind, I held them to their agreements.

In my past, I was a clever punisher and suspect that, if we're honest about it, we've all been, to some degree. I came to admit how I had punished friends, family, co-workers, strangers, and basically anyone I wanted to manipulate toward my idea of what was most important. The blows were often quiet but still cruel. I could ignore, diminish with a look, gossip, lie, and pretend not to care, make fun of others' mistakes, blame, disconnect, abandon, and energetically separate myself, all the while smiling. If all else failed, I could withhold sex, a punishment I saved up for my husband, Pat. Whenever someone was wrong and deserved to be punished I was judge and jury.

We all have our variations of right and wrong. People are punished, even killed, for certain actions based on what's considered moral, ethical, and correct by another human or a group of humans. Different countries kill or punish for different things. Actions killed for in one country are considered moral and acceptable in another. Weird. Who's the morally correct killer? Is one country killing incorrectly? Who decides? All of a sudden I realized how serious I had become in my inquiry. I wished for Dad's companionship again, he would have liked this conversation and probably would have been chuckling heartily, making fun of my intensity. He used to say, "Holly, it ain't nothing but a thing," trying to get me to relax so I could have a more objective viewpoint. I smiled as I repeated his words out loud and felt the emotion rising in my throat.

I kept exploring, questioning the value of judgment. Obviously, it had its place in keeping us safe, making decisions, and deciding what we wanted from our lives. Knowing what I didn't want was important because it helped me reach for something different. Disliking where we found ourselves could serve as awesome fuel for manifesting our dreams. Discernment could help blueprint a future and help a person decide what actions were needed to move toward his or her goals, determine what was limiting, and what would be fulfilling. Then I considered how being judgmental was helpful when it came to teaching my children about issues of safety, such as not to dart out in front of cars. But was it optimal? Maybe teaching the kids to make good judgments wasn't as empowering as teaching consequences. Judgment was more akin to bequeathing my own beliefs of what was right or wrong, but having them recognize the potential consequences of their actions would allow *them* to decide and learn to associate their actions with results. This would help them own what they did with their lives and how they turned out. I liked that because it involved guiding them to trust their own abilities instead of looking to me for what was "ethical." Ethical can mean many things depending on whom you were talking to. Being a critical thinker was often equated to being rational and logical. But, at times, isn't one person's idea of "rational" different from another? Who's wrong? Who's the judge? Oh yeah, it's that "big guy in the sky." I laughed at myself.

It drove me crazy how the act of comparing and judging happened so automatically and instantly. Words appeared and disappeared before I had even realized I was thinking them. Someone could walk in front of me and an opinion could pop out of my analytical brain before I had any clue I was doing it. As I sat at my desk looking out at the neighbor's yard, I realized how often I secretly judged, evaluated, sized-up, criticized, and remarked on its condition. I could have listed several useless opinions and observations just in the short time I'd been sitting there. I commented on whatever was in front of me, including people, places, circumstances, and even my own body. I'm not talking about the blatant vocal criticism you hear in the stands of a sporting event. It's those silent observations, the internal scoffing, and secret resistances that happen so fast. *My neighbors needed to pull some weeds.*

I thought about when people are in groups and their criticisms are spoken out loud, how easily accepted judgments could be as a natural part of our conversations. Some people use them as a way to entertain, get attention, be witty, or popular. The not-so-funny part was how readily we justified our judgment of others by saying we were practicing discernment, good taste, shrewdness, prudence, or wisdom, similar to the God on his throne that we kept projecting as the being that determined who was naughty or nice (like a higher-ranking version of Santa Claus). I suspect we all use criticism as a tool to persuade our child, spouse, friend, or politician to see things the way we do. We sling cruelty, push and manipulate, and convince ourselves it's okay because it's for the "greater good"—not admitting or realizing that our definition of the "greater good" comes from our own indoctrination and is slanted conveniently toward our personal interests and beliefs. Others are certain to have a different perception of what is best for all, just ask them.

> *You cannot look at that which you* **do not want** *and not join and perpetuate that vibration. Take your attention from that which is not in harmony with who you are, and in taking your attention from it, your "now vibration" will adjust to who you really are, and then you can uplift others.*
>
> –*Abraham* by Esther and Jerry Hicks

Resistance was actually a sophisticated method of justifying judgment. I resisted some person or situation only after my negative and righteous translation of "it." Someone else may have had a positive experience of the very same thing, another aspect of the projection phenomenon. The opinion I placed on anything or anyone affected how it felt to me. It all depended on how *I* looked at it.

We make people wrong for anything and everything… walking funny, eating loudly, spilling something, falling, slipping, tripping, or making any human mistake as a mother, father, or friend. As people, we can be very mean and hurtful. However, many of us judge others and ourselves the same way we believe our God does. It makes us feel superior, worthy, God-like, and in some assbackwards way, like a good person. We can't blame anyone for it. In too many circles, being critical was learned, indoctrinated, and taught to us as a smart practice. Maybe I'm only talking about myself here, but I thought I'd be bold and include most of humanity.

I would bet the farm there is no "judging God." Judgment is the opposite of love according to Ernest Holmes, author of *The Science of Mind.* When I feel what love feels like—allowing, kind, honoring, believing in, and connecting with, it IS the opposite of judging. To me, being judgmental feels heavy, cruel, resistant, separating, doubtful, fearful, and dishonoring. Criticism is sticky and attaches me to things through my attention while also amounting to a huge waste of my time and energy. I've come to believe that any motion of judgment, since it *is* energy, adds to the overall flow of pain and density on the planet. It has a quality that anyone can feel at anytime. It isn't pleasurable. Out of our mouths and into the collective energy of life, flows all criticism.

I had a fun project in mind! I decided I would do my best to let go of my mental habit of negatively commenting on what I was looking at and see if I could replace it with appreciation, love, or at the very least, allowing and neutrality. Not judging didn't mean I'd be walking into a dark alley, alone, wearing stiletto heels, a miniskirt, and be fully adorned in bling. It meant *I* would be responsible for the quality of my attention, how I perceived, what I perceived, and how I directed my energy and focus on another life form. I wanted to be responsible for how I interpreted reality so I could contribute to it. I knew my focus mattered and affected every single person and just by becoming aware of this never-ending flow helped me to realize that God-energy can live through my eyes, my mind, and use my voice. The love I felt in Christ's hands had changed my world forever, and even though I didn't understand exactly what God, the Holy Spirit, or the Sacred with No Name looked like, longed for, or anticipated, I could feel whenever love was moving through me. It was the gift my image of Christ had given me and the gift I could choose to give to others. I longed to be open and clear enough to allow it to flow through me to whomever I was with.

If the quantum soup that Deepak Chopra speaks of connects us all, how can we deny the power and effect of what we feel, think, and say? What kind of soup are we making? We have family soup, neighborhood soup, community soup, national soup, and global soup. Even if I'm a tiny little drip of broth, I matter. We all do.

As Eckart Tolle says in *Stillness Speaks,* "If her past were your past, her pain your pain, her level of consciousness your level of consciousness, you would think and act exactly as she does. With this realization comes forgiveness, compassion, peace. The ego doesn't like to hear this, because if it cannot be reactive and righteous anymore, it will lose strength."

My ego was the judger and to quiet her I merely had to love. I knew it was easier said than done. I'm human. I would slip and correct myself and then start again. I wasn't one to give up. Simply knowing it was my ego that wanted to compare, be special, and control everything humanly possible, gave me the fortitude I needed to stop the habit. I knew that the more I fed my ego, the hungrier it got and that feeding it always led to suffering, eventually. I might feel queenly or powerful for a second or two once I'd gotten my way and controlled some situation, but it never felt good for very long. Sometimes it never felt good at all. Egos couldn't be satiated anyway; they always wanted more, better, or different stuff. Having a happy ego was a self-perpetuating trap, an endless empty game, and a detour from sharing the depth of love that I knew existed.

So *who* is God? I don't know. Maybe it's more of a *what* than a who. I was sure that any knowing I needed would come from the Universe, the Tao, Spirit, or the Nameless. I trusted the energy to always respond to my honest desire to awaken. It always has and always does. As Jed McKenna says, "Synchronicity is not a rare occurrence at all; it's the basic organizing principle of energy." Even for those of us who have made mistakes along the way, I believe that Sacred energy holds us and is forever responding to our instructions via feeling, vibration, thinking, and believing. We aren't trained to see how all the events that occur each day are a result of what we are *being* but, as soon as one is willing to explore and become aware of the phenomenon, it is undeniable. Energy responds to energy. The cravings of our flesh are often different than the good intentions of Higher Self but they reach and vibrate nonetheless. Expanding then contracting, separating then connecting, and I was learning to dance with the duality. Sometimes I feel like the master of my mind and then there are other times… I become a slave to it. So I watch and learn.

As I finished up my exploration, I was sure we were all equally eligible for the yummy quantum soup. In order to enjoy it, we merely had to accept the law: we get back what we emit. It's the flow of the Tao. It's

Albert Einstein's Theory of Relativity. It's the Bible's "You reap what you sow" and "Do unto others as you would have others do unto you." It's the age-old idea that what goes around comes around. Perhaps these are all good definitions of grace.

> *Once unshackled from the life-sucking demands of ego, we clearly see the unformed creatures we had hitherto been, like children. Not children in the happy, lyrical sense, but in the abrasive, self-absorbed, discordant sense. What we consider bright and beautiful in children is the inherent nature of the fully developed human. Our true state is one of playfulness, innocence, lack of guilt, unboundedness of spirit, robust health and inner light, a natural confidence and unerring sense of right, imperturbability, grace, a calm eye and easy good humor, balance, freedom from malice and pettiness, the absence of fear, the presence of largesse and a permeating sense of gratitude. Creativity. Connectedness. Correctness. This is the clear and rightful state of the human being. One must die of the flesh to be born of the spirit. One's life energy, formerly squandered by ego, can then be turned to the higher purposes and potentials of life in the magnificent amusement park of duality.*
>
> –*Spiritually Incorrect Enlightenment,* Jed McKenna

Wake Up

chapter 22

Where are the people that chose their lives?

... maybe a life of drudgery and carrot-chasing is exactly what we would choose if we did choose, but we don't. That's what it means to be unconscious; to be asleep within the dream. We slip into the lives that are laid out for us the way children slip into the clothes their mother lays out for them in the morning. No one decides. We don't live our lives by choice, but by default. We play the roles we are born to. We don't live our lives, we dispose of them. We throw them away because we don't know any better, and the reason we don't know any better is because we never asked. We never questioned or doubted, never stood up, never drew a line. We never walked up to our parents or our spiritual advisors or teachers or gurus or any other formative presences in our early lives and asked one simple, honest, straightforward question, the one question that must be answered before any other question can be asked:

What the hell is going on here?

–*The Enlightenment Trilogy,* Jed McKenna

Over the next couple of years, I stayed healthy and became more myself.

I came to accept and in some moments even appreciate the impermanence of form and that loss was part of life and death was eminent. The steadiness of change became more a friend then an enemy. Now and then I would contemplate time, be it an hour, a year, or twenty years, considering how long I had before my own body changed into another substance and it continually reminded me to feel the joy of my existence. Looking death in the eye was part of my waking process. It inspired me to love the moment I was in and appreciate how breathing in followed breathing out and that death followed life just as life followed death. I was determined to trust the Tao and comings and goings of all life. I understood that to resist change was futile and not really living at all. I realized every "thing" was in a constant state of change, including all feelings. Some apparently changed quicker than others but if I watched a tree long enough as Eckart Tolle explains, it too would transform into a rotting decaying form that created fertile ground for new life. There was a flow to life and when I was present, I felt it, rolled with it, and everything fit. To allow and trust change was enlivening.

Trusting the Tao was an evolutionary path, one that transformed with each step forward. I was sure it would continue to unfold… forever. It was only a short time ago that I believed trust was a result of controlling and organizing things. Control equaled being able to mold reality, to have things my way, and to be in charge of emotions. I was finally witnessing lessening degrees of desire or any need to micromanage reality. Letting go delivered a new sense of freedom. Trust took on a whole new face, one of relaxation. Some might have called it detachment. I curiously participated in life wondering what was coming next. I presumed that whatever happened to me would be whatever was supposed to happen next, even if it was getting sick, or experiencing another death of a loved one, or some other life altering event. I believed that if it showed up in my reality it was because I had attracted it and, somehow, it would move all things toward where they needed to go, even if it hurt.

Letting go of control had been my life's work and as time went by it seemed to include larger spheres of space and people. The more I trusted my path, the more I trusted humanity's path. I used to believe humans were broken and needed saving until I realized that I was seeing the same brokenness everywhere I looked, unaware that my own belief was filtering my view. In the hospital, I was able to see with unfiltered eyes and it seemed that humanity had changed, but it was actually me who had changed. I began trusting the flow of hurting and awakening. I stopped fighting life and making countries or circumstances wrong, understanding how that energy was merely attracting more of the same. I trusted, as a nation, that the pain we were experiencing would inspire us to search for more meaning and help us realize that our treasure wasn't so much what we owned or how we looked, but how we loved. I believed we were all waking up and even though the process was often painful, somehow what was occurring was piloting us all to live more from our hearts. I knew it was possible for humanity to feel who they are behind it all and strengthen their connection to the Sacred, even if they didn't call it that. I trusted it would happen because it had happened with me. I went from a slightly frantic need to help and save everyone to a state of awe over the ability of people to honor and save their selves, if they wanted to. I heard a story from Abraham of Esther and Jerry Hicks that lightened my load. Abraham explained how Esther had always kept a supply of hangers in her car to help anyone who happen to lock their keys in their vehicle. Not surprisingly, Esther constantly attracted people who were in need of being saved or rescued, parking lot after parking lot. When Esther realized how her longing to help actually resulted in the universe responding with an abundance of people in need she saw the *Law of Attraction* at work. What we vibrate out creates what we get back. This is not to be confused with the natural flow of extending a hand when someone is reaching.

I was determined to do my part by living my joy. For me, this meant owning where I put my attention and inviting others to see the magic they possessed by doing the same. Like Jed McKenna explains, we are a jar of water scooped out of the ocean thinking we are the individual entity, the jar of water, instead of a tiny small part of oceanhood. His analogy invites the question, "How much of our lives do we spend thinking we got the wrong jar or thinking our jar is better, fuller, has more girth or content when, in fact, every jar has the same fundamental properties?" I believe that we all eventually are poured back into the cosmos for another reminder: we are part of one big ocean and we are all in this together, every single jar of us.

Meanwhile, on the home front, I still caught myself pushing the boys or Pat to see things my way or finagling them to want what I wanted. Sometimes, I would even notice I'd be stubbornly stuck on an idea while still smiling at them, all in an effort to make them feel empowered and at least *believe* I trusted their viewpoint—when really I didn't like it at all. I grappled with merging the invisible with the everyday visible. I tried to appreciate my family's ideas, and would give myself a little time to make friends with their viewpoints. I'd offer them as many perspectives as I could muster so they could chose wisely, aware of the consequences. Meanwhile, it was also about me learning to choose wisely and becoming aware of consequences as a mother and a wife. Often, things didn't work out as I envisioned and I continually had to let go of any attachment and simply trust the process. Learning a new level of trust had arrived along with my boys becoming teenagers. It wasn't always easy and was definitely an ongoing practice.

Ever since my near-death adventure, I was determined to learn and trust the process of raising children without turning them into puppets. Half the time, I stunk at it but I never gave up. I surrendered, then fought for control, then let go and then held on, particularly when it came to sex, drugs, alcohol, and driving cars. I fought with Pat and myself over how to empower them. It was really difficult and there were times when I wasn't sure I was traveling down the right road and pulled in the reigns so tightly, I nearly choked everyone to death. When the boys started driving, I even bought a Breathalyzer test kit (aka drunkometer) and told them they'd have to blow in it after every drive and if there was any register of alcohol in their bodies, their car was mine. Then I would turn around and nicely explain that they were Source of their life and could choose to drink and drive once they turned twenty-one, at which point I would no longer be legally liable for their actions. See, I gave them choices. They just had to wait to exercise them.

I recalled an afternoon when Dad had been at the house and I started freaking out about the boys' stubbornness. Dad got such a kick out of it. He reminded me that I had trained them to be their own people, to think for themselves, and that how they were behaving was exactly what I had always hoped for. He turned to me and said, "Don't bring any of that seriousness around me," as though it would rub off on him. He made me laugh all the time, pointing out how a lot of my worry was the result of my judgment making the situation scary and important. He often reminded me, "The boys are very powerful and aware and they will attract exactly what they need to take them to their next level of awareness, just like you did. You may not always like how it feels or what it looks like, but you will learn to trust it." He always helped me retreat from whatever my attention got stuck on so I could see the bigger picture, where it could lead, what they would learn, and how it provided a great opportunity to teach them about choices. That day I remained discouraged and Dad stood up from his chair with a start and announced, "EGBOK!" I asked, "What did you say?" He chuckled, really having fun with himself and explained that he had just invented a new word. "EGBOK," he repeated, "Everything's gonna be okay!" I giggled with him. EGBOK was a perfect word for Dad. He seemed to believe it about everything, and with all his heart. He repeated it several times, laughing till his eyes watered. He was so tickled with himself. Truly, everything fit into the EGBOK category as far as he was concerned. That became his new phrase for life. He taught it to anyone who would listen, explaining how we could put our attention on any idea of our choosing but, to choose wisely because whatever we focused on would definitely become our reality. I smiled, appreciating my brief but potent time with Dad. "EGBOK," I said out loud, just to feel the word roll off my lips.

I had to laugh at my ego's snarling hold on certain positions regarding diet, drugs, or sex and how I wanted to indoctrinate Travis and Drake with my numerous resistances. I'd prodded them to have *my* beliefs! Long after they moved out and had places of their own, I was still repeating over and over, "Don't drink and drive, say no to drugs, and use a condom." They laughed at me. I intended for it to become an embedded recording in their heads, hoping it would eventually be the message they couldn't turn off. Trusting them to make decisions so that nothing would hurt them was a huge challenge for me. Letting them fall down when I could have protected them from skinning their knees was never easy. I wanted to save them, decide for them, and protect them from pain, as most mothers naturally do. Knowing they needed to learn how to choose, every once in a while, when I knew the lion was sleeping, I'd let them walk into the den and get gnawed on just little so they could learn about life. Pat didn't always agree. I believed the best parent was the one that taught a child to know himself and discover his own magic, even if it didn't match the parent's idea of what was good or important and even if it meant getting bit sometimes.

The boys fell plenty and got bruised and battered from some poor choices, but I was right there hurting along with them and loving them through it. They were quick learners and figured out how to brush themselves off and make better choices with their next steps. Travis and Drake helped me realize one very important thing: that if I controlled and directed their lives with my beliefs, then they could feel justified in blaming me for how their lives turned out. If I pushed them to become some image I held of them, they could sidestep their own responsibility and hold me accountable for their experiences. Sure, I had ideas about each of them becoming president someday, but I had to let that go after they'd both inhaled.

My goal was for the boys to realize they were in charge of manifesting their dreams or nightmares and that it was always up to them which one they chose. Being reminded there was never anybody to blame was a big help. As a family we did our best to eliminate blame as an option. All four of us were aware that it merely postponed ownership of where we found ourselves and attracted a repeat experience. Blame prolonged suffering because in order to continually prove someone else was wrong, a person very often had to keep suffering.

I prayed nothing would happen that would cause me to lose them, but it could have. I admitted the possibility and felt my resistance to living without them. They weren't perfect by any stretch and I wasn't into perfect, so that was okay. I was, however, very committed to them both understanding that what they believed and felt on the inside is what created their life experiences. I was always exploring new ways to drive that point home, constantly lecturing about how their ability to feel had everything to do with their physical and mental health. I did my best to teach them that each decision they made created their own world and what they put out would always come back to them. As John Rosemond encourages in his marvelous book *Teen-Proofing*, when the boys were young I tried to give them just enough rope to hang themselves so they could figure out how to avoid hangings and understand that they were in charge of how their necks felt.

The boys knew they had to feel, admit, and experience where they were in order to move out of it and on to what was next. They didn't always cop to it, but the understanding that they were Source of their lives was in them, and served as the background to whatever was happening. Being in the boys' presence continues to be one of the greatest pleasures of my life.

I had relaxed into being a mom and a wife, and was probably behaving as normal as I ever did, at least in Pat's eyes. I hadn't been writing, studying, or teaching much at all. I felt a little guilty about it sometimes, wondering if I was missing my boat and getting lazy. I understand now it was all part of the rhythm leading me to my next dose of clarity: I received quite a wake-up call from the Universe reminding me of my promise to keep moving forward.

Given that I was going to be forty-five any minute, I decided to have a colonoscopy (particularly since my doctor told me I should have one every year and I hadn't had one since being in the hospital over ten years ago). I felt it was time for a checkup. I hadn't had a single problem with my colon since Dad died. But I wanted the procedure to ensure I wasn't filled with polyps, having been warned about them in the hospital. I decided to find a doctor that had no record of my previous colon issues and I deliberately withheld my medical history when filling out the forms. It was all very easy. Pat dropped me off on his way to the airport to attend a meeting in Texas and Mom was set to pick me up. I got settled into my small cubicle, as I was being prepped for rectal inflation, and strongly persuaded the doctor to remove every single polyp she found because I wouldn't be coming back to do this again, not for a very a long time, hopefully never. I pushed her, and she agreed and promised to remove any polyps. I adored her; she was a new mom and a fairly new physician.

Everything went great, and she told me it looked like I'd had a little colitis in the past, and I told her, "Yes, I had." She said it all looked healthy and that she'd removed about twenty-one polyps and would send a couple to the lab to make sure they weren't cancerous. Then she added, "They all looked non-threatening." I said, "Coooool," still a little goofy from the drug. My new doc sent me home with a clean bill of health and told me I was good for five to ten more years and that I would hear from her if there were any problems with the biopsies. I was released and my mom took me home to rest and hang out with Drake. Pat was going to be gone for a couple days.

I napped and relaxed. A few hours later I began to feel a little strange. Something was off, but I couldn't quite put my finger on it. I scanned my body trying to see if everything was okay. I turned my feelers way up searching for what might be happening. I wondered if the medication was getting to me but it felt different than that. I started hearing a weird sound, like a hum from far away inside me. I thought it must be the medication. Then I felt something happening in my colon and ran to the restroom. An entire cup of blood gushed out. I know it was blood because my colon was completely empty from the prep I had just drank for the colonoscopy procedure. I sat there for a moment confused and wondering if I could use my mind-management tools to make my colon stop bleeding. I told myself to just relax, not freak out, to breath, and that I could get this under control. A voice in my head said, "No way, not this time." I tried to think and my mind wasn't cooperating, and then another cup of blood came out. I wondered how many cups a person could lose before dying. It was my last thought before I passed out.

I woke up on the floor, and I don't know how much time had lapsed but I was in a pool of blood. The door was closed and Drake would never hear me from the other side of the house. My next thought was that I had to reach the door and open it, and I wasn't sure I could. I yelled, "Get up Holly!" At least I think it was me yelling. I crawled the three feet to the door, opened it and screamed "Drake!" as loudly as I could. It came out just above a whisper but Drake heard me and came running. I could only open the door a few inches because I was stuck in front of it. All I could get out of my mouth was "Call 911." Then I collapsed again and Drake, being an Eagle Scout well trained for emergencies probably saved my life that day by not messing with me but making a beeline to the phone.

Then something very interesting happened. A strong message came from somewhere inside me, and consumed every particle of my attention. I opened my eyes very certain I could not die on Drake's clock. It would kill him. I kept repeating the words, "I can't die on Drake's clock. I can't die on Drake's clock." He could somehow imagine himself responsible. There was no way I'd let that happen. Then a voice, maybe mine, told me to **look in the mirror,** that I had to look in the mirror **NOW!** I immediately shuffled my body around to execute the demand. It was so strange an instruction to occur in that moment yet, I didn't question it. I grabbed onto the counter above me and used every bit of energy I possessed to pull myself up the two feet necessary to view my face. The second I peeked over the edge of the counter I knew. I met myself and I don't mean the personality. I saw and felt who I actually was. Not the body, not the reflection, but my spirit, the real me that exists behind it all. I looked into my eyes and saw the puppeteer. I felt the truth of me, the being, the light, as though I was looking directly into my soul. It was the most remarkable experience. It felt like the larger part of me was embracing the smaller pasty white me. I experienced the preciousness of being human from this serene perspective and I understood I was seeing the preciousness of every living thing. It was the element all life on Earth had in common. It was what I had been born to share.

I let go of the counter and trusted. I wasn't afraid to die and absolutely knew Drake would end up with the perfect experience for his very sweet heart. I fell to the floor and went unconscious, knowing I was in the hands of the Sacred. The invisible had met the visible.

I don't know how much time had passed before I found myself moving away from my body. There was light everywhere and something was coming toward me. Or maybe I was moving toward it. I couldn't see clearly. It was hazy and fuzzy like clouds. An opening was revealed and I looked ahead down a hallway of sorts and there was a large group of people. They were so happy. They were laughing and celebrating with such pleasure, cheering and standing close to one another. It seemed like fifty or so people in a gathering, a circle with everyone facing one another. I was trying to see the faces clearly but they kept falling in and out of focus, as though they were just out of my visual range. I tried to move closer but I seemed to be moving too slowly. I wanted to know what the hubbub was about and needed to find someone I recognized; it was very important to me. Then I saw one face I knew and I remember being very comforted by this. I tried to make my way closer to him but something was making it really difficult to move forward. I couldn't quite place who it was but I needed to get closer to him; he was my friend.

Suddenly, a man in the circle with his back to me turned to face me and then so did everyone else, and they were so happy I was there. They expressed such joy at me showing up. It was pure adoration flowing between everyone. It was a big party and I was thrilled to attend. The man that first saw me seemed a bit surprised by my appearance and he walked over and politely, solemnly, waited by my side for what seemed like a long while so everyone could hug me and include me in the celebration. Then, without waiting for all the people to finish, the man standing next to me gently took my shoulders, one in each hand and turned me around, away from the circle, so I was facing back in the direction from where I'd come. It was like I wasn't supposed to be there with the group and he slowly began walking me back to where I had started from. I didn't recognize him at all and I remember staring at him, wanting to know whom the amazing being next to me was. His smile was so complete and whole. He knew I was baffled but he never answered any of my questions. He just showered me with love and kindness.

Peace washed through me and my questions disappeared as he led me to an opening of muted colors and light at the end of the cloud-like hallway we traveled in. He caressed me with that same vibration of love that Christ had. We moved in silence, connected, flowing, peaceful, and calm. We were almost at the opening and I could see through it now; it was my house, my body, with an EMT leaning over me. My mom and Drake were standing on the step into the living room and my body was on the floor in the hallway next to the bathroom door about five feet in front of them. They were all watching, with two other rescue guys on my left and one more on my right.

I watched Drake and was mesmerized by his energy field. It was so vast that I couldn't see where it ended. I followed it to try and find an edge but there wasn't one. It had no ending. My mom also had an energy field that extended quite a distance but I could see the encasement of hers. In that moment I knew that both of them, on some level, were fully aware and that they were more than their bodies and more than the lives they were living. I felt their understanding of all of this, they knew the truth. In the expanded part of themselves (the invisible) they were connected to where I was. I had no doubt they would be okay no matter what happened to my body. I could see it in their energy fields. It was like their physical body was a very small part of who they were in totality. The bulk of their being was outside their body rather than in it, as though the body was a point where energy expressed itself. It blew me away. It made perfect sense and somehow it seemed like I had known this all along. In that moment, the truth of who we were was unmistakable, and the man standing next to me was glad that I could see it.

Then, I looked at the medical technician leaning over my body and couldn't believe what I saw. He was the only body that had no energy field around him, no extension into the invisible that bonded us all. He had no connection to anything that I could see, only a very faint, wispy thread that seemed to disappear into nothing. He was alone and separate and had a very bleak life force pulsing in his body. He seemed empty. I could feel it so acutely. I turned to the man on my arm and the words that came out of my mouth or my mind were, "He thinks it's real." The man on my arm agreed, nodding his head, without saying a word. I said, "He doesn't know." Of everyone standing there, he was the one that concerned me. All the others had a field of energy around them, some larger and more brilliant than others but they all had them.

The man standing next to me quietly watched as I let the understanding soak in. The EMT taking care of me was dense energetically, so much thicker than Drake or Mom. All his energy was turned in on himself. He had no flow or connection toward his Higher Self. I longed to comfort the paramedic and tell him that everything was going to be okay, that he was more than his pain, his body, or his despair. I had to go, right away, and make sure he knew he wasn't alone; it was very important. The man next to me had tremendous compassion flowing to all of us. But he said nothing. He touched my arm one last time, like he was infusing me with love, and then he turned me toward my body.

The next thing I knew, I was back in it.

The Tao says that the sage sees people as straw dogs, and that's what it means; all exterior, no interior. Empty costumes populating the stage like zombies. All appearance, no substance. Yes, the unenlightened look like zombies to the enlightened; like fictional characters animated by mysterious forces. No one home. If a person were born enlightened, rather than going from unenlightened to enlightened and having the experience of being made of straw, I think he'd find this a damn spooky place. Busy, populated, yet strangely uninhabited.

–*The Enlightenment Trilogy,* Jed McKenna

Love What YOU Love

chapter 23

The soul, like the body, accepts by practice whatever habit one wishes it to contact.

–Socrates

I opened my eyes and the EMT had his hand pressing on my neck trying to insert an IV line. I gently touched his arm, loving him with all my heart, and reassured him, "It's okay, and I am going to be okay." I felt him relax and a big whoosh of air escaped his body like he'd been holding his breath for a very long time. Beads of sweat covered his forehead. "I have to go into a vein in your neck area and I need you to be very still." I was energetically caressing him with appreciation, not because I thought I should, or believed it was the right thing to do, or because I needed to save him. I felt genuine indisputable love for him. It was real, with no agenda, and it didn't matter what he did, what he believed, or if he'd ever felt the presence of the Sacred. I loved him and it filled the space that we both occupied. I was calm and connected to him as though we were the best of friends and that having my life resting in his hands now was pure and total perfection. While acutely aware and fascinated by his flow of energy toward me, I heard him say, "We haven't been able to get a line in your arm." My eyes remained locked on his, yet I could feel the invisible swirling, intertwined all around us as though my Higher Self was merging with his Higher Self and his words were decorating the exchange between us with bursts of power. Each word carried its own vibration and density. I had never experienced this before. The combination of our energies was profound. I had never felt this with a stranger and only to a lesser degree with my family. I looked deeply into him and spoke as Source, "You will be able to find the vein in my arm now." He felt the certainty of what I said as though he had said it to himself, instantaneously pulling the catheter-type needle away from my neck and scanning for a vein in my arm with the tourniquet. He spoke softly, "I can't see it very well but I know it's there," and then gently, almost effortlessly inserted the device into one of my veins. It was magic and neither of us was surprised.

Nervously he told me that my blood pressure was really low, something like 55 over 35 and I pulled him close and whispered quietly so Drake couldn't hear, "You need to get my son in the other room right now and make sure he knows I am fine, and that I am going to be fine! Please assure him, because we both know it's true!" I had no doubts of a full recovery, regardless of the circumstances. The fireman standing to his right responded immediately as though he knew the importance of my request and guided Drake into the other room with his arm lovingly around my son's shoulder. "We need to take you to the hospital," said the EMT, "you need a blood transfusion and we have to get this bleeding stopped to get you stable." I knew he was right and responded, "No problem." I looked over at Mom, so glad she was there. She was trying so hard not to freak out but fear was oozing from her physical location like a gushing river. I took a moment to look through her eyes. I was sprawled on the floor in an awkward area between the bathroom door and the door to my office and there was quite a bit of blood where I'd been lying. It was scary. I motioned for Mom to come close, and I pulled her to me and held her. I wanted her to feel how much I loved her, physically, spiritually, and emotionally. I looked her in the eyes to make sure she could merge with me as I said, "I had a great trip Mom, not to worry." She was so beautiful, and so much more than her body communicated. I told her how much I appreciated her, and I watched her swallow and feel my words. I told her I was grateful for everything from the very beginning of our time together and that it was all-perfect. I assured her I was all right and the truth of it was in the air. I invited her to feel the magic embracing us and trust that everything was okay with me. As we connected, she had so much love in her eyes that she filled me up with it. For a second, we met on a level beyond what was happening in the room. Mom was somewhat soothed but didn't relax quite as much as I had hoped. I could feel her vibration as though it was my own, and I was also keenly aware of everyone's energy in the room. Each soul was unique.

Mom had become a very big part of our family and a dear friend to me. She was Grandma! Pat and the boys adored her. She was always there for us just as you would hope a mom would be. When I called to let her know that I wasn't feeling right, just before heading into the bathroom, she knew the way that mothers often do that she'd best drop everything and come right away. For me to see her wholeness on that day was a tremendous gift of peace. We were complete, best friends, and companions. The last several years had been so precious to us.

Mom backed away with her eyes still on me to allow the guys with the gurney into our space. I looked at all the faces staring down at me and smiled saying, "Relax, I am fine. No worries." They picked me up and loaded me onto the bed and were getting ready to carry me out. I called out to Drake and he came around the corner, shook up but stable, and walked up right next to me. The gurney was raised now so we were face to face. He leaned into me wanting the security of our connection and gave me a huge hug. I placed my hand on his heart as he tenderly pulled away and let it rest there while I thanked him for saving my life. Energetically, something moved between us that I could only explain as pure knowing. We both felt it. It was a calm, old, wise sureness, as though we were aware of the Tao of life, in unison, with full honor for the comings and goings, at least for a second anyway. I couldn't stop staring at Drake, his energy and his presence in the room was so solid and grounded. I was in awe of everyone and how each of us had a unique connection to the invisible. I saw it clearly. The vast invisible world held this small visible world. I removed my hand from his chest and looked deeply into his eyes with a grateful smile and assured him I was fine. Through our energetic link he experienced the truth of it.

Since that night, I haven't worried much about Drake. I sensed how he would always move toward whatever was next and remain plugged into divine intelligence. On a psychic level, I was certain that Drake had some awareness of who he was behind the mask and that he would live his life by feel and intuition. It wasn't that I thought things would always be peachy-keen for him, but rather that I just trusted his Higher Self to guide him to his perfect next spot in the timeline of his journey here. It may not match my images, or anyone else's, of what's best in the world of human costumes, but, it would be perfect.

The twenty-minute ride to the hospital was a love-fest, and I was doing the loving. The EMT leaning over me, whose name I had learned was Mike, rode by my side. I took the opportunity to engage him and see who he was to himself. I listened closely as he answered a few of my probing questions as though he had been expecting them. He very comfortably revealed that he was unhappy and had ended up in a life he hadn't planned for. He felt trapped by a career choice built out of "shoulds" as opposed to following his heart, believing that he couldn't make as much money if he pursued what he wanted. He'd been pretty depressed and his wife and daughter had moved out, leaving him alone to figure out what he wanted from life. He missed them terribly and spent all of his paychecks supporting them, yet he rarely saw them. Mike felt trapped in a life he didn't want to live and was very alone.

I asked him if he wanted to hear an interesting viewpoint. He was staring into space and didn't seem to have much of his attention on me. I continued anyway and gently spoke of what I saw regarding his energy when I was returning to my body. He heard me now and turned to look at me as though something clicked in him and he understood. I explained the emptiness I felt in him and he said it felt the same way from where he stood. I asked Mike if he wanted to change things or keep them the same. He looked at me like I was nuts. He said he couldn't change them. I told him I believed that he could. I think my energy got his attention. I was so electric, so full of the Sacred and acutely present that he couldn't ignore me. I explained to him that he could shift his energy whenever he wanted to and asked if he would give me a few minutes to explain. I told him I didn't believe in coincidences. I looked carefully at him to see how willing he was to feel and explore. There was a crack in his armor. I went on to tell him that most of my life had been spent encouraging people to realize how precious they were and that, with his permission, I could do that right now. I smiled at him and he chuckled, opening up a bit more. I asked Mike directly if he was open to feeling goodness in himself and that if he would allow me a few moments, I might be able to help. He grinned, a little leery of this, but said, "Okay" to the middle-aged crazy woman in his ambulance. After all, that was about all he could do besides jump from the moving vehicle. I might have had an advantage over the situation since he was my captive audience. I believed it was what I was there to do, so I rolled with it.

I invited Mike to think about what he loved in life, what he enjoyed. He told me a few things but they felt empty as though he hadn't experienced them in a long, long while. I told him it was really valuable to notice when something made his heart happy, something that filled him with a good feeling, a worthy feeling. I invited him to make time in his life to find his joy and asked him to honestly commit to focusing some attention on it, to consider it an utterly valuable project. He said he didn't know what I meant. I continued, "Make a list of things you enjoy, search for them, and ask yourself what feelings you prefer. Do you like physical exertion, emotional drama like a good movie, or maybe adventure, being outdoors, or being quiet and reading, or building things? What do you like to do Mike?" He said he had never given it much thought because he'd spent most of his time just trying to survive and pay the bills.

I had an idea. I asked him if he knew what it felt like to let love into his heart and receive kindness. He said, "Not really, not for a long time." I asked him if he could remember a time when he did, no matter how young he was. I invited, "Think of a time when you felt adored and cherished." He was quiet and after a bit he said he couldn't think of one. I knew there was one in there, that it was just smothered in a feeling I will call angry sorrow. I felt him almost reach it, so I nudged him a bit more, giving him an example of how nature filled me up with love, how it was my refuge, and I described how the trees, birds, and ocean opened something up in me that could receive the flow of goodness. A familiar look shot across his face and he said the same was true for him. I asked him if he remembered the last time he'd experienced being touched by nature like that. He traveled back to a fond memory and his energy immediately shifted. He spoke of a time when he'd been hiking and came upon a beautiful group of soft-wooded aspens. He described his hike, the leaves changing colors, and how he had always loved trees. There was a creek he described explaining how the sound of it was very soothing to him and that he felt peaceful there. The moment he said it a calm washed over him. I asked, "Wow, did you feel that?" He laughed, admitting that he did. I touched his arm with my free hand and pinched him a little saying, "You can create that feeling anytime you decide to. Feeling those feelings is what will guide you more toward your heart." He was more interested now.

"Mike, you can put your attention on how difficult life is or become skilled at moving it over to what you would **like** to create. Wherever you place your attention, an experience is sure to follow. You need to get your butt out into the woods more, don't cha?" I asked. He laughed. "When you allow joy in and receive the goodness around you, you're connecting with the Sacred with No Name! That's where you will find the door to your dreams… its inside, nobody else can give you your path. You have to listen to yourself, think for yourself, and honor how you feel; that is the only way you can truly love another. BE YOU TO FULL!" I asked him if he got it and he laughed at how goofy I was.

I realized I was jamming a lot of information into a short amount of time but our ride would soon be over, so I continued, "Mike, if you could allow yourself to enjoy the treasures of life and feel the sensations of satisfaction and peace like you do when you're in nature, your vibration will change. People outside of you will reflect what you feel inside. They already are now, right?" He agreed. "What I mean is, how you allow love and receive care serves as a beacon emitting a vibration that acts as an instruction to the universal energy that screams, "Treat me like I treat myself," "Believe in me like I believe in myself," and "Respect me like I respect myself!" I exclaimed enthusiastically, "Divine Intelligence will always match you, that's why it is divine!" He chuckled and I dove into his twinkling eyes with appreciation, wanting him to feel the magic of his own being. "If you don't take time to acknowledge yourself, how can you expect anyone else to? People are basically treating you the way you treat yourself."

Mike was so precious and innocent. Just a few years older than Travis was my guess, with platinum blond hair, blue eyes, and hungry for self-love. I was feeling weak but I had to keep going as it was pouring through me now, "If you begin to appreciate your Self, like you said you appreciated the trees and the Earth during the hike, your heart will automatically open. It will open to you like a dear friend who you have treated well and honorably. As you allow yourself room for mistakes, you will become forgiving of others, and trust will become your friend. This appreciation of yourself opens the door that will lead you to who you are meant to be." He countered, "I can't see leaving my job and taking off to travel the world. I have responsibilities, my daughter and my wife." I went on, "You may be surprised how things change and flow into place once you are honest with yourself and in integrity with your heart. As you listen to your intuitive knowing your world will change. I bet if you practiced for one month, opening and receiving love, a path would reveal itself to your dreams. You have all the time in the world! You're just a puppy. Imagine people starting to realize at the age of sixty or seventy that they could be in charge of their experience of life. You have it made!

"You are learning how to manifest dreams, so are most people on this planet, and one of the ways we do that is by waking up in a nightmare and deciding we're in the wrong place! It's not a bad thing to find yourself in a nightmare, but it is painful if you don't take responsibility for where you find yourself and get moving. You got the message and now you can schedule some serious time to do more of what makes you feel good about yourself. Your life is in your hands, and the world will always reflect how you feel about yourself, so you better get busy falling in love with the guy walking around in your shoes!" I felt his spirit waking up as I continued. "Mike, please remember to be kind to yourself as you learn; don't expect perfection, you're human, and you're going to blow it now and then. You just have to believe in yourself and the idea that you can become whoever you want to be. You have will power and the more you use it, the stronger it gets. You have everything you need.

"Have you ever noticed how your love for nature and trees is unwavering even though nature is forever changing, crumbling, transforming, and disappearing back into the compost of life that births another form? You don't dislike a tree or judge it as wrong for decaying, burning, or being infested with beetles. You accept and maybe even appreciate its cycle of birth and death. You don't think of a rotting tree as a stupid tree. You respect its process, realizing every aspect of it contributes to the overall forest, don't you?" He nodded. "You are very much like the tree. You offer much to the fabric of the world by being you and moving through your own becoming, your own cycle of birth and death. You matter. Look what you did for me today. You saved my life and my guess is you have done a lot of kind things in your life. Be at least as honoring of yourself as you are to a tree!

"If you treat yourself with disrespect, not recognizing how hard you work to figure life out, make ends meet, and be a good father or husband, and only see negativity, guess what you are energetically inviting everyone else to see? Guess what you vibrate at?" Mike understood and admitted he hadn't been good to himself for quite a long time. I could feel his guilt over something in the past and I nudged him again. I explained how he could let the past go whenever he got tired of lugging it around. I wagered that he had already punished himself plenty over past mistakes. He stared at me and said, "Probably." We only had a few minutes before arriving so I talked fast. I explained how love and forgiveness could heal anything and that the most important step was committing to love and committing to forgiveness. I invited him to take a second and feel what it would feel like if he released the past and admitted every mistake he had ever made. He put his head down as if contemplating this and then looked up at me with a smile. He wasn't sure it could be that easy but he certainly liked the idea. I assured him, "It *is* that easy. Decide to drop the past like you would a hot potato. It really is a conscious decision! Let it go, unless you want to suffer some more. That is a choice, too. Some people like suffering." He was considering the idea and then grew solemn and whispered, "It's all easier said than done." I agreed. "You're right, you have to do what it takes to manage your mind, and you have to put in the effort to pay close attention to any habit you have of making yourself wrong or punishing yourself. You have to notice if on some level you aren't keeping yourself from being happy as some form of punishment. You have to observe yourself, relentlessly for a while, and then it becomes easier and more natural to start noticing how *you* are in charge of what you feel, and how fabulous you feel in those moments when you are open and receiving. The contrast is profound and after a while you won't be willing to nestle in guilt and sadness anymore. It won't feel good and you will become clear that it's your attention making it so.

"Mike, I bet you will be very good at catching yourself whenever you're heading down a negative and dark road with your thoughts. You're trained to not miss any signs when it comes to someone's body right?" He nodded in agreement. "It's the same thing only you're going to do this by scanning yourself, your thoughts, mind, and actions with your own attention. You will notice when something isn't feeling good and you will begin to catch the negative ramblings when they first appear!"

Pushing the point home, I asked him one more time if he was sure he wanted to let go of the past. He nodded yes. I continued, "That is the first step; let yourself feel your desire to let it go. Feel how your life would be if you were free of the past, feel the joy you could share with your daughter, feel what you could be teaching her by enjoying life. Start over right now simply because you say so! You are the one in charge of your responses to life. Yes, bad things can happen, and yes, they can hurt deeply but there is a point where you get to move on and you get to choose exactly when that moment is. Feeling your determination to be a good person will lead you to more and more awareness of yourself and what is possible. The attention you direct to your dreams will always open a door to their fulfillment. Progress may seem slow at times but you will look back after a year or two and be amazed at how far you've come. Never give up!

"You may find some people you need to apologize to or make amends with in order to be totally free, but that will come with your honest determination to release whatever is there. You will intuitively know what to do to create peace in your heart. The knowing comes when you are honest about what happened and you take responsibility for your part in it—even if your part was simply vibrating in such a way that attracted blame and pain. Being responsible for what you are emitting to the Universe is the ultimate form of responsibility because it admits that anything you're receiving is coming from what you're putting out. He said, "Whoa, you mean to say anything that happened to me with my wife was what I wanted to happen?" I answered, "I am not talking about wanting on a conscious level or deciding deliberately all the details of how life rolls out. I am speaking of the emotions and feelings we have tried to stuff down or push away from an incident that occurred in the past. They are often still there, vibrating and hurting us from the inside out. They call to divine intelligence, too, and they summon more of themselves until they're acknowledged and deliberately released. A better way to look at it is that anything you were experiencing with your wife had a lot to do with what you were feeling about yourself. If she was disrespectful then my bet is somewhere or another, you were disrespectful to yourself. Does that make sense?" He nodded yes again. I went on, "If you find yourself in a life of suffering, I am just saying that the place to start is with *you,* what you are being, rather than blaming your predicament on anyone else. At some point, a person may realize that they no longer want to stay in a painful situation and very deliberately decide they are done. That is a very different course of action then behaving as though you are a victim of circumstances. Deciding and changing your mind, without blame or any need to punish someone else is more like following your heart and letting yourself love what you love, without a drop of guilt. As a matter of fact, it's a very joyous and liberating experience that inspires everyone around you, its truth living through you!" He seemed to like that idea, as though it gave him permission to be faithful to something other than the unhappy life he found himself living.

I invited Mike to make a list of things he was grateful for and passionate about experiencing. "One thing you can do every time you catch yourself in that old conversation of guilt and being wrong is to practice just dropping it. Stop the conversation mid-stream and put your attention on one of the items on your list. It will change your vibration from guilt to gratitude and you will start emitting a different message into the world. You will begin to attract what you are vibrating at. What we send out always comes back," I repeated. "Placing your attention on the negative aspects of your life is just an old habit that will be fun for you to break. You like a challenge, right?" I made a bet with him that if he dropped that old conversation for one solid week and put attention on something from his gratitude list every time he caught himself wallowing in negativity, at the end of seven days, his life would feel differently. Smiling, I added, "It may take a month but it's a really fun thing to practice. You might even end up doing it for the rest of your life because you enjoy the process. And, it feels really good to give yourself something so sweet and to allow yourself to be human." He laughed at my enthusiasm.

I told him that the best medicine I had ever found for sadness and fear was to admit and be honest about what I felt inside and allow myself to fully be me. I explained how we were usually taught to believe what someone else believed and were never really encouraged or led to discover our own feelings and dreams. I went on, "Allowing ourselves to take the time to discover whom we are and where our spot is in the Universe is actually the only way we can connect with the divine and live out our life's purpose." I continued, "It's understandable that many of us skipped discovering ourselves because if we didn't do as mom believed was best, follow the clan, agree with the church, the political party, or even our friends in school, we were ostracized or punished. It hurt, so we didn't tell our truth and many of us even hid it from ourselves. As children most of us considered it wrong or selfish to listen to our heart's song for fear of being punished." I looked up at him, "In many ways, it's the same with adults, just less blatant. We are quietly judged and diminished for being self-absorbed or different, mostly by people who, just like us, were never taught to feel their own dreams. They aren't bad people; they just haven't been shown that it's a gift to do what they love and that it's one of the best ways to contribute to others. People often think we are arrogant or selfish for caring about ourselves. Which is ironic because it's one of the most important ways to care about the rest of the world. The Bible says, 'Love they neighbor as thyself'… assuming we love ourselves. I think most of us forget about the aspect of self and just strive to love our neighbors. When we really do love and honor our Self, we are connected to God. Then the neighbor part isn't something to strive for, it's simply the result and it comes naturally."

Mike was now connected to something bigger than himself. I sensed it. He was willing and open and the Universe was responding to his reach while holding us dearly. I continued, "The process of going for your dream and forgiving yourself restores faith in the Sacred for everyone who is near you. People feel when friends believe in themselves, especially children because it gives them permission to do the same. A lot of folks have kept their innermost feelings secret, never allowing time to feel their passions. It can take a little self-prodding to answer the question, 'What do I love, what makes my heart sing and be fulfilled?' After being immersed in living up to old preconditioned standards for so long, it calls for new thinking. It takes great courage to acknowledge your dreams and go after them."

Mike was listening intently, and as we pulled into the hospital,

I hurried to wrap it up, "You can put your attention on anything you want in life; do what you enjoy, find out what you love, count all the blessings around you and watch your world transform. It only takes a few moments a day to succeed. Make a commitment to yourself and schedule time to feel your desires. Take five minutes when you wake up, or right before sleep, and anytime in between," I coached. "It's a practice! Never give up on your dreams, never!" He had to get organized to get me out of the vehicle so his attention was dwindling. I thanked him for being there for me and helping to save my life. He looked at me with soft eyes and I felt his sweet heart. I was happy.

The Universe never ceased to amaze me, offering the perfect scenario to prompt my next wake-up. Mike was a reminder for me to move more toward whatever was next. He was my nudge. He did it by showing me to me. As I spoke to him I didn't realize all that would come out of my mouth, but it had to. There was no stopping the flow, it was moving *through* me more than from me. I love teaching and helping people see how amazing they are. It had been a long time since I had engaged in a dialogue that was playful, prodding, and inspiring like that. I loved the whole experience, and it reminded me how much I treasured working with people. I had wandered off alone since Dad died, not branching out and not connecting with anyone besides my family. I'm not saying this was bad or wrong, but that it was exactly how it should have been. I noticed a chapter of my life closing. I was complete with my period of introspection and ready for something different, a new dream. I grew a little excited, thinking about taking my own advice and creating a new project, one that blew my skirt up! But first things first, I had to get released from the hospital.

The emergency room was packed. I waited in my tiny cubicle for several hours before being admitted. I decided against a blood transfusion because it just didn't feel right. I ended up arguing with two physicians about it because I was acting against their strong recommendations. They threatened me with all kinds of possible consequences including the warning that it would take me up to six months to regain my strength. But they didn't know me.

I used the waiting period in the ER to visit with my body's cells and inspire them to perk up and multiply and to not listen to what the docs had said. Thank goodness I had the sense to do this silently or they may have moved me to a different ward. I felt responsible in a new way. I believed in myself and was thrilled by the visual understanding I now had of our connection to the invisible, to Source. I knew what to do and how to heal and got started right away. I wasn't the least bit concerned about the bleeding and trusted that I would be fine, better than ever, actually. I also believed my colon was strong and healthy. The doctors offered to summon the on-call enterologist (the intestines specialist) to check me out (scope my colon again) and discover the problem. I declined. I promised them I would have a blood-free pile of pooh for them very soon so they could all stop wasting time on me and instead help the people who were really suffering. I explained that the bleeding was a result of the polyp removal I had insisted the doctor perform during my colonoscopy. I told them I had persuaded her, against her better judgment, to excise every single one of them, professing I would never drink another glass of that nasty prep fluid as long as I lived. Nobody was to blame but me. The docs finally surrendered, mostly because they had bigger fish to fry. I escaped fairly easily.

I was so glad to finally be left alone in the quietness so I could re-feel the preciousness of the day. The loving man from the invisible who had welcomed me when I had left my body was fixed in my mind. Something about him felt so familiar but I didn't recognize his face. I tried to feel into his being and see what, if anything, was revealed that was memorable, but nothing came to me. I wondered if it was Dad in a different costume, but ruled that out, believing that I would have known. After racking my brain for a few moments, I decided that it didn't matter what costumes everyone in the invisible wore because the vibration they emitted was who they really were. I caught myself smiling into the dark as I relived the love of all the people huddled together. The feeling from them was astounding, huge, and all-encompassing! It included the same feeling I experienced when I had melted into Christ's hands, on top of the feeling of excitement and joy I experienced with Dad. It was similar to the Sacred that I felt whenever I was quiet and connected. It was all Godness. Pure love was the theme of the invisible. I felt so blessed to be near that vibration, nearer those beings. It was like a kiss from heaven. Then, to get a peek at everyone's extension of energy from his or her bodies, particularly Drake's was beyond belief. However, seeing Mike, the EMT, so empty and disconnected was the real gift. Not because I liked seeing him that way but because of what happened to me when I saw him. He awakened something in me that had been fast asleep. Witnessing his separateness was like witnessing some part of my Self.

A few hours after wheeling me in, Mike came to check on me while I was still in the ER cubicle. He was softer, more open, and it was a treasure to feel him. He made light conversation at first and then looked at me seriously for a second before saying, "Thank you." I let it in, to the delight of both of us. He was so precious, such a gift. I shared my gratitude for him being the perfect person to rescue me and explained to him the blessing he was to my world. "Thank you," I said as I peered into his sky-blue eyes. We smiled at one another and I was reminded of the grace of existence. I had a feeling we would meet again someday and that, somehow, we were old friends who had just met. So much of what had poured through me had been for *my* ears as well as his.

What a day! A profound trip into the invisible and a perspective-altering ride to the hospital. The synchronicity was a hoot and contained plenty of evidence and inspiration for Mike and myself to begin a new chapter of life. The joy of being able to touch a fellow human being and point him toward his own path made my heart smile. That was what Mike had done for me.

Even though I couldn't see it in my own body, in my small emergency room cubicle, I knew that every drop of my attention and how I focused it was somehow linking to everyone else's energy, as theirs did mine. Visibly experiencing the vibration that connected us in the invisible had fed my desire to become more responsible for whatever I deposited into the mix. Over the last couple years, my definition of responsibility had changed immensely and continued to transform as I became more aware. I figured it would keep on shifting, and smiling to myself, I wondered what was next.

Intending, feeling, believing, allowing, trusting, and managing my mind was the key to creating magic. I was convinced. Again, Divine Intelligence responded to my strong and ancient desire to be awake. I bet the Sacred patiently waits for each of us to be kind to ourselves and open our hearts to what we love, so it can joyously deliver it! There was so much gratitude filling my little space and my soul felt it too!

Divine Love through me,
blesses and multiplies all that I have,
all that I give and all that I receive.
I give joyously with a consciousness of Abundance.

–A Prayer from Circle's Edge
Church of Religious Science, Reno, NV
Rev. Dr. Sandy Jacob

To Tao or To Doubt

chapter 24

Those who do things by the Pooh Way find this sort of thing happening to them all the time. It's hard to explain, except by example, but it works. Things just happen in the right way, at the right time. At least they do when you let them, when you work with circumstances instead of saying, "This isn't supposed to be happening this way," and trying hard to make it happen some other way. If you're in tune with The Way Things Work, then they work the way they need to, no matter what you may think about it at the time. Later on, you can look back and say, "Oh, now I understand. That had to happen so that those things could happen, and those had to happen in order for this to happen...." Then you realize that even if you'd tried to make it all turn out perfectly, you couldn't have done better, and if you'd really tried, you would have made a mess of the whole thing...

In order to take control of our lives and accomplish something of lasting value, sooner or later we need to learn to Believe. We don't need to shift our responsibilities onto the shoulders of some deified Spiritual Superman, or sit around and wait for Fate to come knocking at the door. We simply need to believe in the power that's within us, and use it. When we do that, and stop imitating others and competing against them, things begin to work for us.

–*The Tao of Pooh,* Benjamin Hoff

The Tao includes all things, all thoughts, all hopes, and all fears. My adventure into the invisible brought more clarity to the concept, "all for one and one for all." Everyone's connected. Some people may appear or feel barely plugged in, but they're still part of the whole. Perhaps they abandoned themselves at some point, like we all have, and the Universe responds by mirroring back emptiness for however long it takes the experience to be acknowledged and owned by us, the original abandoner. As I looked upon the people standing around my body, I realized that whatever happened in one person's energy field affected the surrounding beings. Not in a bad way, more in an evolving way. We were all energetically connected and the ocean of invisible that held us was absorbing everything we emitted like a sponge. Whatever a single being felt became a part of the whole ocean and whatever the ocean held, touched us all. I imagined that humans were like fingers on a hand. They look like separate entities; the fingers could separate from each other, even move independently, but they were connected to a larger, all-inclusive reality. If a finger got smashed, the hand (the inclusive reality) would feel it and be impacted. Whether it knows it or not, the finger is part of a larger reality. So are we. The Tao includes all things.

Within a week of going home I was feeling pretty chipper. I had to take naps for a while and be patient, but I was okay with that. I was so inspired by my peek into the invisible and my connection with Mike that I was eager to create a project that turned me on, made life fun, and allowed me to ooze joy! My mind was on constant scan-mode, searching for my passionate new endeavor. I was excited and felt incredibly enthused by the myriad of possibilities. I was considering teaching, empowering children, contributing, being artistic, writing, golfing, and making money (unfortunately golfing and making money didn't go together in the same sentence). I played with all the ideas, imagining and feeling myself experiencing them. I was anxious to see where this was leading. I concluded that my favorite experience was engaging people and pointing them toward their joy, just like Dad had done with me. Mike reminded me what a treasure this was. In hot pursuit of taking more responsibility and fulfilling my own dream, I went back to delivering the Avatar tools. It was a wonderful time and a huge privilege assisting others in knowing their preciousness, particularly alongside my old friends. However, I kept noticing a nudge to question my commitment and level of joy. Intuitively I knew there was another direction calling me. Frequently I found myself exploring possibilities. I pondered what I might invent or pull together that would be totally new and adventurous. I desired a project that would provide an arena in which I could be more creative and independent while contributing to children and parents. I imagined, felt, tasted, and tried on several ventures… creating a ranch for children to have a thirty-day study program to embrace their potential, designing simple pamphlets on parenting guides for joy, and gathering like-minded people and developing a safe house for children of addicted parents. Even joining the Peace Corps had crossed my mind (this last one was quite an eye roller for Pat).

As the months passed, I let it all brew and kept envisioning possibilities. I felt something wonderful coming. I believed in this with all my heart. It was exciting contemplating the details such as what kind of environment I'd enjoy, how many hours a day I wanted to invest, and the types of people I'd have a blast creating with. I imagined manifesting dreams with a group of friends who had awesome control of their attention, people who thought for themselves, and held personal integrity in high esteem. Whoever I was going to be inventing with had to be committed to being awake! Knowing how to take responsibility was number one.

Operating in integrity was a concept worth exploring. There were so many perspectives of the meaning and experience of the word that it was baffling. Every teacher I had studied with defined it somewhat differently and over time my own interpretation had changed significantly.

I was certain of only one thing… nobody could determine what living in integrity should look like for another. We all had our own ideas about what was true and most important. God knows I've tried to make others adopt my notions, just as religions have tried and countries have tried, but integrity comes from within. As Wayne Dyer said in *Ten Secrets for Success and Inner Peace,* "Inside each and every one of us we must find our own way of fulfilling and actualizing ourselves as human beings and no one else out there can direct us or tell us how to do that. It has to be something that comes from within." Dad often reminded me to look inside for what felt most authentic. He said that when I was present and connected to the invisible that held us all, I would be able to intuitively and inclusively respond to any situation life offered. The people I loved, the organizations I joined, and of course any infomercial I got sucked into, were all quite willing to tell me what I "ought to do" to be happy and harvest a life of integrity. Everyone had a suggestion or an answer. I got distracted more than a few times.

I learned about the mechanics of integrity by acting from my own heart and getting to know myself better. As a personality or "not I," integrity was more about defending and protecting some image I held of myself and often was an act of ego. For my entire life I totally believed that integrity was more about following imposed rules, coloring inside the lines drawn by others, and doing it better than them. But now, when in "feel" and connected to the awareness of Higher Self, my understanding of integrity was much more intuitive. My actions compassionately transformed to include the environment and the people inhabiting it and I acted from inner guidance. Both stages were an integral piece of the evolution of my understanding, yet so different. As I learned more about the Tao and embraced the Yin and the Yang of existence, I became more a product of my inner being than anything being imposed on me as right or wrong from an outside source. Not fitting into someone else's picture of correctness was increasingly okay with me. What had been true for me at one point in my life simply no longer was. I respected the very likely prospect that this was accurate for others as well. Understanding that what someone holds as absolute truth would probably change over their lifetime makes room for a lot of perspectives. Mankind used to believe the earth was flat! I appreciated understanding that everything was in a constant state of change and that we weren't wedded to old choices unless we believed we were. I had room for people to change their minds. My relationships continually evolved to match my inward state.

I got fairly good at recognizing my Higher Self's voice compared to that of my ego. Even though, over time, my ego seemed to grow cleverer and had become quite a skilled ventriloquist, my awareness kept expanding. Although I was constantly challenged by my earthly ambitions, I maintained my commitment to stay on my toes. I used many techniques to check in on myself. I began paying close attention to motivations and intentions behind my words and actions. That was very useful and revealing. Whenever my ego was at the helm, it was usually focused on what others were thinking of me or weighing how I could gain approval. If I questioned what it was I was trying to gain from any action or relationship, it helped me to get more honest and discover often buried intentions. My ego searched for ways to dominate or control a situation, to be the star! It used disagreement and argument as its platform. If I was positional, critical, or righteous about anything and I caught myself, I politely apologized and admitted my mistake. Humiliation helped me to quiet the ego.

Whenever acting from my Higher Self, I was calm and intuitive, with a keen awareness of what was best for all concerned and I was open to whatever the Universe (my vibration) put in my path. I trusted, understanding that the world was constantly transforming, that bad fortune could follow good and vice versa. I didn't need to dominate or compete to be special when I was consciously present. Living in non-attachment allowed me to respect and honor all events. When I was in feel and dancing with the flow of the Tao, there was no urge to manipulate or control reality. I acted from integrity and did my best to take responsibility for every single moment. As Byron Katie says in *Loving What Is,* "When you know better, you do better." When viewing reality from the eyes of Higher Self, I trusted the process of everyone's awakening. I deeply appreciated each moment that I was able to act from this awareness.

I believe that Highest Self keeps getting higher. To recognize that all people are in a state of becoming creates a lot of room for different definitions of integrity to exist. Not to excuse dishonesty, but to be alert to the level of responsibility we are operating from, is smart. What may appear integral to one identity may not be to another. For example, a father who does something dishonest in order to secure a loan to feed his children while internally promising to pay it back with interest may feel in integrity. To the CEO of the financial institution making the loan, the father is out of integrity. Understandably it could become a battle of who is right and who is wrong. Yet, they could both believe they are acting out of integrity, at least in their minds and hearts. I'm not justifying behaviors or criminal acts because someone felt they were in integrity; I'm simply recognizing the different faces of truth. People know, unless mentally unstable, when they are manipulating and being dishonest. Whether they acknowledge it or not, the knowing is in them. If they claim it was an act of integrity, but physically, mentally, or emotionally harmed someone, I suspect they had their ego mixed up with their Highest Self. It happens.

I used to be an integrity policeman constantly searching for bad guys, the ones who were committing transgressions. I had so much attention on what people were doing "wrong" that I missed seeing all the decency and kindness around me. To have so much attention on what was NOT working in the world was very disheartening and painful. I was consumed with exposing dishonesty as though I could fix life and change people by pointing my finger at them. I was relieved to finally realize Divine Intelligence was in charge of integrity, not me. What flows out flows in; the world is always moving into balance.

I was increasingly inspired to create a fun project with my new understanding of human potential. Thinking about what I wanted to explore was exhilarating because I believed whatever I finally chose would come to life. I spent a little time each day contemplating possibilities, wanting to be mindful of what I wished for. I decided the project would include working alongside people who understood integrity in the same vein as me and also operated in life with the benefit of others in mind. This way, when we hit obstacles (which we would), we'd agree on the benefit of taking responsibility for where we found ourselves. This would allow us to effectively move toward a solution and get back on track without wasting energy and time in the kingdom of blame. Making mistakes was part of the human experience but taking full responsibility was more a learned behavior. I just needed someone like-minded to play with. I kept feeling it!

After just a few more weeks of exploring, I received a call from my dear friend, Shakti Cain. She shared some information she had learned from a film called *What the Bleep Do We Know!?* It partly featured Dr. Masuro Emoto's research with water and the powerful effects that spoken and written words have on the actual structure of water crystals. She had read Emoto's book, *Messages from Water,* in which there were photographs showing how water responded differently to certain words. High vibration words such as harmony, gratitude, and peace created expansive and beautiful crystals while low vibration words such as hate, jerk, or idiot produced dingy crystal images that seemed to collapse or shrink. Based on his groundbreaking research, Dr. Emoto believes that words energetically transform their environment. This made perfect sense to me given how everything was made of energy. I loved the whole idea and a project came to mind: to create a water bottling company that offered a variety of positive words on its bottles so people could pick the vibration they wanted for that particular day and put some attention on their goals—instead of their obstacles!

Shakti mentioned how sweet it would be, since humans are mostly made of water, to intentionally put specific words on our clothes that would raise the vibration of our bodies, support healing, inspire courage, or whatever a soul was hungry for. As she spoke I saw a baby wrapped in a blanket with the word PEACE across it. I got so excited that my mind began racing. I loved her idea! I said, "Why not create a clothing line where people could pick words they wanted to wear? They could touch their own lives in a positive way by choosing a word or phrase to inspire them." At this point, I was nearly hyperventilating! We threw around the idea of creating a company and how it might work, what it would cost, and I nudged her to be my partner, but her plate was already too full. I hung up the phone and knew—this was my next project. I felt it being born. I saw it happening. In search of the perfect partner, I scanned my relationships and thought of everyone I could think of. I wanted someone to invent and create with!

I went to bed that night tickled in my knowing that this clothing company adventure would provide so much of what I had imagined possible. I could hardly sleep. I was picturing a website, organic products, and linens, and I imagined every boutique carrying high vibration clothing. I imagined us going international, and then I almost jumped out of bed with excitement when I decided a portion of the proceeds should go to feed, clothe, and love children around the world. Ideas were running through my head at breakneck speed.

I wondered who would be the one to partner with. I wasn't getting any picture or idea of who this person could be. I was certain I didn't want to do it alone. I had asked Pat, the boys, and even my mom and sisters, yet none of them were interested. I finally relaxed, took some breaths, and remembered to trust that the perfect person would appear. In fact, they were already on their way. I was pulling them in with my vibration. I smiled, closed my eyes, and requested that a dream from the invisible guide me.

I woke up early the next morning thinking, *I don't know a darn thing about retail and the Internet is an alien to me,* and then I realized that if I let my mind look for what is wrong instead of what is right, I'd get all caught up in the impossible versus the possible. So I chose to stop the negative dialogue and refused to let the doubt monster get me. I could Tao or I could doubt. I wanted to keep my attention on the goal so I would let the ideas flow freely, writing them down even if they seemed outrageous. I then made a list of the attributes I would love in a partner: kindness, honesty, fun, brilliant, high level of integrity, energetic, Internet savvy, happy, and lots of money to invest. It was exciting!

Over the next few days, I gathered information about everything—retail, website designs, fees, organic clothing vendors, etc., and I asked a couple of my close buddies if they were interested. No luck. Another week passed before I ran into a dear friend I hadn't seen in many years, Masen. Over lunch, I asked him what he did for a living and he reminded me: he owned a company that designed and managed websites. I smiled broadly and delighted in the Universe's timing. I told Masen about my idea. He said he would love to join me on this adventure. We had a great deal of respect for one another and we both knew immediately it was a perfect fit. He wanted to be part of a business that was fun, not with heavy attachment and pushing-pressures, but in the flow. I giggled with pleasure and bathed in the serendipity of the afternoon.

It turns out, Masen knew all the things I didn't know when it came to launching our business, so item after item on our checklist was easily handled. Our mission was to bring some goodness into the world, have fun, contribute to organizations that empower children, and make money doing what we loved! He was the perfect partner and our belief systems were aligned when it came to integrity and being able to create dreams by following our hearts. I was in awe of the ease with which the perfect network of people came together to create this company. I had to laugh as I scoured the nation to find a fulfillment organization we could train to imprint our products with love, one that would be as excited as we were about the project. I had interviewed many companies without success. After numerous calls and not knowing where to go next, I saw the resistance as my signal to stop pushing and to simply relax. So I did. The very next day my husband mentioned he had played golf with a guy he thought might work out for us and that his company was located about thirty minutes from our house! I was freakin' ecstatic! I called and met with the owner and, I know this sounds cliché, but it was a match made in heaven. Everything slid into place, from first thought to ultimate manifestation. That was how I knew it was in alignment with the Tao. I believe that because the project came from our hearts, with a goal that benefited everyone, with no pushing or resisting, magic was allowed to happen. Masen and I knew we had the name the moment we both spoke it out loud, "Be Aware Clothing."

Masen's intention was a perfect match to mine. We agreed that Be Aware Clothing could be the beginning of something much more inclusive. Being firm believers that whatever was going on inside of our hearts and minds would manifest on the outside, we came up with the trademark, Peace in Peace out®.[2] Ahhh… sweet synchronicity!

We believed anything was possible when our actions were geared toward assisting others as well as ourselves. I thought of Dad and how he must be chuckling from the invisible. Then I imagined five big letters on the front of one of our shirts, EGBOK! Everything's gonna be okay. I laughed out loud, truly believing things were already okay. Faith and patience were the only requirements.

When you are inspired by some great purpose, some extraordinary project, all your thoughts break their bonds: Your mind transcends limitations, your consciousness expands in every direction and you find yourself in a new, great and wonderful world. Dormant forces, faculties and talents become alive, and you discover yourself to be a greater person by far than you ever dreamed yourself to be.

–Patanjali

2 Peace in Peace out is a registered trademark of Be Aware Clothing. All rights reserved 2009

Allowing

chapter 25

When you begin to understand Law of Attraction, and you understand that which is like unto itself is drawn, then it is easier and easier to understand that you are offering a signal, and the entire Universe responds. And when you finally get that, and you begin to exercise some deliberate control about the signal that you offer, then it really begins to be fun, because then you recognize that nothing happens outside of your creative control. There are no things that happen by chance or by circumstance. There is nothing that is happening because of something you vibrated a long time ago or in a past life. It is not about what you were born into. It is only about what you are, right now, in this red hot fresh moment emitting.

–*Abraham* by Esther and Jerry Hicks

A dear companion of mine used to say, "Holly, let it be easy." At the time, I couldn't comprehend what she meant. In fact, it confused me. I judged her for not being as ambitious as me and secretly wondered if she was lazy.

I fought against simplicity for years due to a belief that I had to struggle and suffer before I could reap great benefits and reach my deserved pot of gold. I believed I *had* to work so hard that it hurt if I truly wanted to get anywhere. I flaunted suffering and sacrifice as evidence for my efforts as though pain should be rewarded. I would move from thing to thing constantly managing an inventory of what needed to be done, emotionally as well as materially, never finishing one list without starting another. I even reported to Pat how much I had accomplished each day and secretly waited for his praise. Of course I never let the praise in because another part of me said I still hadn't done or suffered enough. That's probably because I wasn't bleeding… yet.

I never stopped to smell flowers on my way to wherever I was going. If I got a whiff of an aromatic rose from my garden, I'd cut it and display it in the house because I thought it would help teach my family about the beauty of nature and the value of gardening. I was busy… and my heart was empty. Every day, my greatest accomplishment was that scribbled checkmark showing that I had completed a task.

Somehow, the more I struggled, the more I felt like I mattered and deserved a prize. One I was hoping to receive from the big guy in the sky as I approached the pearly gates. Eckhart Tolle calls it the psychological need for the next moment describing how we think something coming in the future will finally bring us the joy we have always longed for. Explaining how we entirely miss the pleasure that can only come from being alive in the now. The only place pleasure exists is in the present moment. I engaged "time" with fervor, as a means to an end rather than as an opportunity to feel the wonderment of being human. Just as Eckhart described I had been consumed by my desire for the next moment believing that would be the one that would finally bring me joy. I constantly longed for what I hoped was coming, fully expecting the fruit of all my agony. My completed lists being my pathway to some imagined nirvana that could never arrive. Being happy was always a "future" event.

After lying in bed for several months and smelling the fumes of a dying body, Spirit had helped me realize that I never took a second to smell and enjoy the precious flowers in my own backyard, or sit quietly with the song of the birds, or enjoy long looks into the eyes of my beloved. I had never allowed myself to linger in the quiet and stillness of the Divine. It was everywhere and, yet, I didn't recognize it. Nowadays, you can't get me out of it.

Crohn's disease was a very painful wake-up call, a difficult route toward joy and one I don't recommend. My path was grueling and required a great deal of energy and commitment to traverse because I had desperately resisted all feeling and refused to honestly take responsibility for where I found myself. "Not experiencing" had caused my physical body and emotional armor to thicken into a dense creation that took a long time to peel away at. Taking responsibility was my only road to freedom. Once something becomes physical there's no way out but through. With so much history and massive effort into avoiding feeling any pain, I had become numb to life and I didn't even know it. My body had to scream bloody murder in order for me to hear it. For many years, it had suffered my unconsciousness and denial and as a result, it reeked of abuse. It took years to make amends to my body for closing the door on my inner most feelings. I worked long hours to discover and release all the patterns and memories neatly tucked away and held within my brain, blood, and bones. It was a painful and difficult process because I never knew (at the time) how simple it could be. I didn't know that all I had to do as a child was become willing to feel, be as honest as possible, and not pretend. I truly believed feelings could kill me. I wish someone had taken me aside and explained the mechanics of energy and resistance. I believe I could have understood the uncomplicated instruction to admit the truth and feel my feelings. If I had been told this practice would help me become free of what hurt and lead me toward happiness, it could have been so easy.

We either feel or resist feeling. Feeling is being aware of our bodies, our environment, and other people. It's fully accepting what is so we may eventually transform it. It's being connected and getting a sense of our pockets of density or lightness in the energy around us, near us, in our bodies and our homes. There is always a vibration in the air. If we pay close attention and silence the mind chatter, we can feel it. It's present when we walk into a room, when we're near someone we love, when we're in the woods or by the ocean. It's always there. It's just difficult to notice the multitude of sensations in our space when our mind is busy calculating or comparing. When we shrink into thought or become our ego's need for approval or control, we lose conscious presence. We miss the magic of connecting with a fellow human and fail to honor the gift each moment offers or appreciate the amazing planet we live on. Conscious presence holds the key to allowing and mother Earth is the greatest of all teachers, ever present, like our cats, dogs, and other pets. They have much to teach us about being in the moment, becoming more aware, and receiving the love from the invisible that is constantly embracing us.

We can grow more in tune, more inclusive, and sense the energy that connects us simply by desiring to and then deciding to. This practice of feeling is not to be mistaken with the habit of wallowing in our emotions or suffering. That's often an ego's endeavor to attract more of the same. The ego loves drama, conflict, and turmoil. The ego loves to be right and make others wrong. We can always tell if the ego is at the helm by how we react to the world and respond to the feelings inside of us; if we are judging or resisting, the ego is driving the bus. When our negative, grumpy, or positional response goes unnoticed by us it compounds. Our denial then substitutes for honest feelings and the honest feelings rarely get acknowledged or experienced, which ensures nothing will change. The company we crave is that of our own true Self. Resistance and judgment create ongoing separation and are the game of the ego, while criticism provides the food.

We know the difference between something lightening up or weighing heavier because we can feel it. The heavier and denser, the more it consumes our creative energy. We become tired, discouraged, and eventually depressed. Truly experiencing what resides in our hearts will always lead to more peace, relief, optimism, and further trust. Resisting what we feel in our hearts leads to conflict, fear, and emotional havoc. We know how to allow. It's soft, expansive, and opens doors. It's about being honest with our many selves, and although unwieldy at first, the resulting freedom after a short time of practice is undeniable.

I believe we are all hungry for this connection to the Sacred and long for this innate wisdom to illuminate our paths through our personal existence. I believe this energy is the pure potentiality that Deepak Chopra speaks of, the stillness that Eckhart Tolle so beautifully empowers us to access, and the Source energy—the Vortex that Esther Hicks (Abraham) so magically invites us to embrace with our desire. I believe it is the awareness that Harry Palmer compassionately guides us to claim so that we may take responsibility for living our lives *deliberately.*

I trust this energy and use my life circumstances and challenges to deepen my connection to it. My prayer is that it moves through me into the world. This essence is our truest home. I believe it's there to embrace each and every one of us, if we decide to allow it. As we begin to feel life and coalesce with the heart of a lover, a child, a pet, or even a tree, our relationship and connection to all living things begins to be revealed. It is always there in moments we enjoy the flow of love to and from our beingness. When our hearts open we sense how we are an aspect of something much larger and more encompassing. I believe we can learn how to move through our existence intuitively and compassionately by simply feeling and becoming more allowing of ourselves and others. Feeling is our bond with the Sacred and will always guide us to our perfect next step. Free of a mind that's clamoring with judgment, we are more able to merge with Higher Self and act out of care for all living things. This stillness is expansive and inclusive in ways we cannot know when consumed with owning, conquering, and winning. Not that any of that is bad, it is a path well traveled and ultimately leads to reaching for something more fulfilling.

This vast awareness will wait patiently, lifetimes if necessary, for us to allow its magic into our hearts. It stands silent and vigilant, fully expecting us to experience ourselves as Source, so we may own our power, and joyfully manifest passionate dreams. Once the vibration of the Sacred is embraced, even for a short time, we transform. Relationships change as the door to our heart opens permitting love to flow in and flow out, essentially filling us with the truth of ourselves and all beings. Creating abundance becomes easy and friendships take on new depths. Our willingness to feel enlightens us.

Resistance is the opposite of feeling and is a great signpost that we need to become more self-aware. The properties of resistance close down our connection and we become contracted and alone/separate while trapped in a mind that judges. Resistance leads us to noticing more of what is wrong with ourselves and the world, which energetically attracts more of the very thing we resist. Resistance is what glues us to unhappiness.

I was an expert at resisting. I resisted being unloved, alone, poor, abandoned, rejected, ugly, stupid, and I'm sure a zillion other things. I resisted anyone knowing that I was resisting. I was afraid of looking or acting stupid or being judged. I was consumed with managing my image in the eyes of others which was impossible because everyone had a different definition of what was best, good, or how I should behave to close a deal or get a dose of approval. I was whoever I needed to be rather than becoming the aspect of the Nameless that only I could become in the fabric of life. I sold my soul to avoid my fear of failure. I pretended that life was perfect so expertly and thoroughly that nobody ever knew how much I resisted making mistakes. Pretense and resistance annihilated my creative energy. I actually believed resisting was smart and that pushing against all the above was the most effective path for succeeding in life.

I couldn't have been more wrong. It took every ounce of energy I could gather to keep all those emotions and notions at bay, which meant I had nothing left to put toward manifesting my dreams or creating health and abundance. I was exhausted and depleted from resisting.

I see now that dreams cannot be created by resisting nightmares. It's clear that we need to put our attention and energy toward our desires, whatever makes our hearts sing, so that the Universe can bring it to us. When we believe in ourselves and trust, magic happens. We must learn to feel and ooze expectation and deservability. The Universe has no judgment; it merely delivers whatever we vibrate at. What we request energetically will always come to us. Therefore, knowing what we are emitting (or requesting) becomes monumentally important. Feeling is the only path to this intuitive understanding. A strong and heartfelt belief that we deserve to be happy (without any doubt) sends a signal to the Universe so it can deliver that to our door. And, our belief that we don't deserve to be happy sends a signal to the Universe as well and it also delivers THAT to our door. The Universe honors all our requests with equal passion. Responsibility is being honest and aware enough to own our signals to the world. Divine intelligence will always reflect our innermost patterns and tendencies. When honestly examined this is a miraculous process allowing us to know ourselves completely. We may not like what we see, we may fight it, we may deny it, we may medicate ourselves so we can avoid it, and still, it will wait for us until we recognize and experience our life as our own to orchestrate. This is the human process of becoming real.

I didn't want to be sick. I deeply desired to be awake, to understand and learn how to love without conditions. From a very early age I had prayed for this. Obviously, I ignored a few of the kinder proddings because the signposts the Universe sent me along the way didn't make it into my heart. When given opportunities to forgive, I held grudges, when held responsible I often blamed, and when faced with a choice to tell the truth or lie and protect my image, frequently I opted for a splash of dishonesty. All because I was afraid of failure, disapproval, abandonment, and the underlying thread woven throughout my choices was the fear of being alone. Which when viewed from where I am now, I was anyway. I was too busy being numb and too afraid of vulnerability to feel or let anyone into my heart, including the invisible. I wasn't able to receive any information from the Nameless or from my Higher Self because I was shut down and guilt ridden believing I was unworthy of such good fortune.

So, the message got louder and the Universe (Higher Self) appropriately selected a sledgehammer for the next communication. It definitely wasn't the easiest way for me to reach my dreams, but it worked. The Sacred was merely responding to my intention to be awake. It had to, that's how vibration works. My desire for awakening had been transmitting outward to All That Is for my entire life and maybe even before that. Divine Intelligence was merely doing its job, and I am forever grateful.

Ever since my health traumas and near-death experiences, I am positive that everyone is part of an all-inclusive design, bigger than all of us put together—an intricate web of life that works in a collective fashion as well as individually. Imagine a piece of fabric with each thread being fundamentally a part of the whole. Each offers a very important ingredient of the overall function, every single thought or intention of each tiny aspect affects the integrity and ability of the entire cloth. We each make an impression of joy or sorrow, peace or war, love or hate, and it moves through the entire fabric of life adding to the overall energy of existence. From the level of Source we understand and enjoy being responsible for what we bring to the cloth because ***we are*** the fabric of life.

We can create a wave of peace in our surroundings by being peaceful. *Peace in, Peace out.* We can increase understanding in the world through our efforts to understand. I have always found with tragedy that there's an inherent possibility to transform the pain through reaching for something better, easier, and kinder. This simple act of desiring or wanting is revitalizing and spontaneously inspires and strengthens the entire fabric of life. Reaching for something that feels better is our nature and as we dream and imagine possibility we add hope to the overall vibration that encompasses humanity. Dream big!

Whether the goal is conscious or not, on some level of awareness perhaps we attract strange and difficult situations knowing they will somehow lead us to our true nature and remind us to be more compassionate with one another while simultaneously inspiring us to take more responsibility for our experience of life. Whenever hardship occurs, we seem to move more toward what matters most and more in the direction of our own truth. Through death, loss, and failure, something in the heart of humanity awakens, our care for one another deepens and we strive to offer any relief imaginable. Maybe collectively we believe we need to suffer or go to painful lengths to attain heightened awareness. However true, this doesn't make something difficult or painful any less hurtful, and still, I'm certain there is great wisdom at work on some level of how we are all creating reality. I am equally confident we can awaken by becoming consciously present and choosing to feel instead of transforming as a result of debilitating pain and hurting.

Life doesn't have to be so hard and painful. We may hurt and suffer at times but we don't *have* to suffer to wake up. We can choose to become SELF aware, without enduring a tragedy. We can exercise self-discipline, create a daily practice, and manage our minds so we attract more goodness into our environments and allow success to become our teacher. Each one of us deserves joy in our lives no matter what mistakes we've made and no matter who we've hurt or damaged in the past. We can clean up our messes and forgive ourselves and everyone else, too! Today is a good day to stop punishing someone for our pain, including ourselves. We can change our lives and those of others by abstaining from holding toxic grudges that attract a repeat of whatever we were resisting in the first place. I have done it, against all odds, so I know it can definitely be done! Through forgiveness, I healed a supposedly "incurable" disease. I fell in love with my adversaries, and as I became honest about my own faults, I developed a deep compassion for all people. Life became the heaven I dreamed it could be and it wasn't because someone outside of me finally changed.

Resisting reality creates hell on Earth. I attracted abuse again and again until ultimately turning on my self to finish the task, which of course, invited the Universe to assist me. With great respect for our beliefs, the Universe always cooperates by responding to our intentions. That's why I now pay close attention to the messages I send out. I check my actions and clean up my mistakes as quickly as I'm able. I let the Universe know when I've blown it and hurt another or myself and take responsibility for it by telling the truth. I pledge to be more aware and do better next time. And I do it over and over again. I fail and start over. I practice being more honest and courageous every day. It's a discipline. Some days I'm better at it than others, but I never give up on living from Higher Self knowing. The process is forever teaching me to love more deeply, honestly admit what I feel, and allow.

We can *decide* to let the past go. Paying punishment forward merely adds to the collective pain in the world and, eventually, it finds its way back to the punisher.

We can do better. We can admit our mistakes and make up for them by raising our vibration to one of love, honor, and acceptance for our fellow humans and also for ourselves. We can flow care and compassion to people as we drive, shop, garden, and as we breathe. We can add some kindness to the world as our amends for any pain we've caused another. We can begin to raise our vibration by simply having more compassion for ourselves, considering the obstacles we've had to move through and overcome. We can transform our lives by putting some attention on the goodness in our own hearts, acknowledging the determination that we have each new day to do the right thing. As we individually invite and embrace our connection to Highest Self, our actions in the world are instinctively for the benefit of everyone. When we live intuitively, caring is effortless and becomes our natural state of being. Conscious presence is tremendously powerful, focusing it toward goodness in Self and others offers the opportunity to heal broken hearts, families, and bodies.

Our energy affects the world. It adds to the collective stream that touches every soul. It's very much like water to a fish. Every thought, action, vibration, and intention we have makes up all that we swim in. Whether it's focused inward or outward, our presence and joy is the greatest gift we can offer the planet. We can all add something yummy to the quantum soup so that life tastes even better! Feeling pleasure not only opens our hearts, it creates a vibration that nudges all hearts. "Pleasure is free," as my dear sister Patricia likes to say. To give the world a gift, simply take a moment and feel happy because you decide to. One moment of your joy is a present to everyone.

We don't have to suffer or pay some heavy price for freedom. We can enjoy life *now.* We can become aware of what we're sending out by noticing what's coming in. It may not make sense and we may not like what we see and the idea may offend us, but we don't have to waste time arguing with reality anymore. If we keep attracting some experience we don't prefer, we need to take responsibility for who we are being and stop blaming others. We can correct our dishonesties and move on to what's next with a daily practice of simply putting our attention on something we appreciate or feel grateful for. *We* are in charge of our experience of joy and freedom! We can manage our minds and make a difference in our families, communities, and ultimately our world. We are powerful beings so why not experiment and see how life can change simply by becoming more aware of what we are thinking. Take a chance and admit obvious patterns, revel in joys, and take time to discover what truly delights us. It's a fun and enlightening exploration. Play with it for a week, a month, a few years, or the rest of your life! What do you have to lose? Ooze your desires!

If you just give it a go, I'll bet you'll catch a smile on your face in no time. And perhaps a wink will slip from your eye during your next visit to the mirror. You may even become your own best friend and experience your own preciousness, if even for a few seconds here and there. You might even acknowledge how determined you've always been to do the right thing and suddenly feel all the good intentions inside your own heart. Once you see the beauty of your soul, there's a good chance you'll begin to honor and respect the same in others. But watch out… this will instruct the Universe to bring you more of the same… so get ready for love.

If you're brave and decide to venture into connecting with all things and feel life fully, then it's very likely you'll allow the intuitive knowing of Higher Self to guide you closer toward joy. There's no stopping it once you're there! Health often improves, you feel adored, connected to the

Divine, and end up a wise, old being, highly skilled in managing your mind. Dreams come true so quickly that most people decide to use their knowing to assist others in experiencing how magnificently powerful and precious they are… and how glorious life can be.

As we awaken, our care for others is multiplied and we begin to feel how we all belong to each other in a very sacred way. As we trust and strengthen our connection to the Divine we're able to hold that same vibration for others and provide an energetic pathway, one that allows them to access their own magic. Sounds like love to me.

All you need to do is feel life, stop punishing yourself and others for mistakes, and let go of the past. Decide to forgive everything and everyone. Be done with it. Enjoy your SELF. Love your Selves, all of them, and the Universe is sure to love you back.

We're forever unfolding. So, **feel free,** bask in this savory morsel from Abraham-Hicks, and enjoy the magic of *Allowing...*

"As always, we are infinitely, happily, and eternally, incomplete."

With Love,
Holly

Begin now with the words,
Knowing that the experience will follow,
The experience preceding certainty,
And the awareness of what you are.
Begin with the words, the ideas, the thoughts
Which tell you that your world IS YOU.
Every aspect of what you label OTHER,
Whether it be another being, another animal,
Another plant, another chair, a distant star—
Everything which you call "other"
Is, indeed, your Self.
For you have become your friend.
You have become your enemy.
And neither of those sentences makes any sense.
For you have merely become your Self.

—Journey Beyond Words:
A Companion to the Workbook
of The Course in Miracles,
Brent Haskell, Ph.D., D.O

Celebrations

On to the limb
Of the no limit being
The singing bird has come

And I,
In this everywhere sky
Am laughter
Creating now forever after

All unlocked
From the prison of myself

And on the course of Avatars
I chart the uncharted
I steer by the stars

Now, the tides come not for me
For I am the ship,
I am the sea
I am the harbor wherever I be

Howard Wayne Goss
1934–1996

Quote Alley

"Spiritual awakening" is about discovering what's true. Anything that's not about getting to the truth must be discarded. Truth isn't about knowing things—you already know too much. It's about un knowing. It's not about becoming true, it's about unbecoming false so that all that's left is truth. If you want to become a priest or a lama or a rabbi or a theologian, then there's a lot to learn—tons and tons. But if you want to figure out what's true, then it's a whole different process and the last thing you need is more knowledge."

Jed McKenna

A round man cannot be expected to fit in a square hole right away. He must have time to modify his shape.

Mark Twain

If we examine every stage of our lives, we find that from our first breath to our last we are under the constraint of circumstances. And yet we still possess the greatest of all freedoms, the power of developing our innermost selves in harmony with the moral order of the Universe, and so winning peace at heart whatever obstacles we meet.

Johann Wolfgang von Goethe

The most valuable skill that you could ever develop is the skill of directing your thoughts toward what you want—to be adept at quickly evaluating all situations and then quickly coming to the conclusion of what you most want—and then giving your undivided attention to that. There is a tremendous skill in directing your own thoughts that will yield results that cannot be compared with results that mere action can provide.

Abraham-Hicks

Wherever you go, go with all your heart.

Confucius

Having access to that formless realm is truly liberating. It frees you from bondage to form and identification with form. It is life in its undifferentiated state prior to its fragmentation into multiplicity. We may call it the Unmanifested, the invisible Source of all things, the Being within all beings. It is a realm of deep stillness and peace, but also of joy and intense aliveness. Whenever you are present, you become "transparent" to some extent to the light, the pure consciousness that emanates from this Source. You also realize that the light is not separate from who you are but constitutes your very essence.

Eckhart Tolle

Emotions are your body's response to your mind.

Meister Eckhart

Rather than recoil from the horror of nothingness, plunge headlong into it. What is there to lose?

Jed McKenna

The only time we suffer is when we believe a thought that argues with what is. When the mind is perfectly clear, what is is what we want.

Byron Katie

He most honors my style who learns under it to destroy the teacher.

Walt Whitman

When you are in alignment with who-you-really-are, (with your Inner Being or Source), you cannot help but uplift those with whom you come into contact. Your value to those around you hinges upon only one thing: your personal alignment with Source. And the only thing you have to give to another is an example of that alignment—which they may observe, then desire, and then work to achieve—but you cannot give it to them... Everyone is responsible for the thoughts they think and the things that they choose as their objects of attention.

Abraham-Hicks

Personal reality reflects what a person really believes—not always the same as what he/she may be pretending to believe.

Harry Palmer

Pretending is resisting what you really believe.

Harry Palmer

Parents can't choose the mates for their children or the behavior of their children. You actually can't choose anything for your children without disempowering them.

Abraham-Hicks

All children have a sense of what is incomplete in their 'parents' way of life. After all, that's the system: We chose our parents in part to be awakened to what is missing, to what needs to be added to human understanding, and we begin that process by being dissatisfied with what we find in our lives with them.

James Redfield

You are the creator of your own life experience, and as the creator of your experience, it is important to understand that it is not by virtue of your action, not by virtue of your doing—it is not even by virtue of what you are saying—that you are creating. You are creating by virtue of the thought that you are offering…

You cannot speak or offer action without thought-vibration occurring at the same time; however, you are often offering a thought-vibration without offering words or action. Children or babies learn to mimic the vibration of the adults who surround them long before they learn to mimic their words.

Abraham-Hicks

When you lose touch with inner stillness, you lose touch with yourself. When you lose touch with yourself, you lose yourself in the world.

Eckhart Tolle

Pain is inevitable suffering is optional.

The Dalai Lama

The Compassion Exercise

by Harry Palmer, author of the Avatar Materials

Increase the amount of compassion in the world.

Instructions: This exercise can be done anywhere that people congregate (airports, malls, parks, beaches, etc.). It should be done on strangers, unobtrusively, from some distance. Try to do all five steps on the same person. Expected results are a personal sense of peace.

Step 1 With attention on the person, repeat to yourself:

Just like me, this person is seeking some happiness for his/her life.

Step 2 With attention on the person, repeat to yourself:

Just like me, this person is trying to avoid suffering in his/her life.

Step 3 With attention on the person, repeat to yourself:

Just like me, this person has known sadness, loneliness and despair.

Step 4 With attention on the person, repeat to yourself:

Just like me, this person is seeking to fulfill his/her needs.

Step 5 With attention on the person, repeat to yourself:

Just like me, this person is learning about life.

Variations:

1. May be done by couples and family members to increase understanding of each other.
2. May be done on old enemies and antagonists still present in your memories.
3. May be done on other life forms.

This is one of thirty exercises that can be found in ReSurfacing®: Techniques for Exploring Consciousness by Harry Palmer. Excerpted with permission.

The body is just a rental car and this planet is just a motel. This is nobody's home, though some treat it like a permanent residence, as if the worst thing that can possibly happen is that you pick up and move on. How absurd, and yet, how absolutely vital to the experience. Look at things in this light and you'll see the countless ways in which society encourages the externalized self and mocks, discourages and combats the very notion of turning inward. Alan Watts called it the taboo against knowing who you are.

Jed McKenna

There is no truth to forget about anything until someone creates some.

Harry Palmer

The point is to wake up, not earn a Ph.D. in waking up. Simply put waking up is job one, and then, if you still want to liberate all beings or promote world peace or save the whales, great… lucky beings, lucky world, lucky whales.

But the bottom line remains the same; you're either awake or your not.

Jed McKenna

What the caterpillar calls the end of the world, the rest of the world calls a butterfly.

Lao Tzu

Knowing others is intelligence.
Knowing yourself is true wisdom.
Mastering others is strength.
Mastering yourself is true power.
If you realize that you have enough,
you are truly rich.
If you stay in the center
and embrace death with your whole heart,
you will endure forever.

Tao Te Ching #33

You're picky about the car you drive. You're picky about what you wear. You're picky about what you put in your mouth. We want you to be pickier about what you think.

Abraham-Hicks

Each one sees what he carries in his heart.

Johann Wolfgang von Goethe

When I argue with reality, I lose—but only 100% of the time.

Byron Katie

Through allowing, you become what you are; vast, spacious. You become whole. You are not a fragment anymore, which is how the ego perceives itself. Your true nature emerges, which is one with the nature of God.

Eckhart Tolle

No human would ever do anything to harm another if Connected to Source because when you're Connected, you're empowered; you don't feel insecure. And when you don't feel insecure, you don't need to do something to somebody else that you're afraid of, because you're not afraid. You understand that Well-Being is yours.

Abraham-Hicks

In your system of reality you are learning what mental energy is, and how to use it. You do this by constantly transforming your thought and emotions into physical form. You are supposed to get a clear picture of your inner development by perceiving the exterior environment. What seems to be a perception, an objective concrete event independent from you, is instead the materialization of your own inner emotions, energy, and mental environment.

The Seth Material, Jane Roberts

The Truth is far more all-encompassing than the mind could ever comprehend. No thought can encapsulate the Truth. At best, it can point to it. For example, it can say: "All things are intrinsically one." That is a pointer, not an explanation. Understanding these words means feeling deep within you the truth to which they point.

Eckhart Tolle

As I observed the actions of my day, wanting to be thought of as a "good person" was the primary motivating factor. I wondered who I would be if all the things I did for approval and acceptance were removed. Who would be left?

Holly Riley

Those who danced were thought to be quite insane by those who could not hear the music.

Angela Monet

Power in general, such an absence of external restriction and limitation that it depends only upon the inward determination of the subject whether or not it will act.

Integrity unimpaired condition, wholeness, entireness, purity, completeness.

Harry Palmer

Any man who can drive safely while kissing a pretty girl is simply not giving the kiss the attention it deserves.

Albert Einstein

Many think success means getting everything I want. And we say, that's what dead is, and there is no such thing as that kind of dead. Success is not being done; not being complete. Success is still dreaming and feeling positive in the unfolding.

Abraham-Hicks

The belief that something is wrong is the fire under the ass of humanity.

Jed McKenna

Spirit is truly and always one; but its manifestations on different planes of creation are different. Just as ice, water and vapor are not three things but only three forms of the same thing, similarly Spirit is one, but its forms are many. In the very highest transcendent realms, it abides as an extremely fine and subtle entity; but as we descend toward less subtle regions, this Spirit also takes less subtle forms.

Rumi

Believe nothing, no matter where you read it or who has said it, not even if I have said it, unless it agrees with your own reason and your own common sense.

Buddha

Indoctrinate to fill someone with beliefs.

Harry Palmer

Think for yourself. That's the golden rule. Think for yourself. Make it your mantra. Tattoo it on the inside of your eyelids.

Jed McKenna

When my goals are motivated by what others consider the priority rather than listening to my heart, I am unfulfilled.

Holly Riley

Empty your mind of all thoughts.
Let your heart be at peace.
Watch the turmoil of beings,
but contemplate their return.
Each separate being in the universe
returns to the common source.
Returning to the source is serenity.
If you don't realize the source,
you stumble in confusion and sorrow.
When you realize where you came from,
you naturally become tolerant,
disinterested, amused,
kindhearted as a grandmother,
dignified as a king.
Immersed in the wonder of the Tao,
you can deal with whatever life brings you,
and when death comes, you are ready.

Tao Te Ching #16

I am the awareness that is aware that there is attachment. That's the beginning of the transformation of consciousness.

Eckhart Tolle

A man is a god in ruins. When men are innocent, life shall be longer, and shall pass into the immortal, as gently as we awake from dreams.

RalphWaldo Emerson

Your conclusion that there isn't enough of something—whether it is enough land, or money, or clarity—stems from you learning, without meaning to, a vibration that holds you apart from what you want. There is not limitation. If you identify a desire for it, Source recognizes your desire, and immediately begins to deliver it to you. And it will manifest in the variety, in the fullness, and in the way that you, and only you, learn to allow it.

Abraham-Hicks

Lao Tzu On Being In The Moment
The master gives himself up
to whatever the moment brings.
He knows that he is going to die,
and he has nothing left to hold onto:
No illusions in his mind,
no resistances in his body.
He doesn't think about his actions;
they flow from the core of his being.
He holds back nothing from life;
therefore he is ready for death,
as a man is ready for sleep
after a good day's work.

Lao Tzu

One grand great life throbs through earth's giant heart,
And mighty waves of single Being roll
From nerve-less germ to man, for we are part
Of every rock and bird and beast and hill,
One with the things that prey on us, and one with what we kill.

Oscar Wilde

Every negative assumption or expectation… that we make about another human being is a prayer that goes out and acts to create that reality in that person. Remember our minds connect—our thoughts and expectations go out and influence others to think the same way we do… Our prayer-field is working constantly in the world, sending out our expectations, and in the case of another person, the effect is almost instantaneous.

James Redfield

The realization that something is not as you want it to be is an important first step, but once you have identified that, the faster you are able to turn your attention in the direction of a solution, the better, because a continuing exploration of the problem will prevent you from finding the solution. The problem is a different vibrational frequency than the solution—and all thoughts (or vibrations) are affected by (or managed by) the Law of Attraction.

Abraham-Hicks

Feeling is the language that speaks to the Divine Matrix (the Universe). Feel as though your goal is accomplished and your prayer is already answered.

Gregg Braden

All the misery on the planet arises due to a personalized sense of "me" or "us." That covers up the essence of who you are. When you are unaware of that inner essence, in the end you always create misery. It's as simple as that. When you don't know who you are, you create a mind-made self as a substitute for your beautiful divine being and cling to that fearful and needy self. Protecting and enhancing that false sense of self then becomes your primary motivating force.

Eckhart Tolle

Even if you find someone to assign the blame to it doesn't solve the problem.

Jed McKenna

But who prays for Satan? Who, in eighteen centuries, has had the common humanity to pray for the one sinner that needed it most…?

Mark Twain

Absolute miracles happen when I can trust enough and be vulnerable enough to get honest feelings out of my mouth to another person.

Kathy Kendall

What is it to wake up to the truth about reality? Is it to realize that we're made of the same subatomic as a starfish or the stars?

Is it to drop our preoccupation with ourselves and watch the walls between me and you, mine and yours disappear?

As our suspicious softens, a clear view of the universe emerges. When we can see past superficial differences, we feel at home wherever we are. The world is no longer a room full of wary strangers but a vast cosmic block party to which everyone and everything—is invited.

Adapted from the teachings of Zen Master Dogen

The 14th century Tibetan master, Longchenpa who, upon awakening, made this pronouncement: Since things neither exist nor don't exist, are neither real nor unreal, are utterly beyond adopting and rejecting—one might as well burst out laughing.

Longchenpa

Anger is an acid that can do more harm to the vessel in which it is stored than to anything on which it is poured.

Mark Twain

Accepting means you allow yourself to feel whatever it is you are feeling at that moment. It is part of the is-ness of the NOW. You can't argue with what is. Well, you can, but if you do, you will suffer.

Eckhart Tolle

Though we seem to be sleeping, there is an inner wakefulness that directs the dream, and that will eventually startle us back to the truth of who we are.

Rumi

Get deeper and deeper into yes. Say yes to each and everything. Say yes to good and bad, to day and night, to summer and winter. Say yes to success and to failure, say yes to life and to death. Forget everything else; just remember one word, yes, and it can transform your whole being. It can become a radical change, a revolution.

Osho

How do I know the wind should be blowing? It's blowing.

Byron Katie

As we let our own light shine, we unconsciously give other people permission to do the same. As we are liberated from our own fear, our presence automatically liberates others.

Marianne Williamson

I cannot tell you any spiritual truth that deep within you don't already know. All I can do is remind you of what you have forgotten.

Eckhart Tolle

Gratitude unlocks the fullness of life. It turns what we have, into enough and more. It turns denial into acceptance, chaos to order, confusion to clarity. It can turn a meal into a feast, a house into a home, a stranger into a friend. Gratitude makes sense of our past, brings peace for today, and creates a vision for tomorrow.

Melody Beattie

Don't you think it's reasonable to ask to know a teacher's success rate? The proof is in the pudding, right? Didn't you ask them about the fruit of their teachings when you started with them?

Jed McKenna

If you cannot find the truth right where you are, where else do you expect to find it?

Dogen Zenji

They're Singing Your Song

When a woman in a certain African tribe knows she is pregnant, she goes out into the wilderness with a few friends and together they pray and meditate until they hear the song of the child. They recognize that every soul has its own vibration that expresses its unique flavor and purpose. When the women attune to the song, they sing it out loud. Then they return to the tribe and teach it to everyone else. When the child is born, the community gathers and sings the child's song to him or her. Later, when the child enters education, the village gathers and chants the child's song. When the child passes through the initiation to adulthood, the people again come together and sing. At the time of marriage, the person hears his or her song.

Finally, when the soul is about to pass from this world, the family and friends gather at the person's bed, just as they did at their birth, and they sing the person to the next life.

To the African tribe there is one other occasion upon which the villagers sing to the child. If at any time during his or her life, the person commits a crime or aberrant social act, the individual is called to the center of the village and the people in the community form a circle around them. Then they sing their song to them.

The tribe recognizes that the correction for antisocial behavior is not punishment—it is love and the remembrance of identity. When you recognize your own song, you have no desire or need to do anything that would hurt another.

A friend is someone who knows your song and sings it to you when you have forgotten it. Those who love you are not fooled by mistakes you have made or dark images you hold about yourself. They remember your beauty when you feel ugly; your wholeness when you are broken; your innocence when you feel guilty, and your purpose when you are confused.

You may not have grown up in an African tribe that sings your song to you at crucial life transitions, but life is always reminding you when you are in tune with yourself and when you are not. When you feel good, what you are doing matches your song, and when you feel awful, it doesn't. In the end, we shall all recognize our song and sing it well.

You may feel a little warbly at the moment, but so have all the great singers. Just keep singing and you'll find your way home.

"Sing Your Song" from Wisdom of the Heart, Alan Cohen

For more information on Alan Cohen's books and programs, visit www.alancohen.com

Do unto others the way you would have them do unto you because how you treat them or think about them is exactly how they are going to treat you. The prayer that you send out with your feeling or action tends to bring out in them exactly what you expect.

James Redfield

As you look for a better-feeling way to approach whatever you are giving your attention to; as you continue to ask yourself, from your ever-changing vantage point, "What is it that I do want?" eventually you will be standing in a very pleasing place—for you cannot continually ask yourself what it is that you do want without your point of attraction beginning to pivot in that direction.... The process will be gradual, but your continued application of the process will yield wonderful results in only a few days.

Those old habits don't have to be erased, they just become replaced by a new habit that is more in vibrational harmony with who you are and what you want.

Abraham-Hicks

Will the power of making a reasoned choice or decision or of controlling one's own actions.

Harry Palmer

Nothing will work unless you do.

Maya Angelou

The Universe knows all things and is responding to the vibration that you are sending. When you are sending your vibration on purpose, you are orchestrating what the Universe is aligning for you.

Abraham-Hicks

Respect your SELF enough to feel your way to your own truth.

Holly Riley

To be or not to be. *Shakespeare*

To be is to do. *Rousseau*

To do is to be. *Sartre*

Doo bee doo bee doo. *Frank Sinatra*

Taken from the movie Leap! www.leapmovie.com

HOLLY'S NEW ALLOWING HANDBOOK IS NOW AVAILABLE!

The Handbook contains a simple Catch & Release strategy that transforms pain into peace, doubt into self-confidence, and allows solution to replace blame. Each chapter opens a doorway that leads the reader to their dreams.

YOU'RE INVITED

Let Life Love You....

For reminders of your power and preciousness, join our Facebook community at Allowing - Holly Riley. To be included in our mailing list and recieve random inspiration and event updates.

Send us a note at www.HollyRiley.com

Please enjoy this

15% OFF COUPON

for books and CD's

visit us at www.HollyRiley.com
and enter coupon code - hollybook10

peace in - peace out - peace in - peace out

ALSO VISIT

www. qmusing.com and receive a

15% OFF COUPON

coupon code quantum15

inside: now all you need is a cake

inside: vision is the art of seeing things invisible

inside: thank you thank you thank you

Visit our website and have a look at full color inspiring, thought provoking and humorous greeting cards. For whatever the occasion, for whatever the reason, or for no reason at all, there's an original greeting card that says it and we have it.

quantumusing

interesting thoughts printed on stuff

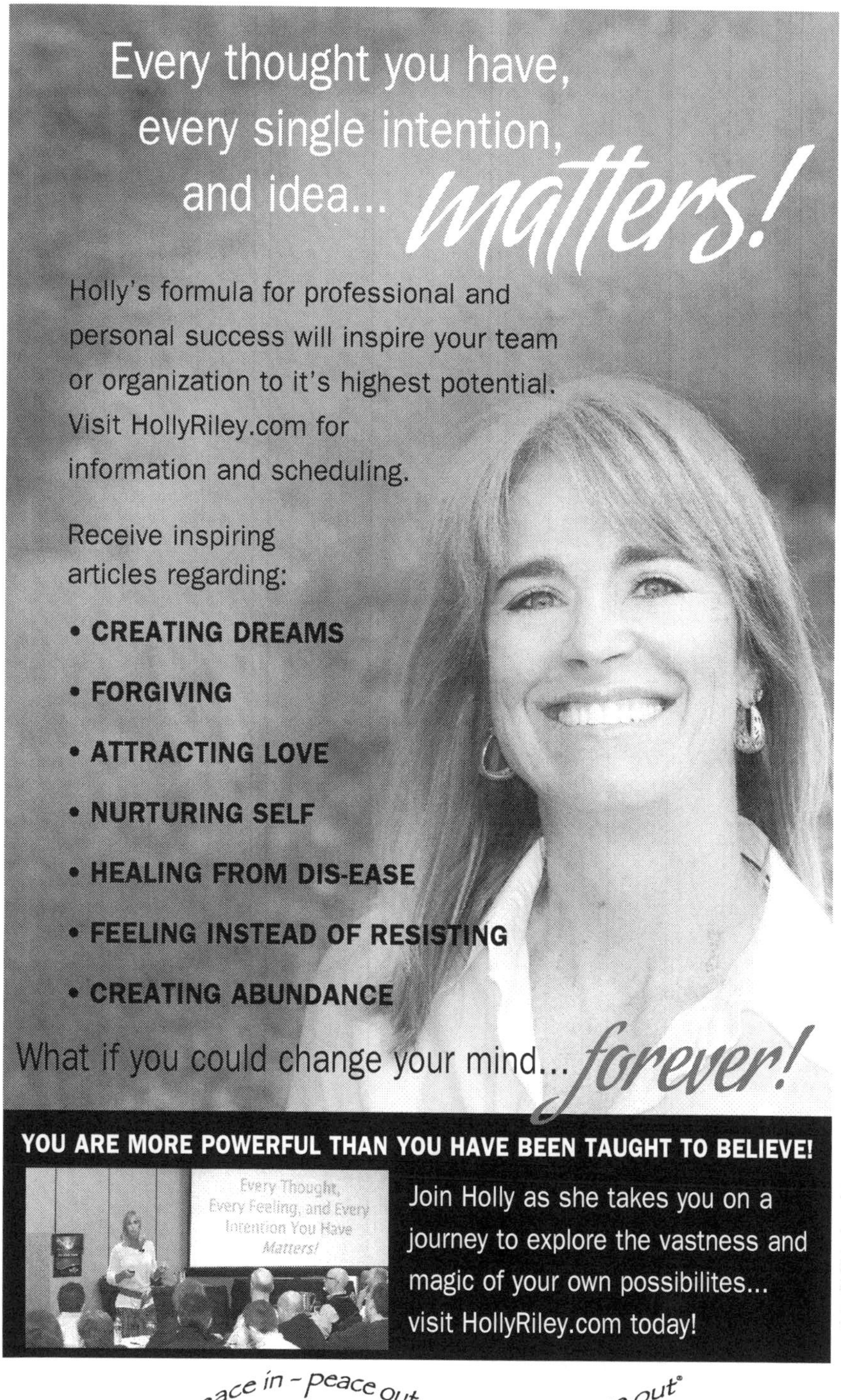

peace in - peace out - peace in - peace out®

Acknowledgments

This book is filled with people that I love dearly! I would like to thank them all for permitting me to reveal myself at their expense, particularly my husband, who believed in my writing long before anyone else considered it palatable. I want to thank Travis and Drake from the bottom of my heart for being my greatest teachers as well as such good sports when held captive during those many long drives where I often read parts of Allowing out loud.

I would also like to acknowledge all the teachers who lit a fire in my heart: Jane Roberts, Ram Dass, and Butch Nelson for showing me there was a door smack-dab in the middle of the wall I had created; Werner Erhard, Arnold Siegel, and Donna Hamilton for being the first to show me how to feel; Robert Kirby for his commitment to truth; Deepak Chopra for every word he ever spoke; Neale Donald Walsh for an inclusive and loving perspective; Abraham via Esther and Jerry Hicks for inspiring guilt-free joy; Eckhart Tolle for exemplifying presence and illustrating how to live life in the moment; Harry Palmer for his profound grace and wisdom on the mechanics of attention and consciousness; Avra Honey Smith for showing me what it feels like to be believed in, Gary Renard for being a clear conduit to the invisible; Byron Katie for the simplicity and magic of 'The Work"; Kayt Campbell for holding my balloon string through a hurricane; Ishana Bai for being a wizard of energy and teaching me to trust my heart above all else; Dr. Kam Yuen for making it easy; Jed McKenna for single-handedly crumbling the foundation of what I believed mattered most, leaving only one place to turn… toward myself. And, my dad, the greatest teacher of all, for never giving me his own answers but forever inspiring me to find my own.

I am especially grateful for an amazing and aware support team including my sister Patricia Rich who can make art out of anything; my dear friend Shakti Cain whose relentless commitment to allowing the book to unfold kept me in sync with my heart; CJ Schepers whose editing skills were heaven-sent; Ram Magen for being the most empowering friend a person could ever have; and most of all Josephine Mason because without her this book would not be. Her passion for this story moved mountains.

Resources

I am eternally grateful for all the wisdom and love the following authors have put into words. These resources have provided me with inspiration throughout the journey I've just shared with you. They have encouraged me to awaken through many difficult experiences. If one attracts your attention, I bet it would lead you gracefully toward your own preciousness.

A Course in Miracles, Dr. Helen Schucman

Ask and It Is Given, Esther and Jerry Hicks

A Thousand Names for Joy: Living in Harmony with the Way Things Are, Byron Katie and Stephen Mitchell

A New Earth: Awakening to Your Life's Purpose, Eckhart Tolle

The Disappearance of the Universe: Straight Talk About Illusions, Past Lives, Religion, Sex, Politics, and the Miracles of Forgiveness, Gary Renard

The Education of Oversoul Seven, Jane Roberts

The Fourth Way, P.D. Ouspensky

Freedom: The Courage To Be Yourself, Osho

I Need Your Love—Is That True? Byron Katie and Michael Katz

Journey Beyond Words, Brent Haskell, Ph.D., D.O

Awareness: The Key to Living in Balance, Osho

Living Deliberately: The Discovery and Development of Avatar, Harry Palmer

Love Precious Humanity: The Collected Wisdom of Harry Palmer, Harry Palmer, edited by Kayt Kennedy

Loving What Is: Four Questions That Can Change Your Life, Byron Katie and Stephen Mitchell

Meetings With Remarkable Men (All and Everything), G.I. Gurdjieff

Power vs. Force, David R. Hawkins, M.D., Ph.D.

The Path of the Mystic, Osho

Reinventing The Body, Resurrecting The Soul: How to Create a New You, Deepak Chopra

ReSurfacing® Workbook: Techniques for Exploring Consciousness, Harry Palmer

Seth Speaks: The Eternal Validity of the Soul, Jane Roberts and Robert F. Butts

Spiritual Enlightenment: The Damnedest Thing, Jed McKenna

Spiritual Warfare, Jed McKenna

Spiritually Incorrect Enlightenment, Jed McKenna

Stillness Speaks, Eckhart Tolle

Your Immortal Realty: How to Break the Cycle of Birth and Death, Gary Renard

Workshops

Ishana Bai – Yuen Method, Levels 1, 2, 3 - www.te-energetics.com

Donna Hamilton MFT – Professional training in Clinical Hypnotherapy and Neuro Linguistic Programming - www.P.A.U.S.E.com

Robert Kirby – Integrating Body-Mind-Spirit & Soul - www.robertkirby.com

Harry Palmer – The Avatar Course Sections 1, 2, 3, 4, 5 - www.AvatarEPC.com

Dr. Kam Yuen – Yuen Method seminars - www.yuenmethod.com

Audios/DVDs

Abraham by Esther and Jerry Hicks – *The Teachings Of Abraham The Master Course CD Program*

Abraham by Esther and Jerry Hicks – *The Law of Attraction CD Collection*

Abraham by Esther and Jerry Hicks – *The Art of Allowing Workshop*

Abraham by Esther and Jerry Hicks – *Ask and It Is Given*

Eckhart Tolle – *Findhorn Retreat: Stillness Amidst the World*

Eckhart Tolle – *Living a Life of Inner Peace*

Eckhart Tolle – *The Power of Now*

Gregg Braden – *Speaking the Lost Language of God*

The Movie Leap! – *www.LeapMovie.com*

The Living Matrix – *www.TheLivingMatrixMovie.com*

Web Addresses

Abraham-Hicks – www.Abraham-Hicks.com

Byron Katie – www.thework.com

Carl Jung – www.carljung.com

Douglas Harding – www.headless.org

Eckhart Tolle – www.eckharttolle.com

The Art of Ascension – www.theishayatradition.org

Jed McKenna – www.jedmckenna.com

Kryon Channeling – www.kryon.org

Ralph Waldo Emerson – www.transcendentalists.com

Ramana Maharshi – www.sriramanamaharshi.org

Rumi – www.rumi.net

Seth/Jane Roberts – www.ImagineNoLimits.com/seth.html

References

Campbell, Kayt 2011. *Me, not Me – Living the Difference Between Who We Are and What We're Not.* Joy Publications.

Chopra, Deepak, 2009. *Reinventing the Body, Resurrecting the Soul.* New York: Harmony Books.

Emoto, Masaru, 2004. *The Hidden Messages in Water,* Hillsboro, OR: Beyond Words Publishing,.

Gurdjieff, G.I., 1963. *Meetings with Remarkable Men (All and Everything).* London: Penguin Press.

Gurdjieff, G.I., 1973. *Views from the Real World, Early Talks of Gurdjieff.* New York: Dutton.

Haskell, Brent, Ph.D., D.O., 1994. *Journey Beyond Words: A Companion to the Workbook of the Course in Miracles.* Los Angeles: DeVorss & Company.

Harding, Douglas E., 2005. *Open To The Source: A Practical Guide for Seeing Who You Really Are.* Carlsbad, CA: Inner Directions Publishing.

Hawkins, David R., 1995. *Power vs. Force.* Carlsbad, CA: Hay House.

Hicks, Esther and Jerry, 2004. *Ask and It Is Given: Learning to Manifest Your Desires.* Carlsbad, CA: Hay House.

Hicks, Esther and Jerry, 2009. *The Vortex: Where the Law of Attraction Assembles All Cooperative Relationships,* Carlsbad, CA: Hay House.

Hoff, Benjamin, 1998. *The Tao of Pooh.* London: Mandarin Publishing.

Katie, Byron, and Stephen Mitchell. 2007. *A Thousand Names for Joy: How to Live in Harmony with the Way Things Are.* New York: Harmony Books.

Katie, Byron, and Stephen Mitchell, 2003. *Loving What Is: Four Questions That Can Change Your Life.* New York: Three Rivers Press.

Katie, Byron, and Michael Katz, 2005. *I Need Your Love—Is That True?* New York: Three Rivers Press.

Kennedy, Kayt, 1999. *Love Precious Humanity: The Collected Wisdom of Harry Palmer.* Altamonte Springs, FL: Star's Edge International.

McKenna, Jed, 2009. *Spiritual Enlightenment: The Damnedest Thing.* Fairfield, IA: Wisefool Press.

McKenna, Jed, 2009. *Spiritually Incorrect Enlightenment.* Fairfield, IA: Wisefool Press.

McKenna, Jed, 2009. *Spiritual Warfare.* Fairfield, IA: Wisefool Press.

Ouspensky, P.D., 1971. *The Fourth Way.* London; Vintage Books.

Nicoll, Maurice, 1984. *Psychological Commentaries on the Teaching of Gurdjieff & Ouspensky, Vol. 1, 11.* Boston: Shambhala Publications.

Osho, 1977. *The Path of the Mystic.* Pasadena, CA: Theosophical University Press.

Osho, 2004. *Freedom: The Courage to Be Yourself.* St. Martin's Press.

Palmer, Harry, 1994. *Living Deliberately: The Discovery and Development of Avatar.* Altamonte Springs, FL: Star's Edge International.

Palmer, Harry, 1994. *ReSurfacing: Techniques For Exploring Consciousness.* Altamonte Springs, FL: Star's Edge International.

Redfield, James, 1999. *The Secret of Shambhala: In Search of the Eleventh Insight.* New York: Warner Books.

Renard, Gary, 2002. *The Disappearance of the Universe: Straight Talk About Illusions, Past Lives, Religion, Sex, Politics, and the Miracles of Forgiveness.* Carlsbad, CA: Hay House.

Renard, Gary, 2006. *Your Immortal Reality: How to Break the Cycle of Birth and Death.* Carlsbad, CA: Hay House.

Robbins, Mike, and Richard Carlson, 2007. *Focus on the Good Stuff: The Power of Appreciation.* San Francisco: Jossey-Bass.

Roberts, Jane, 1969. *Seth Speaks.* San Rafael, CA: Amber-Allen Publishing.

Roberts, Jane, 1970. *The Education of Oversoul Seven.* Upper Saddle River, NJ: Prentice Hall Trade.

Russell, Bertrand, 1997. *Principles of Social Reconstruction.* 2nd Ed., London: Routledge.

Schucman, Helen, 1976. *A Course In Miracles.* Mill Valley, CA: Foundation for Inner Peace..

Seuss, Dr., 1958. *The Cat in the Hat Comes Back.* New York: Random House.

Tolle, Eckhart, 2005. *A New Earth: Awakening to Your Life's Purpose.* New York: Dutton.

Tolle, Eckhart, 1999. *The Power of Now: A Guide to Spiritual Enlightenment.* Vancouver, Canada: Namaste Publishing.

Tolle, Eckhart, 2003. *Stillness Speaks,* Vancouver, Canada: Namaste Publishing.

Williamson, Marianne, 1992. *A Return to Love.* New York: HarperCollins.

18062361R00195

Made in the USA
Lexington, KY
16 October 2012